Control Theories of Crime and Delinquency

Advances in Criminological Theory
Volume 12

Control Theories of Crime and Delinquency

Chester L. Britt
Michael R. Gottfredson
editors

Transaction Publishers
New Brunswick (U.S.A.) and London (U.K.)

This book is printed on acid-free paper that meets the American National Standard for Permanence of Paper for Printed Library Materials.

Library of Congress Catalog Number: 2003040220
ISBN: 0-7658-0180-9
ISSN: 0894-2366
Printed in the United States of America

Library of Congress Cataloging-in-Publication Data

Control theories of crime and delinquency / Chester L. Britt and
Michael R. Gottfredson, editors.
p. cm. — (Advances in criminological theory; v. 12)
Includes bibliographical references (p.) and index.
ISBN 0-7658-0180-9 (cloth : alk. paper)
1. Criminology. I. Britt, Chester L. II. Gottfredson, Michael R. III. Series.

HV6018.C66 2003
364—dc21

2003040220

Contents

List of Tables vii

List of Figures viii

Editors' Introduction 1
Chester L. Britt and Michael R. Gottfredson

1. Self-Control and Opportunity 5
Michael R. Gottfredson and Travis Hirschi

2. Self-Control Pathology: The Elephant in the Living Room 21
Matt DeLisi

3. The Effect of Learning on Crime: Contrasting *A General Theory of Crime* and Social Learning Theory 39
Todd A. Armstrong

4. The Interactive Effects of Social Control Variables on Delinquency 53
Robert Agnew

5. A Control Theory of Gender Difference in Crime and Delinquency 77
Barbara J. Costello and Helen J. Mederer

6. Genocide and General Theory 109
Augustine Brannigan and Kelly H. Hardwick

7. Sexual Harassment and Low Self-Control: A Proposed Application of the General Theory of Crime 133
Kevin M. Thompson and Leana Allen Bouffard

8. Punishment of Children from the Perspective of Control Theory 151
Travis Hirschi and Michael R. Gottfredson

9. Self-Control, Group Solidarity, and Crime: An Integrated Control Theory 161
Chester L. Britt

10. Comparative Criminology: Content or Simply Methodology? 179
Alexander T. Vazsonyi

11. Crime as Risk-Taking: Co-occurrence of Delinquent Behavior, Health-Endangering Behaviors, and Problem Behaviors 213
Marianne Junger and Maja Deković

12. The Versatility vs. Specialization Debate: Different Theories of Crime in the Light of a Swiss Birth Cohort 249
Henriette Haas and Martin Killias

Contributors 275

Index 277

Tables

4.1 Correlations between the Social Control, Delinquent Peers, and Delinquency Measures 64

4.2 General and Serious Delinquency Regressed on the Social Control and Delinquent Peer Measure (Standardized effects shown, with unstandardized effects in parentheses) 64

4.3 General and Serious Delinquency Regressed on the Social Control, Delinquent Peer, and Interaction Measures, with the Interactions Added One at a Time 66

4.4 General and Serious Delinquency Regressed on the Social Control, Delinquent Peer, and Interaction Measures, with the Interactions Added Together 66

10.1 Descriptive Statistics of Demographic Variables, Low Self-Control, and Deviance by Country 197

10.2 Model Fit for Individual Groups by Sex and by Country 203

11.1 Relationships between Risk-Taking Behaviors 224

12.1 Incidence of Different Types of Offenses among the 21,314 Recruits during the Twelve Months Preceding Recruit Training 253

12.2 Serial and Serious Offenders among the 21,314 Recruits in a Twelve-Month Period 254

12.3 Incidence of Different Offenses Committed by Serial and Serious Offenders over a Twelve-Month Period 256

12.4 Overlapping of Different Types of Specializations among Different Types of Serial and Severe Offenders over a Twelve-Month Period 257

12.5 Listing of the Independent Variables Introduced into the Logistic Regression Algorithm 261

12.6 Resulting Model for Bodily Injury 263

12.7 Model Fitting Information for Table 12.6 on the Logistic Regression of Bodily Injury 265

12.8 Resulting Logistic Regression Model for Forcible Rape 267

12.9 Model Fitting Information for Table 12.8 on the Logistic Regression of Rape 269

Figures

10.1 Scatter Plot of Low Self-Control and Total Deviance by Country (Males) 198, 199

10.2 Scatter Plot of Low Self-Control and Total Deviance by Country (Females) 200, 201

Editors' Introduction

Chester L. Britt and Michael R. Gottfredson

By most measures, control theories continue to be among the most popular explanations for crime and delinquency. Polls of criminologists place control theories at the top of the list of theories thought to be most viable (Ellis and Walsh, 1999). Citation studies indicate that control theory authors are among the most frequently cited scholars in the field (Cohn, Farrington, and Wright, 1998). Textbooks designed for undergraduates routinely include sections dedicated to control theory explanations. Today, scholarly debates about the causes of crime and delinquency are often debates within control theory rather than debates between control theories and other explanations, and long-time oppositional theories seek to incorporate control theory into their explanations more frequently than they seek to deny its validity.

Perhaps the principal source of this popularity is that control theory accommodates both of the great traditions in criminology: the positivist and the classical schools. The positivistic side of control theory focuses on the causes of crime being determined by differences among people in their dispositions to engage in crime and delinquency. Thus, control theories welcome efforts to measure crime and delinquency more effectively, to assign people different probabilities of engaging in criminal behavior according to their individual and social characteristics, and to study such differences at various points across the life-course. As such, control theories are appealing to social and behavioral scientists from a wide range of disciplines who study empirical differences in the causes of behavior. The generally accepted findings that most problem behaviors of interest to sociologists and psychologists are highly related among subjects and, of course, have common antecedents and consequences for life events, are findings easily accommodated by control theories. Whether or not the terms favored by various control theorists are employed in this work, the combination of a vast body of empirical research focused on identifying early childhood experiences as causing multiple problem behaviors, the distribution of these behaviors by age, and the persistent effects of parents and peers in the causal chain are the *sine qua non* of modern control theories. Scholars working in the seemingly diverse fields of epidemiology, developmental psychology, accidents, schooling, and delinquency find enormous common ground in the commonality of the causes of their specific foci of interest.

Control theories are also friendly to the classical school's image of a rational actor making decisions when confronted by gains and losses in the presence of assorted temptations. The developments in opportunity theory based on victimization surveys (e.g., Hindelang, Gottfredson, and Garofalo, 1978), on efforts to account for crime rate trends (e.g., Cohen and Felson, 1979), and on crime prevention methods (Clarke and Cornish, 1985) closely parallel the themes of control theories. In control theories, the presence of a temptation in the absence of restraint increases the chances of crime, all the more so if the individual so tempted lacks self-control. Consequently, control theories have captured the attention of researchers interested in how offenders make decisions, how opportunities can affect the probability of crime, and the connection between the timing of punishments and the probability of influencing the decision to engage in crime. Unlike other social theories of crime causation, control theories assume motivation for crime, and view its study as unnecessary. Individuals are not pressured to commit a crime by culture, by strain, by frustration, or by class. People engage in crime for the same reasons that they engage in all other forms of behavior—they expect to benefit or experience pleasure from the act in some way. From the perspective of control theory, the more interesting research question focuses on why people do *not* engage in crime. The now impressive empirical literatures on choice, opportunity, and indirectly, on deterrence all find linkages back to control theory. Modern control theories embrace studies of criminal justice as well as studies of crime, having application in either arena of study.

Part of the appeal of control theory internationally may be due to control theorists having adopted an almost radical, non-relativistic position on the causes of crime. That is, the causes of crime and delinquency are not seen as the products of unique cultures, peoples, settings, historical periods, or even variable legal definitions of crime itself. Rather, control theory assumes that the causes of crime are the same everywhere and at all times. Modern control theory defines crime as the use of force or fraud in the pursuit of short-term benefits without consideration of long-term negative consequences. Crime sours interpersonal relations, is evidence of lack of socialization (regardless of the culture responsible for the socialization), and is the anathema of all social control efforts, formal as well as informal. Control theory expects cross-national criminology to be successful, anticipates that the causes and correlates of delinquency and crime (as defined above) are the same everywhere, and encourages research investigating crime in different settings. So far, the evidence seems supportive of this stance.

Undoubtedly, another part of the appeal of control theory is that it is very friendly toward scientific testing, to the gathering of data and their application to hypotheses derived from the theory. Control theory is, above all else, a theory of the facts. For example, recent versions have been constructed explicitly to account for the nature of crime and the characteristics of offenders as revealed by the empirical literature (Gottfredson and Hirschi, 1990). The modern control theory tradition has attempted to draw explicit connections between the theory and the data about delinquency and crime, a tradition that can be traced directly to the work most responsible for the modern control theory tradition, *Causes of Delinquency* (Hirschi, 1969). Little wonder, then, that scholars interested in empirical science, in statistical analyses of crime, and in measurement have centered much of their attention on control theory.

Although researchers are finding control theory increasingly useful and valid, by one measure, it may also be said that control theories have had quite limited influence on public policy, at least in the United States. The dominant policies for dealing with crime and delinquency in the United States have decidedly favored other explanations, explanations that rely on the deterrent and incapacitative functions of the criminal justice system. Politically popular sentencing schemes (such as "Three Strikes and You're Out") and other efforts to identify and punish career criminals are inconsistent with the basic assumptions underlying modern control theories. Similarly, manipulations of public policing—by intensive patrols, random stops, "hot spot" saturations, and so-called community policing—are far removed from the policies suggested by a theory that focuses on informal socialization by family and friends.

Why do control theories fare so well in scientific settings and in textbooks but so poorly in public policy considerations? On this question, the blame seems to lie with the positivistic side of control theory, which believes in root causes for problem behaviors that come years before the problems become of interest to the political authorities. For control theories, important causes of crime come ten to fifteen years before the police and the courts become interested in the case. These causes also illustrate the inability of political authorities to have much of a meaningful impact on crime in the near term. The seeds of policy dissatisfaction are planted deep within control theory itself. A theory that focuses on prevention through informal socialization, rather than legal intervention, is a theory too far removed in time from the immediacy of contemporary policymakers. Ironically, a theory that stresses short-term gratification over long-term consequences may be as applicable to the explanation of contemporary crime policy as it is to the explanation of crime.

References

Clarke, Ronald V., and Derek Cornish. 1985. "Modeling Offenders' Decisions: A Framework for Research and Policy." In M. Tonry and N. Morris (eds.), *Crime and*

Justice: An Annual Review of Research, Vol. 6. Chicago: University of Chicago Press.

Cohen, Lawrence E., and Marcus Felson. 1979. "Social Change and Crime Rate Trends: A Routine Activity Approach." *American Sociological Review* 44: 588–608.

Cohn, Ellen G., David P. Farrington, and Richard A. Wright. 1998. *Evaluating Criminology and Criminal Justice*. Westport, CT: Greenwood Press.

Ellis, Lee, and Anthony Walsh. 1999. "Criminologists' Opinions About Causes and Theories of Crime and Delinquency." *The Criminologist* 24(1): 1–6.

Gottfredson, Michael R., and Travis Hirschi. 1990. *A General Theory of Crime*. Palo Alto, CA: Stanford University Press.

Hindelang, Michael J., Michael Gottfredson, and James Garolfalo. 1978. *Victims of Personal Crime*. Cambridge, MA: Ballinger Press.

Hirschi, Travis. 1969. *Causes of Delinquency*. Berkeley: University of California Press.

1

Self-Control and Opportunity

Michael R. Gottfredson and Travis Hirschi

One of the most influential twentieth-century books on crime was entitled *Delinquency and Opportunity* (Cloward and Ohlin, 1960). At the time it was written, students of crime and delinquency understood that opportunity referred to access to legitimate and illegitimate avenues of advancement in American society. Legitimate opportunities were of course conventional educational and occupational careers; illegitimate opportunities were positions within an organized criminal subculture. Lack of either kind of opportunity had profound consequences for the likelihood and nature of a delinquent career. Delinquent acts themselves did not really require opportunities. Delinquents made their own.

Cloward and Ohlin were not alone in their view of the role of opportunity. On the contrary, they were well within the long-standing position that crime and delinquency are the product of positive and strong motives, the view that offenders are driven to their crimes by socially engendered needs or beliefs (definitions) that only crimes can satisfy (see also Parsons, 1951; Merton, 1938; Cohen, 1955; Sutherland, 1939).

At the beginning of the twenty-first century, much of criminology has abandoned this image of a "constrained" offender required to do what he does (Matza, 1964) in favor of an image of a "potential" offender who may or may not commit the crime depending on the objective and perceived opportunities available to him. Collectively, rational choice theories (Cornish and Clarke, 1986), routine activity–lifestyle/exposure theories (Cohen and Felson, 1979; Hindelang, Gottfredson, and Garofalo, 1978), control theories (Gottfredson and Hirschi, 1990), and even such offshoots of differential association as social learning theory (Akers, 1998) command considerable attention. All are in varying degrees opportunity theories, where the opportunities of interest have no connection to those found in earlier theories of crime.

As might be expected, this shift of focus from the offender to the situation or "setting" (Felson and Clarke, 1998) has brought with it natural tendencies to emphasize or even exaggerate differences between past and current perspectives and thus to miss opportunities to capitalize on their complementarities. As a theory of both crime and criminality, our self-control theory (Gottfredson and Hirschi, 1990) attempts to address the interplay of potential offenders and criminal opportunities without giving an exclusive role to either. Given the considerable research supportive of opportunity theory in recent years (Felson and Clarke, 1998), (and—if we may—the not inconsequential empirical success of self-control theory during the same period), this chapter attempts to reexamine and clarify the concept of opportunity from the perspective of self-control theory.

Self-control theory assumes that the nature of the offender may be inferred from the nature of criminal acts, and vice versa. In other words, it assumes a fit between acts and individuals such that we can learn the salient characteristics of one by examination of the other.

Traditionally, criminology looked at offenders and allowed the characteristics imputed to them to determine the nature of crime. Thus, in a famous example, delinquents were said to be lower-class boys whose wish to be liked by middle-class teachers had not been granted, all of which explained the malicious, negativistic, and non-utilitarian nature of their delinquent acts (Cohen, 1955). Perhaps partly in response to the persistent tendency of the traditional approach to downplay or even deny the relevance of the immediate setting, modern opportunity theorists have been reluctant to attribute characteristics to offenders over and above their willingness to commit crimes under favorable circumstances. But there is a more important reason for such reluctance. Opportunity theory is seen by its advocates as a practical crime prevention strategy tested by modifying a setting and observing the results. As such, it is not bound by the rules usually applied to abstract social science theories. The principles it follows are analogous to those that apply to searches for safer cars, for means of reducing the risks of drunk driving, or even for a light bulb that works. Success is all the proof one needs, and failure—even repeated failure—cannot gainsay the effort.

We have no qualms about the practical value of this strategy, or about the benefits accruing to it from its reluctance to pursue the implications of its results for the nature of offenders. At the same time, we believe its results can be further exploited by scholars interested in understanding the interaction between individual predispositions and the opportunities available to them. We begin with a sketch of the offense and the offender from the perspective of self-control theory.

The Offense in Self-Control Theory

Self-control theory sees criminal acts to be as "easy as falling down a mountain." No special skill or preparation and no planning are required to snatch a purse, throw a rock through a car window, open an unlocked door or cash drawer, or fire a gun at a stranger. All that is required for the acts described is the degree of physical strength normally attained by early adolescence. Otherwise, all of them would be within the capabilities of children. Self-control theory sees crimes as split-second events, requiring such little time for their execution that many different crimes can be committed simultaneously or consecutively in a matter of minutes, and only rarely will one crime because of the time and effort involved preclude commission of another. Self-control theory sees criminal acts as exciting, risky, or thrilling. The house may be occupied; the victim may possess a lethal weapon; the audit may discover the discrepancy; the witness may get the word to the police in time for them to appear on the scene; the drug may not have been cut to the degree assumed. Self-control theory sees crime as producing only meager short-term benefits. The victim's purse, however it was obtained, may contain only a few dollars; the stolen jewelry or electronic equipment may be declared worthless by the pawnbroker; the next morning it may be impossible to remember what provoked the stabbing at the bar.

Available data abundantly support the view that crimes are rarely products of extensive planning, effort, or skill. Most occur in close proximity to the offender's residence or within his daily round. The "burglar" walks to the scene of the crime, the "robber" victimizes available targets on the street, the "embezzler" steals from his own cash register at the fast food restaurant, the "car thief" drives away cars with keys left in the ignition. The "burglar" searches for an unlocked door, an open window, an unoccupied, single-story house. (Once inside, he looks for easily portable goods of interest to himself without concern for their potential value in a larger market.) The truant merely stays home and watches television or sleeps a few extra hours. The abuser gets his way by using force against a child or a weaker adult. Indeed, the major requirement for successful completion of crimes of violence is superior strength or command of instruments of force—a gun, a knife, a club, or a table lamp. Some property crimes may require physical strength or dexterity, but in most cases no more than that necessary for the ordinary activities of life. Likewise, sex, drugs, and alcohol require no special training, little teaching, and no particular skill. Quite the contrary—learning to defer pleasures of mood, to attend to obligations, to wait one's turn in line, to negotiate needs with others, to respect the rights of the weak, requires diligent training and teaching, accomplished by someone who cares about the outcome.

The Offender in Self-Control Theory

Control theories are restraint theories. They are not motivational theories. They take the benefits of crime as obvious, and consider search for hidden motives, reasons, or benefits to be at best unrewarding and at worst clearly misleading. (For example, if the offender is found to have needs or wants that explain a particular crime, he would be expected to engage in other offenses consistent with these peculiar needs or wants—i.e., he would be expected to specialize in particular crimes and expend if necessary special effort to accomplish them. Unfortunately for this approach, offenders do not specialize and, as we have just seen, they tend to be strangely disinclined to crimes that entail much in the way of inconvenience.) So, in control theories, differences among people in criminal behavior reflect differences in the restraints confronting them (including those in the immediate environment) rather than differences in motivation to offend. In self-control theory, individuals are restrained from crime because they care about the long-term or broader consequences of their behavior. Because they take the easy way, because they gain little from their crimes and risk much from committing them, offenders are characterized as having relatively little self-control (Gottfredson and Hirschi, 1990).

Research and the facts about criminal behavior tell us that self-control is generated in the early years of life, primarily through parental action (Hirschi, 1983, 2002; Glueck and Glueck, 1950; Loeber and Stouthamer-Loeber, 1986; McCord and McCord, 1959; McCord, 1979). In families in which parents care about their children's behavior, in which they monitor their children's actions, in which they recognize deviant behavior, and in which they penalize illegitimate use of force and fraud, self-control becomes a stable characteristic of the child. To some degree, the school also plays a role in the development of self-control. Children attached to school develop long-term aspirations and commitments to the future inconsistent with self-serving impulses and behavior that are costly to others (Hirschi, 2002). In the absence of early training in the family and compensatory interest in the school and further education, the individual will be relatively low on self-control—that is, relatively susceptible to the lures of momentary pleasure.

Opportunity in Self-Control Theory

Opportunities are sets of circumstances favorable to crime. At one extreme, such circumstances make crime possible. At the other extreme, they make crime virtually necessary. Between these extremes, circumstances make crime more or less likely and, together with the propensities of potential offenders, account for variations in crime rates. Even where circumstances are least favorable to crime, possibilities of crime may add up to the probability of crime. This is because criminal acts are mainly momentary events, and life is full of moments. As a result, it is possible to say that crime is an "ever-present possibility in human affairs" (Gottfredson and Hirschi 1990: 4), that "crime can happen to anyone," that "everyone is capable of crime."

Put another way, criminal acts are possible whatever the propensities of potential offenders—and isolated or single criminal events may as a result say very little about those responsible for them. At the same time, criminal and analogous acts are so numerous that measures of the criminal propensity of the actor constructed from the number of different acts in which he participates are not invalidated by variation in opportunity across individual offenses. At the extremes, then, and at all points between, it is reasonable to say that with respect to evaluation of the criminal propensity of individuals, opportunities for crime are ubiquitous (Marcus, 2000; Marcus, in press). *This fact answers the criticism of self-control theory that it does not deal sufficiently with the concept of opportunity.* It confirms that self-control can be measured and the theory assessed without undue concern for differences in opportunities to commit criminal, deviant, or reckless acts.

Early tests of self-control theory (e.g., Grasmick et al., 1993) misunderstood this point, interpreting the theory as giving equal causal significance to self-control and opportunity. We interpreted the theory otherwise:

> In the view of the theory, opportunities to commit one or another crime or analogous acts are limitless. Opportunities to commit a particular act may be severely limited, however (Hirschi and Gottfredson, 1987). Self-control and opportunity may therefore interact for specific crimes, but are in the general case independent. For example, driving under the influence (DUI) should be largely a function of self-control. But not entirely. . . .[W]here legal restrictions on the availability of alcohol are enforced (such as age restrictions on purchasing), the DUI rate is reduced. Further, in many cases, self-control and opportunity are not independent. In order to embezzle from banks, one needs first to be employed in one, a condition that depends in part on (high) self-control and its consequences. Access to information on how to smuggle drugs is enhanced by a term in prison, a condition too that depends in part on (low) self-control and its consequences. The generality of the theory thus stems from its conception of the offender, a conception that must be taken into consideration before situational or "structural" influences can be understood. (Hirschi and Gottfredson, 1993:50)

Along the same lines: In our understanding, circumstances cannot require crime because the offender must by definition participate in the act—that is, he or she is always the element that transforms conditions necessary for crime into conditions collectively sufficient to produce the act in question. In this sense, the idea that "opportunity makes the thief" is as destructive of social policy directed at offenders as the idea that "poverty makes them do it" is of social policy directed at reduction of criminal opportunities.

Factors Affecting Opportunity

To say that opportunities for crime are ubiquitous is not to say that opportunities for any particular crime are ubiquitous. Each crime or type of crime has a unique opportunity structure or set of conditions necessary for its performance. Here, for example, is a discussion of the logical structure of auto theft, and its implications for prevention of this particular crime:

> Auto theft is an especially complex crime. In order for car theft to occur, there must be an automobile that is accessible, drivable, and attractive. There must also be an offender who is both capable of driving and insufficiently restrained. For auto theft, as opposed to joyriding, it is also necessary that the offender possess the means to maintain and store the vehicle. . . .
>
> Auto theft can therefore be prevented by reduction in the number of automobiles, by making access to automobiles more difficult, by making them more difficult to drive, and by making them less attractive to offenders. Auto theft can also be reduced by increasing restraints on people who tend toward criminality, perhaps by making eighteen the minimum age for a driver's license. (Gottfredson and Hirschi, 1990:35)

To say that everyone is capable of crime is not to say that everyone is capable of *every* crime. Indeed, opportunities for *particular* crimes may vary immensely over time and place, and from one individual to another. Thus, most 12-year-olds are incapable of auto theft because they have not learned to drive, and most 30-year-olds are incapable of truancy because they are no longer enrolled in school. Thus, most British citizens are incapable of murder with a handgun, and most of us are incapable of insider trading. By the same token, when automobiles came on the scene, they quickly replaced horses as criminal opportunities, and no object now outweighs the airplane as a focus of opportunity restriction.

Such shifts in the opportunity structure for particular crimes say nothing about the relation between self-control and crime. The 12-year-old who cannot steal a car may well steal a bicycle; the 30-year-old who cannot be truant from school may well be truant from work and family obligations. The British citizen with low-self control may find many other ways to let his tendencies be known, as may those of us barred from insider trading. The horse thief of yesterday is today's auto thief. Insofar as he tends to act on behalf of a nation-state, a political group, or even his own family, the skyjacker may be something else again. But here too it makes little sense to focus on opportunity restriction without concern for the tendencies and capabilities of potential offenders.

Indeed, even from this brief list of examples it is apparent that opportunities for crime are affected by technological, political, and economic factors, and by properties of the individual other than self-control. Age matters, and so does sex. Indeed, sex differences in crime depend in good measure on the offense in question, so much so that Zager was led to conclude that "gender is best seen as an opportunity [rather than a motivational or self-control] factor" (1994: 77). And so do size and strength matter. As Felson (1996) puts it, big people hit little people. As the Gluecks would put it, mesomorphs are more likely to be delinquent (Glueck and Glueck, 1950: 181–97). It was once thought that intelligence was an opportunity factor. Bright or informed people were better able than not-so-bright-or-informed people to conceive and execute crimes. We know now that crimes requiring keen insight are extremely rare, that anticipation of consequences works against commission of inherently costly acts.

The specification of the interaction of varying individual predispositions for delinquency and logically possible opportunities is one of the most significant and complex problems confronting modern criminology. Environmental criminologists emphasize the simplicity and practicality of their approach and its consequent value for crime prevention. At the same time, they characterize criminological theory as extremely complicated and consequently irrelevant to everyday practice. Perhaps it would be of value to consider particular settings in which self-control theory might contribute to practical crime prevention and to compare its recommendations with those stemming from other perspectives, especially environmental criminology.

Violent Crime in the University

One of the authors, during a Ph.D. oral exam, once asked a campus police officer how he would explain the extremely low rate of crime on the university campus. The police officer quickly listed the various crime prevention strategies and tactics of his department—e.g., frequent patrols, rapid response time, broad dissemination of crime prevention information. Today, the same university (Arizona) is grieving over the murder by a student of three professors in the school of nursing, and is devoting a great deal of effort to strategies and tactics for preventing the recurrence of such an event. The killer committed suicide. A letter written by him has been closely examined for the insights it might reveal about his mental state. A local expert on violence has published a call for a "forensic inquiry" on "specimens" left behind by the killer's record and body. And of course the university's various counseling services and reporting procedures are being reexamined for clues as to how they might have prevented the crime.

What can self-control theory tell us the about the university's crime rate and about this crime in particular? It can tell us that individually and collectively the explanations and approaches thus far advanced have no foundation in experience or research. The police are an insignificant factor in crime control, especially on university campuses (see below). On the campus in question, what scores of police officers could not do to achieve crowd control at football games was fully accomplished by banning alcohol from the stadium. (Give full credit to opportunity theory.) For all the resurgence of the biological perspective on crime, no serious scholar believes that criminal behavior can be predicted from chemical traces in the blood or tissue of living (or dead) human beings. Counseling of course assumes something not in evidence since the invention of evaluation research—that treatment, especially "talk therapies," actually work. More important, self-control theory can tell us that universities have very low rates of crime because they recruit and employ industrious people with records of academic achievement and law-abiding behavior. Such people have miniscule rates of crime wherever they are found. (The best predictor of crime is prior crime. One of the best non-crime predictors of crime is academic performance.) The straightforward way to maintain a safe campus is thus to maintain high standards of academic accomplishment and zero-tolerance of criminal, especially violent behavior. It turns out that the killer of the professors would have been removed had either standard been met. He was failing his classes and had previously threatened one of the teachers he killed.[1]

Self-control theory and opportunity theory agree that preventing crime in one location does not typically create compensatory crime in other locations. Offenders do not require crime. They especially do not require particular criminal acts. Therefore, institutions should feel free to do internally whatever they can to control crime without worrying about the consequences for crime rates in other settings.

Crime on the Border

In contrast to college populations, U.S. Border Patrol agents appear to have a high rate of crime. For example, the thousand or so agents in the Tucson region produce an average of one criminal complaint a day, whereas the twenty-one thousand or so students at the University of California, Irvine produce about two offenses a day (including bike thefts.) Some of this difference is attributable to sex and education differences between the two populations. Border Patrol agents are largely men, and have at least a high school education. College students are about equally men and women. The age distribution of the two groups is roughly identical. Both are beyond the peak age of crime, but not far beyond it. The major difference would appear to be opportunities for crime, which are considerably greater for patrol agents, encountering as they do on a regular basis people intent on violating the law and willing to pay for it by whatever means available.

So, what would be the wisest practical policy for reducing the crime rate of agents on the border? It may be failure of our imaginations, but we see no advantage in further analysis of the opportunities available to them, and here as elsewhere examination of their motives would seem to be if anything counterproductive. This leaves careful screening of applicants as the primary method of crime reduction. Such screening would be based on prior involvement in criminal or analogous acts obtained from official records, self-reports, and the reports of others in a position to know.[2] Here is a preliminary report on the potential effectiveness of such screening from a thorough study of this issue:

> you may be interested to hear that self-control alone (as measured by the RBS [Retrospective Behavioral Self-Control Scale]) accounted for more variance in the dependent variable (deviance in the work place) than the entire set of 23 alternative predictors, including opportunity as well as situational and personality factors of motivation. (Marcus, 2002)

Broader Policy Implications

Recent research on the effectiveness of general deterrence, of the police, and of opportunity-based crime reduction strategies would seem to offer further opportunities for understanding the implications of self-control theory for environmental approaches to crime control.

General deterrence refers to the crime prevention effects of criminal sanctions (fines, imprisonment, execution) for the population as a whole. Self-control theory predicts that change in the certainty, severity, or alacrity of such punishments will have little effect on crime rates. This is especially true with respect to changes in the severity of punishments. Criminal justice penalties are typically too far removed in time for individuals low on self-control to incorporate them into their decision-making, however harsh such penalties might be. A shift from one to five years in prison as the penalty for a crime will have little effect on those who do not think beyond their immediate circumstances. (People who pay little heed to the consequences of reckless driving and hard drug use are unlikely to be overly concerned about the possible criminal justice consequences of their actions.) At the same time, the theory suggests that increasing the certainty of sanctions may produce the desired effects, especially if such increases also reduce the time-delay in their implementation. Under such conditions, certainty becomes an opportunity factor as we have defined it. Because immediate costs and benefits dominate the thinking of individuals with low self-control, even they will tend to be intimidated by the prospects of rapid reaction by the criminal justice system.

Our view seems consistent with widely accepted reviews of the deterrence literature (Blumstein et al., 1978) suggesting that within the context of hard to find deterrence effects, certainty had better support than severity. Recent reviews claim more than this for deterrence. Indeed, Nagin concludes that "evidence of a substantial deterrence effect is much firmer than it was two decades ago" (1998: 1) and even that "the collective actions of the criminal justice system exert a very substantial deterrent effect" on the crime rate (1998: 3). Given this shift in interpretation of the evidence, we should look again at how self-control notions square with the findings of deterrence research.

Nagin divides the empirical deterrence literature into three data- or research-design categories: ecological, interrupted time-series, and studies of perception. The first examines the effect of targeted and specific policy interventions such as police crackdowns on so-called hot-spots—e.g., sports bars frequented by large numbers of young people. His conclusion here is that "the evidence suggests that such interventions have at least a temporary effect, although decay is commonplace" (Nagin, 1998: 2). In terms of opportunity notions as understood by control theory, it might be said that the immediate presence of the police can reduce the opportunity for crime and thus curtail it in specific places at particular times, but the lack of opportunity will quickly evaporate when the surveillance is gone. Rather than evidence of classical deterrence, such findings are supportive of the idea that offenders tend to have low self-control.

The second type of study examines natural variations in crime rates and sanction levels across time and space. These studies, which sometimes show negative associations between crime rates and sanction levels, and sometimes do not, were the basis of the 1978 National Research Council review that concluded "evidence is more consistent with the idea of deterrence than not." Such studies are the central to the deterrence literature, but they remain inherently ambiguous, because social trends other than sanction levels (such as measures of attitudes toward crime and deviance and changes in demography) produce similar correlations over time. As Walker (2001) notes, these social and demographic trends are equally compatible with trends in unemployment, welfare caseloads, new AIDS cases, and births to teenage women. We may not agree that these indicators are causes of crime-rate trends, but Walker's conclusion is as defensible as deterrence conclusions based essentially on the same correlations. Thus, Walker's conclusion that "[c]rime is down because of the general social and economic health of the country, not because of any particular crime policy or policies" seems as consistent with these data as the claim of deterrence. In fact, in a recent review of the data on the deterrent and incapacitative effects of imprisonment trends, Blumstein and Wallman write, "[t]here has been a massive growth in prison populations since the early 1970s with no comparable effect on crime rates" (2000: 480).

The third type of deterrence study reviewed by Nagin is the so-called perceptual deterrence study. These are surveys (usually of college students) that show that people who perceive that sanction risks and costs are relatively high have lower self-reported crime levels than do people who perceive that sanction risks and costs are relatively low. In a series of studies, Nagin and Paternoster found such differences for a wide range of offenses, including tax evasion, drunk driving, theft, corporate crime, and sexual assault.

Such findings are exactly what self-control theory has always predicted. Those who least "need" deterrence (those with self-control) are those who are most likely to find the risks of crime unacceptable. Unlike deterrence theory, control theory predicts this outcome not because self-controlled individuals are intimidated by sanctions, but because they are already socialized. As a matter of fact, Nagin seems to agree: "these studies suggest that the deterrent effect of formal sanctions arises principally from fear of the social stigma that their imposition triggers." This is not quibble. In control theory, restraint is produced by family action during the first few years of life (creating self-control and concern for social stigma). In the deterrence model, restraint is produced by the contemporaneous fear of criminal justice sanctions. The data from such studies may fit both explanations, but only the deterrence model suggests manipulation of criminal justice penalties as a crime reduction strategy.

Policing. In control theory terms, variations in policing should be understood as efforts to reduce opportunities. Their effects should therefore be limited to the extent they alter in obvious and immediate ways opportunities for crime. Put another way, they should produce no lasting learning or deterrence effects. In our view, such predictions are consistent with the now considerable evidence from police research:

> There is. . . a substantial body of research evidence . . ., suggesting that policing resources and tactics have at best a tenuous relationship to levels of crime. (Reiner, 2000: 1037);
>
> The police do not prevent crime. . . . Experts know it, the police know it, but the public does not know it. Yet the police pretend that they are society's best defense against crime and continually argue that if they are given more resources, especially personnel, they will be able to protect communities against crime. This is a myth. (Bayley, 1994, cited in Eck and Maguire, 207);
>
> There is one thing that is a myth: The police have a substantial, broad, and independent impact on the nation's crime rate" (Eck and Maguire, 2000: 249);
>
> the limited evidence available suggests that it is possible that focused attention on small areas with very high numbers of crimes contributed to the overall reduction in violent crime (Eck and Maguire, 2000: 248);
>
> most of the claims about the police contribution overstate the available evidence. Some of the policing strategies that have received the most attention (for example, Compstat and zero-tolerance policing) are the least plausible candidates for contributing to the reduction in violent crime. (Eck and Maguire, 2000: 245)

Indeed, it is difficult to discover in the serious literature about policing effects any empirical support for policies directed at making policing more visible or intrusive.

Reductions in opportunity for impulsive crimes. Situational crime prevention, or target hardening, operates directly on the notion of opportunity. If the focus is on denying immediate benefits, spontaneous activity, and obvious temptations, situational crime prevention methods should be effective. Similarly, to the extent that they provide short-term or immediate sanctions, they have greater prospect of working. On the other hand, efforts to effect crime prevention in the community generally, by changing attitudes, civility, or collaborative behavior, are less likely to have noticeable impact on crime because they presume an incorrect image of the offender. A recent review of crime prevention programs seems to conclude as much: "There is substantial evidence to show that situational crime prevention works at the level of the situation. But there is much less evidence that any of these successes have ever permeated through to the level of the neighborhood, the city, the region, or the country. . . . There is much less evidence to show that community crime prevention works" (Bennett, 1998: 398).

Conclusions. Modern control theories of crime are not theories of justice. That is, they are not designed to provide guidance about all appropriate uses of criminal sanctions. Certainly criminal sanctions can be justified on numerous grounds, from retribution and reprobation to deterrence and incapacitation. All societies condemn and seek to control similar conduct by means of criminal sanctions, even though attempts to control conduct by criminal law varies by time and place. For this reason, among others, we decided to define crime for the purposes of the theory and independent of criminal law (Gottfredson and Hirschi, 1990). Most of the behavior proscribed by criminal law falls within the theory's definition, but some does not; and some behavior not criminalized is well within the intended scope of the theory. By definition, then, much of what goes on in criminal law and in efforts to reform it are outside the scope of control theory.

For example, the justice system continuously adjusts the penalties for criminal acts. When such adjustments are undertaken for the purpose of enhancing the deterrent effects of the law or to increase the incapacitative effect of sanctions, the domains of control theory and of the criminal law overlap and the effort may be said to be either correct or mistaken from the point of view of the theory. Often, however, penalties in criminal law are adjusted for purposes other than crime control—to condemn, to publicize, or to express reprobation. In such instances, the domains do not overlap. The policy is not right or wrong, according to the theory, and is not evidence one way or another about the theory. Invocation of the theory in such cases is illegitimate.

Take, for example, the now-common identification of some criminal acts as "hate crimes." What control theory says about the value of enhancing penalties because a crime was stimulated by hate, rather than by some other common motive for the use of force or fraud, depends on the purpose thought to be served by such enhancements. If the purpose is to signal condemnation, social disapproval, and blameworthiness, control theory is not particularly relevant. After all, as we have repeatedly noted, control theory explicitly eschews consideration of motives in its efforts to understand crime, assuming that all human motives and emotions (hate included) are capable of finding expression in crime. Is it worse to murder out of hate or out of greed, and should the state punish one murder more than the other? Are people who have committed four crimes more deserving of punishment than those who have committed two? Important as these questions may be for the functioning of the justice system, and for politics, these are not questions that control theory is particularly qualified to answer.

On the other hand, as we have argued in this chapter, elements of control theory do make strong predictions about utilitarian uses of criminal sanctions, particularly for deterrence, incapacitation, and rehabilitation (see Gottfredson and Hirschi, 1988, 1995).

A crime-derived description of opportunities also begins to help focus attention on the potential for various strategies for crime reduction. Because individual differences in predisposition are established prior to involvement in the opportunity structure (by and large), attempting to alter the course of these dispositions is a potentially powerful way to reduce opportunities. The growing empirical work on the long-term effects of early childhood interventions suggests that considerable improvement in self-control is possible with focused efforts (see Greenwood, 2002, for a review of early childhood prevention programs).

Policies based directly on control theory may have benefits in addition to those already noted. Because control theory tends to emphasize the role of childrearing rather than state police powers, common problems associated with more intensive policing may be avoided. Assisting single mothers to provide capable care for their children is substantially less likely to raise the problems of bias and heavy-handed police tactics that the intensive policing, mandatory arrests, or "hot spots" movements have generated. Apart from the dubious effectiveness of such intensive enforcement plans, the controversy around racial profiling that surrounds these efforts is the best current example. And of course bias is not the only problem with intensive police practices. As Justice Stevens has remarked: "even if these data were race neutral they would still indicate that society as a whole is paying a significant cost in infringement in liberty by these virtually random stops." (Cited in Mears and Harcourt, 2000, citing a study of New York City's Street Crimes Unit that made 45,000 stops, only 20 percent of which resulted in arrest.) Intensive policing has nearly always generated citizen opposition, charges of brutality, and unfairness. Such claims are surely less likely to surround efforts to provide targeted resources to enhance the life-chances of children.

Notes

1. According to press reports, the killer's threats to himself and others had at one time been reported to the campus police. Further action was not taken because a phone call from the police was not answered.
2. At one time (and perhaps still in some locations today) people denying involvement in criminal or analogous acts were considered liars and thus less trustworthy than those admitting such offenses! Modern research confirms that replies to such questions meet standard criteria of reliability and validity.

References

Akers, R. 1998. *Social Learning and Social Structure*. Boston: Northeastern University Press.

Bayley, D. 1994. *The Police for the Future*. New York: Oxford.

Bennett, T. 1998. "Crime Prevention." In M. Tonry (ed.), *The Handbook of Crime and Punishment*. New York: Oxford.

Blumstein, A., J. Cohen, and D. Nagin. 1978. *Deterrence and Incapacitation: Estimating the Effects of Sanctions on Crime Rates*. Washington, DC: National Academy Press.

Blumstein, A., and J. Wallman. (eds.) 2000. *The Crime Drop in America*. New York: Cambridge University Press.

Cloward, R., and L. Ohlin. 1960. *Delinquency and Opportunity*. New York: Macmillan.

Cohen, A. 1955. *Delinquent Boys*. New York: Macmillan.

Cohen, L., and M. Felson. 1979. "Social Change and Crime Rate Trends: A Routine Activities Approach." *American Sociological Review* 44: 588–608.

Cornish, D., and R. Clarke. 1986. *The Reasoning Criminal*. New York: Springer-Verlag.

Eck, J., and E. Maguire. 2000. "Have Changes in Policing Reduced Violent Crime?" Chapter 7 in A. Blumstein and J. Wallman (eds.), *The Crime Drop in America*. New York: Cambridge.

Felson, M., and R. Clarke. 1998. *Opportunity Makes the Thief*. Police Research Series Paper 98. London: Home Office.

Felson, R. 1996. "Big People Hit Little People: Sex Differences in Physical Power and Interpersonal Violence." *Criminology* 34: 433–452.

Glueck, S., and E. Glueck. 1950. *Unraveling Juvenile Delinquency*. Cambridge, MA: Harvard University Press.

Gottfredson, M., and T. Hirschi. 1988. "Career Criminals and Selective Incapacitation." Pp. 199–209 in J. Scott and T. Hirschi (eds.), *Controversal Issues in Crime and Justice*. Beverly Hills, CA: Sage.

Gottfredson, M., and T. Hirschi. 1990. *A General Theory of Crime*. Stanford: Stanford University Press.

Gottfredson, M., and T. Hirschi. 1995. "National Crime Control Policies." *Society* 32: 30-36.

Grasmick, H., C. Tittle, R. Bursik, and B. Arneklev. 1993. "Testing the Core Empirical Implications of Gottfredson and Hirschi's General Theory of Crime." *Journal of Research in Crime and Delinquency* 30: 5–29.

Greenwood, P. 2002. "Juvenile Crime and Juvenile Justice." In J. Wilson and J. Petersilia (eds.), *Crime*. Oakland, CA: ICS Press.

Hindelang, M., M. Gottfredson, and J. Garofalo. 1978. *Victims of Personal Crime*. Cambridge, MA: Ballinger.

Hirschi, T. 1983. "Crime and the Family." In J. Wilson (ed.), *Crime and Public Policy*. San Francisco: ICS Press.

Hirschi, T. 2002 [1969]. *Causes of Delinquency*. New Brunswick, NJ: Transaction Publishers.

Hirschi, T., and M. Gottfredson. 1987. "Causes of White Collar Crime." *Criminology* 25: 949–974.

Hirschi, T., and M. Gottfredson. 1993. "Commentary: Testing the General Theory of Crime." *Journal of Research in Crime and Delinquency* 30: 47–54.

Loeber, R., and M. Stouthamer-Loeber. 1986. "Family Factors as Correlates and Predictors of Juvenile Conduct Problems and Delinquency." Pp. 29–149 in M. Tonry and N. Morris (eds.), *Crime and Justice: An Annual Review of Research*, Vol. 7. Chicago: University of Chicago Press.

Marcus, Bernd. 2000. *Measuring Gottfredson and Hirschi's 1990 Construct of Self-Control*. Tuebingen, Germany: University of Tuebingen.

Marcus, Bernd. in press. "An Empirical Assessment of the Construct Validity of Two Alternative Self-Control Measures." *Educational and Psychological Measurement*.

Marcus, Bernd. 2002. Personal communication.

Matza, D. 1964. *Delinquency and Drift*. New York: Wiley.

McCord, J. 1979. "Some Child-Rearing Antecedents of Criminal Behavior in Adult Men." *Journal Personality and Social Psychology* 37:1477-86.

McCord, W., and J. McCord. 1959. *Origins of Crime*. New York: Columbia University Press.

Meares, T., and B. Harcourt. 2000. "Forward: Transparent Adjudication and Social Science Research in Constitutional Criminal Procedure." *Journal of Criminal Law and Criminology* 903: 733.

Merton, R. 1938. "Social Structure and 'Anomie'." *American Sociological Review* 3: 672-682.

Nagin, D. 1998. "Criminal Deterrence Research at the Outset of the Twenty-First Century." In *Crime and Justice: A Review of Research* 23: 1–43.

Parsons, T. 1951. *The Social System*. New York: Macmillan.

Reiner, R. 2000. "Policing and the Police." In M. Maguire et al. (eds.), *The Oxford Handbook of Criminology*. Oxford: Oxford University Press.

Sutherland, E. 1939. *Principles of Criminology*. Philadelphia: Lippincott.

Walker, S. 2001. *Sense and Nonsense about Crime and Drugs*. Belmont, CA: Wadsworth.

Zager, M. 1994. "Gender and Crime." Pp. 71-80 in T. Hirschi and M. Gottfredson (eds.), *The Generality of Deviance*. New Brunswick, NJ: Transaction Publishers.

2

Self-Control Pathology: The Elephant in the Living Room

Matt DeLisi

It would be an overstatement to say "once a criminal always a criminal," but it would be closer to the truth than to deny the evidence of a unifying and long-enduring pattern of encounters with the law for the most serious offenders. Richard Herrnstein (1995: 41)

"The elephant in the living room" is a cliché whereby people avoid discussing uncomfortable issues that plague them. No matter how evident this problem, it is tactfully avoided. It might seem strange to use this cliché given the attention accorded to self-control theory, indeed, dozens of scholars have studied it. While the bulk of the scholarly attention to self-control theory has been supportive (Hirschi and Gottfredson, 1993, 2000), others (e.g., Akers, 1991; Barlow, 1991; Geis, 2000) have grave concerns about purported deficiencies of the theory. These include that it is tautological and therefore ridden with fatal error, that it is no better than competing theories (e.g., social learning and differential association), that it explains little variation in crime, and that it is rife with alleged methodological problems which, not coincidentally, are the outcome of a scrutiny to which other theories are not subjected. Unfortunately, these concerns are academic red herrings that avoid the potentially more interesting and relevant aspects of self-control theory. Namely, self-control theory hits the bulls-eye. Other scholars do not want to admit this. In grand and yet cogent form, the theory parsimoniously matches the empirical reality of crime. Still, important things about self-control have remained unsaid.

The current thesis is that self-control is homologous to psychopathy and that the socialization processes that fail to instill self-control are analogous to sociopathy. The interconnectedness between these constructs underscores five criminological truisms. First, the family is the fundamental socialization agent and is most responsible for inculcating pro-social and antisocial values, beliefs, and behaviors. Consequently, familial dysfunction is the most profound criminogenic force. Second, the individual-level is the appropriate unit of analysis for studying crime. Sociological root causes are spurious because they are self-selected by individuals. Third, the stability and omnibus generality of self-control and psychopathy explain criminal versatility and other negative life outcomes for criminal offenders. Fourth, the criminal justice system, because of its delayed application, is generally unable to mollify criminal behavior, evidenced by the failure of most offenders. Fifth, the essence of self-control, psychopathy, and sociopathy reflect the Hobbesian assumptions of human nature that underwrite control theories. Each proposition accentuates the unquestionably negative nature of force and fraud and the individuals who commit such acts. This undeniably grim information forecasts the continued inability of society and the criminal justice system to appropriately control crime.[1]

The Salience of the Family

Everybody knows that the family has an enormous impact on criminal behavior. Common sense and the nightly news convey that it is no coincidence that the preponderance of chronic offenders and persons who commit atrocious criminal acts were often themselves the victims of considerable abuses at the hands of their own family. Based on the same logic, it is understood that caring, diligent, loving, responsible, righteous parents generally do not produce children who are prone to engage in generalized problematic behavior. Toward this end, Gottfredson and Hirschi (1990: 97) have acknowledged the "belief of the general public (and those who deal with offenders in the criminal justice system) that 'defective upbringing' or 'neglect' in the home is the primary cause of crime."

Childhood abuse, neglect, maltreatment, and the like have been linked to an assortment of problems including juvenile delinquency, antisocial personality, substance abuse, mental illness, poor self-image, alcoholism, and chronic criminality (Glueck and Glueck, 1930; Hirschi, 1994, 1995; Levy, 1942; McCord, 1979; Moffitt, 1990, 1993; Muller, Lemieux, and Sicoli, 2001; Widom, 1989). Haapasalo and Pokela (1999) reviewed several longitudinal studies of delinquency including the Cambridge-Somerville Youth Study, Cambridge Study in Delinquent Development, Christchurch Health and Development Study, Dunedin Multidisciplinary Health and Development Study, and the Oregon Youth Study. They consistently found that chronic adult criminals had experienced harsh, punitive, overly lax, and neglectful parenting; had been significantly more likely to be rejected by their parents;

and had suffered child abuse victimization. These findings were mirrored by data from the Pittsburgh Youth Study (Stouthamer-Loeber et al., 2001) and Rochester Youth Development Study (Thornberry, Ireland, and Smith, 2001). Family violence begets many problems.

Self-control theory is palatable to sociologists because of its focus on family socialization processes in causing problem behaviors. Effective parents are caregivers who monitor the child's behavior, recognize deviant behavior when it occurs, and punish such behavior. These socialization processes differentially produce self-control by age eight.[2] Parental attachment to the child, parental criminality, family size, and the single-parent family differentially constitute effective parenting and affect delinquency. For example, Farrington (2000) found that children at age ten who experienced adverse child-rearing, and had many siblings, convicted parents, family disruption, and young mothers were significantly more likely to be antisocial at age thirty-two. Similarly, McCord (1979) examined the family backgrounds of 201 men reared in the 1930s and 1940s. Studying their criminal records thirty years later, she found that home atmosphere was a significant antecedent of adult crime. Both lend retrospective support to the prospective claims of self-control theory.

Since the family is the primary arena of socialization it is the most significant determinant of an individual's life chances. Consequently, one of the most pivotal contributions of self-control theory is the explicit discussion of the role that abject parenting plays in producing criminal and largely unsuccessful persons (see Cochran et al., 1998; Gibbs, Giever, and Martin, 1998; Hay, 2001; Polakowski, 1994). This has enormous implications for criminological theory. What self-control theory says is that *one's own parents are most responsible* for consigning them to a life of failure. Moreover, the socialization processes instilling self-control occur so early in life (before the child has any real sense of agency) and are so profound, that they are ostensibly ontogenetic processes. This makes the causes of self-control and self-control itself largely intractable. Consider prenatal care as an example. Taking prenatal vitamins; consulting with doctors; getting sufficient sleep; eating a balanced diet; and avoiding stress, excessive physical exertion, smoking, alcohol, and substance use are just some of the things that an expectant mother can do to produce a healthy environment for her child. After birth, parents engage in an array of behaviors with significant consequences for their child (see Hirschi, 1995: 135; Moffitt, 1990).

The socialization processes that engender low self-control are more disturbing than Gottfredson and Hirschi theorize because they are in effect producing sociopathic children, the feral products of indifferent, incompetent, or overburdened parents (Lykken, 1995: xviii). Failing to effectively teach and monitor children has implications far more serious than simply producing youngsters who are unable to appreciate long-term tasks. Abject parenting promotes hyperactivity, fidgetiness, outbursts, and having a short-temper—all are simple examples of choosing "me" and "now" over "others" and "later." Teachers frequently describe such children as cheating, crafty, cruel, disobedient, impudent, lying, boredom-prone, and rude (McCord, 2000). These qualities pose life-long problems. Herpertz and Sass (2000) have suggested that severe familial difficulty helps engender the emotional deficiencies demonstrated by psychopaths. Specifically, children with poor conditioning fail to appreciate the consequences of their actions leading to a deficit of avoidance behavior. This emotional detachment compromises the child's ability to experience feelings such as guilt, which can inhibit violent impulses. Additionally, their emotional void contributes to under-arousal or chronic boredom, leading to the need for sensation seeking.

In sum, the parenting styles implicated by self-control theory are fertile ground for the production of sociopathy. Knowing this, it is difficult to imagine a more criminogenic environment than a home governed by abusive, ambivalent, indifferent, lazy, and selfish parent(s). Childhood problems such as inattentiveness in school, irritability, aggressiveness, hyperactivity, impulsiveness, and possessing a generally rancorous disposition are the likely outcomes of this environment, traits that are the harbingers of juvenile delinquency, adult criminality, and personal malaise (Loeber, 1987; Loeber and Farrington, 1998; Loeber and Stouthamer-Loeber, 1996; Robins, 1966). Once established, these traits are rarely undone, making dysfunctional family socialization the most destructive crime-causing force in contemporary society.[3]

Individuals, Self-Selection, and Crime

The following anecdote is useful when introducing students to self-control theory. Imagine that a female loved-one (e.g., daughter, sister, or mother) has brought home her fiancé. While the fiancé is in the other room, your loved-one briefly describes his personality and lifestyle. He is sporadically employed and generally stays at a job for only one to three months. While he has no official vocational training, he prefers work in the areas of construction and landscaping. He frequently quits or is fired because of disagreements with coworkers and supervisors. Indeed, it is often the case that the fiancé has a clear vision of how to improve the company, but meddling and conspiring bosses always get in the way. He recurrently collects unemployment benefits because he chooses to avoid underemployment. For the record, the fiancé, who described school as "not his thing," did manage to graduate high school, but found his two months in college unrewarding and quit.

Socially, the fiancé enjoys going to bars and is an enthusiastic drinker. He also smokes cigarettes, dabbles recreationally with illicit drugs (when they are provided by his friends), prefers to eat at fast-food restaurants rather than cook at home, and does not exercise. He is frequently bored and annoyed by others' expectations of him. The fiancé is friendly and only abusive, sullen, or irritable when intoxicated or when "things are not going his way." He has been "common-law married" twice and briefly engaged once before, but your loved-one is confident that their impending relationship is "the one."

Students find this exercise darkly humorous and, unfortunately, can immediately envision someone in their own lives who fits the profile. This resonance is the main allure of self-control theory, which suggests that multi-faceted behaviors and life outcomes are primarily the consequences of an interpersonal deficiency that coalesces in certain individuals. For example, Evans and his colleagues (1997: 490–91) found that self-control was related in the expected direction to "quality of family relationships, attachment to church, having criminal associates and values, educational attainment and occupational status, and residing in a neighborhood perceived to be disorderly. Self-control is also significantly related to quality of friendships and the analogous behavior measure is negatively related to marriage and positively related to nights out." DeLisi (2001a: 7) assessed that persons with low self-control "compromise their life chances by constantly living in the now and abjuring long-term benefits, are wholly self-absorbed and unconcerned with the welfare of others, are more likely to abuse alcohol and illicit drugs, and are generally hot-tempered." Hirschi and Gottfredson (1994: 261) noticed that "throughout the twentieth century, evidence has accumulated that people who tend to lie, cheat, and steal also tend to hit other people; that the same people tend to drink, smoke, use drugs, wreck cars, desert their spouses, quit their jobs, and come late to class."

In other words, lightning continually strikes persons who lack self-control. It is perhaps the only criminological theory that can realistically explain the profound failure that continually characterizes the lives of criminal offenders. It is not simply coincidence that criminal offenders (or the fiancé in the current example) are such profound losers. This brute reality is guaranteed to roil others in the academic community. For example, Evans and his colleagues (1997: 495) concluded that, "The general theory is a controversial perspective that many criminologists may, for ideological reasons, prefer to be proven false. Its emphasis on enduring individual differences and its disdain for social causation are out of step with the ways of thinking about crime now dominant in the discipline."

Abusive, neglectful, criminal, or simply lackadaisical parenting fails children long before that child can associate with delinquent peers, be labeled at school, be profiled by the police, feel strain, or decide to embrace a putative subculture. The damage is done early, and the individual selects most processes occurring afterward. It is this realization and the protean implications of it that constitute the "general" in *A General Theory of Crime*. This is a major concern since other theoretically relevant variables often claim credit for self-control. Gottfredson and Hirschi (1990: 167–68) have suggested, "It is hard to overstate the magnitude of this problem in criminology because of the tendency of people with low self-control to avoid attachment to or involvement in all social institutions—a tendency that produces a negative correlation between institutional experience and delinquency. This gives all institutions credit for negative effects on crime, credit they may not deserve."[4]

The problem with sociological root causes (e.g., poverty, minority status, discrimination, social inequality, neighborhood disorganization, socioeconomic strain) is that they most commonly typify persons *not involved in crime*. The majority, to use the aforementioned examples, of the impoverished, minority, discriminated against, have-nots, dwellers of disorganized neighborhoods, and strained individuals are not criminals. Conversely, individuals who lack self-control routinely demonstrate some involvement in problem behaviors. From this vantage, the social context is largely incidental since poorly controlled persons will find a way to manifest their individual-level deficiency. The same can be said of psychopaths who continually and volitionally injure others and engage in criminal conduct. They are what Robins and O'Neal (1958: 170) described as "a relatively circumscribed segment of the population distinguished by a life-long failure to conform to the social mores . . . it seems probable that [their] criminal activities are more frequently only one expression of a grossly disturbed life pattern of which transiency, violence, and unstable family relations, as well as crime, are typical." Individuals matter. Self-control theory and the psychopathy literature make this perfectly clear, especially given the staggering per capita human, social, and criminal costs of the worst offenders.

Versatility/Generality

Part and parcel of the consistently disadvantaged situations that persons with low self-control place themselves in is the idea of criminal versatility or generality. Gottfredson and Hirschi (1990) purport that self-control is a stable, enduring tendency (akin to criminal propensity) that manifests in different expressions of behavior depending on social circumstances. These behaviors are quick and relatively easy ways to satisfy some immediate desire, whether normative or criminal. They include sleeping through the morning alarm, cutting in line, choosing to skip appointments, silencing an annoying person, in short, following one's id. There is no rhyme or reason to the nature of the offense committed. Persons simply choose to commit violent, property, white-collar, nuisance, drug, or victimless crimes depending on their mood and immediate wants, the presence of suitable victims or objects of desire, the likelihood of easy gain, and the absence of police or other sanctioning agents. Consequently, aggravated assault, burglary, embezzlement, disorderly conduct, marijuana smoking, and prostitution are similar because they are borne from the same animus.

The stability and versatile manifestations of self-control are reconcilable with the general offending habits of criminal offenders. This is contrary to the idea of offense specialization which posits that criminals near-obsessively engage in specific types of crimes as if to satisfy some fixation. A popular example of this specialized offender is the serial killer, the seemingly functioning person by day who over time preys on other people and kills them. A cursory examination of the rap sheets of serial killers, however, reveals that they engage in an assortment of criminal acts in concert with the actual killing. These include abduction or kidnapping, rape, robbery, auto theft, theft, and drug use. Empirical research consistently supports the idea of criminal versatility (Britt, 1994; DeLisi, 2001c; Herrnstein, 1995; Hindelang, 1971; Hirschi, 1969; Loeber and Farrington, 1998; Simon, 2000; Wolfgang, Figlio, and Sellin, 1972), particularly among psychopaths (Black and Larson, 1999; Glueck and Glueck, 1943: 64/120, 1950: 239–40; Hare, 1993, 1996; Hare, McPherson, and Forth, 1988; Harris, Rice, and Cormier, 1991; Harris, Skilling, and Rice, 2001; Hart, Kropp, and Hare, 1988; Hemphill et al., 1998; Lykken, 1995).

A careful reading of Gottfredson and Hirschi's (1990: 91–94) discussion of the manifestations of self-control also reveals the isomorphism between their construct and psychopathy.[5] Particularly telling is the passage they cite from Harrison Gough's (1948: 362) early sociological investigation of psychopathy:

> Unconcern over the rights and privileges of others when recognizing them would interfere with personal satisfaction in any way; impulsive behavior . . . ; inability to form deep or persistent attachments to other persons or to identify in interpersonal relationships; poor judgment and planning in attaining defined goals; apparent lack of anxiety and distress over social maladjustment . . . ; a tendency to project blame onto others and to take no responsibility for failures . . . ; almost complete lack of dependability and unwillingness to assume responsibility; and, finally, emotional poverty.

The diagnostic overlap between psychopathy and self-control is alarming, and both constructs denote a generally problematic disposition that does not lead to happy endings. For example, Cleckley's (1941) seminal criteria included items such as failure to follow any life plan, unresponsiveness in relationships, pathological egocentricity and incapacity for love, poor judgment, and lack of remorse or shame, insincerity, and unreliability. This profile was ultimately reformulated by Robert Hare (1991, 1993, 1996), whose Psychopathy Checklist-Revised (PCL-R) is the definitive measure of psychopathy. The PCL-R is a twenty-item index comprising two types of factors, interpersonal/affective and socially deviant lifestyle. The interpersonal/affective factors includes glibness/superficial charm, grandiose sense of self-worth, pathological lying, conning/manipulative, lack of guilt or remorse, shallow affect, callousness/lack of empathy, and failure to accept responsibility for one's actions. The socially deviant lifestyle factor includes proneness to boredom/need for stimulation, parasitic lifestyle, poor behavioral controls, sexual promiscuity, impulsivity, irresponsibility, lack of realistic long-term goals, early onset of problems, marital problems, juvenile delinquency, noncompliance with the criminal justice system, and *criminal versatility.*

In other words, psychopaths and persons lacking self-control will, by definition, serve themselves at the expense of others regardless of the context. Criminal versatility enhances the idea that the ultimate driving force of crime lies within the individual, making the claims of individual pathology approaches like self-control and psychopathy more believable. Mendacious claims with social psychological approaches (e.g., social learning) simply cannot compete with the consistency posed by individual-level defects.

Criminal Justice: Too Little, Too Late

Gottfredson and Hirschi are less than enthusiastic about the ability of the state to deter or control crime. In their words (1990: 269), "Given the ineffectiveness of natural learning environments in teaching self-control, we would not expect the artificial environments available to the criminal justice system to have much impact." Indeed, self-control theory anticipates criminal justice systems' failure to correct delinquent behavior for two reasons. First, the invariant effect of age on crime (Hirschi and Gottfredson, 1983) posits that offenders will cease and desist from offending as they pass through the crime-prone years during adolescence and early adulthood. Particularly for the purpose of deterrence, sanctions are largely redundant if individuals will quit crime on their own. Furthermore, based on the logic of the invariant age-crime curve, selective incapacitation efforts are futile because they constitute warehousing persons, even high-rate offenders, whose criminal offending careers are undeniably on the wane (see LeBlanc, 1997).

Second, the etiology of self-control occurs in early childhood. Once established, it remains a stable individual characteristic for life. In fact, Gottfredson and Hirschi (1990: 108) suggest, "The stability of criminality is a staple of pragmatic criminology." This means that once engendered, low self-control cannot be undone (Arneklev, Cochran, and Gainey, 1998). The inexorable nature of low self-control is reconcilable with the failure of criminal justice policy to effectively reduce recidivism. Concepts such as correction and rehabilitation literally mean to restore to a prior state or condition of health, functioning, or capacity. To be corrected, an individual must have been functioning in the first place. Theoretically, the purpose of sanctions is to compel the deviant to relinquish their deviance and recommit to conformity. But, what if they have never conformed? Can individuals learn to do something (e.g., behave) that was precluded by their socialization experiences? Persons who have never had a caregiver in their life are, simply, "designed to fail" (DeLisi, 2001b). Well-meaning social scientists, judicious probation officers, earnest mental health counselors, firm but supportive parole officers, or liberal judges cannot realistically rectify these voids.

The application of self-control to criminal justice system issues is in its infancy, but already the empirical evidence of self-control's detrimental effects is daunting. Just as self-control has been found to be predictive of crime in student or community samples (review Pratt and Cullen, 2000), it is also inversely related to acts of force and fraud among high-risk offender samples (DeLisi, 2001a, 2001b; Longshore, 1998; Longshore and Turner, 1998; Longshore, Turner, and Stein, 1996). Moreover, low self-control is helpful in explaining why many offenders do not successfully comply with criminal justice system agents. For example, DeLisi (2001a) suggested that the use of aliases and alternative/fraudulent dates of birth, places of birth, and social security numbers should be used to behaviorally operationalize self-control since attempting to deceive the police is risky, shortsighted, impulsive, and irresponsible. Empirically, offenders who employ numerous aliases and other forms of deception were significantly more involved in violent, property, white-collar, and nuisance offending than persons with greater self-control. Also, offenders who used multiple fraudulent identifiers also tended to miss court appearances, violate probationary and parole sentences, escaped, and were more frequently convicted of felonies and sentenced to prison (DeLisi, 2001b).

Low self-control might explain why only a fraction of persons who engage in illegal behavior are actually arrested. Perhaps impulsivity (e.g., frequenting bars, going out at night, driving after drinking alcohol) differentiates arrestees from secret deviants, or perhaps the lackluster personality traits (e.g., hot-tempered demeanor) of persons with low self-control mobilizes police attention. Self-control might prove helpful in explaining why many defendants prefer the relatively immediate results of a plea agreement rather than endure a trial, are unable or unwilling to abide by bond conditions such as sobriety, or generally have difficulty with the responsibilities posed by community corrections. Within the parameters of self-control theory, it is clear why the criminal justice system is largely ineffectual: It is applied far too late in life to benefit the criminal defendants it is designed to correct.

Unfortunately, "too little, too late" might be optimistic if the pathology posed by self-control approaches the criminal justice track record of psychopathic offenders. Psychopaths, by their very nature are not amenable to treatment or correction, thus their recidivism is a certainty (Black and Larson, 1999; Cleckley, 1941; Hare, 1993; Harris, Skilling, and Rice, 2001; Lykken, 1995; Robins, 1966). Reid and Gacono (2000: 648) have expressed the reason for this "therapeutic nihilism:"

> Psychopaths feel pain, but it is temporary and poorly remembered after it is gone. They may feel anxiety associated with immediate danger, but their anticipation of danger is more often a stimulation and not particularly uncomfortable. Getting caught and punished for a crime is to be avoided, but the combination of the low probability of being caught and the even lower probability of being punished makes the stimulation of antisocial behavior easily worth the gamble. In fact, the "gamble" itself, within a personality structure characterized by proneness to boredom, makes the antisocial behavior itself appealing.

It is not difficult to superimpose this passage into the logic of *A General Theory of Crime.* The idea that poorly controlled offenders will ever turn it around is a liberal will-'o-the wisp, and a compelling reason why the criminal justice system is primarily in the business of warehousing and incapacitating rather than rehabilitating and treating.

Hobbes and Crime

Most theories of delinquency offer explanations about the mechanisms by which individuals are propelled toward committing crime. The core assumption inherent to these theories is that actors are generally good and therefore not predisposed to commit bad acts. Environments or social conditions on the other hand are potentially bad if for no other reason than they may entice normally good persons to do bad things. These extra-individual phenomena include poverty, unfair labeling, discrimination, strain, and associating with people who already commit delinquent acts. Control theories are diametrically different. They assume that people are simply self-interested and therefore not concerned with the feelings of others or the community. In short, control theory posits a more cynical and mean view of human nature in which maximizing pleasure and minimizing pain are the "sovereign masters" of man. Crime, then, is a priori expected. The task at hand for criminologists of this orientation is to explain why people do not engage in crime: What situations or phenomena cause them to resist their natural impulses and behave?

Control theory is squarely in the classical tradition, specifically the thought of Thomas Hobbes. Writing in the seventeenth century, Hobbes held a rather pessimistic view of human beings. Man was framed as a competitive, quarrelsome, diffident creature in search of glory who was not adverse to "use violence to make themselves master of other men's persons, wives, children, and cattle" (Hobbes, 1987[1651]: 64–65). This profile was characteristic of all persons, not just wrongdoers; therefore human nature itself was unutterably bad. Hobbes' famous proclamation is that the life of man is solitary, poor, nasty, brutish, and short.

Because of his intrinsic hate, lust, ambition, and covetousness, man must somehow be kept in line to avoid a degenerative "war of all against all." The sanctioning mechanism is the state or *Leviathan* and its necessary institutions including law and criminal justice. According to Hobbes (1987[1651]: 158), "of all the passions that which inclines man least to break the laws is fear. Nay, excepting some generous nature, it is the only thing (when there is appearance of profit, or pleasure by breaking the laws) that makes men keep them." Therefore, it is the state's function to strike fear and impose penalty since self-sanctioning will not naturally occur.

The way to ward off such disagreeable tendencies is for parents or caregivers to effectively socialize their children. This entails investing in children, instilling pro-social beliefs and values, and closely monitoring children to recognize and adjust their aberrant behavior. Fundamentally, this teaches children that there is more to life than the hasty and immediate gratification of one's desires, that some desirable outcomes take longer to achieve, that verbal articulation rather than a physical tantrum or primal scream is a more civilized way of handling discomfort, and that other people matter and are worthy of consideration. Ineffective parenting will have difficulty surmounting the feral tendencies described by Hobbes. Furthermore, it makes sense that children who are neglected, beaten, malnourished, abandoned, bartered for some other commodity, kept in a closet, or subjected to continual victimization will not thrive.

Gottfredson and Hirschi spend an entire chapter describing the logical structure of crime as self-serving acts of force and fraud that "provide benefits with similar qualities such as immediacy, brevity of obligation, and effortlessness" (1990: 21). They do not, however, provide discussion about the moral and social nature of crime and thus do not go far enough in linking the characteristics of criminal acts to the character of persons with low self-control. Force and fraud are not simply physical and immediate means to achieving self-serving ends; force and fraud are negative, bad, mean-spirited, and misanthropic. In other words, self-control, pathological offenders, and the moral and social nature of crime are textbook Hobbes.

Crimes are unquestionably bad things. This simple point is lost by media reports that bombard weary residents, criminal justice practitioners who cannot afford to be weighted down by the endlessly depressing nature of their job, and criminologists immersed in generally arcane research. Yet, the commission of crime and the resulting victimization purely reflect the malicious drama characterized by Hobbes. The loss and pain that result from murder are incalculable as are the physical and emotional distress, embarrassment, shame, and anger felt by rape victims. Armed robbery is a visceral gun-in-the-face in which perpetrators use the threat of lethal force to obtain usually scant amounts of money. The common victim of armed robbery is the person whose unfortunate circumstance was showing up for work at a gas station, convenience store, or bank. Aggravated assault is an attack in which serious bodily injury is incurred, such as shooting, stabbing, bludgeoning, or stomping another person.

Burglary victims must live with the knowledge that an unwanted person has occupied the intimate confines of their home. Theft, the universal crime, is loss of something of value, taken by someone else who wanted it. Auto theft is this to a greater degree, although given our reliance on automobiles in the United States, losing one's car has several unfortunate implications. Forgery commits an absolute mess for the victim whose checkbook was used. Disorderly conduct, public intoxication, and vagrancy frighten citizens and expose onlookers to drunken, disrespectful behavior. The list of deviance and the devastation wrought is endless: price-fixing, infidelity, substance abuse, domestic violence, extortion, prostitution, child abuse, ethnic intimidation, tax evasion, pimping, etc. Crime is serious business that creates pain, instills fear, ruins life chances, contributes to balkanization, devalues communities, and necessitates ugly state intervention. This is Hobbes' script.

Criminals are morally and socially reprehensible. This realization is devastating to those intent on lionizing offenders and absolving their individual-level flaws. Indeed, after a decade of empirical research, could one come to the conclusion that persons with low self-control (read criminals) are not flawed? Self-control is facilitative of failure in traffic (Junger and Tremblay, 1999; Keane, Maxim, and Teevan, 1993), school (Cochran et al., 1998; Gibbs and Giever, 1995; cf. Tibbetts and Myers, 1999), work (Gibson and Wright, 2001), family (Evans et al., 1997; Gibson, Wright, and Tibbetts, 2000), dating (Sellers, 1999), and complying with the criminal justice system (DeLisi, 2001b). Moreover, drinking alcohol; substance abuse; smoking; gambling; violent, property, white-collar, and nuisance offending; and being victimized are significantly more likely for persons with low self-control (Arneklev et al., 1993; Brownfield and Sorenson, 1993; DeLisi, 2001a; Gibbs, Giever, and Martin, 1998; Piquero and Tibbetts, 1996; Schreck, 1999; Sorenson and Brownfield, 1995).

Thirty years ago, Hirschi (1973) published a wry, reflexive article about the ideological games that criminologists play and how these dogmatic procedural rules often fly in the face of empirical reality (also see Gottfredson and Hindelang, 1980). Self-control theory has raised the ire of criminologists because it proudly violates these rules (e.g., avoids "kinds-of-people" theory and the "evil causes evil fallacy"). But unfortunately, both of these are grimly true. A multitude of problems are likely for persons with low self-control, and their dysfunction is the outcome of an earlier one, abject parenting. Taken together, self-control evokes the messages of Hobbes: People are bad creatures who do bad things to one another. Indeed, this message is the moral undercurrent of crime.

Conclusion

Gottfredson and Hirschi (1990: xiii) were motivated to create self-control theory because they were "unhappy with the ability of academic criminology to provide believable explanations of criminal behavior." What they sought was a theory complete with the "ring of truth." They have succeeded. The empirical support of self-control theory is all the more surprising since so many scholars have been sniping at it. These claims of refutation are the usual academic fare: alternative and better theories, concerns over conceptualization, measurement, model specification, tautology, applicability to "diverse" subjects, and so on.

What has not, until now, been adequately discussed are the linkages between self-control and pathological conditions like psychopathy and sociopathy. These are frighteningly real phenomena that are significantly engendered by familial dysfunction and parents unwilling or unable to sensibly rear their children. The products are selfish, mean-spirited, socially lacking children who will grow to fail in all arenas of life. This failure rears its ugly head regardless of context. Pathologies like self-control lend themselves to disparate criminal and analogously negative behaviors and constitute tremendous human, social, and fiscal costs. Furthermore, the early-life etiology of self-control makes it a largely intractable problem that renders the criminal justice system powerless. Until the pernicious problems that plague the American family are genuinely addressed, pathology will flourish, and the painful relevance of self-control theory will remain all too clear.

Notes

1. Psychopathy, sociopathy, antisocial personality disorder, and low self-control are similar phenomena. However, they are not the same. The former three constructs in particular are often and incorrectly used interchangeably. Briefly, psychopathy is a personality disorder defined by a distinctive cluster of behaviors and inferred personality traits, most of which society views as pejorative (Hare, 1993: ix). It is a lifelong condition found in approximately 5 percent of males. Psychopaths are conscienceless predators whom, it has been estimated, commit over 50 percent of the violent crime in the United States. The etiology of psychopathy is not completely known, however strong evidence suggests that it is partially but substantially heritable. Sociopathy is prototypically akin to psychopathy, however its etiology is social. Abusive, abject, or abysmal parenting like those implicated by self-control theory produces sociopaths. Antisocial personality disorder is a diagnosis used by the American Psychiatric Association and published in the *Diagnostic and Statistical Manual (DSM)*. A "pervasive pattern of disregard for and violation of the rights of others occurring since age 15" and three or more psychopathic-like personality traits are needed to meet a diagnosis of ASPD. ASPD is much more common than psychopathy; 90 percent of psychopaths meet the criteria for ASPD, but only 30 percent of the latter meet the guidelines for psychopathy (Shipley and Arrigo, 2001: 409). For a look at the history of these related concepts, see (Arrigo and Shipley, 2001; Hare, 1993; Harris, Skilling, and Rice, 2001; Lykken, 1995; Shipley and Arrigo, 2001).
2. Self-control is actually developmental, not static as is generally and incorrectly expressed in the literature (for an exception, see Sampson and Laub, 2001: 247).

3. Cochran and his colleagues (1998: 247) found mixed empirical support for self-control theory. They admonished that "it appears that other factors beyond effective parenting may also play a role in the development of self-control." They are probably correct in their assessment; however this is not necessarily a damaging criticism of the theory. Indeed, it is probable that children who demonstrate psychopathy are very difficult to govern and thereby compromise the ability of parents to instill self-control. The idea that children can demonstrate psychopathy has been supported empirically (Edens et al., 2001; Farrington, 2000; Harris, Skilling, and Rice, 2001; Lynam, 1996).
4. Wilson and Herrnstein (1985: 42) are aligned with this line of reasoning: "Whatever factors contribute to crime . . . they must all affect the behavior of individuals if they are to affect crime. If people differ in their tendency to commit crime, we must express those differences in terms of how some array of factors affects their individual decisions."
5. In addition to the influence of Gough's (1948) work, Gottfredson and Hirschi (1990) also heavily reference Lee Robins' (1966) research on sociopathy. The interest in psychopathy is also evident in Hirschi's (1969: 17–18, 24) *Causes of Delinquency.*

References

Akers, Ronald L. 1991. "Self-Control as a General Theory of Crime." *Journal of Quantitative Criminology* 7: 201–211.

Arneklev, Bruce J., John K. Cochran, and Randy Gainey. 1998. "Testing Gottfredson and Hirschi's 'Low Self-Control' Stability Hypothesis: An Exploratory Study." *American Journal of Criminal Justice* 23: 107–127.

Arneklev, Bruce J., Harold G. Grasmick, Charles R. Tittle, and Robert J. Bursik, Jr. 1993. "Low Self-control and Imprudent Behavior." *Journal of Quantitative Criminology* 9: 225–247.

Arrigo, Bruce A., and Stacey Shipley. 2001. "The Confusion over Psychopathy (I): Historical Considerations." *International Journal of Offender Therapy and Comparative Criminology* 45: 325–344.

Barlow, Hugh D. 1991. "Explaining Crime and Analogous Acts, or the Unrestrained Will Grab at Pleasure Whenever They Can." *Journal of Criminal Law and Criminology* 82: 229–242.

Black, Donald W., and C. L. Larson. 1999. *Bad Boys, Bad Men: Confronting Antisocial Personality Disorder.* Oxford: Oxford University Press.

Britt, Chester L. 1994. "Versatility." Pp. 173–192 in Travis Hirschi and Michael Gottfredson (eds.), *The Generality of Deviance.* New Brunswick, NJ: Transaction.

Brownfield, David, and Ann Marie Sorenson. 1993. "Self Control and Juvenile Delinquency: Theoretical Issues and an Empirical Assessment of Selected Elements of a General Theory of Crime." *Deviant Behavior* 24: 243–264.

Cleckley, Hervey. 1941. *The Mask of Sanity.* St. Louis, MO: Mosby.

Cochran, John K., Peter B. Wood, Christine S. Sellers, Wendy Wilkerson, and Mitchell B. Chamlin. 1998. "Academic Dishonesty and Low Self-Control: An Empirical Test of a General Theory of Crime." *Deviant Behavior* 19: 227–255.

DeLisi, Matt. 2001a. "It's All in the Record: Assessing Self-Control Theory with an Offender Sample." *Criminal Justice Review* 26: 1–16.

———. 2001b. "Designed to Fail: Self-Control and Involvement in the Criminal Justice System." *American Journal of Criminal Justice* 26: 131–148.

———. 2001c. "Extreme Career Criminals." *American Journal of Criminal Justice* 25: 239–252.

Edens, John F., Jennifer L. Skeem, Keith R. Cruise, and Elizabeth Cauffman. 2001. "Assessment of 'Juvenile Psychopathy' and Its Association with Violence: A Critical Review." *Behavioral Sciences and the Law* 19: 53–80.

Evans, T. David, Francis T. Cullen, Velmer S. Burton, Jr., R. Gregory Dunaway, and Michael L. Benson. 1997. "The Social Consequences of Self-control: Testing the General Theory of Crime." *Criminology* 35: 475–504.

Farrington, David P. 2000. "Psychosocial Predictors of Adult Antisocial Personality and Adult Convictions." *Behavioral Sciences and the Law* 18: 605–622.

Geis, Gilbert. 2000. "On the Absence of Self-control as the Basis for a General Theory of Crime: A Critique." *Theoretical Criminology* 4: 35–54.

Gibbs, John J., and Dennis Giever. 1995. "Self-control and Its Manifestations among University Students: An Empirical Test of Gottfredson and Hirschi's General Theory." *Justice Quarterly* 12: 231–256.

Gibbs, John J., Dennis Giever, and Jamie S. Martin. 1998. "Parental Management and Self-control: An Empirical Test of Gottfredson and Hirschi's General Theory." *Journal of Research in Crime and Delinquency* 35: 40–70.

Gibson, Chris, and John Wright. 2001. "Low Self-control and Coworker Delinquency: A Research Note." *Journal of Criminal Justice* 29: 483–492.

Gibson, Chris L., John Paul Wright, and Stephen G. Tibbetts. 2000. "An Empirical Assessment of the Generality of the General Theory of Crime: The Effects of Low Self-control on Social Development." *Journal of Crime and Justice* 23: 109–134.

Glueck, Sheldon, and Eleanor T. Glueck. 1930. *500 Criminal Careers.* New York: Knopf.

Glueck, Sheldon, and Eleanor Glueck. 1943. *Criminal Careers in Retrospect.* New York: The Commonwealth Fund.

———. 1950. *Unraveling Juvenile Delinquency.* New York: The Commonwealth Fund.

Gottfredson, Michael R., and Michael J. Hindelang. 1980. "Trite But True." *American Sociological Review* 45: 338–340.

Gottfredson, Michael R., and Travis Hirschi. 1990. *A General Theory of Crime*. Stanford, CA: Stanford University Press.

Gough, Harrison. 1948. "A Sociological Theory of Psychopathy." *American Journal of Sociology* 53: 359–366.

Haapasalo, Janna, and Elina Pokela. 1999. "Child-Rearing and Child Abuse Antecedents of Criminality." *Aggression and Violent Behavior* 4: 107–127.

Hare, Robert D. 1991. *The Hare Psychopathy Checklist–Revised.* Toronto: Multi–Health Systems.

———. 1993. *Without Conscience: The Disturbing World of the Psychopaths Among Us.* New York: The Guilford Press.

———. 1996. "Psychopathy: A Clinical Construct Whose Time Has Come." *Criminal Justice and Behavior* 23: 25–54.

Hare, Robert D., Leslie M. McPherson, and Adelle E. Forth. 1988. "Male Psychopaths and Their Criminal Careers." *Journal of Consulting and Clinical Psychology* 56: 710–714.

Harris, Grant T., Marnie E. Rice, and Catherine A. Cormier. 1991. "Psychopathy and Violent Recidivism." *Law and Human Behavior* 15: 625–637.

Harris, Grant T., Tracey A. Skilling, and Marnie E. Rice. 2001. "The Construct of Psychopathy." Pp. 197–264 in Michael Tonry and Norval Morris (eds.), *Crime and Justice: An Annual Review of Research*. Chicago: University of Chicago Press.

Hart, Stephen D., Philip R. Kropp, and Robert D. Hare. 1988. "Performance of Male Psychopaths following Conditional Release from Prison." *Journal of Consulting and Clinical Psychology* 56: 227–232.

Hay, Carter. 2001. "Parenting, Self-control, and Delinquency: A Test of Self-control Theory." *Criminology* 39: 707–736.

Hemphill, James F., Ron Templeman, Stephen Wong, and Robert D. Hare. 1998. "Psychopathy and Crime: Recidivism and Criminal Careers." Pp. 375–399 inn D. Cooke, A. Forth, and R. Hare (eds.), *Psychopathy: Theory, Research, and Implications for Society*. Boston, MA: Kluwer Academic Publishers.

Herpertz, Sabine C., and Henning Sass. 2000. "Emotional Deficiency and Psychopathy." *Behavioral Sciences and the Law* 18: 567–580.

Herrnstein, Richard J. 1995. "Criminogenic Traits." Pp. 39–64 in James Q. Wilson and Joan Petersilia (eds.), *Crime*. San Francisco, CA: ICS Press.

Hindelang, Michael J. 1971. "Age, Sex, and the Versatility of Delinquent Involvements." *Social Problems* 18: 522–535.

Hirschi, Travis. 1969. *Causes of Delinquency*. Berkeley: University of California Press.

———. 1973. "Procedural Rules and the Study of Deviant Behavior." *Social Problems* 21: 159–173.

———. 1994. "Family." Pp. 47–69 in Travis Hirschi and Michael R. Gottfredson (eds.), *The Generality of Deviance*. New Brunswick, NJ: Transaction.

———. 1995. "The Family." Pp. 121–140 in James Q. Wilson and Joan Petersilia (eds.), *Crime*. San Francisco, CA: ICS Press.

Hirschi, Travis, and Michael Gottfredson. 1983. "Age and the Explanation of Crime." *American Journal of Sociology* 89: 552–584.

———. 1993. "Commentary: Testing the General Theory of Crime." *Journal of Research in Crime and Delinquency* 30: 47–54.

———. 1994. "Substantive Positivism and the Idea of Crime." Pp. 253–270 in Travis Hirschi and Michael R. Gottfredson (eds.), *The Generality of Deviance*. New Brunswick, NJ: Transaction Publishers.

———. 2000. "In Defense of Self-Control." *Theoretical Criminology* 4: 55–70.

Hobbes, Thomas. 1987[1651]. *Leviathan.* London: The Guernsey Press.

Junger, Marianne, and Richard Tremblay. 1999. "Self Control, Accidents, and Crime." *Criminal Justice and Behavior* 26: 485–501.

Keane, Carl, Paul S. Maxim, and James J. Teevan. 1993. "Drinking and Driving, Self Control, and Gender: Testing a General Theory of Crime." *Journal of Research in Crime and Delinquency* 30: 30–46.

LeBlanc, Marc. 1997. "Socialization or Propensity: Does Integrative Control Theory Apply to Adjudicated Boys?" *Studies on Crime and Crime Prevention* 2: 200–223.

Levy, David M. 1942. "Psychopathic Personality and Crime." *Journal of Educational Sociology* 16: 99–114.

Loeber, Rolf. 1987. "The Prevalence, Correlates, and Continuity of Serious Conduct Problems in Elementary School Children." *Criminology* 25: 615–642.

Loeber, Rolf, and Magda Stouthamer–Loeber. 1996. "The Development of Offending." *Criminal Justice and Behavior* 23: 12–24.

Loeber, Rolf, and David P. Farrington (eds.), 1998. *Serious and Violent Juvenile Offenders: Risk Factors and Successful Interventions.* Thousand Oaks, CA: Sage.

Longshore, Douglas. 1998. "Self-control and Criminal Opportunity: A Prospective Test of the General Theory of Crime." *Social Problems* 45: 102–113.

Longshore, Douglas, and Susan Turner. 1998. "Self-Control and Criminal Opportunity: A Cross–Sectional Test of the General Theory of Crime." *Criminal Justice and Behavior* 25: 81–98.

Longshore, Douglas, Susan Turner, and J. Stein. 1996. "Self-Control in a Criminal Sample: An Examination of Construct Validity." *Criminology* 34: 209–228.

Lykken, David T. 1995. *The Antisocial Personalities.* Hillsdale, NJ: Lawrence Erlbaum Associates.

Lynam, Donald R. 1996. "Early Identification of Chronic Offenders: Who Is the Fledgling Psychopath?" *Psychological Bulletin* 120: 209–234.

McCord, Joan. 1979. "Some Child–Rearing Antecedents of Criminal Behavior in Adult Men." *Journal of Personality and Social Psychology* 37: 1477–1486.

———. "Developmental Trajectories and Intentional Actions." *Journal of Quantitative Criminology* 16: 237–253.

Moffitt, Terrie E. 1990. ""Juvenile Delinquency and Attention Deficit Disorder: Boys' Developmental Trajectories." *Child Development* 61: 893–910.

———. 1993. "Adolescence–Limited and Life–Course Persistent Antisocial Behavior: A Developmental Taxonomy." *Psychological Review* 100: 674–701.

Muller, Robert T., Kathryn E. Lemieux, and Lisa A. Sicoli. 2001. "Attachment and Psychopathology among Formerly Maltreated Adults." *Journal of Family Violence* 16: 151–169.

Piquero, Alex, and Stephen Tibbetts. 1996. "Specifying the Direct and Indirect Effects of Low Self-control and Situational Factors in Offenders' Decision Making: Toward a More Complete Model of Rational Offending." *Justice Quarterly* 13: 481–510.

Polakowski, Michael. 1994. "Linking Self– and Social Control with Deviance: Illuminating the Structure Underlying a General Theory of Crime and Its Relation to Deviant Activity." *Journal of Quantitative Criminology* 10: 41–78.

Pratt, Travis C., and Francis T. Cullen. 2000. "The Empirical Status of Gottfredson and Hirschi's General Theory of Crime: A Meta–Analysis." *Criminology* 38: 931–964.

Reid, William H., and Carl Gacono. 2000. "Treatment of Antisocial Personality, Psychopathy, and Other Characterologic Antisocial Syndromes." *Behavioral Sciences and the Law* 18: 647–662.

Robins, Lee N. 1966. *Deviant Children Grown Up: A Sociological and Psychiatric Study of Sociopathic Personality*. Baltimore, MD: Williams and Wilkins.

Robins, Lee N., and Patricia O'Neal. 1958. "Mortality, Mobility, and Crime: Problem Children 30 Years Later." *American Sociological Review* 23: 162–171.

Sampson, Robert J., and John H. Laub. 2001. "Understanding Variability in Lives Through Time: Contributions of Life–Course Criminology." Pp. 242–258 in Alex Piquero and Paul Mazerolle (eds.), *Life–Course Criminology: Contemporary and Classic Readings*. Belmont, CA: Wadsworth.

Schreck, Christopher. 1999. "Criminal Victimization and Low Self-Control: An Extension and Test of a General Theory of Crime." *Justice Quarterly* 16: 633–654.

Sellers, Christine. 1999. "Self-Control and Intimate Violence: An Examination of the Scope and Specification of the General Theory of Crime." *Criminology* 37: 375–404.

Shipley, Stacey, and Bruce A. Arrigo. 2001."The Confusion over Psychopathy (II): Implications for Forensic (Correctional) Practice." *International Journal of Offender Therapy and Comparative Criminology* 45: 407–420.

Simon, Leonore M. J. 2000. "An Examination of the Assumptions of Specialization, Mental Disorder, and Dangerousness in Sex Offenders." *Behavioral Sciences and the Law* 18: 275–308.

Skilling, Tracey A., Vernon L. Quinsey, and Wendy M. Craig. 2001. "Evidence of a Taxon Underlying Serious Antisocial Behavior in Boys." *Criminal Justice and Behavior* 28: 450–470.

Sorenson, Ann Marie, and David Brownfield. 1995. "Adolescent Drug Use and a General Theory of Crime: An Analysis of a Theoretical Integration." *Canadian Journal of Criminology* 37: 19–37.

Stouthamer-Loeber, Magda, Rolf Loeber, D. Lynn Homish, and Evelyn Wei. 2001. "Maltreatment of Boys and the Development of Disruptive and Delinquent Behavior." *Development and Psychopathology* 13: 941–955.

Thornberry, Terence P., Timothy O. Ireland, and Carolyn A. Smith. 2001. "The Importance of Timing: The Varying Impact of Childhood and Adolescent Maltreatment on Multiple Problem Outcomes." *Development and Psychopathology* 13: 957–979.

Tibbetts, Stephen B., and David L. Myers. 1999. "Low Self-control, Rational Choice, and Student Test Cheating." *American Journal of Criminal Justice* 23: 179–200.

Widom, Cathy Spatz. 1989. "The Cycle of Violence." *Science* 244: 160–166.

Wilson, James Q., and Richard J. Herrnstein. 1985. *Crime and Human Nature*. New York: Simon and Schuster.

Wolfgang, Marvin E., Robert M. Figlio, and Thorsten Sellin. 1972. *Delinquency in a Birth Cohort.* Chicago: University of Chicago Press.

3

The Effect of Learning on Crime: Contrasting *A General Theory of Crime* and Social Learning Theory

Todd A. Armstrong

The tension between control theory and social learning theory is exemplified by the disagreement between Akers (1998) and Gottfredson and Hirschi (1990). Gottfredson and Hirschi contend that the two theories and the causal propositions contained within them are incompatible. In contrast, Akers argues that the propositions contained in *A General Theory of Crime* are consistent with learning theories of crime. Akers (1998) states, "[Gottfredson and Hirschi (1990)] view self control as the result of childhood socialization. If socialization is not a social learning process, what is it? Therefore, it seems to be self contradictory to claim, as Gottfredson and Hirschi do, that self-control explains crime in a way that is inconsistent with differential association and later learning theory" (p. 39). This chapter will assess the veracity of this statement. To this end, the human nature assumptions in both social learning theory and *A General Theory of Crime* will be reviewed, followed by a discussion of the effect of learning on propensity from within social learning and control theories. Finally, the implications of this discussion for research on the relationship between peers and delinquent behavior will be assessed.

The Assumptions of Social Learning Theory and *A General Theory of Crime*

In response to criticisms of differential association theory, Akers developed social learning theory by combining the basic elements of differntial association theory with principles borrowed from psychological explanations of learning. Consequently, a clear understanding of social learning theory's human nature assumptions is predicated on an understanding of the human nature assumptions of differential association theory. Kornhauser (1978) provides the most succinct description of the human nature assumptions implicit in differential association theory, concluding that within differential association theory "man has no nature, socialization is perfectly successful, and cultural variability is unlimited" (p. 34). This conclusion is largely a function of the attribution of motivation to a learned excess of pro-criminal definitions in the sixth statement of differential association theory. This statement asserts, "a person becomes delinquent because of an excess of definitions favorable to the violation of law over definitions unfavorable to violation of law" (Sutherland et al., 1992). As Kornhauser (1978) notes, this proposition is offered in the absence of the specification of any other source of motivation leading to the conclusion that within differential association theory man has no natural tendency toward acts of crime and deviance. Without learning, there is no motivation. Consequently, man is motivated only to the extent that he learns to define acts of crime and deviance as favorable through exposure to a delinquent belief structure. Kornhauser realized that the attribution of motivation to learned definitions was tantamount to a disavowal of deviance. In the absence of other sources of motivation, an individual will not act in contradiction to the belief structure to which he or she is exposed. Crime is not deviance; it is simply conformity to delinquent culture.

Recently, Akers (1996) attempted to address Kornhauser's assessment of the human nature assumptions implicit in differential association theory. Akers argued it is inaccurate to suggest that Sutherland proposed "there is no possibility of violation of internal group norms by individuals" (p. 233). While this is true, an assessment of the human nature assumptions of differential association theory must be based on the causal propositions that are actually included in the theory. Nowhere does Sutherland suggest that individuals commit acts of crime and delinquency in violation of group norms as a product of inadequate socialization. Absent any source of motivation other than learned definitions we are left to conclude that in differential association theory man's motivation is entirely defined by a positive learning process. In this process an individual exposed to pro-criminal definitions in an interaction with sufficient duration, priority, and intensity will necessarily engage in acts of crime and deviance in conformity to the delinquent subculture to which the individual has been exposed. An eleventh hour claim to a causal process that is the hallmark of control theory is not enough to undo Kornhauser's criticism. Within differential association theory, man "has no nature (and) socialization is perfectly successful" (Kornhauser, 1978: 34). In the absence of learning, motivation is lacking, in the presence of particular learning processes, motivation is a necessary consequence.

As Akers (1996) notes, Sutherland never clearly specified the human nature assumptions of differential association theory. Fortunately, Kornhauser addressed this deficiency, deriving the assumptions described above from the causal propositions contained in the theory. While this was a reasonably straightforward task, this is not the case with social learning theory. The human nature assumptions of social learning theory are obfuscated by the incorporation of causal processes from disparate theoretical traditions. In contrast to the deterministic assumptions of differential association theory, psychological theories of learning and in particular the principle of operant conditioning assume that man's actions are motivated by utilitarian considerations. Seemingly, this would make Kornhauser's criticism of differential association theory inapplicable to social learning theory by offering a second source of motivation, the benefits of the act itself. Indeed, this is true to the extent that social learning theory attributes motivation to the intrinsic rewards of an act. Unfortunately, Akers stops short of taking the human nature assumptions of psychological learning theories to their logical conclusion, instead offering a theory where culture determines utility, the consequences of acts being determined in large part by learned societal reaction. While its primacy is eroded somewhat, learning and culture still remain the primary determinants of human behavior in social learning theory, and man, having no natural tendency with regard to acts of crime and delinquency, is free to learn or unlearn motivation and/or restraint.

The human nature assumptions of the control theory tradition stand in stark contrast to those of social learning theory. Control theory assumes man is a rational actor attempting to maximize utility. Motivation toward an act is inherent in the consequences of the act itself, not learned. As there is little variation in our sensitivity to the consequences of a given act, there is minimal variation across individuals in motivation toward equivalent acts. In the absence of meaningful differences in motivation, differences in restraint define individual variation in the propensity to commit acts of crime and delinquency. In *A General Theory of Crime* (1990), individuals differ in restraint to the extent that they differ in self-control. This description of individual propensity is combined with a clear description of the nature of criminal acts. Such acts provide an immediate benefit that serves as the source of motivation; however, they offer comparatively little in the way of profit and have profoundly limited long-term or lasting benefits (Gottfredson and Hirschi, 1990: 20). Taken in conjunction with control theory's assumption regarding man's utilitarian nature, this definition of criminal acts leads to the conclusion that man learning motivation toward acts of crime and deviance is extremely unlikely. If it is indeed man's nature to seek to maximize pleasure and minimize pain and if he is "learning" at all, in any conventional sense of the word, his motivation toward acts that do not represent an efficient way to maximize utility will decrease.

The Effect of Learning on Crime in Social Learning Theory

Within social learning theory, crime is no different from any other act and man, having no natural tendency with regard to crime, is free to learn or unlearn a propensity toward such acts. As a result, social learning theory's description of the effect of learning on crime is a complex web of conditional causal processes in which increases and/or decreases in motivation and/or restrain can be learned and/or unlearned, sometimes. Differential association theory was criticized for its failure to specify the learning process that lead to changes in definitions. Social learning theory addressed this deficiency by incorporating psychological learning principles with differential association theory's emphasis on definitions. The psychological learning processes incorporated in social learning theory include "all of the behavioral mechanisms of learning in operant theory that had been empirically validated as well as Bandura's (1977) conceptualization of imitation" (Akers, 1998: 57). Empirically validated behavioral mechanisms of learning from operant theory include:

> (1) operant conditioning, differential reinforcement of voluntary behavior through positive and negative reinforcement and punishment; (2) respondent (involuntary reflexes), or "classical" conditioning; (3) unconditioned (primary) and conditioned (secondary) reinforcers and punishers; (4) shaping and response differentiation; (5) stimulus discrimination and generalization, the environmental and internal stimuli that provide cues or signals indicating differences and similarities across situation that help elicit, but do not directly reinforce, behavior; (6) types of reinforcement schedules, the rate and ratio in which rewards and punishers follow behavior; (7) stimulus-response constellations; and (8) stimulus satiation and deprivation. (Akers, 1998: 57)

In this laundry list of behavioral mechanisms, operant conditioning is the basic principle around which all the others are organized. Operant conditioning holds that positive reinforcement subsequent to a particular behavior will increase the likelihood that the behavior will occur again. "Whether individuals will refrain from or initiate, continue committing or desist from criminal and deviant acts depends on the relative frequency, amount, and probability of past, present, and anticipated rewards and punishments perceived to be attached to the behavior" (Akers, 1998: 66). In social learning theory, the principle of operant conditioning is integrated with Bandura's (1977) conceptualization of imitation. "That is imitation is a separate learning mechanism characterized by modeling one's own actions on the observed behavior of others and on the consequences of that behavior (vicarious reinforcement) prior to performing the behavior and experiencing its consequences" (Akers, 1998: 58). Imitation has a stronger effect on the acquisition of a behavior than on the probability that the behavior will be repeated, though according to Akers (1998), "it continues to have some facilitative effect in maintaining or changing behavior" (p. 75).

There are three main processes that describe the effect of learning on criminal propensity in social learning theory. These processes are (1) the effect of learning on the anticipated rewards and consequences of crime, (2) the effect of learning on "definitions," and (3) the effect of learning on the actual consequences of an act. The first process, is directly derived from the work of psychological learning theorists. This process makes no assumptions beyond those present in behavior theory. Learning results in a change in the likelihood of a criminal act through a change in the anticipated rewards and consequences that occurs as a product of individual's direct or indirect experience with an act. If experience demonstrates that the consequences of an act are more positive than previously believed, the likelihood of engaging in the act will increase. Conversely, if experience demonstrates that the consequences of an act are more negative than previously believed, the likelihood of engaging in the act will decrease.

In the second learning process identified above, learned changes in definitions regarding acts of crime and delinquency are equivalent to changes in individual criminal propensity. Definitions "label the commission of an act as right or wrong, good or bad, desirable or undesirable, justified or unjustified" (Akers, 1998: 78) and are "learned through reinforcement contingencies operating in the socialization process" (Akers, 1998: 84). In social learning theory, the effect of learned changes in definitions on propensity is conditional, depending on the type of definition learned. Definitions favorable to the violation of the law may be positive or neutralizing. "Positive definitions are beliefs or attitudes that make the behavior morally desirable or wholly permissible. . . . Neutralizing definitions favor violating the law or other norms not because they take acts to be positively desirable but because they justify or excuse them" (Akers, 1998: 79). Thus, learned increases in positive definitions are equivalent to learned increases in motivation toward crime, while learned increases in neutralizing definitions are equivalent to learned decreases in restraint. In any case, a learned increase in positive or neutralizing definitions will increase the likelihood an individual will engage in delinquent acts. Social learning theory is also comfortable with the possibility that both positive and neutralizing definitions may be unlearned leading to a decrease in the likelihood of delinquent behavior. Additionally, social learning theory allows that changes in definitions favorable to conformity may influence propensity, leading to an increase or decrease in criminal propensity depending on the nature of change in these definitions.

In the third learning process included in social learning theory, learning experiences alter the consequences of an act. In describing the effect of learning on the consequences of drug use, Akers (1998) states, "whether or not these effects are experienced positively or negatively is partially contingent upon previously learned expectations. Through social consequences, one learns to interpret the effects as pleasurable and enjoyable or as frightening and unpleasant" (p. 71). Thus, someone who has learned to interpret the euphoric effects of drugs as positive would experience more pleasure attendant to the ingestion of drugs than someone who has not had this learning experience. This difference in pleasure attendant to the commission of an act is equivalent to a learned a difference in motivation. An individual who has learned to interpret the effects of drugs as positive will be more motivated toward acts of drug use than someone who has not had this learning experience. In social learning theory, this type of process is an important determinant of motivation. Akers states (1998) "even those rewards that we consider to be very tangible, such as money and material possessions, gain their reinforcing worth from the symbolic prestige and approval value they have in society" (p. 72). Motivation is determined by our learned reaction to the consequences of an act, not the consequences themselves.

Curiously, contemporary social learning theory also asserts that learning processes influence criminal behavior through their effect on self-control. Akers (1998) argues self-control is the product of "social learning in which individuals learn from parents, peers, and others, and take on as their own concepts of the right and wrong things to say and do in given contexts" (p. 73). A person exercises self-control by reinforcing or punishing his or her own behavior. This reinforcement or punishment is contingent upon an individual acting in a manner consistent with his or her definitions. Self-control in this case appears to be more analogous to the concept of shame or to the beliefs element of Hirschi's (1969) control theory than the concept of self-control embodied in Gottfredson and Hirschi's (1990) *A General Theory of Crime*.

Despite the incorporation of the principle of operant conditioning and its emphasis on the consequences of an act, social learning theory remains, in large part, deterministic. While the theory does emphasize an act's consequences, it argues that learning and culture play an important part in determining these consequences. The casual influence of learning and culture in social learning theory is a result of the deterministic legacy of differential association theory. This legacy is evident in social learning theory's treatment of the concept of definitions. Contemporary versions of social learning theory downplay the causal importance of the normative component of definitions, however, the theory remains deterministic, allowing that "strongly held beliefs may 'motivate' crime in the sense that they direct one to what 'ought' to be done or not done in certain situations" (Akers, 1998: 82). More tellingly, social learning theory argues that holding definitions favorable to the violation of the law may be sufficient to cause the commission of an act. "If the act is congruent with or allows one to demonstrate adherence to a certain norm or set of values that may provide enough positive motivation to do it" (Akers, 1996: 240). Thus, while the absolute determinism of differential association theory is relaxed somewhat by the incorporation of psychological learning processes, social learning theory remains in large part deterministic.

The Effect of Learning on Crime in *A General Theory of Crime*

Gottfredson and Hirschi (1990) note, that "the essential features of learning theories of crime are consistent with the classical model as these theories assume that behavior is governed by its consequences. Behavior that is rewarded has an increased probability of repetition, whereas behavior that is punished has a decreased probability of repetition" (pp. 70–71). Despite this basic compatibility, there are important differences between the classical model and positive learning theories of crime. Gottfredson and Hirschi (1990) explain "In the classical view of human nature, positive learning theories of crime are redundant or superfluous because they seek to explain something unproblematic—that is, the benefits of crime" (p. 71). Thus, it is not the idea that learning influences the likelihood of the commission of a criminal act that is inconsistent with classical theory. Instead, the incompatibility of classical theories with positivist theories of crime lies within the positivist assumption that we need to learn in order to appreciate the benefits of crime.

Within the context of *A General Theory of Crime*, learning results in a decrease in criminal propensity through its effect on self-control. Individuals who are low in self-control tend to be "impulsive, insensitive, physical (as opposed to mental), risk-taking, shortsighted, and nonverbal" (Gottfredson and Hirschi, 1990: 90). These characteristics are summarized as "factors affecting the calculation of the consequences of one's acts" (Gottfredson and Hirschi, 1990: 95). Underlying these factors is an inability to fully appreciate the consequences of one's actions coupled with a lack of sensitivity to the potential long-term consequences of these actions. Gottfredson and Hirschi's (1990) definition of propensity is complemented by their description of the characteristics of criminal acts. These acts: (1) provide immediate gratification of desires, (2) are easy or simple, (3) are exciting, risky, or thrilling, (4) provide few or meager, long-term benefits, (5) require little skill or planning, and (5) often result in pain or discomfort for the victim. As defined, criminal acts offer a distribution of costs and benefits consistent with the behavioral tendencies of those who are low in self-control. These individuals are vulnerable to the temptation of the moment and have an inability to appreciate the long-term consequences of an act. Therefore, they are more likely to engage in acts that offer immediate benefit and have negligible or negative long-term consequences than individuals who have higher levels of self-control.

Although Gottfredson and Hirschi (1990) avoid the word "learning" (preferring to refer to the processes that results in self-control as socialization), it is clear that in *A General Theory of Crime* different learning experiences lead to differences in self-control. Self-control is learned through parental behavior "directed toward teaching the child about the rights and feelings of others, and of how these rights and feelings ought to constrain the child's behavior"

(p. 97). Gottfredson and Hirschi (1990) explain "in order to teach the child self-control, someone must: (1) monitor the child's behavior; (2) recognize deviant behavior when it occurs; and (3) punish such behavior" (p. 97). Individuals who are raised in environments where these three conditions occur more often will tend to have more self-control. The end result of which is a child "more capable of delaying gratification, more sensitive to the interests and desires of others, more independent, more willing to accept restraints on his activity, and more unlikely to use force or violence to attain his ends" (Gottfredson and Hirschi, 1990: 97).

Within *A General Theory of Crime* learning processes do not lead to meaningful increases in criminal propensity. Learned intra-individual differences in self-control are time stable after early adolescence. Gottfredson and Hirschi's (1990) theory also precludes learned increases in propensity as a function of an increase in motivation. The classical tradition attributes motivation toward crime to the benefits that criminal acts provide. Consistent with this view, *A General Theory of Crime* asserts that motivation toward crime is inherent in the benefits of the act itself. No unique learning is necessary to appreciate these pleasures/benefits. Further, control theories assume motivation toward crime is relatively equally distributed across the population arguing, "there will be little variability among people in their ability to see the pleasures of crime" (p. 95). Absent meaningful variation in motivation, there is nothing for positive learning processes to explain.

The language used in the discussion of the assumptions regarding the distribution of motivation in *A General Theory of Crime* is very important. Gottfredson and Hirschi (1990) state, "there will be *little* (italics added) variability among people in their ability to see the pleasures of crime" (p. 95) followed by the assertion, "the pleasures of crime are *reasonably* (italics added) equally distributed over the population" (p. 95). Clearly, these statements allow some minor variation in the distribution of the pleasures of crime across the population. The importance of these minor differences and the processes that may explain them is implied in Gottfredson and Hirschi's (1990) treatment of these differences. Inter-individual differences in ability to appreciate the benefits of crime are trivial. This leads to the conclusion that positive learning processes attempting to explain differences in motivation are also trivial, and therefore unimportant to an explanation of crime and deviance. Nonetheless, it is relatively easy to construct a scenario where experience with a particular criminal act can lead to an increase in the probability that the actor will repeat the act in question. Consider the example of a young man in his mid-teens whose family recently moved into a rough neighborhood. In his previous neighborhood, this young man rarely engaged in serious acts of aggression. In his new neighborhood, the young man quickly realizes that acts of aggression are a relatively routine part of life and are rewarded with the respect of one's peer group. Additionally, he realizes that in this new neighborhood parents are less likely to find out about misbehavior. As he learns about these differences, the rate at which he engages in serious acts of aggression increases. Understanding our hypothetical young man's increased frequency of serious acts of aggression from within the context of *A General Theory of Crime* requires an emphasis on this theory's distinction between crime and criminality. Crime is an event, while criminality is an enduring disposition/propensity. The likelihood of a criminal event is the product of the interaction between criminal propensity and opportunity. Consequently, change in criminal propensity or change in the opportunity structure both influence the likelihood of a criminal event. In the above case, the increase in the likelihood of serious acts of aggression is not due to a learned increase in enduring individual propensity, rather it is the product of a change in the opportunity structure. In his new neighborhood the young man has an increased opportunity to engage in serious acts of aggression that will be rewarded by peers and have a minimal likelihood of being detected by his parents. It is the different opportunity structures in the respective neighborhoods, not a learned change in propensity, which explains the increased likelihood of serious acts of aggression.

Implications for the Interpretation of Recent Research

Social learning theory holds that exposure to pro-criminal definitions of sufficient priority, duration, and intensity will lead to an increase in motivation toward criminal and delinquent acts. Arguably, the peer group is the primary setting in which individuals are exposed to pro-criminal definitions and motivation is learned. If indeed learning from peers plays such an important role in defining motivation, it would seem to require that the influence of peers increases while criminal behavior increases. A reasonably strong body of evidence indicates that this is the case. Warr (2002) notes, a number of researchers have "commented on the strong similarity between the age distribution of peer influence and delinquent behavior itself" (p. 14). As delinquent behavior increases in early adolescence, so does time spent with peers (Warr, 2002: 11). This increase in exposure is paralleled by an increase in the importance of the peer group along with a decrease in the relative influence of parents (Warr, 2002: 13, 28). Concordant increases in criminal behavior and peer influence in early adolescence suggest that peer influence plays an important role in explaining criminal behavior.

While a substantial body of literature has found a strong correlation between one's own delinquent behavior and the delinquency of one's peers, the cause of this correlation remains at issue. Social learning theorists argue an important part of the relationship between delinquency and peers is explained by the causal influence of peers on propensity. In contrast, control theorists have argued that the relationship between delinquency and peers may be attributable to the process of homophily or to a measurement artifact.[1] As a product of these competing explanations, it is widely recognized that the correlation between individual delinquency and peer delinquency does not necessarily provide support for the social learning theory assumption that exposure to delinquent peers leads to a learned increase in propensity toward acts of crime and deviance. In an attempt to disentangle the different explanations of the correlation between delinquent peers and delinquency, Matsueda and Anderson (1998) offer a three-wave cross-lagged panel model that accounts for many of the deficiencies of prior research. This model estimates both the lagged effect of delinquency on peers and the lagged effect of peers on delinquency. The model also accounts for the "measurement artifact" explanation by allowing correlated errors and estimating the effect of respondent delinquency on indicators of peer delinquency. Control variables accounting for age, race, gender and an indicator of a broken home are included along with stability effects for delinquent peers and delinquent behavior. In their discussion of the literature, Matsueda and Anderson (1998) argue theories within the control tradition assume that the correlation between delinquency and delinquent peers should be entirely explained by the effect of delinquency on peers and/or a measurement artifact. Accordingly, a significant relationship between peers and delinquency net of the effect of delinquency on peers and any measurement artifact should be interpreted as support for theories that argue exposure to delinquent peers results in a learned increase in propensity.

When models are estimated, Matsueda and Anderson (1998) find that the influence of delinquency on peers is roughly twice that of the influence of peers on delinquency. This clearly demonstrates the process of homophily is a stronger explanation of the correlation between peers and delinquency than any causal effect of peers on delinquency. Nonetheless, consistent with their reading of the literature Matsueda and Anderson (1998) interpret the relatively small effect of peers on delinquency as support for social learning theory stating, "contrary to control theories, and consistent with learning theories, we find that delinquent peer associations exert a nontrivial effect on delinquent behavior" (p. 299). Unfortunately, Matsueda and Anderson's (1998) study does not allow the determination of why exposure to delinquent peers leads to an increase in deviance. Both social learning and control theories contain propositions that are capable of explaining the weak but significant effect of peers on delinquency. One such proposition is the "pro-criminal definitions process" in social learning theory. This proposition assumes that the effect of peers on delinquency is a product of a learned increase in propensity. While untested in Matsueda and Anderson's (1998) study, past research suggests that the relationship between peers and delinquency is not attributable to learned changes in pro-criminal definitions. In a review of the literature on peers and delinquency, Warr (2002) concluded "in most studies, the correlation between subjects' behavior and friends' behavior does not appear to be the result of (or primarily the result of) any attitude transference between individuals" (Warr, 2002: 76).

Gottfredson and Hirschi's (1990) theory is comfortable with the possibility that exposure to delinquent peers can cause minor, though non-trivial increases in delinquency. In *A General Theory of Crime* (1990), the likelihood of a criminal act is the product of the interaction of propensity and opportunity. If delinquent peers result in increased opportunities for delinquent behavior, then consistent with the example offered earlier in this chapter, an individual may "learn" about these increased opportunities, increasing the likelihood of the occurrence of a criminal act without a change in enduring individual propensity. In this case, the increased likelihood of a criminal act would be the product of an increase in opportunity, not a change in propensity. Thus, it is possible the effect of peers on delinquency found by Matsueda and Anderson (1998) is entirely consistent with control theory. Osgood et al. (1996) provide evidence supporting the argument that delinquent peers influence the likelihood of crime through a change in opportunity. Their test of the relationship between routine activities and deviant behavior found increases in opportunity were associated with increases in deviant acts. Specifically, time spent in unstructured socializing with peers in the absence of responsible authority figures was positively related to five measures of crime and deviance including scales measuring criminal behavior, heavy alcohol use, marijuana use, other illicit drug use, and dangerous driving. The authors used opportunity measures that did not carry connotations of deviance in order to minimize the possibility of alternative theoretical interpretations. Using such measures greatly reduced the possibility that the relationship between opportunity measures and delinquency measures were due to a change in pro-criminal definitions or the effect of crime on routine activities.

Given the evidence on the relationship between peers and delinquency, it seems *A General Theory of Crime* is preferable to social learning theory as an explanation of the correlation between delinquent behavior and delinquent peers. Matsueda and Anderson (1998) find the effect of delinquency on peers is twice as large as the effect of peers on delinquency, demonstrating that the learned increase in propensity explanation emphasized by social learning theory can at best play a minor role in explaining the correlation between peers and delinquency. More importantly, it is possible that variation in opportunity, a process entirely consistent with the human nature assumptions and causal processes within *A General Theory of Crime*, explains this relatively small effect. In addition to its consistency with the evidence, Gottfredson and Hirschi's (1990) theory is also superior by virtue of it parsimony. Absent conclusive evidence in favor of a more complicated explanation, the simpler explanation is preferable.

Conclusion

This chapter used a statement from *Social Learning and Social Structure: A General Theory of Crime and Deviance* as its stepping off point, we return to it now to offer some focus for the conclusion. Akers (1998) states, "[Gottfredson and Hirschi] view self-control as the result of childhood socialization. If socialization is not a social learning process, what is it? Therefore, it seems to be self-contradictory to claim, as Gottfredson and Hirschi do, that self-control explains crime in a way that is inconsistent with differential association and later learning theory" (p. 39). This argument is only partially correct. While self-control may be conceptualized as being the product of a learning process, it remains incompatible with social learning theory. In part, this incompatibility is attributable to differences in the functioning of learning between the two theories. The explicit human nature assumptions of *A General Theory of Crime* preclude learned decreases in self-control. In contrast, restraint can be learned and unlearned in social learning theory (as can motivation).

In addition to differences with regard to the potential effects of learning on self-control, the concept of self-control as defined in *A General Theory of Crime* is consistent with social learning theory due to the conflicting background assumptions of the two theories. Arguing that self-control is compatible with social learning theory because it is the product of a learning process ignores these background assumptions. The human nature assumptions of *A General Theory of Crime* are an extension of classical assumptions regarding crime and human nature. The classical tradition holds that "Nature has placed mankind under the governance of two sovereign masters, pain and pleasure" (Bentham, 1948 [1789]: 1). This conceptualization of man's nature is embraced and reiterated by Gottfredson and Hirschi (1990) who state, "in this view, all human conduct can be understood as the self-interested pursuit of pleasure or the avoidance of pain" (Gottfredson and Hirschi, 1990: 5). In *A General Theory of Crime*, the classical definition of man's nature is complimented by a description of criminal acts as a subset of acts that tend to have some small immediate benefit and the potential for future cost. The only feature that distinguishes criminal acts from the broader category of acts that do not tend to result in the realization of utility is the fact that criminal acts are against the law. This description of criminal acts is also linked to the classical tradition. In *The Principles of Morals and Legislation*, Bentham describes "mischievous acts" as acts that tend to result in disutility (more pain than pleasure), and argues that the purpose of the law is to augment the total happiness of the community by prohibiting mischievous acts. As defined by Bentham, criminal acts are acts leading to net disutility that should be prohibited by the government. Thus, it is clear that traditional and contemporary classical theories define man as a rational actor that seeks to maximize utility, and crime as part of a class of acts that do not tend to result in much utility. If we accept these definitions, we are lead to the conclusion that it is unlikely learning will cause a meaningful increase in motivation toward acts of crime and deviance. It is hard to conceive of a creature, whose conduct can be understood as the self-interested pursuit of pleasure or avoidance of pain, learning an increased propensity toward a class of acts that by definition do not tend to result in the realization of utility.

The classical human nature assumptions present in control theories are clearly contradictory to the tabula rasa approach to man's nature inherent in social learning theory. While social learning theorists seem content to ignore the human nature assumptions implicit in their own theories and those explicit in the theories of others, the willingness to incorporate processes with contradictory assumptions comes with a price. The folly of ignoring the human nature assumptions of theory is illustrated by the parable of the ostrich boy. Originally put forth as an example of the logic of social learning theory in a criminological text, Hirschi (1996) again offers the tale of the ostrich boy as an example of the consequences of continuing to ascribe causal importance to cultural variability. This tale demonstrates what happens when the human nature implications inherent in causal propositions are downplayed, deemphasized, or outright ignored. As the story goes, ostrich boy was raised by ostriches in the Australian outback, "he had grown up with them, run with them as fast as they did, acted on their signals, and adopted their feeding habits. He could not speak human, but he communicated perfectly with his ostrich family, using their sounds" (Hirschi, 1996: 255). Ignoring human nature assumptions and integrating casual propositions without careful consideration of their implications can lead to examples like ostrich boy, a story that is entirely consistent with the human nature assumptions of social learning theory. Perhaps more troubling, ignoring human nature assumptions when assessing the compatibility of causal processes can also lead to theories that are quite comfortable with the proposition that man can learn anything including the ability "to run 40 miles an hour, go long periods without water, (and) subsist on alfalfa" (Hirschi, 1996: 255).

Note

1. In the process of homophily people befriend people like themselves; this is also known as the "birds of a feather" explanation. The measurement artifact argument suggests that the correlation between self-report measures of delinquency and delinquent peers is attributable to co-offending. Teens often commit offenses in groups, therefore it is entirely possible that a single act of delinquency would be individual and peer delinquency simultaneously.

References

Akers, Ronald L. 1996. "Is Differential Association/Social Learning Cultural Deviance Theory." *Criminology* 34: 229–245.

———. 1998. *Social Learning and Social Structure: A General Theory of Crime*. Boston, MA: Northeastern University Press.

Bandura, Albert. 1977. *Social Learning Theory*. Englewood Cliffs, NJ: Prentice Hall.

Bentham, Jeremy. 1948 [1789]. *The Principles of Morals and Legislation*. New York: Hafner Press.

Gottfredson, Michael R., and Travis Hirschi. 1990. *A General Theory of Crime*. Stanford, CA: Stanford University Press.

Hirschi, Travis. 1969. Causes of Delinquency. Berkeley, CA: University of California Press.

Hirschi, Travis. 1996. "Theory without Ideas: Reply to Akers." *Criminology* 34: 249–256.

Kornhauser, Ruth R. 1978. *Social Sources of Delinquency: An Appraisal of Analytic Methods*. Chicago: University of Chicago Press.

Matsueda, Ross L., and Kathleen Anderson. 1998. "The Dynamics of Delinquent Peers and Delinquent Behavior." *Criminology* 36: 269–308.

Osgood, D. Wayne, Janet K. Wilson, and Patrick M. O'Malley. 1996. "Routine Activities and Individual Deviant Behavior." *American Sociological Review* 5: 635-655.

Sutherland, Edwin H. 1947. *Principles of Criminology*. Fourth Edition. Philadelphia, PA: J. B. Lippincott.

Sutherland, Edwin H., Donald R. Cressey, and David F. Luckenbill. 1992. *Principles of Criminology*. Dix Hills, NY: General Hall.

Warr, Mark. 2002. *Companions in Crime*. New York: Cambridge University Press.

4

The Interactive Effects of Social Control Variables on Delinquency

Robert Agnew

Survey data from American criminologists suggest that social control theory is the most popular theory of crime and delinquency (Walsh, 2002: 13–16). Reflecting this fact, social control variables are routinely included in studies on the causes of delinquency and are frequently targeted in delinquency prevention and control programs (see Agnew, 2001; Kempf, 1993). The empirical evidence on social control theory, however, is decidedly mixed. Some studies suggest that social control variables have a relatively large direct effect on delinquency (e.g., Costello and Vowell, 1999; Dukes and Stein, 2001; Junger and Marshall, 1997; Junger-Tas, 1992; Sampson and Laub, 1993; Simons et al., 1998), while other studies suggest that they have a relatively small or no direct effect (e.g., Agnew, 1985, 1991a; Elliott et al., 1985; Erickson et al., 2000; Greenberg, 1999; Jang and Smith, 1997; Marcos et al., 1986; Matsueda and Heimer, 1987; Menard and Morse, 1984; Paternoster et al., 1983; Polakowski, 1994).

Several explanations have been offered for these mixed results. Among other things, social control variables are said to have weak effects when there are controls for other relevant variables, like delinquent peer association and self-control. Association with delinquent peers is frequently said to mediate the effect of social control on delinquency, while self-control is said to account for both social control and delinquency during adolescence (see Elliott et al., 1985; Erickson et al., 2000; Evans et al., 1997; Gottfredson and Hirschi, 1990: 154–68; Hirschi and Gottfredson, 1995; Sampson and Laub, 1993; Matsueda and Heimer, 1987; Simons et al., 1998; Wright et al., 1999). Social control variables are said to have weak effects in longitudinal studies, because such studies take account of the causal effect of delinquency on social control (e.g., Agnew, 1985, 1991a; Jang and Smith, 1997; Paternoster et al., 1983; Thornberry et al., 1998). In addition, social control variables are said to have weak effects because they are poorly measured in certain studies (e.g., Agnew, 1991a; Costello and Vowell, 1999). All of these explanations may have some merit, but they are not able to fully explain the mixed results on social control theory. Social control variables *sometimes* have relatively large direct effects on delinquency in longitudinal studies, in studies that control for association with delinquent peers and/or self-control, and in studies that employ social control measures similar to those used in non-supportive studies (e.g., Costella and Vowell, 1999; Hay, 2001; Junger and Marshall, 1997; Nagin and Paternoster, 1991, 1993, 1994; Sampson and Laub, 1993; Simons et al., 1998; Wright et al., 1999, 2001).

As a consequence, there is much uncertainly over the empirical status of what is perhaps the most influential theory in the discipline. This uncertainly is evident in reviews of the theory, which routinely discuss the mixed results of empirical research (e.g., Akers, 2000; Gottfredson, 2001; Hawkins et al., 1998; Kempf, 1993; Kercher, 1998; Thornberry, 1996). And it is evident in much recent theoretical work, some of which denies the importance of social control variables during adolescence and some of which assigns a central place to such variables (see Evans et al., 1997; Gottfredson, 2001:45–61; Gottfredson and Hirschi, 1990; Hirschi and Gottfredson, 1995; Nagin and Paternoster, 1993; Paternoster and Brame, 1997; Sampson and Laub, 1993; Simons et al., 1998). This chapter does not attempt to fully resolve the mixed results of past research, but it does explore another possible reason for such mixed results: The impact of social control variables on delinquency may be conditioned by other factors, such that control variables have a large effect in some circumstances and a small effect in others.

This is not a new argument. Several criminologists have argued that the effect of social control variables on delinquency is conditioned by the respondent's motivation for delinquency. Low social control is said to free adolescents to engage in delinquency, but it is claimed that adolescents will not commit delinquent acts unless they also are positively motivated to do so. There have been a few tests of this idea, with the motivation for delinquency usually being measured in terms of association with delinquent peers. Most data suggest that social control variables have a small effect or no effect on delinquency when association with delinquent peers is low, but a much stronger effect when association with delinquent peers is high (Agnew, 1993; Conger, 1976; Elliott et al., 1985; Hirschi, 1969: 158; Linden and Hackler, 1973; Poole and Regoli, 1979; Stanfield, 1966; Warr, 1993). Such studies, however, usually focus on selected types of social control. This study builds on the previous research by examining whether each of the major types of social control—direct control, stake in conformity, and beliefs—interacts with a measure of delinquent peer association in its effect on delinquency.

This study also builds on previous research by examining whether the major types of social control interact with one another in their effect on delinquency. In particular, is a given type of social control more likely to affect delinquency when other types of social control are high or low? As indicated below, there are good reasons to expect interactions between the major types of social control, although such interactions are seldom examined in the literature. It is also possible that social control variables interact with other factors in their effect on delinquency, with limited data suggesting that social control variables are more likely to affect delinquency when strain is high (Agnew, 1993; Mazerolle and Maahs, 2000) and self-control is low (Wright et al., 2001; although see Nagin and Paternoster, 1994, and Nagin and Pogarsky, 2001, who find that the threat of legal sanctions may be more likely to affect delinquency when self-control is high). We might also expect social control to be more likely to affect delinquency when delinquent opportunities are more common (Agnew, 2001: 202–09; Briar and Piliavin, 1965; Osgood et al., 1996). It is not possible to investigate these additional interactions with the data used in this study, but this study nevertheless advances a growing literature that suggests that social control variables are more likely to affect delinquency in some circumstances than in others.

The first part of this chapter describes the major types of social control and discusses the possible ways in which these types may interact with one another and delinquent peer association to affect delinquency. The second part describes the data and measures that are used to examine these interactions. The third part presents the results. The examination of such interactions is important not only for the light it may shed on the empirical status of a major theory, but also because of its policy implications. Efforts to reduce delinquency often attempt to increase social control, and such efforts can clearly benefit from knowledge about those factors that condition the effect of social control on delinquency.

The Major Types of Social Control and Their Interactive Effects on Delinquency

The Three Major Types of Social Control

Several typologies of the major types of social control have been presented, the most prominent of which is Hirschi's (1969) description of attachment, commitment, involvement, and belief. Hirschi's typology, however, suffers from certain problems, including the fact that it does not adequately distinguish direct control from attachment (see Hirschi, 1969: 88–90; Wells and Rankin, 1988) and that measures of involvement appear to be unrelated to delinquency in most studies, unless such measures also tap commitment (e.g., time spent on homework, see Kempf, 1993). For that reason, this chapter draws on the work of several social control theorists, including Hirschi, to present a more generic description of the major types of social control (see Agnew, 2001; Briar and Piliavin, 1965; Gottfredson and Hirschi, 1990; Kornhauser, 1978; Patterson, 1982; Sampson and Laub, 1993; Wells and Rankin, 1988). Three major types of social control are presented, with each type having two or more components.

Direct Control refers to the efforts of others to monitor the juvenile's behavior and sanction deviance. Parents, school officials, neighbors, police, and others may exercise direct control; but data suggest that parents are the most important source of direct control given their long-standing and intimate relationship with the juvenile. Direct control has at least four components: (1) Setting clear rules that prohibit delinquency and that limit the juvenile's exposure to temptations/opportunities for delinquency. (2) Monitoring the juvenile's behavior to detect rule violations, with this monitoring being direct (e.g., watching the juvenile after school) and indirect (e.g., keeping track of the juvenile by questioning him or her and others familiar with the juvenile). (3) Recognizing delinquency/rule violations when they occur. (4) Sanctioning rule violations in a consistent and meaningful manner, but one that is not overly harsh. Direct control reduces the likelihood of delinquency through the consistent sanctioning of delinquent acts and acts conducive to delinquency, like associating with delinquent peers.

Stake in Conformity refers to what the juvenile has to lose by engaging in delinquency. Stake in conformity has two components: (1) The juvenile's emotional attachment to conventional others, like parents and teachers. Juveniles who like or respect conventional others have more to lose by engaging in delinquency, since they risk jeopardizing valued relationships and hurting people they care about. (2) The juvenile's actual or anticipated investment in conventional activities, with this investment being indexed by such things as good grades, material possessions, a good reputation, and the anticipation of obtaining a good education and getting a good job. Juveniles with large investments in these areas also have more to lose by engaging in delinquency.

Internal Control refers to the ability of juveniles to exercise *self-restraint* in the face of delinquent impulses or temptations. Such control is partly a function of beliefs regarding delinquency, with social control theorists arguing that some juveniles condemn delinquency while others have an amoral orientation toward delinquency. This amoral orientation stems primarily from poor socialization, although certain theorists also stress the fact that some juveniles are resistant to socialization for biological reasons (Brennan and Raine, 1997). *Self*-control may also be seen as a type of internal control, with self-control being a function of several personality traits, like impulsivity and irritability. Gottfredson and Hirschi (1990) argue that low self-control results from low attachment between parent(s) and child and low direct control by the parent(s) during the childhood years. Gottfredson and Hirschi, however, view self-control as distinct from social control and they further argue that social control has little effect on delinquency once levels of self-control are established in childhood (also see Hirschi and Gottfredson, 1995; Taylor, 2001). Recent data cast doubt on this latter argument, suggesting that social control may impact delinquency even after levels of self-control are taken into account (Hay, 2001; Nagin and Paternoster, 1993, 1994; Simons et al., 1998; Wright et al., 1999, 2001). It would therefore be desirable to examine whether self-control interacts with the types of social control listed above, but it is not possible to measure self-control in this study. Wright et al. (2001), however, find that social control variables measuring "stake in conformity" have a greater effect on crime when self-control is low, although limited data from the deterrence literature suggest that the threat of official sanctions (a type of direct control) *may* have a greater effect on crime when self-control is high (Nagin and Paternoster, 1994; Nagin and Pogarsky, 2001).

The types of social control listed above are related to one another, partly because they are caused by common factors (e.g., parental criminality, family size, self-control) and partly because they have causal effects on one another. For example, direct control and stake in conformity help produce beliefs that condemn delinquency (see Hirschi, 1969). But the relation is far from perfect, since each type of social control is also influenced by unique factors (e.g., Agnew, 2001). Also, an increase in one type of social control may reduce other types of social control in certain circumstances. For example, a high stake in conformity may sometimes reduce the direct control to which juveniles are subject (see Agnew, 1990; Hagan et al., 1990; Sherman and Smith, 1992; and the case study of the "Saints" in Chambliss, 1973). As a consequence, there is some independent variation in the major types of social control, making the examination of interaction effects possible.

Interactions between the Social Control Variables and Delinquent Peer Association

Several predictions can be made regarding the interactions between the major types of social control and delinquent peer association.

There is some basis for predicting that the major types of social control will have a greater effect on delinquency when delinquent peer association is high. Several criminologists claim that while low control may free the juvenile to engage in delinquency, delinquency is unlikely unless the motivation for delinquency is also high (e.g., Agnew, 1993; Conger, 1976; Kornhauser, 1978; Elliott et al., 1985; Wright et al., 2001). Delinquent peer association is widely viewed as the best measure of delinquent motivation, with data suggesting that delinquent peer association has a relatively large effect on delinquency, even after the possibility of reciprocal causal effects and/or correlated measurement error are taken into account (Agnew, 2001; Akers, 1998: 117–26; Elliott and Menard, 1996; Erickson et al., 2000; Matsueda and Anderson, 1998; Thornberry et al., 1998). The few tests for this predicted interaction have been generally supportive. Most commonly, researchers focus on social control measures which index stake in conformity, particularly attachment to parents. Elliott et al. (1985) employ a more global measure of social control that indexes selected types of involvement and moral beliefs, while Agnew (1993) employs a global measure that indexes stakes in conformity and moral beliefs. Studies usually find that social control variables have a much stronger effect on delinquency when association with delinquent peers is high (Conger, 1976; Elliott et al., 1985; Hirschi, 1969: 158; Linden and Hackler, 1973; Poole and Regoli, 1979; Stanfield, 1966; Warr, 1993).

Many control theorists, however, would predict that social control variables will *not* interact with delinquent peer association in their effect on delinquency. Such theorists argue that most people are strongly motivated to engage in delinquency and that this motivation does not vary much from person to person. That is, most people have strong needs and desires that are more easily satisfied through delinquency than through conventional means. What determines variation in levels of delinquency is not variation in the motivation for delinquency, which is limited, but variation in the controls or restraints against acting on delinquent motives (e.g., Agnew, 1993; Kornhauser, 1978: 46–50, 140–42). According to this argument, the effect of social control variables on delinquency should *not* be conditioned by those variables that allegedly index the motivation for delinquency. Variables like delinquent peer association do not have a major impact on the motivation for delinquency. The effect of delinquent peer association on delinquency is said to be spurious for several reasons: both peer association and delinquency are caused by low control, delinquency causes delinquent peer association, and delinquent peer association is a surrogate measure of delinquency (see Gottfredson and Hirschi, 1990; Hirschi, 1969; Hirschi and Gottfredson, 1995; Kornhauser, 1978; Sampson and Laub, 1993). There is, in fact, good evidence that the effect of delinquent peer association on delinquency has been exaggerated (although the best data suggest that delinquent peer association does have some causal effect on delinquency [see above references]). Further, a few studies suggest that certain social control variables do *not* interact with measures of peer/sibling delinquency in their effect on delinquency (Sampson and Laub, 1993: 117 for school attachment; Warr, 1993 for parental attachment). The control argument for the absence of interaction effects, then, has some theoretical and empirical plausibility.

Finally, it might be argued that social control variables will have a *weaker* effect on delinquency when delinquent peer association is high. Although the evidence is somewhat mixed, certain data suggest that adolescents in delinquent peer groups and gangs are resistant to parental, school, and other conventional influences (Agnew, 2002a; Decker and Van Winkle, 1996). Ultimately, delinquent peer association may cause a reduction in direct control, stake in conformity, and conventional beliefs. But for a time, adolescents in delinquent peer groups may still be subject to some conventional controls. The impact of such controls on delinquency, however, may be much diminished due to the strong influence of the delinquent peer group. Delinquent peers, in particular, may lead one another to evade and resist the conventional controls to which they are subject. Some social control theorists might dispute this, claiming that the relations among delinquent peers are "cold and brittle," with such peers exerting little independent effect on the juvenile (e.g., Hirschi, 1969 :138–61). Limited data, however, suggest that delinquent peers and gang members sometimes have close relations with and exert strong influences on one another (Agnew, 1991b; Giordano et al., 1986).

In sum, there is some basis for arguing that social control variables will have a larger, smaller, or the same effect on delinquency when delinquent peer association is high. While limited data favor the first argument, only a few studies have been conducted in this area and these studies do not examine all of the major types of social control. There is a clear need for further research.

Interactions of the Social Control Variables with One Another

The major types of social control may also interact with one another in affecting delinquency, although this type of interaction is seldom examined (but see Rankin and Wells, 1990, on the interaction between parental attachments and direct controls; and Sherman and Smith, 1992, on the interaction between "legal and informal threats of punishment"). As above, different predictions can be made regarding the nature of the interactions that might emerge.

One might predict that a given type of control will have a *larger* effect on delinquency when other types of control are high. That is, the different types of control reinforce one another. When one or more types of control are high, the juvenile will be more aware of, accepting of, and/or concerned with the other types of control. The best example involves direct control and stake in conformity (see Rankin and Wells, 1990; Sherman and Smith, 1992). Direct control should have a larger effect on delinquency when stake in conformity is high, since the juvenile has more to lose if delinquency is detected and sanctioned. Certain research from the child development literature suggests that parental direct control is more effective when parental attachment is high (see the review in Rankin and Wells, 1990). And certain research from the deterrence literature supports this argument (Nagin, 1998: 20–23). For example, arrest reduces domestic violence among employed individuals but increases it among the unemployed (Sherman, 1993; Sherman and Smith, 1992). Likewise, one can argue that stake in conformity should have a larger effect on delinquency when direct control is high, since one's stake in conformity is only in jeopardy if there is a reasonable chance that delinquent acts will be detected and sanctioned. Chambliss (1973) found some support for this argument in his study of the "Saints" and the "Roughnecks," two delinquent groups in a high school. The Saints had a high stake in conformity, but engaged in much delinquency because they were low in direct control. Similar interactions can be predicted for other combinations of the major types of control. For example, one might predict that direct control will have a larger effect on delinquency among those with conventional beliefs, since these individuals are more likely to accept conventional rules, grant legitimacy to the control efforts of conventional others, and be concerned about the consequences of detection and sanction. Among other things, such individuals may be more concerned about the embarrassment and shame that might result from detection (see Piquero and Tibbetts, 1996, for a discussion of the role of shame in deterrence theory).

An equally plausible case, however, can be made for the argument that a given type of control will have a *smaller* effect on delinquency when the other types of control are high. In particular, one type of control may wholly or partly function as a substitute for other types of control (see Rankin and Wells, 1990, and the discussion of the "replacement hypothesis" in Sherman and Smith, 1992). The best example involves direct control and internal control. It has been argued that direct control is unnecessary or less necessary when internal control is high. Individuals high in internal control will refrain from delinquency regardless of their level of direct control. So direct control should have its largest effect on delinquency when internal control is low.

Finally, it is possible that the major types of control will not interact in their effect on delinquency. That is, each type of control may have an independent effect on delinquency that does not vary across levels of the other types of control. Certain studies find that parental direct control and parental attachment do *not* interact in their effect on delinquency (see Rankin and Wells, 1990). Rankin and Kern (1994) find little evidence that mother and father attachment interact in their effect on delinquency, although mother and father attachment appear to have independent additive effects on delinquency. And certain data from the deterrence literature suggest that the perceived certainty of official sanctions does not interact with stake in conformity in its effect on offending (e.g., Nagin and Paternoster, 1992; see Sherman and Smith, 1992 for an overview).

In sum, there is some theoretical and (very limited) empirical basis for arguing that a given type of social control will have a larger, smaller, or the same effect on delinquency when other types of control are high. So more research is needed in this area as well.

Data and Measures

Data

Data are from the first wave of the "Youth and Deterrence" survey conducted by Paternoster (Paternoster, 2001). All tenth grade students in attendance at nine high schools in the Columbia, South Carolina area were surveyed in the fall of 1979. The schools were selected to include rural, suburban, and urban students and to reflect the race, gender, and social class characteristics of the area high schools. Over 99 percent of those in attendance the day the survey was administered agreed to participate in the study, yielding a sample size of 2703 (see Paternoster, 1988; Paternoster and Piquero, 1995 for further information). This data set is used because it has excellent measures of the major types of social control, delinquent peer association, and delinquency.

Measures

The social control and delinquent peer association measures were created in several steps. Items measuring social control and delinquent peer association were selected from the data set. Groups of items similar in content were then factor analyzed using principal components analysis and an oblique method of rotation. Twenty-two items measuring family relations were factored; eighteen items measuring school and community experiences; four items measuring the respondent's moral beliefs about delinquency; eight items measuring the respondent's perceived likelihood of getting caught by the police if they engage in delinquency and, if caught, how much of a problem the punishment would "create for [their] life"; and eight items measuring friends' delinquency and friends' moral beliefs about delinquency.[1] Scales were created based on the factor loadings, with each item loading at least .45 on one and only one scale (most loadings were much higher). One measure of delinquent peer association and twelve measures of social control emerged from these analyses. There are seventy-eight potential interactions between such measures; analyzing such a large number of interactions would pose several problems, including problems of multicolinearity between many of the interactions and their component parts.

For that reason, the twelve measures of social control were subject to a second-order factor analysis. Three master scales emerged from this analysis, indexing direct control, stake in conformity, and moral beliefs. Each master scale was creating by standardizing the items/scales that loaded on the master scale and then taking their sum (each item/scale loads at least .46 on its master scale). The items/scales in each master scale are listed below:[2]

Direct Control: The measure of direct control is the sum of three scales. High scorers on the two-item "parental supervision" scale state that their parents "always" know where they are when they are away from home and who they are with (alpha reliability=.81). High scorers on the eight-item "parental disapproval of delinquency" scale state that their father and mother would "strongly disapprove" if they engaged in the delinquent acts of shoplifting, vandalism, drinking under age, and marijuana use (alpha=.89). High scorers on the four-item "probability of police capture" scale state that there is a very high probability that they would be caught by the police if they engaged in shoplifting, vandalism, drinking under age, and marijuana use (alpha=.81). In sum, high scorers on the master "direct control" scale state that their parents closely monitor their activities, their parents strongly disapprove of delinquency, and they will probably be caught by the police if they engage in delinquency.

Stake in Conformity: The measure of stake in conformity is the sum of four scales and items. High scorers on the nine-item "parental attachment" scale state that they feel close to their mother and father, want to be like their mother and father, feel it is important that their mother and father approve of the things they do, feel that it helps to talk to their mother and father about things that are worrying or bothering them, and care what their parents think of them (alpha= .80). (Note: this scale measures attachment to one parent for those respondents who only report data for one parent.) High scorers on the single-item "grades" measure state that they get "mostly A's" in school. High scorers on the six-item "school attachment" scale state that they like school a lot, like their teachers a lot, feel that they could go to their teachers for advice, feel that their teachers understand them, feel that it is important that their teachers approve of the things they do, and want to be like their favorite teacher (alpha=.67). High scorers on the three-item "community activities" scale state that it is very important to participate on athletic teams, in school clubs and activities, and in church group activities (alpha=.45). In sum, high scorers on the master "stake in conformity" scale state that they are strongly attached to their parents, teachers, and school; are doing well in school; and are involved in or at least feel it is important to be involved in community activities.

Conventional Moral Beliefs: High scorers on the four-item conventional moral beliefs scale state that it is always wrong to steal things worth less than $10, destroy others' property, drink alcohol under age, and smoke marijuana. Low scorers state that it is "never wrong" to engage in such acts (alpha =.74). It should be noted that while this scale is treated as a social control measure, it can also be taken as a social learning measure. It is not possible to determine whether those with low scores on the beliefs scale are immoral due to poor socialization (as control theorists argue) or have been taught beliefs conducive to delinquency (as social learning theorists argue). This is a common problem with beliefs scales in the literature (e.g., Akers, 1998; Costello and Vowell, 1999; Elliott et al., 1985).

Delinquent Peer Association: High scorers on the eight-item delinquent peer association scale state that all of "the people [they] hang around with" have damaged private property, stolen things worth less than $10, drank liquor under age, and used marijuana. Further, they state that their "best friends" think it is "never wrong" to engage in each of these four offenses. This scale has 1,004 missing cases, much more than the other variables in the analysis. For that reason, missing values were estimated using the "impute" procedure in Stata 6 (StataCorp, 1999). In particular, missing values were estimated based on the pattern of responses to those individual items in the scale for which data were available. The results below are largely the same regardless of whether the scale with the imputed data is used or cases with missing data are excluded; so for that reason results are reported for the scale with the imputed data (alpha reliability=.88).

Delinquency: Two measures of delinquency are employed. The fifteen-item "general delinquency" scale measures the number of times during the past year that respondents have drunk liquor under age, used marijuana, used other drugs, stolen something less than $10, stolen something $10 to $50, destroyed somebody's property, broken into a building and taken something, taken a car for a ride without permission, threatened to or beaten somebody up to get money or something else, damaged or destroyed school property, thrown objects at cars or people, carried a hidden weapon, sold marijuana or other drugs, stolen things from other students, and beaten somebody up badly. Variation in this general measure is largely a function of the more frequently occurring, less serious items (especially drinking under age, smoking marijuana, carrying a hidden weapon like a gun or knife, damaging property, and throwing objects at people or cars).

It has been argued that social control theory is better able to explain minor rather than serious delinquency (see Agnew, 1985). For that reason, a separate scale of "serious delinquency" is also employed, with this scale measuring the number of times that respondents have stolen something worth $10-$50, broken into a building to steal something, threatened to or beaten somebody up to get money or something else, sold marijuana or other drugs, and beaten somebody up badly. These two delinquency measures are positively skewed, with a small percentage of respondents reporting very high frequencies. For that reason, we follow the practice of Paternoster and Piquero (1995: 284, n.7) and truncate higher frequencies "to the frequency corresponding to the 90th percentile."

Socio-demographic Control Variables: All regression analyses were run with controls for sex, age, race (African American, White), family status (live with both natural parents versus other living arrangements), welfare status (not on welfare, uncertain, receive welfare benefits), and mother and father's education. These controls had little impact on the results, so regression results without the controls are reported for the sake of simplicity.

Results

Table 4.1 shows the correlations between the scales measuring the major types of social control, delinquent peer association, and general and serious delinquency. As expected, the social control measures are positively correlated with one another, although none of these correlations exceeds .46. The control measures are negatively correlated with delinquent peer association and both measures of delinquency, with the correlation being somewhat higher for general than serious delinquency. Delinquent peer association is positively correlated with both measures of delinquency, with the correlation also being somewhat higher for general delinquency. The lower correlations with serious delinquency may reflect the fact that there is less variation in serious delinquency to explain, as well as the fact that the moral beliefs and delinquent peer measures focus on minor delinquency. (Note: even though the respondents are not a random sample of a larger population, significance levels are reported for interpretive purposes).

Table 4.2 shows the results of regressing general and serious delinquency on the social control and delinquent peer association measures. Each of the

Table 4.1
Correlations between the Social Control, Delinquent Peers, and Delinquency Measures

	Direct Control	Stake in Conformity	Moral Beliefs	Delinquent Peers	General Delinq.	Serious Delinq.
Direct Control	1.0					
Stake in Conformity	.39	1.0				
Moral Beliefs	.46	.42	1.0			
Delinquent Peers	-.55	-.45	-.58	1.0		
General Delinquency	-.41	-.39	-.51	.55	1.0	
Serious Delinquency	-.36	-.31	-.39	.41	.57	1.0

Note: All correlations significant at $p < .01$.

Table 4.2
General and Serious Delinquency Regressed on the Social Control and Delinquent Peer Measure (Standardized effects shown, with unstandardized effects in parentheses)

	General Delinquency	Serious Delinquency
Direct Control	-.08(-2.73)	-.12(-.10)
Stake in Conformity	-.12(-2.73)	-.12(-.07)
Moral Beliefs	-.24(-5.14)	-.18(-.10)
Delinquent Peers	.32(3.64)	.20(.06)
Adjusted R^2	.368	.248

Note: All effects significant at $p < .01$.

social control measures has a significant negative effect on general and serious delinquency, although these effects are smaller than delinquent peer association. The effects of direct control and stake in conformity are small in absolute size, while the affect of moral beliefs is moderate in size. (Although somewhat arbitrary, small effects are defined as standardized effects less than .15, moderate effects are from .15 to .25, and large effects are above .25). Direct control and stake in conformity have roughly comparable effects on general and serious delinquency, although beliefs and delinquent peer association have smaller effects on serious delinquency.

An Examination of Interaction Effects

As suggested earlier, it may be that social control variables have larger effects on delinquency in some circumstances than others. This possibility is explored by examining whether the social control variables interact with one another and with delinquent peers in their effect on delinquency. Following Aiken and West (1991), interaction terms were created by first standardizing all variables and then multiplying one variable by another. Six interactions were created: direct control X stake in conformity, direct control X moral beliefs, stake X beliefs, delinquent peers X direct control, delinquent peers X stake, and delinquent peers X beliefs. These interaction terms were then added to the regression equations for general and serious delinquency. Since all variables are standardized, the unstandardized regression results are comparable to the standardized results. This standardization procedure has the advantage of reducing multicolinearity—a potentially serious problem when examining interactions. It should be noted, however, that there is a strong bias *against finding significant interaction effects* in non-experimental research (see Jessor et al., 1995; McClelland and Judd, 1993 for fuller discussions). This test for interactions, then, should be viewed as a conservative one.

Given the concern with multicolinearity, interaction terms were first added *one at a time* to the regression equations for general and serious delinquency. Results for these regression equations are shown in Table 4.3. Multicolinearity was not a problem in any of these regressions, with variance inflation factors (VIF) for the independent variables never exceeding two. Next, the six interactions were added *as a group* to the regressions for general and serious delinquency. Results for these equations are shown in Table 4.4. Certain of the VIFs approached 3.0 in these analyses. While there are no firm guidelines for what is an unacceptably large VIF, the precision of parameter estimates is reduced by almost half when variance inflation factors are in the 3.0 range (see Fox, 1991: 12). Although not shown in the tables, the standard errors for the interaction terms in Table 4.4 are about 50 percent higher on average that the standard errors for the comparable terms in Table 4.3. For that reason, the results in Table 4.4 should be viewed with caution.

Table 4.3
General and Serious Delinquency Regressed on the Social Control, Delinquent Peer, and Interaction Measures, with the Interactions Added One at a Time

	General Delinquency						Serious Delinquency					
Direct Control	-.08	-.09	-.08	-.08	-.08	-.08	-.12	-.15	-.13	-.13	-.13	-.13
Stake in Conformity	-.12	-.12	-.12	-.12	-.12	-.12	-.10	-.11	-.10	-.11	-.10	-.11
Moral Beliefs	-.24	-.22	-.22	-.23	-.23	-.18	-.16	-.12	-.13	-.15	-.15	-.08
Delinquent Peers	.33	.33	.33	.33	.33	.35	.21	.21	.21	.21	.20	.23
Direct X Stake	.07						.13					
Direct X Beliefs		.06						.12				
Stake X Beliefs			.05						.11			
Direct X Peers				-.09						-.14		
Stake X Peers					-.09						-.15	
Beliefs X Peers						-.09						-.13
Adjusted R^2	.372	.371	.371	.376	.376	.376	.267	.262	.262	.270	.272	.263

Note: All effects significant at $p < .01$.

Table 4.4
General and Serious Delinquency Regressed on the Social Control, Delinquent Peer, and Interaction Measures, with the Interactions Added Together

	General Delinquency	Serious Delinquency
Direct Control	-.08*	-.13*
Stake in Conformity	-.12*	-.10*
Moral Beliefs	-.21*	-.12*
Delinquent Peers	.35*	.22*
Direct X Stake	.00	.03
Direct X Beliefs	-.06	.00
Stake X Beliefs	-.03	-.01
Direct X Peers	-.06*	-.08*
Stake X Peers	-.07*	-.08*
Beliefs X Peers	-.05**	-.03
Adjusted R^2	.379	.279

*$p < .01$, ** $p < .05$.

Interactions between the Social Control Measures

Let us first focus on the interactions between the social control measures, as shown in Table 4.3. All of these interactions are statistically significant and positive, meaning that as one social control variable increases in size, the negative effects of the other control variables on general and serious delinquency become *smaller*.[3] The effect of each control variable on delinquency can be estimated with an equation of the following type (see Aiken and West, 1991):

$$\text{Delinquency} = B1(\text{ControlVar1}) + B2(\text{ControlVar2}) + B3(\text{ControlVar1})(\text{ControlVar2})$$

B3 refers to the coefficient for the interaction term. Recall that each variable is standardized, with a mean of zero and a standard deviation of one. Using this information, we can estimate the standardized effect of a given control variable on delinquency when another control variable is set at various levels. For example, stake in conformity has an effect of -.19 on general delinquency when direct control is set at one standard deviation below its mean (-1), an effect of -.12 when direct control is set at its mean (0), and an effect of -.05 when stake is set at one standard deviation above its mean (+1). Similar interpretations can be given for the other interactions between the control variables.

Taken as a whole, the data in Table 4.3 suggest that a given control variable has a much larger negative effect on delinquency when the other forms of control are low, with this negative effect usually being moderate to large in size. A given control variable tends to have a small negative effect on delinquency when the other forms of control are at their mean. And a given control variable tends to have little or no effect on delinquency when the other forms of control are high. These findings apply to both general and serious delinquency. To give another illustration, the effect of beliefs on serious delinquency is -.24 when direct control is low (one SD below its mean), -.12 when direct control is at its mean, and .00 when direct control is one standard deviation above its mean. These results, however, should be viewed with caution because the interactions between the control variables are not significant in the equations where all interaction terms are entered together (see Table 4.4), although the high VIFs in these equations may partly account for this.

There is some evidence, then, that a given type of control has a larger effect on delinquency when other types of control are *low*. The different types of control, then, may substitute for one another to a certain extent. While this finding is tentative given the results in Table 4.4, there is no evidence that a given type of control has a larger effect on delinquency when the other types of control are *high*. So, for example, there is no evidence that direct control has a larger effect on delinquency when stake in conformity is high.

Interactions between the Social Control and Delinquent Peer Measures

The data in both tables 4.3 and 4.4 indicate that the effects of the social control variables on general and serious delinquency are conditioned by delinquent peer association (although the delinquent peers X beliefs interaction for serious delinquency is not significant in Table 4.4). All of the interactions are negative, meaning that as delinquent peer association increases, the social control measures have an increasingly larger negative effect on delinquency. For example, the data in Table 4.3 indicate that direct control has an effect of .01 on serious delinquency when delinquency peers is set at one standard deviation below its mean, an effect of -.13 when delinquent peers is at its mean, and an effect of -.27 when delinquent peers is at one standard deviation above its mean. Similar interpretations can be given for the other interactions. A given social control variable typically has little or no effect on delinquency when delinquent peer association is low, a small negative effect when delinquent peer association is at its mean, and a moderate to large negative effect when delinquent peer association is high. This confirms the limited research conducted by others in this area, and *suggests* that variations in levels of social control have little effect on delinquency unless the motivation for delinquency is high. Variations in social control can be quite consequential when this is the case.

It should be noted that the converse is also true: the effect of delinquent peer association on general and serious delinquency is conditioned by the social control variables. For example, data in Table 4.3 indicate that delinquent peer association has an effect of .35 on serious delinquency when direct control is set at one standard deviation below its mean, an effect of .21 when direct control is at its mean, and an effect of .07 when direct control is at one standard deviation above its mean. The other interactions are similarly interpreted, suggesting that delinquent peer association has a large positive effect on delinquency when social control is low and a small effect when social control is high. So these data also suggest that variations in the motivation for delinquency have little effect on delinquency unless social controls are weak.

Conclusion

The data suggest that the major types of social control interact with delinquent peer association and *may* interact with one another in their effect on both general and serious delinquency. These interactions are such that a given type of social control tends to have little or no effect on delinquency when delinquent peer association is low and other forms of social control are high. A given type of social control, however, has a moderate to large effect on delinquency when delinquent peer association is high and other forms of social control are low. These findings can be explained by arguing that (1) social control does not impact delinquency unless there is some positive motivation for delinquency, and (2) one form of social control substitutes for another to some extent. It should be kept in mind, however, that direct control, stake in conformity, and moral beliefs are broadly measured in this study. Stake in conformity, for example, includes grades, participation in community organizations, and parent, teacher, and school attachments. More specific measures of social control may not substitute for one another to the same extent.

These findings, of course, need to be confirmed with studies employing alternative measures, including both general measures of the major types of social control (e.g., stake in conformity) and more specific measures (e.g., parental attachment, grades). It would also be useful to control for levels of self-control, as well as to examine additional interactions between social control and measures of self-control, strain, and opportunity for crime. Further, longitudinal studies should be done, with such studies ideally examining contemporaneous effects and taking account of the possibility of reciprocal effects and correlated measurement error between variables (see Agnew, 1991a; Matsueda and Anderson, 1998). Longitudinal studies might also explore whether the effect of social control is conditioned by *prior* levels of delinquency, since prior delinquency is perhaps the best measure of one's motivation for delinquency. Unfortunately, such studies are not easily done. Finally, researchers should examine a range of more specific predictions regarding interactions. It has been suggested, for example, that the combination of strong parental attachment and poor supervision leads to covert delinquency like theft, while weak attachment and poor supervision leads to overt delinquency like aggression (Patterson, 1982). The nature of interactions, then, may differ by type of crime. Nonlinear interactions (see below) and asymmetric interactions are also a possibility. Criminologists have neglected interaction effects in their theory and research and much work needs to be done in this area (see Agnew, 2002b; Cullen, 1984).

At the same time, it should be noted that the findings from this study are compatible with the results of certain longitudinal research that has examined the interaction between selected types of social control and delinquent peer association, strain, and self-control (Mazerolle and Maahs, 2000; Wright et al., 2001). These findings are also compatible with studies suggesting that risk and protective factors interact in their effect on delinquency, with protective factors having a greater effect on delinquency when risk is high (e.g., Jessor et al., 1995). Protective factors are broadly defined in such studies, but they typically include certain types of social control like parental and school attachment, conventional beliefs, and direct controls. Risk factors are also broadly defined, but they often include measures of strain and delinquent peer association. Further, these findings are compatible with research on delinquency prevention and rehabilitation programs (see Agnew, 2001; Andrews and Bonta, 1998 for overviews). Many of these programs involve effects to increase social control, and data suggest that such programs are most effective among those already inclined to engage in delinquency (often because they are low in social control, high in strain, and/or associate with delinquent peers).

Given such data, we might suggest the following general proposition: social control variables will have larger negative effects on delinquency among individuals at high-risk for delinquency—with high-risk individuals being those who are low in other types of social control and/or positively motivated for delinquency. This proposition, however, does run counter to certain of the research cited earlier in the chapter, particularly the deterrence research. Several studies find little or no evidence for interaction effects, although this may be due to the difficultly of detecting interactions in non-experimental research (see McClelland and Judd, 1993). And some studies suggest that legal sanctions have a larger negative effect among individuals who are *high* in self- and social control (e.g., Nagin and Paternoster, 1994; Nagin and Pogarsky, 2001; Sherman and Smith, 1992). As indicated, for example, arrest reduces subsequent domestic violence among employed offenders, but increases it among unemployed offenders. While the interaction effects in such studies sometimes fail to reach statistical significance, these studies are nevertheless at odds with the proposition just advanced.

These studies might be reconciled with the above proposition by arguing that there is a nonlinear interaction between social control and the risk for crime. Increases in a particular type of social control—especially a rather specific type like arrest—may not reduce crime among those with a *very high risk* for crime (like unemployed offenders). (Very high-risk offenders may respond to arrest with *increased* offending for several reasons, including the fact that arrest may function as a source of strain for them [see Sherman, 2000, for a fuller discussion]). Increases in social control may reduce crime among those with a *moderately high risk* for crime (like employed offenders and most of the "at-risk" juveniles in this study). And increases in social control may have little or no effect among those with a *low risk* for crime (like most of the juveniles in this study). Nagin and Paternoster (1993) make a similar argument regarding the interaction between social control and self-control; claiming that social control is most relevant for "marginal offenders"—those whose "self-control is not so high as to virtually preclude offending, nor so low that they would offend regardless of the inducements or disincentives" (Nagin and Paternoster, 1994: 585). Future research should examine whether this type of nonlinear interaction exists, although it may be difficult to do so with school samples that contain few very high-risk offenders.

While much more research is needed on interaction effects, the results from this study are nevertheless important for both theoretical and policy-related reasons. They suggest that the effect of social control variables on delinquency varies a good deal across individuals, and so they advance our understanding of the causes of delinquency. They also point the way toward an integrated theory of delinquency, since they suggest that the major types of social control and the other causes of delinquency not only influence one another, but they also interact with one another in their effect on delinquency. Most integrated theories devote little or no attention to such interaction effects, but they clearly play an important role in the explanation of delinquency (see Agnew, 2002b; Cullen, 1984; Elliott et al., 1985; Tittle, 1995 for further discussions of the role of interaction effects in integrated theories).

The results from this study also shed some light on the mixed results of past research. These mixed results may be *partly* due to differences in the nature of the samples being examined. Samples that contain large numbers of conventional adolescents may be more likely to find that social control measures have weak direct effects on delinquency. This is because the adolescents in such samples tend to have moderately high levels of social control and low levels of association with delinquent peers. Unfortunately, as Hagan and McCarthy (1997) point out, most data sets used in the delinquency research fit this description since they are based on school samples (also see Kempf, 1993: 152). Indeed, the data from the school survey used in this study suggest that social control variables have weak direct effects on delinquency (see Table 4.2, where main effects are reported). Data sets that examine samples at higher risk for delinquency may find stronger support for social control theory, since variation in a given type of social control is likely to be more consequential when other forms of social control are low and delinquent peer association is high. This may help explain why Sampson and Laub (1993) find such strong support for social control theory in their analysis of the Gluecks' data, which focuses on deprived juveniles, many of whom are at high risk for delinquency. It may also explain why Hagan and McCarthy (1997) find social control theory so relevant in their study of street youth. To be sure, other factors also influence the mixed results of past research, since results regarding social control theory are mixed across school samples and different analyses from the same sample (e.g., Costello and Vowell, 1999).

These results are also important for policymakers. They suggest that increases in a single type of social control, albeit a broad type, can have an important impact on delinquency among high-risk juveniles. That is an encouraging finding, because it suggests that it is possible to achieve substantial reductions in delinquency without increasing all types of control and eliminating all association with delinquent peers.

Notes

1. Items were factored in these clusters because much data suggest that items such as these tend to cluster into domains organized around family, school, community, and peer group (e.g., Wiatrowski et al., 1981).
2. The number of factors was limited to two, since a scree test suggested that two factors best fit the data (the third factor had an eigen value of 1.05, just satisfying the somewhat arbitrary criteria of 1.0). The following should also be noted: The moral beliefs scale loads on the direct control master scale, but moral beliefs are treated separately from direct control for theoretical reasons. And three of the social control measures are excluded from the analysis. A measure of the perceived problems that would result from arrest is excluded because it loads on the direct control scale, even though it should index stake in conformity. A measure of occupational and educational expectations is excluded because it has a high number of missing values (including this measure in the stake in conformity master scale, however, does not change the results). A measure of educational aspirations is excluded because it does not load on any of the master scales.
3. The addition of the interactions increases the amount of explained variance in delinquency by about 2 percent on average, which is typical for non-experimental studies that find significant interaction effects (e.g., Jessor et al., 1995: 931). It must be remembered, however, that there is a strong bias against finding significant interactions in non-experimental research (McClelland and Judd, 1993).

References

Agnew, R. 1985. "Social Control Theory and Delinquency: A Longitudinal Test." *Criminology* 23: 47–61.

_____. 1990. "Adolescent Resources and Delinquency." *Criminology* 28: 535–566.

_____. 1991a. "A Longitudinal Test of Social Control Theory and Delinquency." *Journal of Research in Crime and Delinquency* 28: 126–156.

_____. 1991b. "The Interactive Effects of Peers Variables on Delinquency." *Criminology* 29: 47–72.

_____. 1993. "Why Do They Do It? An Examination of the Intervening Mechanisms Between 'Social Control' Variables and Delinquency." *Journal of Research in Crime and Delinquency* 30: 245–266.

_____. 2001. *Juvenile Delinquency: Causes and Control*. Los Angeles: Roxbury.

_____. 2002a. "An Integrated Theory of the Adolescent Peak in Offending." Unpublished manuscript.

_____. 2002b. "Moving Toward an Integrated Theory of Delinquency." Unpublished manuscript.

Aiken, L. S., and S. G. West. 1991. *Multiple Regression: Testing and Interpreting Interactions*. Newbury Park, CA: Sage.

Akers, R. L. 1998. *Social Learning and Social Structure*. Boston: Northeastern University Press.

_____. 2000. *Criminological Theories*. Los Angeles: Roxbury.

Andrews, D. A ,and J. Bonta. 1998. *The Psychology of Criminal Conduct*. Cincinnati, OH: Anderson.

Aseltine, R. H., Jr. 1995. "A Reconsideration of Parental and Peer Influences on Adolescent Deviance." *Journal of Health and Social Behavior* 36: 103–121.

Brennan, P. A., and A. Raine. 1997. "Biosocial Bases of Antisocial Behavior: Psychpysiological, Neurological and Cognitive Factors." *Clinical Psychology Review* 17: 589–604.

Briar, S., and S. Piliavin. 1965. "Delinquency, Situational Inducements, and Commitment to Conformity." *Social Problems* 13: 35–45.

Chambliss, W. J. 1973. "The Saints and the Roughnecks." *Society* 11: 24–31.

Conger, R. D. 1976. "Social Control and Social Learning Models of Delinquent Behavior: A Synthesis." *Criminology* 14: 17–40.

Costello, B. J., and P. R. Vowell. 1999. "Testing Control Theory and Differential Association: A Reanalysis of the Richmond Youth Project Data." *Criminology* 37: 815–842.

Cullen, F. T. 1984. *Rethinking Crime and Deviance Theory*. Totowa, NJ: Rowan and Allanheld.

Decker, S. H., and B. Van Winkle. 1996. *Life in the Gang*. New York: Cambridge University Press.

Dukes, R. L., and J. A. Stein. 2001. "Effects of Assets and Deficits on the Social Control of At–Risk Behavior Among Youth." *Youth and Society* 32: 337–359.

Elliott, D. S., D. Huizinga, S. S. Ageton. 1985. *Explaining Delinquency and Drug Use*. Beverly Hills: Sage.

Elliott, D. S., and S. Menard. 1996. "Delinquent Friends and Delinquent Behavior: Temporal and Developmental Patterns." Pp. 28–67 in J. D. Hawkins (ed.), *Delinquency and Crime: Current Theories*. New York: Cambridge University Press.

Erickson, K.G., R. Crosnoe, and S. M. Dornbusch. 2000. "A Social Process Model of Adolescent Deviance: Combining Social Control and Differential Association Perspectives." *Journal of Youth and Adolescence* 29: 395–425.

Evans, T. D., F. T. Cullen, V. S. Burton, Jr., R. G. Dunaway, and M. L. Benson. 1997. "The Social Consequences of Self-Control: Testing the General Theory of Crime." *Criminology* 35: 475–501.

Fox, J. 1991. *Regression Diagnostics*. Newbury Park, CA: Sage.

Giordano, P. C., S. A. Cernkovich, and M. D. Pugh. 1986. "Friendships and Delinquency" *American Journal of Sociology* 91: 126–132.

Gottfredson, D. 2001. *Schools and Delinquency*. New York: Cambridge University Press.

Gottfredson, M. R. and T. Hirschi. 1990. *A General Theory of Crime*. Stanford: Stanford University Press.

Greenberg, D. F. 1999. "The Weak Strength of Social Control Theory." *Crime & Delinquency* 45: 66–81.

Hagan, J., A. R. Gillis, and J. Simpson. 1990. "Clarifying and Extending Power-Control Theory." *American Journal of Sociology* 95: 1024–1037.

Hagan, J., and B. McCarthy. 1997. "Anomie, Social Capital, and Street Criminology." Pp. 124–141 in N. Passas and R. Agnew (eds.), *The Future of Anomie Theory*. Boston: Northeastern University Press.

Hawkins, J. D., T. Herrenkohl, D. P. Farrington, D. Brewer, R. F. Catalano, and T. W. Harachi. 1998. "A Review of Predictors of Youth Violence." Pp. 106–146 in R. Loeber and D. P. Farrington (eds.), *Serious & Violent Juvenile Offenders*. Thousand Oaks, CA: Sage.

Hay, C. 2001. "Parenting, Self-Control, and Delinquency: A Test of Self-Control Theory." *Criminology* 39: 707–736.

Hirschi, T. 1969. *Causes of Delinquency*. Berkeley: University of California Press.

Hirschi, T., and M. R. Gottfredson. 1995. "Control Theory and the Life-Course Perspective." *Studies on Crime and Crime Prevention* 4: 131–142.

Jang, S. J., and C. A. Smith. 1997. "A Test of Reciprocal Causal Relationships among Parental Supervision, Affective Ties, and Delinquency." *Journal of Research in Crime and Delinquency* 34: 307–336.

Jessor, R., J. Van Den Bos, J. Vanderryn, F. M. Costa, and M.S. Turbin. 1995. "Protective Factors in Adolescent Problem Behavior: Moderator Effects and Developmental Change." *Developmental Psychology* 31: 923–933.

Junger, M., and I. H. Marshall. 1997. "The Interethnic Generalizability of Social Control Theory: An Empirical Test." *Journal of Research in Crime and Delinquency* 34: 79–112.

Junger-Tas, J. 1992. "An Empirical Test of Social Control Theory." *Journal of Quantitative Criminology* 8: 9–28.

Kempf, K. L. 1993. "The Empirical Status of Hirschi's Control Theory." Pp. 143–185 in F. Adler and W. S. Laufer (eds.), *New Directions in Criminological Theory, Advances in Criminological Theory*, Vol. 4. New Brunswick, NJ: Transaction.

Kercher, K. 1988. "Criminology." Pp. 294–316 in E. F. Borgotta and K. S. Cook (eds.), *The Future of Sociology*. New York: Wiley.

Kornhauser, R. 1978. *Social Sources of Delinquency*. Chicago: University of Chicago Press.

Linden, E., and J. C. Hackler. 1973. "Affective Ties and Delinquency." *Pacific Sociological Review* 16: 27–46.

Marcos, A. C., S. J. Bahr, and R. E. Johnson. 1986. "Test of a Bonding/Association Theory of Adolescent Drug Use." *Social Forces* 65: 135–59.

Matsueda, R. L., and K. Anderson. 1998. "The Dynamics of Delinquent Peers and Delinquent Behavior." *Criminology* 36: 269–306.

Matsueda, R. L., and K. Heimer. 1987. "Race, Family Structure, and Delinquency: A Test of Differential Association and Social Control Theories." *American Sociological Review* 52: 826–840.

Mazerolle, P., and J. Maahs. 2000. "General Strain Theory and Delinquency: An Alternative Examination of Conditioning Influences." *Justice Quarterly* 17: 753–778.

McClelland, G. H., and C. M. Judd. 1993. "Statistical Difficulties of Detecting Interactions and Moderator Effects." *Psychological Bulletin* 114: 376–390.

Menard, S., and B. J. Morse. 1984. "A Structuralist Critique of the IQ-Delinquency Hypothesis: Theory and Evidence." *American Journal of Sociology* 89: 1347–1378.

Nagin, D. S. 1998. "Criminal Deterrence Research at the Outset of the Twenty-First Century." Pp. 1–42 in M. Tonry (ed.), *Crime and Justice: A Review of Research*, Vol. 23. Chicago: University of Chicago Press.

Nagin, D. S., and R. Paternoster. 1991. "The Preventive Effects of the Perceived Risk of Arrest: Testing an Expanded Conception of Deterrence." *Criminology* 29: 561–587.

_____. 1993. "Enduring Individual Differences and Rational Choice Theories of Crime." *Law & Society Review* 27: 467–496.

_____. 1994. "Personal Capital and Social Control: The Deterrence Implications of a Theory of Individual Differences in Criminal Offending." *Criminology* 32: 581–606.

Nagin, D. S., and G. Pogarsky. 2001. "Integrating Clerity, Impulsivity, and Extralegal Sanction Threats into a Model of General Deterrence: Theory and Evidence." *Criminology* 39: 865–892.

Osgood, W. D., J. K. Wilson, P. M. O'Malley, J. G. Bachman, and L. D. Johnston. 1996. "Routine Activities and Individual Deviant Behavior." *American Sociological Review* 61: 635–655.

Paternoster, R. 1988. "Examining Three-Wave Deterrence Models: A Question of Temporal Order and Specification." *Journal of Criminal Law and Criminology* 79: 135–179.

_____. 2001. "Youths and Deterrence: Columbia, South Carolina, 1979–1981, ICPSR Study #8255." Ann Arbor, Michigan: Inter-University Consortium for Political and Social Research.

Paternoster, R., and R. Brame. 1997. "Multiple Routes to Delinquency? A Test of Developmental and General Theories of Crime." *Criminology* 35: 49–84.

Paternoster, R., and A. Piquero. 1995. "Reconceptualizing Deterrence: An Empirical Test of Personal and Vicarious Experiences." *Journal of Research in Crime and Delinquency* 32: 251–286.

Paternoster, R., L. E. Saltzman, G. P. Waldo, and T. E. Chiricos. 1983. "Perceived Risks and Social Control: Do Sanctions Really Deter?" *Law & Society Review* 17: 457–479.

Patterson, G. 1982. *Coercive Family Processes*. Eugene, OR: Castalia.

Piquero, A., and S. Tibbetts. 1996. "Specifying the Direct and Indirect Effects of Low Self-Control and Situational Factors in Offenders' Decision Making: Toward a More Complete Model of Rational Offending." *Justice Quarterly* 13: 481–510.

Polakowski, M. 1994. "Linking Self-and Social Control with Deviance: Illuminating the Structure Underlying a General Theory of Crime and Its Relation to Deviant Activity." *Journal of Quantitative Criminology* 10: 41–78.

Poole, E. D., and R. M. Regoli. 1979. "Parental Support, Delinquent Friends, and Delinquency: A Test of Interaction Effects." *Journal of Criminal Law & Criminology* 70: 188–193.

Rankin, J. H., and R. Kern. 1994. "Parental Attachments and Delinquency." *Criminology* 32: 495–515.

Rankin, J. H., and L. E. Wells. 1990. "The Effect of Parental Attachments and Direct Controls on Delinquency." *Journal of Research in Crime and Delinquency* 27: 140–165.

Sampson, R. J., and J. H. Laub. 1993. *Crime in the Making*. Boston: Harvard University Press.

Sherman, L. W. 1993. "Defiance, Deterrence, and Irrelevance: A Theory of the Criminal Sanction." *Journal of Research in Crime and Delinquency* 30: 445–473.

_____. 2000. "The Defiant Imagination: Consilience and the Science of Sanctions." Presented at the University of Pennsylvania, Philadelphia.

Sherman, L. W., and D. A. Smith. 1992. "Crime, Punishment, and Stake in Conformity: Legal and Informal Control of Domestic Violence." *American Sociological Review* 57: 680–690.

Simons, R. L., C. Johnson, R. D. Conger, and G. Elder, Jr. 1998. "A Test of Latent Trait versus Life-Course Perspectives on the Stability of Adolescent Antisocial Behavior." *Criminology* 36: 217–244.

Stanfield, R. E. 1966. "The Interaction of Family Variables and Gang Variables in the Aetiology of Delinquency." *Social Problems* 13: 111–417.

StataCorp. 1999. *Stata Statistical Software: Release 6.0*, Vol. 2. College Station, TX: Stata Corporation.

Taylor, C. 2001. "The Relationship between Social and Self–Control." *Theoretical Criminology* 5: 369–388.

Thornberry, T. P. 1996. "Empirical Support for Interactional Theory: A Review of the Literature." Pp. 198–235 in J. D. Hawkins (ed.), *Delinquency and Crime, Current Theories*. Cambridge: Cambridge University Press.

Thornberry, T. P, M. D. Krohn, A. J. Lizotte, C. A. Smith, and P. K. Porter. 1998. "Taking Stock: An Overview of Findings from the Rochester Youth Development Study." Paper presented at the annual meeting of the American Society of Criminology, Washington, DC.

Tittle, C. R. 1995. *Control Balance: Toward a General Theory of Deviance*. Boulder, CO: Westview.

Walsh, A. 2002. *Biosocial Criminology*. Cincinnati: Anderson Publishing.
Warr, Mark. 1993. "Parents, Peers, and Delinquency." *Social Forces* 72: 247–264.
Wells, E. L., and J. H. Rankin. 1988. "Direct Parental Controls and Delinquency." *Criminology* 26: 263–284.
Wiatrowski, M. D., D. B. Griswold, and M. K. Roberts. 1981. "Social Control Theory and Delinquency." *American Sociological Review* 46: 525–541.
Wright, B. R. E., A. Caspi, T. E. Moffitt, and P. A. Silva. 1999. "Low Self-Control , Social Bonds, and Crime: Social Causation, Social Selection, or Both?" *Criminology* 37: 479–514.
_____. 2001. "The Effects of Social Ties on Crime Vary by Criminal Propensity: A Life-Course Model of Interdependence." *Criminology* 39: 321–352.

5

A Control Theory of Gender Difference in Crime and Delinquency*

Barbara J. Costello and Helen J. Mederer

There is a mounting body of literature criticizing mainstream theories of crime for their inattention to female crime and the gender gap in criminal and delinquent behavior, and to their overall ignorance of the value of feminist approaches to studying social phenomena. While it is difficult to argue with these claims, we hold that feminist scholars have spent too much time criticizing "masculinist" approaches to the study of crime and too little time trying to improve upon them. Our goal in this chapter is to elaborate a control theory of gender differences in criminal behavior that addresses the important feminist criticisms of mainstream theories of crime. In the process, we provide a more complete framework for understanding and explaining gender differences in crime than has currently been developed, and thus further our understanding of the etiology of criminal behavior as a whole.

To briefly summarize our perspective, we develop a multilevel control theory that explicitly incorporates considerations of gender and the patriarchal nature of human societies. As Naffine (1987) notes, control theory is particularly well-suited to explain the greater conformity of women and girls relative to men and boys given its focus on explaining conformity rather than crime. Drawing on Risman's (1998) argument that gender inequality is created and maintained on the individual, interactional, and structural levels, we hold that females are more constrained than males through gender socialization, through the communication of gender expectations in interactions with others, and through institutional barriers to gender equality such as occupational segregation and inequality in the household division of labor.

* We thank Leo Carroll, Constance Chapple, and Travis Hirschi for their helpful comments on an earlier version of this chapter.

Starting with the control theory assumption of an asocial human nature, the crux of our argument is that males and females are by nature equally inclined to commit criminal and analogous acts, but females are more constrained than males in virtually all aspects of life. Thus, males are freer to deviate than females. Our arguments lead to the conclusion that the most fruitful approach to gender equality in crime and other aspects of social life is not to *focus* on increasing the freedoms accorded to women, but rather on decreasing the freedoms accorded to men.

Criminological Theories and Feminist Perspectives

Perhaps the most common complaint about existing theories of crime is that they were developed and largely tested by men with male offenders in mind (Daly and Chesney-Lind, 1988; Naffine, 1987; Smart, 1976). We do not take issue with this fact. However, we do take issue with the conclusion that because these theories were designed by and about men, that they cannot explain female crime or the gender gap in criminal behavior. We believe that this conclusion is simply not supported with convincing evidence. For example, attempts to include consideration of females in mainstream theories have been derided as "domesticated feminism" in that they do not explicitly incorporate considerations of patriarchal social organization (Daly and Chesney-Lind, 1988). Such conclusions imply that nonfeminist theories cannot be transformed into feminist theories simply because the theories were originally developed by and about men. The problem with this line of reasoning is that it leads to the outright rejection of "masculinist" theories before attempts have been made to integrate them with feminist approaches. Another problem with this "separatist" position is that it conceptualizes men's and women's behavior as having different antecedents and consequences, which reduces the possibility that we can develop truly general theories of human behavior (Epstein, 1988). By assuming that there are basic differences between the sexes that are deeply rooted and that result in different approaches to the world, this position also tends to support and justify gender inequality. By viewing gender differences as "inevitable and even desirable" rather than as social constructions, such theories rationalize women's subordination to men (Epstein, 1988: xi). We thus agree with Epstein's position on this issue—that the two sexes are similar, and that gender differences are socially constructed. "This view ascribes observed differences in behavior to a social control system that prescribes and proscribes specific behaviors for women and men" (1988: 25), and implies that feminist scholarship can be produced working in conventional paradigms.

Feminist scholars have criticized mainstream criminology's methods as well as its theories. Many feminist researchers advocate more qualitative approaches to studying crime, and "are more interested in providing texture, social context, and case histories; in short, in presenting accurate portrayals of how adolescent and adult women become involved in crime" (Daly and Chesney-Lind, 1988: 518). Clearly, qualitative approaches are of great value and provide types of data that are simply beyond the capacity of quantitative approaches. However, we believe that the focus on qualitative approaches in lieu of quantitative approaches presents further problems for the potential impact of feminist thought on mainstream criminology. In essence, some feminist scholars reject both the dominant theories and methods of the discipline, which leaves little room to convince its practitioners of the errors of their ways, and practically ensures that feminist and "mainstream" scholars will continue to speak different languages (see also Yllo, 1988). Further, qualitative methods in themselves are not sufficient to address one of the central variables of some feminist theories, patriarchy itself. We believe that demonstrating the effects of patriarchy, a macro-level variable, requires the use of methods better suited to measuring macro-level variables than are small-scale qualitative studies. Moreover, we do not believe that there are any necessary connections between feminist theory and particular methods of research (Collins, 1999; Epstein, 1988; Jayaratne and Stewart, 1991). Instead, we argue that a complete understanding of the impact of gender on crime requires the use of mixed methods, simply because gender inequality is so pervasive in human societies that it is impossible to fully measure it using only quantitative or only qualitative methods. Again, then, we believe that the feminist rejection of the approach of mainstream criminology is premature, and that the possibilities of integrating "masculinist" and feminist approaches have not been fully explored.

Feminist Criticisms of Control Theories

Control theory, particularly Hirschi's (1969) social control theory, has been widely criticized due to its lack of attention to female crime. For example, Messerschmidt holds that it is "incapable of deciphering the gendered nature of crime" (1993: 3). Again, we argue that this claim is quite premature, and further that it is not backed with sufficient evidence to be convincing. Specifically, Messerschmidt's "evidence" that control theory cannot explain both male and female crime is merely that Hirschi, "remarkably and without explanation" excluded girls from his test of the theory in *Causes of Delinquency* (Messerschmidt 1993: 3). We see once again that the fact that females have not been studied is taken as evidence that females' behavior or the gender gap in crime *cannot* be understood in the context of control theory.[1]

Naffine also argues that Hirschi (1969) is "not even-handed in his treatment of the sexes" (1987: 66). Her argument rests on the claim that other criminologists, like Sutherland and Cohen, had portrayed male offenders in a positive, romanticized light, thereby portraying female conformists as passive, uninteresting, or unintelligent. Hirschi, on the other hand, "performs an almost undetectable sleight of hand" by portraying the conforming male in a positive light, as hard-working, dedicated, and concerned for the opinions of others (1987: 66). It is difficult to argue that Hirschi performed a "sleight of hand" given his claim that his theory was asking a different question than those of his predecessors, namely why people conform rather than why they deviate. It is also difficult to make this argument given his explicit rejection of the unspoken procedural rule of the time to "appreciate deviance" (Hirschi, 1973: 170–71). Ultimately, however, Naffine's criticisms of Hirschi seem to be centered around the idea that he missed a good opportunity to develop a theory that explicitly incorporated considerations of gender. She advocates an approach to studying crime that views conforming women as "responsible, hardworking, engrossed in conventional activities and people and perfectly rational in their calculation not to place all this at risk by engaging in crime" (1987: 131; see also Simpson, 1991), just as Hirschi viewed conforming men. This is the view of conforming men and women we take in this work.

Problems in the Current Literature

The Typological Approach

Our goal with the current work is to explain both male and female crime, and more importantly to explain the gender gap in criminal and analogous behaviors. We do not believe it is fruitful to approach the study of crime by creating typologies of offenders or offenses and offering different explanations for each type. This approach is exemplified in explanations of male violence against females (Brownmiller, 1975), in the work of socialist feminist approaches that make distinctions between "street crime" and "corporate crime" (Messerschmidt, 1986), in approaches that focus on masculinity as the cause of male crime (Messerschmidt, 1993), and in explanations of female homicide (Ogle, Maier-Katkin, and Bernard, 1995) or violent crime (Heimer and DeCoster, 1999). Rather, we concur with Gottfredson and Hirschi (1990) that it is more useful to work toward general theories that attempt to explain a unified phenomenon with a single set of theoretical constructs. This avoids the lack of accumulation of knowledge that is risked with a radical empiricist approach (Gottfredson and Hirschi, 1990), avoids the problems associated with allowing the state or those in powerful positions in society to define the dependent variable of interest to criminology (Gottfredson and Hirschi, 1990; Messerschmidt, 1986), and allows us to avoid the problem so often cited in feminist literature that criminologists only focus on one sex (males, historically) in developing explanations of crime.

Again drawing on the work of Gottfredson and Hirschi (1990), we define criminal and analogous acts as those that provide immediate, quick, and easy gratification of desires, that often cause pain and suffering to others and to the offender him- or herself in the long run, and that are often exciting or risky. This definition is broad enough in scope to include offenses committed by males or females, young or old, rich and poor, and can include offenses ranging in seriousness from drinking too much to illegally dumping toxic waste and killing hundreds of people.

While we recognize the importance of one's social position on life chances and behavior, we reject the implicit claim made by many theories of crime that social position necessarily determines the *types* of variables or causal mechanisms that influence the likelihood and types of criminal behavior in which one engages. These sorts of explanations are not satisfying theoretically, and they tend to be refuted by the simple fact of versatility in offending. For example, radical feminists focus on patriarchy as a cause of male violence against women, and view such violence as a means for men to retain control over women (MacKinnon, 1987; Russell, 1998). This argument is not supported with evidence that men who assault their girlfriends or wives are more likely to also have a history of violence against their parents and peers (Malone, Tyree, and O'Leary, 1989), and are more likely to engage in other forms of violent and nonviolent deviant behaviors (Simons et al., 1995) than are men who do not assault their partners. These types of explanations are also inconsistent with evidence that male and female offenders report "strikingly similar" motives for robbery (Miller, 1998: 47).

In a more complicated typological approach, Messerschmidt (1986) argues that crimes committed by the bourgeoisie are an attempt to maintain their social positions and the status quo, while crimes committed by those with less power are attempts to either resist their oppression or accommodate it. The ways in which males and females resist and accommodate oppression vary due to differences in males' and females' relative levels of power. For example, young males resist by eschewing working for low wages at dead-end jobs and embracing a street culture in which a tough-guy reputation confers status. At the same time, however, their conformity to the norms of the street culture results in their accommodation to their powerless position in society. Females resist through drug addiction or suicide, or accommodate through economic crimes such as prostitution and shoplifting.

One problem with this perspective is that it overlooks commonalities in the actual behaviors exhibited by people in different social locations, and instead accords primary importance to their social locations. This focus leads us to ignore empirical findings such as that versatility in offending holds for both males and females (Campbell, 1981; Hindelang, 1971; Mazzerole et al., 2000). Similarly, males as well as females most commonly commit minor property crimes (Chesney-Lind, 1997; Weis, 1976), both males and females commit violent crime (Simpson, 1991), and overall patterns of offending are very similar for males and females (English, 1993).

Messerschmidt's approach is to look for variation in his independent variables of interest (class, race, and gender) and posit that the obvious variations in social location among people in the United States must cause variations in the amounts and types of crimes they commit. We argue that a better approach is to first empirically assess the extent to which the behaviors of people in different social locations vary, and then assess the extent to which they vary on independent variables of interest. In this way, we avoid constructing theories that explain differences in behavior that do not actually exist. Poor women engage in prostitution to make money; rich businessmen engage in illegal business practices to make money. The poor steal to get money or items they want but do not have; those in power fix prices to get money they want but do not have. It is difficult to make the argument that these behaviors require different explanations, unless one argues that differences in the independent variables of interest actually create the differences in the dependent variable despite the lack of observable difference in the dependent variable. Clearly, this approach has the effect of confounding the independent and dependent variables of interest, because it holds that differences in behavior (the dependent variable) are only observable through observing differences in the independent variables (race, class, and gender.) Thus, Messerschmidt has created a false typology, based not on observable differences in the dependent variable, but on observable differences in the independent variables. This approach, ironically, bears some resemblance to early attempts to explain female crime with reference to their alleged biological differences from men (see Smart, 1976 for a review), it merely substitutes differences in power for biological differences.

Another way to conceptualize this problem in the literature is to view it as an exercise in reading contingency tables. We might ask the question, as Ogle, Maier-Katkin, and Bernard (1995) do, "What percentage of homicides by women involve killing intimates?" Their review of the literature shows that the answer to this question is about 80 percent, which leads them to construct a theory of why male and female murderers victimize different types of people. In contrast, we might ask "What percentage of women and men kill an intimate?" Rates of intimate homicide are about three times higher for men than for women. Thus, we think it more useful to ask why men commit all types of homicide much more often than women do, rather than begin with the small proportion of women who commit homicide and then ask why they kill who they do.

By focusing on the similarities between the types of crimes committed by males and females rather than on the differences, we work toward a theory of crime that is truly general and that helps avoid the historical problem in criminology of assuming that females commit only certain types of crime such as prostitution and other sexual offenses (Campbell, 1981; Smart, 1976). We argue that to create a gender-inclusive theory of crime, we must first adopt a gender-inclusive conceptualization of the dependent variable of interest. Fortunately, crime and delinquency data support such a conceptualization. Males and females most often commit petty property offenses, and least often commit serious violent offenses. There is clearly a quantitative difference in males' and females' offending, but little evidence for important qualitative differences in offense types. For this reason, we believe it is more useful to focus on quantitative differences in independent variables affecting male and female crime, and less useful to posit qualitative differences in the types of variables or causal mechanisms linking them to crime.[2]

Integrated Theories

A number of attempts to explain the gender gap in criminal offending are similar to our approach in this work in that they incorporate considerations of gender into mainstream theories of crime (Hagan, Gillis, and Simpson, 1985; Hagan, Simpson, and Gillis, 1987; Heimer, 1996; Steffensmeier and Allan, 1996). However, these attempts incorporate elements of a variety of theoretical perspectives that have conflicting assumptions about human nature and social order, and thus lack the consistency that we hope to achieve with our perspective. Following Hirschi (1979), we hold that "separate and unequal is better."

One example of an integrated approach to explaining the gender gap is Heimer's (1996) theory of differential social control. In this work, Heimer draws on control theories by arguing that youths anticipate the reactions of others to their behavior before deciding on their actions. They also consider their own attitudes toward the law, which they have formed largely through the process of taking the role of significant others. Thus, attachment to others and belief in the moral validity of the law are important elements in Heimer's theory, as they are in Hirschi's (1969) social control theory. However, Heimer also draws on Sutherland's differential association theory by arguing that significant others or reference groups can exert pressure toward deviation as well as pressure toward conformity. It is this idea that gives her theory its name, in that differential social control is a result of the differential normative standards of the individual's reference groups. Individuals can be constrained to commit crime just as they can be constrained to conform, and social control in delinquent groups can be transformed into self-control through the process of role-taking (Heimer, 1996: 41).

Heimer thus "uses the terms but ignores the claims" of social control theory (Hirschi, 1979: 34). She rejects the control theory claim that organized groups are by definition organized to increase conformity to norms against the use of force and fraud, and argues that self-control can be conducive to delinquency. Both of these claims are contrary to control theory's assumptions of human nature and social order, and contrary to much empirical evidence. She also argues that the feminine gender role is incompatible with delinquent behavior, and that the opinions of others likely more strongly affect girls than boys. While the latter claim implies that girls would be more influenced by delinquent peers than boys, most of Heimer's discussion of the differential effect of gender on crime focuses on the *deterrent* effect of others' opinions on delinquency. For example, she states that "anticipating that parents and/or peers would disapprove of delinquency may be more consequential for females' than for males' delinquency" (1996: 43). Her theoretical model presumably does not distinguish between others' approval or disapproval of delinquency, but her choice of terminology to describe these effects (as well as the direction of her variables' coding) emphasizes the ability of others to control behavior in conforming rather than deviant directions. We agree with Heimer's approach in this regard, but we find it unsatisfactory in its integration of control and cultural deviance propositions about the direction of group influence.

Similarly, power-control theory draws on control theory concepts to explain gender difference in delinquency, but it does not remain true to control theory's assumption of human nature (Hagan, Gillis, and Simpson, 1985; Hagan, Simpson, and Gillis, 1987). Hagan, Gillis, and Simpson (1985) argue that gender differences in delinquency should be larger among those in upper classes because upper-class boys are being socialized for occupations in which risk-taking is a rewarded attribute, unlike lower-class boys destined for blue-collar occupations. Hagan, Simpson, and Gillis (1987) make a slightly different argument, in that the relative positions of husbands and wives in the class structure will influence children's socialization. Households that are more egalitarian will produce fewer gender differences in delinquency because both girls and boys are encouraged to be more risk-taking. Households that are more patriarchal, in contrast, will foster risk-taking mainly in boys and place greater controls on girls' behavior.

Hagan and colleagues' focus on controls exerted by parents is consistent with the control theory notion that the absence of adequate control leads to delinquency (Jensen, 1993). However, they also argue that risk-taking is "encouraged" for some youths, depending on their class status (Hagan et al., 1987: 793). The idea that risk-taking is encouraged in children of any class background is contrary to the control theory assumption that risk-taking behavior is a consequence of our asocial human nature, and needs to be controlled rather than taught through socialization.[3] Hagan and colleagues, and others who have tested power-control theory's assertions (Grasmick et al., 1996), also conceptualize risk-taking quite differently than do control theories. For example, Gottfredson and Hirschi (1990) argue that crime often requires risk-taking, but criminal risk-taking is generally shortsighted, impulsive, and designed to produce immediate short-term pleasure. In contrast, the power-control conceptualization of risk-taking is of the sort needed to succeed in the business world, which we argue is generally more of a "calculated risk-taking" than an impulsive one. Successful investors tend not to be those who buy large quantities of stock impulsively, because they like the sound of a company's name, and so on. Rather, they spend time learning about companies before they invest, try to diversify their holdings to guard against financial disaster, and expect to profit in the long term rather than making a fortune with a single trade. Obviously, there are those who make business deals without adequate foresight, but we would argue that they tend to be unsuccessful in business much as most criminals are unable to make a good living through criminal behavior. In short, we argue that successful risk-taking in business requires self-control, and bears little resemblance to the sort of risk-taking involved in most types of crime.[4]

Incomplete Theories and Empirical Tests

Another problem in the current literature on gender and crime that we hope to overcome with our perspective is that most theories exclude at least some concepts that are known to be related to crime. As Heimer (1996) notes, most gender-focused theories of crime do not consider the role of attitudes toward crime or peer influence in delinquency causation. Similarly, we are unaware of any gender-focused theory of crime that incorporates a consideration of the individual's level of commitment to school or occupation. Given that commitment to school, working hard in school, and liking school are very robust predictors of delinquency (Costello and Vowell, 1999), the lack of attention to these variables in theories of gender differences in delinquency is potentially problematic. While we do not argue that a theory of gender difference must be able to explain all known correlates of offending, we do argue that it is worthwhile to consider the potential role of robust correlates of offending in explaining gender differences in crime (Jensen 1993).

One of the reasons that the correlates of offending noted above may be overlooked in theories of gender and crime is their focus on macro-level variables, particularly those involving social stratification. For example, Messerschmidt (1986, 1993) argues that capitalism and social inequality are the most important determinants of types and rates of crime committed by people in different social locations. He incorporates consideration of interactional-level variables in his argument that crime provides a way for males to "do gender," but his focus on inequality as the ultimate causal variable leads him to argue that males in different social strata do gender differently (Messerschmidt 1993). Middle-class white boys can demonstrate or achieve masculinity largely through participation in school organizations, but access to such avenues for demonstrating masculinity are not available to lower-class or black boys. Thus, lower-class and minority boys show their masculinity through criminal behavior and defiance of school rules. Messerschmidt's emphasis on the importance of inequality leads him to overlook relevant individual correlates of offending, such as Hirschi's (1969) findings that lower-class boys and black boys do have aspirations for conventional success, and that those who do are less likely to be delinquent. Hirschi also found that middle-class boys with lower academic ability were more likely to accept fatalistic statements, thought to be characteristic of the lower classes (e.g. Miller, 1958), than were lower-class boys with higher academic ability (1969). Just as strain theories tend to overlook such findings, then, Messerschmidt's variation on strain theory (with masculinity as the desired goal rather than money) suffers by a failure to consider important micro-level correlates of offending and within-class variation on these variables.

Important correlates of offending are also often excluded from empirical studies of gender difference in offending, and measures of important theoretical constructs are often lacking in content validity. For example, some studies measure gender differences in parental supervision using only measures of whether respondents' parents know where they are and who they are with when away from home (Hagan et al., 1985, 1987; Jensen and Eve, 1976), or using only three questions asking parents how many of their children's friends and friends' parents they know (Heimer, 1996; Heimer and DeCoster, 1999). Power-control theory classifies households as egalitarian or patriarchal based only on parents' relative occupational location, without directly measuring parents' gender-role attitudes, decision-making power in the family, or the division of household labor (Hagan et al., 1987; McCarthy et al., 1999). Adler's (1975) exposition of the liberation hypothesis did not include sufficient measures of "liberation," and we believe she grossly overestimated the impact of the women's movement on women's lives. Similar criticisms have been leveled against studies of individuals' gender orientation and its relation to crime (Giordano and Cernkovich, 1979). As we argue below, women's increased labor force participation has not led them to "desert those kitchens" and take on the traditional roles of men (Adler, 1975:12). Rather, in many ways women's and girls' lives have remain unchanged over the past fifty years, and in some ways women are even more constrained than they ever were.

Part of the problem of inadequate operationalization of theoretical constructs, of course, lies in limitations of available data, and in limitations in researchers' ability to collect large quantities of data from respondents who may be only reluctantly participating in their studies. We recognize that it is much easier to criticize existing data sets than it is to improve upon them in significant ways. However, we believe that limitations of data have had the effect of limiting theory development, and have contributed to the dismissal of previous attempts to explain the gender gap in offending. For example, some scholars have used Jensen and Eve's (1976) failure to explain all of the gender difference in offending as evidence that control theory cannot explain the gender gap in delinquency, despite the fact that their analysis left only about 2 percent of the gender gap unexplained. Similarly, others have argued that gender ideologies and respondents' gender orientations cannot explain the gender gap because of failures of existing studies to find clear patterns supporting those predictions. As Heimer (1996) notes, it is difficult to reject such explanations given the variety of different ways these concepts have been operationalized.

Another problem with the research on gender ideologies and orientations is that it tends to reduce the "gender structure" to individual-level variables, and neglects to consider the effects of interactional processes and institutional constraints on crime. Our argument is that gender inequality is maintained on all three levels (Risman, 1998), so it is premature to reject role-based theories solely on the results of purely individual-level studies. Similarly, Chafetz (1990) argues that one problem with gender theory is its reliance on single levels of analysis rather than taking a multi-level approach. Specifically, she holds that voluntaristic theories, which emphasize how women come to make choices that lead unintentionally to their subordinate status, focus on the micro level and neglect the mezo and macro levels. Coercive theories, which emphasize men's ability to maintain their power over women due to their greater resources, focus on the mezo and macro levels, and neglect the micro level. We agree with Chafetz's position that these theories are "partial" theories, and lack detailed and systematic ties to other levels of analysis.

Human Nature, Social Order, and Femininity

Control theories of crime start with the assumption of value consensus, or that all human societies prohibit acts of force and fraud undertaken in the pursuit of self-interest. This assumption is consistent with the control theory assumption that humans are by nature self-interested and unconcerned with the consequences of their actions for others. In order to function, social groups must have some mechanisms for controlling the self-interested tendencies of their members. These mechanisms include the formal actions of the state to sanction offenders, informal ones such as parental control and socialization of children, and our tendencies to control each other's behavior in both overt and subtle ways. The cause of criminal, delinquent, and disruptive behavior in the control theory perspective is simply individuals acting on their natural tendencies because of a failure in some aspect of social control.

We argue above that integrated theories are flawed in part because they tend to mix incompatible assumptions about human nature and social order. It would be a mistake, then, to argue that males and females have different natures, and early attempts at explaining gender differences with reference to males' and females' different natures have been rightly criticized (Smart, 1976). Instead, we remain consistent with control theory assumptions by assuming that men and women have exactly the same innate tendencies, which are to pursue self-interest without regard for the interests of others. We also assume that it is not possible to form or maintain human societies unless individuals and ultimately society as a whole work to limit the individual pursuit of self-interest. Given these assumptions, our question is not "Why do men commit so much crime?" (Heidensohn, 1997; Hayslett-McCall and Bernard, 2002), but rather, "Why don't women commit as much crime as men?" Our answer is, quite simply, that women are more effectively controlled than men are through their early socialization, through their interactions with others, and through the operation of social institutions (Risman, 1998). This control over women has the positive outcome of reducing female crime, and hence overall crime rates in society.

The position that women's oppression in society has positive social outcomes is an unpopular one, for good reason. However, as we argue below, only *one* implication of this idea is typically cited in objection to this functionalist argument, and that is the implication that gender inequality should be maintained to keep crime rates from increasing. Ironically, we suspect that this implication is the first to come to mind because of the tendency to view men as "normal" and women as "other"—much of the push toward gender equality focuses on allowing women to be "more like men" in some ways, so arguing that women should not be provided the freedom enjoyed by men seems to imply that women's oppression is a desirable state. However, this is not our argument. We argue that gender inequality is inherently dysfunctional for society, and the dysfunctions associated with it are greater than the benefit it might produce in terms of lower crime rates among women. Our efforts to reduce crime should focus not on maintaining disproportionate control over women, but rather to work toward increasing control over men, or making the constraints experienced by men more similar to those experienced by women.

We have to this point not addressed the question of how gender inequality initially arose, and how such a dysfunctional social arrangement came to be. Drawing on radical feminist perspectives (Firestone, 1970), we tie women's oppression to the one indisputable biological difference between men and women, which is women's ability to bear and nurse children.[5] As Firestone (1970) argues, the unavailability of effective contraception for much of human history meant that birth rates would be high, and due to biological necessity, women were the primary caretakers of infants. It is this initial division of labor that led to women's subordination, because it set limits on their physical mobility, kept them in or near the home (Chafetz, 1990), and limited their ability to obtain scarce and highly valued resources such as meat obtained though hunting large game.

This initial division of labor, born of necessity, had important consequences both for the value of "men's work" and "women's work," and for the differential constraints that came to be placed on men and women. Although women's food collection and production provided more of the daily nutrition needed for survival, men's work focused on obtaining more scarce and thus more valuable goods, and as a result it provided more status and prestige. Hunting has the added benefit of providing immediate and tangible valued goods to the individual himself and his family or larger social unit. In contrast, women's work focused on rearing children, which were not scarce, and which were economically valuable only in the long term. Caring for infants, in particular, was an activity that provides only uncertain benefits (due to high infant mortality rates) and benefits that could not be realized until many years later. When these benefits were realized, they were likely to be realized primarily within the family, for example in the form of economic contributions to the family or prestige that children's accomplishments might bring. Nonetheless, children were economically valuable, and they benefited the family in the long term. Thus, childrearing was a crucial activity for the survival of families and (obviously) for the survival of a social group as a whole.

We thus view childrearing as a necessary activity that requires years of hard work for only distant and somewhat uncertain benefits. In keeping with control theory assumptions, then, it is not an activity that is inherently pleasurable—it does not bring immediate gratification of individual desires, it is not easy, and it is not usually exciting or thrilling. To address the seemingly difficult question of why people do it, some have argued that it must be an evolutionary adaptation, such that a "maternal instinct" is necessary to explain women's willingness to work so hard for such distant and uncertain benefits. While this is a logical argument, and we do not deny that women enjoy many aspects of childrearing, we believe that there is too much evidence against it. For example, many women choose to remain childless, and it is not uncommon for women to abandon or kill their children. If human women as biological entities have evolved to become emotionally invested in children, it is difficult to explain even a few individuals who do not fit the general pattern, unless we resort to an "atavistic" characterization of those who do not. In contrast, a social explanation of women's willingness to care for children need not be so deterministic—if social processes are not effective, then individual women will not be willing to undertake this activity.[6]

Historically, women were the primary childrearers out of sheer necessity. The question then becomes, why have women been willing to allow this social arrangement to continue once it was no longer a biological necessity? Our answer to this question is that the social definition of the feminine gender has come to be intimately associated with the care of children, and more generally, a selfless concern for the well-being of others, and a self-controlled focus on potential long-term consequences of their own and others' behavior. In short, femininity is having strong bonds to family and community, and having self-control.[7]

From a control theory perspective, femininity is further removed from human nature than is masculinity. While selfishness and pursuing short-term pleasure are discouraged for both men and women, we argue that it is actually more important for this to be discouraged among girls and women because of their roles as primary nurturers for children and family (Chodorow, 1978). In short, women are more responsible for the perpetuation of human groups than are men, and as a consequence it has simply been more necessary for women to be self-controlled than for men to be. Initial biological differences between men and women and the concurrent division of labor that arose by necessity have been translated into social norms and structures that perpetuate the gendered division of labor and its inherent inequality. Thus, the social definition of femininity and the social practices that "enforce" it are both functional and dysfunctional. They are functional for the perpetuation and smooth functioning of society and to make women less inclined to commit crime. They are dysfunctional in that they leave men relatively free from the responsibilities of caring for others, they allow boys' socialization to underemphasize the importance of concern for others, and thus they have left men relatively free to commit crime. Of course, they are also dysfunctional because they have served to limit women's opportunities to pursue individual goals that are not necessarily tied to the well-being of their families.

A growing body of literature on gender and caring supports our argument that social practices that maintain femininity constrain women's behavior, and supports our argument that this arrangement has become increasingly dysfunctional. "True womanhood" or "the cult of domesticity" is the identification of women's true nature with nurturance and moral sensitivity (Harrington, 2000; Williams, 2000). Women are most admired and most respected when they fulfill the role of supportive wife or mother and least admired and respected when they enter the world of power, which prevents women from claiming and equal voice in public affairs (Harrington, 2000). Motherhood is a measure of virtue; the good woman is the good mother. "Intensive mothering," the idea that mothers are responsible for all aspects of a child's development, is the norm for women (Hays, 1996). At the same time, the "cultural contradiction" of mothering also places demands on women to be ideal workers, unencumbered by the demands of caring for children (Hays, 1996). The push to make women more like men in terms of ideal workers (Williams, 2000) has resulted in a crisis of caretaking, which has made the dysfunctions of traditional gender arrangements more apparent. We cannot have gender equality and a society in which dependents are adequately cared for by making women more like men—men must become more like women and share the constraints of caretaking. As Harrington puts it,

> "taking care of those who need it is a moral act. Mothering is a moral act. And to the extent that women have carried the mothering assignment through the centuries—

however unfair its terms have been—they have acted as trustees of an ethic of care that is essential to the good society." (2000: 113–114)

The Female Role as a Constrained Role

The essence of our argument is that women and girls are more socially controlled and more self-controlled than men and boys, and these differences in control explain the gender gap in criminal behavior. In Risman's (1998) terms, socialization practices produce differences in males' and females' "gendered selves," so that they develop different preferences, attitudes, and behaviors. Gendered expectations for behavior are reinforced in our interactions with others, so that others' reactions to our behavior lead us to "do gender" by acting in ways consistent with these expectations. The institutional arrangements in our society provide further reinforcement for traditional behavior, and act as barriers to both men's and women's ability to behave in ways inconsistent with traditional gender expectations.

In control theory terms, females are socialized to have greater self-control and to be more concerned with the opinions and feelings of others. Informal social control processes reinforce conforming behavior for both males and females, but operate more strongly on females than males. Similarly, structural-level forces work to maintain conformity for all, but many structural variables disproportionately limit the freedom of women and girls and allow men the freedom to pursue purely individualistic goals, as well as to commit crime.

It is this focus on crime as individualistic but universally undesirable behavior that most clearly distinguishes our perspective from existing theories of gender difference. For example, Heimer's (1996) differential social control theory allows for the possibility that self-control can produce crime if the social context is a deviant one. Our perspective starts with the assumption that crime is the natural result of selfish human tendencies, and that self-control is antithetical to crime. We also view social integration as antithetical to crime, so that more solidary groups have lower rates of force and fraud, and greater influence on their members, than less solidary groups. Similar to Heimer's theory, Hagan's power-control theory holds that deviance requires socialization to risk-taking behavior, again in contrast with the control theory view that risk-taking is unsocialized behavior. Power-control theory also denies the control theory assumption that all social groups discourage force and fraud among their members. Rather, it holds that at least some forms of force or fraud are necessary for occupational success.

Our perspective also differs from other explanations of the gender gap in our argument that processes working on all three levels of analysis operate to maintain and reinforce gender difference and inequality. Most criminological research focuses only on the individual level of analysis, and there is also a strong structural tradition in the literature. Interactional processes, likely due to the difficulty of studying them, have been least commonly studied in criminology, and we argue that this is of great consequence in understanding processes leading to the gender difference in crime. Most importantly, though, we do not believe that evidence of relationships (or lack thereof) between variables operating on one level of analysis and deviance can be taken as definitive. Because the gender structure operates on all three levels (Risman, 1998), we must work toward empirical analyses of processes on all three levels.

We present below a brief review of the criminological and gender literature that addresses the central claims of our perspective. We also provide some suggestions for research at each level of analysis and on the interrelationships between variables operating on each level of analysis.

The Individual Level of Analysis

We argue that girls are, in essence, better socialized than boys, and that these differences will be apparent both in observations of others' treatment of girls, and in personality characteristics that are the outcome of socialization.[8] With regard to others' treatment of girls, there is evidence to suggest that parents supervise and control girls' behavior more than boys' behavior (Hagan, Simpson, and Gillis, 1987).[9] As Gottfredson and Hirschi (1990) note, monitoring of behavior is a crucial first step in correcting misbehavior when it occurs, thus this finding is consistent with the notion that girls' behavior is more effectively controlled than boys' behavior.

Research has also found that mothers give more negative feedback to girls' expressions of anger than to boys', and that girls get more negative feedback overall from both parents and teachers (Harter, 1999). In an observational study of six cultures, Whiting and Edwards (1975) found that others interrupt girls' activities and try to change girls' behavior significantly more than boys' behavior. Given that sex differences in delinquency and crime remain stable over time, it is unlikely that such negative feedback is a reaction to girls' higher rates of misbehavior, and is more likely the result of girls being held to higher standards of behavior than boys are.

Zahn-Waxler and Robinson (1995) report that "other-oriented" disciplinary techniques, such as explaining the negative consequences of misbehavior for other people, are used more often with girls than with boys. Such differential treatment is likely to result in girls being more concerned about the effects of their behavior on others, and we suggest that it may lead to a greater level of concern for others in general, similar to arguments made by Chodorow (1978) and Gilligan (1982). Again, these findings are consistent with control theory, in that concern for others is contrary to the self-centeredness that characterizes criminal behavior (Gottfredson and Hirschi,

1990). Such disciplinary techniques might also be conducive to girls developing a tendency to be more future-oriented and concerned about the negative consequences of their behavior for themselves as well as others, which is consistent with empirical findings of versatility in offending. In this way, it is possible that parental disciplinary techniques can have effects on acts "analogous to crime," such as reckless driving, accidents, and so on.

With regard to outcomes of socialization, there is evidence that girls are more empathic than boys, are more likely to engage in reparative behaviors after harming someone, and are more likely to disapprove of their treatment of others than are boys (Zahn-Waxler and Robinson, 1995). Similarly, studies show that girls experience more guilt and shame than boys do (Harter, 1999; Hoffman, 1975), and are more concerned about others' reactions to their behavior than are boys (Maccoby and Jacklin, 1974). Hagan, Gillis, and Simpson (1990) find that girls express a lower desire for risk-taking than boys do, and measures of self-control as conceptualized by Gottfredson and Hirschi (1990) show that females have significantly higher levels of self-control than males (Burton et al., 1998). These findings are consistent with the patterns of socialization noted above, suggesting that adults' greater efforts to produce prosocial emotions and behaviors among girls are successful.

Additional research bearing directly on our contention that conceptions of femininity are tied to women's roles as mothers is found in Whiting and Edwards's (1975) cross-cultural study. For example, they found that among children aged three to six years, there was no significant sex difference in nurturing behaviors. However, differences in the expected direction emerged among children aged seven to eleven years, suggesting that gendered socialization patterns led to the increase in nurturing among girls. Additional findings suggest that socialization for "responsible" behavior starts at earlier ages for girls than boys, and there is some evidence that these socialization practices are more common in cultures in which girls are required to care for infants such as younger siblings (Whiting and Edwards, 1975).

In sum, there is evidence to suggest that girls are "better socialized" than boys in ways that decrease their likelihood of engaging in criminal or deviant behaviors. These findings are consistent with the prediction derived from control theory that girls are more carefully supervised than boys, that their misbehavior is less tolerated, and that these processes result in girls and women being more concerned for other people, more self-controlled and concerned about the consequences of their behavior, and more responsible and nurturing than boys.

On the face of it, however, there are some problems with our claim that girls are better socialized than boys. For example, some studies of the relationship between attachment to others and deviance show a greater effect of attachment among males than females (Canter, 1982; Hindelang, 1973; Johnson, 1987; Lauritsen, 1994). Similarly, the research on the relationship between delinquency and gender orientations or gender-role attitudes is quite mixed, with no clear relationship between femininity and delinquency for either males or females (see Heimer, 1996 for a review).[10]

However, neither of these apparently contradictory findings can, in themselves, disprove our argument. For example, while we clearly predict that girls are more attached to others and concerned about their opinions, we do not predict that the *effect size* will be greater for girls.[11] This is most clearly illustrated by considering a comparison between an unattached girl and an unattached boy—there is no reason to expect that the lack of attachment will be more consequential for the girl's delinquency than for the boy's. In fact, the opposite finding would be consistent with our perspective. We argue that being female affects delinquency not only because of the individual's internalized gender identity but also because of interactional pressures and institutional constraints that are disproportionately experienced by females. Variables operating on any one level of analysis, then, will be less crucial in explaining girls' delinquency.

Our argument here is analogous to Risman's (1998) point that married couples who are committed to gender equality still often fall into traditional gender roles due to interactional and structural constraints. There is some evidence that gender identity alone is not a very strong predictor of the household division of labor (Coltrane, 2000). To the best of our knowledge, these findings have not led to the argument that gender is irrelevant to the explanation of the household division of labor. Similarly, we argue that the lack of a clear relationship between gender attitudes or gender orientations and crime does not imply that role-based theories cannot explain gender differences in crime. Put simply, there is more to gender than a single set of attitudes or personality characteristics.

Another possible explanation for the failure of existing individual-level explanations of gender difference in crime is that they are limited in scope, as noted previously. It is possible that more detailed analyses of multiple variables operating on the individual level would uncover important sources of gender difference. For example, Krohn and Massey (1980) and Rosenbaum (1987) both found a stronger attachment effect for males, but both studies found that the overall explained variance for their social control models was greater for females than for males. Given that our argument is that girls are better socialized in general, not that they are merely more attached to others, such "holistic" analyses provide a better test of our perspective. Similar improvements in measuring individual-level variables might involve direct measurement of affective reactions such as guilt and shame that are the implicit causal mechanisms linking attachment to others and conformity.

Another example of the potential importance of considering multiple variables on the individual level of analysis is that girls' overall socialization to be more self-controlled and future-oriented may simply make them more likely than boys to consider the costs of their behavior before acting. In this way, differences in levels of self-control may minimize the effect of differences in social control. This possibility provides an important point of contrast between our perspective and Heimer's (1996) differential social control theory. Heimer argues that girls are likely to be more affected by the opinions of others than boys are, and thus that the relationship between anticipated disapproval of others and delinquency will be stronger for girls than for boys. She does not, however, test the hypothesis that girls are simply *more likely* than boys to engage in role-taking. Our perspective, in contrast, views girls as both more concerned about others' opinions and more likely to consider them in the first place.

This would be consistent with another possibility, which is that girls may be more affected by the opinions of others to whom they are not attached, such as strangers in public places. The latter possibility points to an additive effect of an individual-level variable (sensitivity to others' opinions) and an interactional-level one (others' reactions to females' behavior.) It is to such interactional processes that we now turn.

The Interactional Level

The least-studied level of analysis in criminology is the interactional level—systematic studies of group processes, expectations for others, and how they are communicated are rare. Neglect of this area is likely due to measurement difficulty—because many forms of communication and informal sanctioning are subtle, they are difficult to measure with surveys, which is the predominant mode of theory-testing in criminology.[12] Following Risman (1998), we argue that the process of "doing gender" (West and Zimmerman, 1987) influences all forms of gendered behavior, including crime and delinquency. Subtle interactional pressures with regard to crime are likely to operate very differently for males and females. Because crime is less congruent with the feminine gender role, we argue that interactional pressures against criminal and analogous behaviors are likely to be exerted more strongly and more frequently for females than males (Heimer, 1996).

One important source of interactional pressures against crime is the peer group. Most criminological theory and research incorporating peer effects on crime focuses on peers' role in increasing the individual's delinquent behavior. Control theory, in contrast, focuses on the role of others in discouraging or deterring delinquency and crime—as Hirschi (1969) argued, even delinquent peers can deter delinquency. We thus conceptualize the documented peer effect on crime as an indication that delinquent peers offer fewer interactional barriers to the individual's delinquency, and importantly, that nondelinquent groups are more able to effectively control the behavior of their members.

This points to the need for research on group processes that *discourage* delinquency as well as those that might encourage it. It is certainly the case that friends sometimes convince each other not to engage in delinquent or reckless behavior, but to our knowledge, no studies have focused on these processes. This omission is important in light of the obvious fact that most behavior, even among delinquents, is conforming behavior (Short and Strodtbeck, 1965). It is also important because we only have measures of group variables that might foster delinquency but no basis of comparison to group processes that deter delinquency. It is possible, for example, that for every time a group of peers encourages an individual to engage in a delinquent behavior, the same group discourages that individual from engaging in a delinquent behavior. Given the lack of data on such processes, this is of course purely speculative. But consistent with the control theory perspective, we argue that the sum total of all group influence is in the direction of conformity, that this is true for both males and females, but that these processes influence girls' behavior more frequently or more strongly than they influence boys' behavior.

Some evidence in support of this claim is found in studies showing a stronger effect of delinquent peers on delinquency among males (Johnson, 1979; Smith and Paternoster, 1987). One interpretation of such findings is that peers have less influence on girls than on boys. However, it can also be taken as evidence that even delinquent peers sometimes exert pressure against delinquency on female group members. Bottcher (1995) presents evidence that at least in some cases, males discourage their girlfriends from engaging in deviant behavior such as drug sales, even when the males themselves are involved in that activity. One of the participants in Bottcher's study also indicated that others would look down on girls committing crime: "if a girl were to steal a car or commit a robbery, it 'would be looked at funny cause that's like something the guys should do'" (1995: 50). There is also evidence that male gang members try to exclude females from participation in or planning of criminal activities, in part due to chivalrous attitudes toward them, and in part due to suspicion that the girls would reveal their secret plans to others (Campbell, 1991; Klein, 1995). The latter finding again points to a potential area of overlap between individual and interactional processes. The boys' perceptions of girls, likely based on the girls' prior behavior or stated attitudes, is that they are likely to "squeal," which influences their interactions and likely reduces the rate of female participation in gang delinquency.[13]

There is also some evidence that girls' better socialization insulates them from the effects of deviant peer groups, pointing to another source of interaction between levels of analysis. Specifically, Mears, Ploeger, and Warr (1998) find that the effect of delinquent peers among girls with high levels of belief in the moral validity of the law is near zero, and is significantly less than the effect among similar boys. They argue that these findings support Gilligan's

(1982) claim that female socialization emphasizes avoiding harm to others, which is consistent with our arguments. Thus, it is possible that girls are both more resistant to group influence to deviate, and more likely to experience group pressure away from deviation.

It has also been argued that females experience greater levels of stigma for committing crime than do males, or that crime among women is "doubly deviant" (Finley and Grasmick, 1985; Heimer, 1996: 42; Schur, 1984). This idea is supported with evidence that women perceive greater risk of sanctions than men (Richards and Tittle, 1981), and that gang girls have to try to manage their identities to find "acceptably deviant behavior" (Swart, 1991). These findings indicate a perception among girls and women that their behavior is under greater scrutiny than is males' behavior, and perhaps that this is a direct result of their sex. There is also evidence that females who act pro-socially, but who are not perceived as doing so for purely altruistic motives, are viewed less favorably by others than boys engaging in the same behavior with the same motives (Barnett et al., 1987). The latter finding is, we believe, particularly telling in that it reveals how others regard even pro-social behavior among females as less laudable when the motives underlying it are inconsistent with the selflessness expected of women.

The Structural Level

The best-known structural explanations of the gender difference in crime are those developed by Simon (1975) and Adler (1975). This "liberation hypothesis" holds that as women's behavior became more like men's in terms of labor force participation, their behavior would become more like men's in terms of crime. The causal mechanism in both theories is that women's increased opportunities in the labor force provide increased opportunities for them to engage in criminal behavior. The major problem with this perspective is that the convergence in male and female crime rates has not occurred as predicted.

We believe that there are two reasons why this hypothesis has not received empirical support. First, it overemphasized the extent to which women's opportunities were increasing, largely because of its focus on labor force participation to the exclusion of other relevant variables. Adler's claim that "women are no longer indentured to the kitchens . . . there will be no turning back to the days when women found it necessary to justify their existence by producing babies or cleaning houses" (1975: 12) rings shockingly naive in light of evidence that the household division of labor has changed little in the past three decades. Research on this issue has found persistent inequality in allocation of household labor (cf. Coltrane, 2000 for a review). National random samples such as the National Survey of Families and Households show that although women do less housework than in the past and men do somewhat more, women still do three times as much routine housework and childcare as men, regardless of women's employment status. Further, Thompson and Walker's review of this literature concludes that, "women's employment, time availability, resources, conscious ideology, and power do not account for why wives still do the bulk of family work" (1989: 857). Gender remains the main predictor of housework allocation (Berk, 1985; Brayfield, 1992; Hochschild and Machung, 1989; Pleck, 1985), and a major way that the gender structure is maintained in the household is through the division of labor (Coltrane, 1989; Ferree, 1991; Mederer, 1993).

Because we argue that gender inequality is maintained on the individual, interactional, and structural levels, we would not make the prediction that change in one respect (women entering the workforce) would have far-reaching ramifications for gendered behavior. While we believe that opportunity factors are important in explaining crime and the gender gap, we see opportunity as a necessary but not sufficient condition for crime to occur, while Simon and Adler's arguments imply that it is sufficient. In Gottfredson and Hirschi's (1990) terms, differences in crime must be analytically separated from differences in criminality. Women in traditionally male occupations still experience gendered socialization practices, and face interactional pressures toward conformity that are greater than those experienced by men. Thus, if we are correct in our assertion that women are better socialized and more socially controlled than men, we would still expect to find women committing less crime than men even when their criminal opportunities are the same.[14] Further, while we do not deny that women's participation in the workforce can provide opportunities for employment-related crime and other offenses made more possible by their absence from the home, the "double day" many working women face may mean that their overall opportunity to commit crime is lower than in the past. Studies showing that men have more free time per day than women do support this contention (Bond, Galinsky, and Swanberg, 1997; Hochschild, 1997; Hochschild and Machung, 1989).

We believe that there is a second reason why the liberation hypothesis failed, which is distinct from but closely related to the first. The hypothesis focuses on the ways that women's behavior has become more like men's. Given our focus on femininity as a deterrent to crime rather than on masculinity as an incentive to crime, we argue that it may be more fruitful to analyze the extent to which males have increasingly taken on feminine identities, roles, and tasks rather than the extent to which females have taken on masculine roles. As noted above, while women have increasingly worked at paid employment, the extent to which men have taken on the nurturing roles of women is substantially less. As we discuss below, we believe that the gender gap would be substantially smaller, without increases in women's crime rates, if the constraints women face were experienced more by men.

In discussions of gender inequality, it is easy to fall into explanations of gender differences in behavior as the result of inequality that is evident among adult men and women. This is perhaps because gender inequality has more easily visible indicators among adults, such as income and the household division of labor. However, it is important to keep in mind that young people commit most crime. Discussions of structural constraints on girls' behavior focus largely on decreased opportunity for girls to commit crime due to greater parental supervision and the fact that girls tend to spend more time at home than boys (Bottcher, 1995; Felson and Gottfredson, 1984; Mawby, 1980; Smith and Paternoster, 1987). While we agree that gender differences in supervision are important in explaining gender differences in crime, there is evidence that these differences in supervision cannot explain the gender gap (Gottfredson and Hirschi, 1990). Again, then, it is important to recognize that differences in structural opportunities to commit crime are in themselves insufficient to explain the gender gap, and we must consider the effects of "criminality" factors (Gottfredson and Hirschi, 1990) such as gender socialization, as well as interactional pressures.

Recommendations for Research

It is important to note that the three levels of analysis are analytically separable, but not empirically distinct—with regard to criminal opportunity, for example, many have argued that women's opportunity to commit crimes is lower than men's in part because of structural constraints such as girls' and women's ties to home and family. We have suggested that an additional way to view girls' lower opportunity is the possibility that girls are discouraged by their companions from committing crime. Thus, to fully conceptualize the "opportunity" factor, processes operating on both levels must be considered. We must also recognize that the influence of some of these forces is multiple—for example, girls being kept closer to home limits their opportunity to commit crime, but it also likely has further socialization effects, so that girls' preferences over time may be affected by their increased supervision. Similarly, if girls are repeatedly discouraged from criminal and deviant behavior by their peers, we would expect this to also work to socialize girls away from criminal desires, so that over time they are less likely to perceive criminal opportunities, in effect eliminating crime from their behavioral repertoire.

Thus, research designed to explain the gender gap in crime must attempt to measure processes operating at all three levels. This obviously will require the use of multiple methods. We suggest that traditional survey approaches that can measure individual traits be combined with more qualitative approaches designed to measure interactional pressures on males and females. This would allow, for example, tests of the hypothesis that girls at low levels of attachment to parents or commitment to school are nonetheless more constrained from crime by interactional pressures from peers than are similar boys. Measuring such interactional processes might involve direct observation, or perhaps more feasibly, in-depth interviews geared toward uncovering instances of group influence away from crime as well as toward it. Similarly, incorporating the structural level of analysis might involve cross-cultural studies of societies that differ in the extent to which men participate in traditionally female tasks. Taking a different view of the liberation hypothesis, we would expect societies in which fathers do more "mothering" to have somewhat lower rates of male crime and a narrower gender gap than societies in which males' role as parents is minimal. Viewed differently, we would also argue that to the extent to which the gender gap in caring for others has remained stable, the gender gap in crime has remained stable.

Variables operating on the three levels of analysis might also be usefully combined to conduct empirical tests similar to those testing power-control theory. We argue that the parents' labor force participation, their division of household labor including childcare, and the parents' gender identities and gender-role attitudes must all be considered in discussions of the effect of parental socialization on children. We hypothesize that couples who are committed to gender equality and who mutually engage in childcare and other caretaking behavior will be likely to instill more "feminine" traits in their male and female children, leading to more egalitarian socialization practices and interactions within the family regardless of the family's socioeconomic status. We would expect boys' and girls' rates of delinquency in such families to be similar, and more importantly, we would expect such boys to have lower delinquency rates than boys in less egalitarian families, other aspects of socialization held constant. Such a study would, of course, have to consider interactional processes outside of the family, and would have to recognize that a study of a single society cannot control for social structure, just a family's position in the social structure.[15]

Conclusions

We have attempted to set forth a control theory of gender difference in delinquency that addresses feminist criticisms of mainstream criminological theory. We incorporate considerations of the origins of gender inequality and the effects of patriarchy on rates of male and female crime, and we reframe control theory arguments in light of those considerations. We also believe that our arguments point out some of the limitations in existing research on the gender gap in crime, and suggest some new avenues for research that may contribute to our knowledge of crime causation in general.

We also hope that our arguments point to potential areas for social change that would help reduce gender inequality and reduce overall crime rates at the same time. We must deconstruct the idea that men are "normal" and women are "other," and the concomitant view that men's freedom is good and women's constraints are bad. Rather than implying that increased gender equality would lead to higher crime rates among females, our perspective implies that gender equality would lead to reduced crime rates among males. It is unlikely that any society would ever experience a role-reversal, such that men are the caretakers of home and family and women are the breadwinners and heads of households—we believe that gender is too entrenched in human societies for that to be a realistic possibility. Rather, we hope that men as well as women come to be held responsible for the caring work that must be done to ensure the very survival of society. Of course, the crisis in caring has come about largely due to women's desire and need to work at paid employment, so the issue of men's and women's behavior is intimately linked. However, there is no reason to conceptualize either crime or gender as zero-sum games—it is not the case that increases in men caring for others must come at some cost in terms of women's caring behavior or motivations. Certainly, there is no reason to assume that a certain amount of crime must be committed, so that females will "fill in the gap" left by males' decreasing crime rates. In short, we argue that the focus in feminist literature and in feminist perspectives of crime has been misguided—rather than focusing on women becoming more like men, we should focus on ways that men can become more like women.

Notes

1. Ironically, Messerschmidt's (1993) theory is as guilty as social control theory of ignoring women, in that he focuses on explaining how masculinity causes crime for men without discussing the implications of that idea for female crime. This is perhaps a more egregious offense when committed by a scholar who is explicitly interested in the effects of gender on crime (see also Heimer's [1994] review of this book).
2. We distinguish between studying differences in sex ratios for different offenses and creating typologies of "male" and "female" offenses. As Zager (1994) notes, there are nontrivial differences in sex ratios across offense types that have important implications for explaining the gender gap in crime. This does not imply, however, that different variables are necessary to explain the differences in sex ratios.
3. More recently, McCarthy, Hagan, and Woodward (1999) have revised power-control theory to focus less on decreased controls on girls in egalitarian families and more on increasing controls on boys in these families. This perspective is more consistent with control theory assumptions (Jensen, 1993), but McCarthy et al. still argue that risk preferences among children may be "heightened" by parental socialization practices (1999: 769).
4. We would expect that if risk-taking were a positive quality for success in business and other occupations, then risk-taking would be *positively* associated with other measures predictive of success, such as commitment to school. We are not aware of any evidence of such a relationship.

5. Our claim that women's subordination and lower crime rates have been historically rooted in biology should not be taken as an essentialist argument—in keeping with the control theory perspective, we argue that men and women have the same selfish tendencies. The link to women's capacity to bear and nurse children is, we believe, necessary to explain the universality of women's subordination, and, as Gottfredson and Hirschi (1990) note, their universally lower crime rates.
6. We recognize that we are oversimplifying the distinction between evolutionary and sociological perspectives, and that some evolutionary perspectives challenge the control theory assumption of an asocial human nature. Further discussion of these important issues is, unfortunately, beyond the scope of this work.
7. Simpson and Elis (1995) argue that this conception of femininity is based largely on white, middle-class definitions, and that femininity is not defined similarly for women of all races or social classes. However, their position on this issue is challenged by Bottcher's (1995) interviews with white, black, and Hispanic lower-class boys and girls, who indicate that crime is incompatible with the feminine role, and that pregnancy, motherhood, or the need to care for younger siblings all impose constraints on girls' willingness and ability to commit crime.
8. In keeping with our multi-level approach, we do not argue that childhood socialization is the only means through which gender orientations or gender-role attitudes are acquired. Evidence that gender-role attitudes become more liberal with increases in education is sufficient to show that this is not the case.
9. In addition to a possible socialization effect, greater parental supervision of girls also limits girls' opportunity to commit crime. This is the interpretation most commonly made in the criminological literature, and is discussed further below.
10. However, several studies have found a negative relationship between femininity and delinquency while finding no relationship between masculinity and delinquency (e.g., Heimer, 1996; Heimer and DeCoster, 1999; Shover et al., 1979). These findings support our argument that girls are socialized away from crime, but that masculinity or masculine socialization does not encourage crime, as some argue (Messerschmidt, 1993; Hayslett-McCall and Bernard, 2002).
11. We thus agree with Simons, Miller, and Aigner's (1980) call for the explanation of why girls tend to score lower on variables that cause crime rather than focusing on different variables to explain crime for males and females.
12. Even theories that incorporate interactional processes are often tested with survey data that do not necessarily measure group processes. For example, Heimer (1996) uses measures of individuals' attitudes, anticipated disapproval of deviance, and gender definitions as measures of role-taking. These variables may measure the *outcomes* of interaction, but they are in fact measures of individual characteristics.
13. Paradoxically, however, there is also evidence that others' perceptions of females sometimes enable their criminal behavior. For example, Miller (1998) notes that perceptions of women as conforming lend a helpful element of surprise to women armed robbers.
14. It is also possible that women who succeed in traditionally male occupations do so as a result of higher levels of self-control—to the extent that women have to work twice as hard to be judged half as good as men, we would expect a self-selection effect to minimize the extent to which their increased opportunity for crime would lead to criminal behavior.
15. While space limitations preclude a full treatment of the issue, we also believe that our perspective can be usefully applied to differences in crime among other groups in different structural locations in our society. One question raised with our perspective, for example, is why greater structural constraints faced by the poor and

minorities do not significantly reduce their crime rates as compared to middle-class whites. We suggest that one consequential difference in the constraints faced by women and those faced by these disenfranchised groups is that women are the only minority group to experience socialization that intimately links a demographic trait to attitudes and behavior inconsistent with crime. Women are supposed to be nurturing and caring, and some evidence suggests that this is true across racial, ethnic, and socioeconomic groups (Bottcher, 1995). In contrast, the poor and minority groups do not socialize their members to be nurturing and caring due to their status as minority group members. Thus, we predict that the failure of structural constraints to reduce crime rates for the poor and minorities is due in part to the lack of socialization to demographic-specific characteristics that reduce crime. Of course, middle-class women also receive benefits from their roles as wives and mothers that are unavailable to the poor and minority group members.

References

Adler, Freda. 1975. *Sisters in Crime*. New York: McGraw-Hill.

Barnett, Mark A., Vera McMinimy, Gwyn Flouer, and Iriz Masbad. 1987. "Adolescents' Evaluations of Peers' Motives for Helping." *Journal of Youth and Adolescence* 16: 579–586.

Berk, Sara F. 1985. *The Gender Factory: The Apportionment of Work in American Households*. New York: Plenum Press.

Bond, James T., Ellen Galinsky, and Jennifer E. Swanberg. 1997. *The 1997 National Study of the Changing Workforce*. New York: Families and Work Institute.

Bottcher, Jean. 1995. "Gender as Social Control: A Qualitative Study of Incarcerated Youths and Their Siblings in Greater Sacramento." *Justice Quarterly* 12: 33–57.

Brayfield, April. 1992. "Employment Resources and Housework in Canada." *Journal of Marriage and the Family* 54: 19–30.

Brownmiller, Susan. 1975. *Against Our Will: Men, Women, and Rape*. New York: Bantam.

Burton, Velmer S. Jr., Francis T. Cullen, T. David Evans, Leanne Fiftal Alarid, and R. Gregory Dunaway. 1998. "Gender, Self–Control, and Crime." *Journal of Research in Crime and Delinquency* 25: 123–47.

Canter, Rachelle J. 1982. "Family Correlates of Male and Female Delinquency." *Criminology* 20: 149–68.

Chafetz, Janet S. 1990. *Gender Equity: An Integrated Theory of Stability and Change*. Newbury Park, CA: Sage.

Campbell, Anne. 1981. *Girl Delinquents*. New York: St. Martin's Press.

———. 1991. *The Girls in the Gang*. Second Edition. Cambridge, MA: Basil Blackwell.

Chesney–Lind, Meda. 1997. *The Female Offender: Girls, Women, and Crime*. Thousand Oaks, CA: Sage.

Chodorow, Nancy. 1978. *The Reproduction of Mothering: Psychoanalysis and the Sociology of Gender*. Berkeley, CA: University of California Press.

Collins, Patricia H. 1999. "Moving Beyond Gender: Intersectionality and Scientific Knowledge." Chapter 9 in Ferree, Myra M., Judith Lorber, and Beth Hess, (eds.), *Revisioning Gender*. Thousand Oaks, CA: Sage.

Coltrane, Scott. 1989. "Household Labor and the Routine Production of Gender." *Social Problems* 36: 473–490.

———. 2000. Research on Household Labor: Modeling and Measuring the Social Embeddedness of Routine Family Work. *Journal of Marriage and the Family* 62: 1208–1233.

Costello, Barbara J. and Paul R. Vowell. 1999. "Testing Control Theory and Differential Association: A Reanalysis of the Richmond Youth Project Data." *Criminology* 37: 815–842.

Cowie John, Valerie Cowie, and Eliot Slater. 1968. *Delinquency in Girls*. London: Heinemann.

Daly, Kathleen and Meda Chesney-Lind. 1988. "Feminism and Criminology." *Justice Quarterly* 5: 497–535.

English, Kim. 1993. "Self-Reported Crime Rates of Women Prisoners." *Journal of Quantitative Criminology* 9: 357–382.

Epstein, Cynthia F. 1988. *Deceptive Distinctions: Sex, Gender, and the Social Order*. New Haven, CT and New York, NY: Yale University Press and the Russell Sage Foundation.

Felson, Marcus, and Michael Gottfredson. 1984. "Social Indicators of Adolescent Activities Near Peers and Parents." *Journal of Marriage and the Family* 46: 709–714.

Ferree, Myra M. 1991. "The Gender Division of Labor in Two–Earner Marriages: Dimensions of Variability and Change." *Journal of Family Issues* 12:158–180.

Finley, Nancy J., and Harold G. Grasmick. 1985. "Gender Roles and Social Control." *Sociological Spectrum* 5: 317–330.

Firestone, Shulamith. 1970. *The Dialectic of Sex: The Case for Feminist Revolution*. New York: Bantam Books.

Gilligan, Carol. 1982. *In a Different Voice: Psychological Theory and Women's Development*. Cambridge, MA: Harvard University Press.

Giordano, Peggy C., and Stephen A. Cernkovich. 1979. "On Complicating the Relationship between Liberation and Delinquency." *Social Problems* 26:467–481.

Gottfredson, Michael R., and Travis Hirschi. 1990. *A General Theory of Crime*. Stanford, CA: Stanford University Press.

Grasmick, Harold G., John Hagan, Brenda Sims Blackwell, and Bruce J. Arneklev. 1996. "Risk Preferences and Patriarchy: Extending Power-Control Theory." *Social Forces* 75: 177–199.

Hagan, John, A. R. Gillis, and John Simpson. 1985. "The Class Structure of Gender and Delinquency: Toward a Power-Control Theory of Common Delinquent Behavior." *American Journal of Sociology* 90: 1151–1178.

———. 1990. "Clarifying and Extending Power-Control Theory." *American Journal of Sociology* 95: 1024–1037.

Hagan, John, John Simpson, and A. R. Gillis. 1987. "Class in the Household: A Power-Control Theory of Gender and Delinquency." *American Journal of Sociology* 92:788–816.

Harter, Susan. 1999. *The Construction of the Self: A Developmental Perspective*. New York: Guilford Press.

Harrington, Mona. 2000. *Care and Equality: Inventing a New Family Politics*. New York: Routledge.

Hays, Sharon. 1996. *The Cultural Contradictions of Motherhood*. New Haven: Yale University Press.

Hayslett–McCall, Karen L., and Thomas J. Bernard. 2002. "Attachment, Masculinity, and Self-Control: A Theory of Male Crime Rates." *Theoretical Criminology* 6:5–33.

Heidensohn, Frances. 1997. "Gender and Crime." Pp. 761–798 in M. Maguire, R. Morgan, and R. Reiner (eds.), *The Oxford Handbook of Criminology*, Second Edition. New York: Oxford University Press.

Heimer, Karen. 1994. Review of "Masculinities and Crime: Critique and Reconceptualization of Theory," by James W. Messerschmidt. *Contemporary Sociology* 23:860–861.

———. 1996. "Gender, Interaction, and Delinquency: Testing a Theory of Differential Social Control." *Social Psychology Quarterly* 59: 39–61.

Heimer, Karen, and Stacey DeCoster. 1999. "The Gendering of Violent Delinquency." *Criminology* 37: 277–317.

Hindelang, Michael J. 1971. "Age, Sex, and the Versatility of Delinquent Involvements." *Social Problems* 18: 522–535.

———. 1973. "Causes of Delinquency: A Partial Replication and Extension." *Social Problems* 20: 471–487.

Hirschi, Travis. 1969. *Causes of Delinquency*. Berkeley: University of California Press

———. 1973. "Procedural Rules and the Study of Deviant Behavior." *Social Problems* 21: 159–173.

———. 1979. "Separate and Unequal Is Better." *Journal of Research in Crime and Delinquency* 16: 34–38.

Hochschild, Arlie R. with Anne Machung. 1989. *The Second Shift*. New York: Avon.

Hochschild, Arlie R. 1997. *The Time Bind: When Work Becomes Home and Home Becomes Work*. New York: Henry Holt and Company.

Hoffman, M.L. 1975. "Development Synthesis of Affect and Cognition and Its Implications for Altruistic Motivation." *Developmental Psychology* 11: 605–622.

Jayaratne, Toby E., and Abigail J. Stewart. 1991. "Quantitative and Qualitative Methods in the Social Sciences: Current Feminist Issues and Practical Strategies." In Mary M. Fonow and Judith A Cook (eds.), *Beyond Methodology: Feminist Scholarship as Lived Research*. Bloomington, Indiana: Indiana University Press.

Jensen, Gary F. 1993. "Power-Control vs. Social-Control Theories of Common Delinquency: A Comparative Analysis." Pp. 363–380 in F. Adler and W.S. Laufer (eds.), *New Directions in Criminological Theory: Advances in Criminological Theory*, Vol. 4. New Brunswick, NJ: Transaction.

Jensen, Gary F., and Raymond Eve. 1976. "Sex Differences in Delinquency: An Examination of Popular Sociological Explanations." *Criminology* 13: 427–448.

Johnson, Richard E. 1979. *Juvenile Delinquency and Its Origins*. New York: Cambridge University Press.

———. 1987. "Mother's versus Father's Role in Causing Delinquency." *Adolescence* 22: 305–315.

Klein, Malcolm W. 1995. *The American Street Gang: Its Nature, Prevalence, and Control*. New York: Oxford University Press.

Krohn, Marvin D., and James L. Massey. 1980. "Social Control and Delinquent Behavior: An Examination of the Elements of the Social Bond." *The Sociological Quarterly* 21: 529–543.

Lauritsen, Janet L. 1994. "Explaining Race and Gender Differences in Adolescent Sexual Behavior." *Social Forces* 72: 859–884.

Maccoby, Eleanor E., and Carol N. Jacklin. 1974. *The Psychology of Sex Differences*. Stanford, CA: Stanford University Press.

MacKinnon, Catherine A. 1987. *Feminism Unmodified: Discourses on Life and Law*. Cambridge, MA: Harvard University Press.

Malone, Jean, Andrea Tyree, and K. Daniel O'Leary. 1989. "Generalization and Containment: Different Effects of Past Aggression for Wives and Husbands." *Journal of Marriage and the Family* 51: 687–697.

Mawby, Rob. 1980. "Sex and Crime: The Results of a Self-Report Study." *British Journal of Sociology* 31: 525–543.

Mazzerole, Paul, Robert Brame, Ray Paternoster, Alex Piquero, and Charles Dean. 2000. "Onset Age, Persistence, and Offending Versatility: Comparisons Across Gender." *Criminology* 38: 1143–1172.

McCarthy, Bill, John Hagan, and Todd S. Woodward. 1999. "In the Company of Women: Structure and Agency in a Revised Power-Control Theory of Gender and Delinquency." *Criminology* 37: 761–788.

Mears, Daniel P., Matthew Ploeger, and Mark Warr. 1998. "Explaining the Gender Gap in Delinquency: Peer Influence and Moral Evaluations of Behavior." *Journal of Research in Crime and Delinquency* 35: 251–266.

Mederer, Helen J. 1993. "Division of Labor in Two-Earner Homes: Task Accomplishment versus Household Management as Critical Variables in Perceptions about Family Work." *Journal of Marriage and the Family* 55: 133–145.

Messerschmidt, James W. 1986. *Capitalism, Patriarchy, and Crime: Toward a Socialist Feminist Criminology*. Totowa, NJ: Rowman & Littlefield.

———. 1993. *Masculinities and Crime: Critique and Reconceptualization of Theory*. Lanham, MD: Rowman & Littlefield.

Miller, Jody. 1998. "Up It Up: Gender and the Accomplishment of Street Robbery." *Criminology* 36:37–66.

Miller, Walter. 1958. "Lower Class Culture as a Generating Milieu of Gang Delinquency." *Journal of Social Issues* 14: 5–19.

Naffine, Ngaire. 1987. *Female Crime*. Boston: Allen & Unwin.

Ogle, Robbin S., Daniel Maier–Katkin, and Thomas J. Bernard. 1995. "A Theory of Homicidal Behavior Among Women." *Criminology* 33:173–194.

Pleck, Joseph. 1985. *Working Wives/Working Husbands*. Beverly Hills, CA: Sage.

Richards, Pamela, and Charles R. Tittle. 1981. "Gender and Perceived Chances of Arrest." *Social Forces* 59: 1182–1199.

Risman, Barbara J. 1998. *Gender Vertigo: American Families in Transition*. New Haven, CT: Yale University Press.

Rosenbaum, Jill Leslie. 1987. "Social Control, Gender, and Delinquency: An Analysis of Drug, Property, and Violent Offenders." *Justice Quarterly* 4: 117–132.

Russell, Diana E. H.1998. *Dangerous Relationships: Pornography, Misogyny, and Rape*. Thousand Oaks, CA: Sage.

Schur, Edwin M. 1984. *Labeling Women Deviant: Gender, Stigma, and Social Control*. New York: McGraw–Hill.

Short, James F., and Fred L. Strodtbeck. 1965. *Group Process and Gang Delinquency*. Chicago: University of Chicago Press.

Shover, Neal, Stephen Norland, Jennifer James, and William E. Thornton. 1979. "Gender Roles and Delinquency." *Social Forces* 58: 162–75.

Simon, Rita J. 1975. *Women and Crime*. Lexington, MA: Lexington Books.

Simons, Ronald L., Martin G. Miller, and Stephen M. Aigner. 1980. "Contemporary Theories of Deviance and Female Delinquency: An Empirical Test." *Journal of Research in Crime and Delinquency* 17: 42–57.

Simons, Ronald L., Chyi-In Wu, Christine Johnson, and Rand D. Conger. 1995. "A Test of Various Perspectives on the Intergenerational Transmission of Domestic Violence." *Criminology* 33: 141–171.

Simpson, Sally S. 1991. "Caste, Class, and Violent Crime: Explaining Difference in Female Offending." *Criminology* 29:115–135.

Simpson, Sally S. and Lori Elis. 1995. "Doing Gender: Sorting Out the Caste and Crime Conundrum." *Criminology* 33:47–77.

Smart, Carol. 1976. *Women, Crime, and Criminology*. Boston: Routledge & Kegan Paul.

Smith, Douglas A., and Raymond Paternoster. 1987. "The Gender Gap in Theories of Deviance: Issues and Evidence." *Journal of Research in Crime and Delinquency* 24: 140–172.

Steffensmeier, Darrell, and Emilie Allan. 1996. "Gender and Crime: Toward a Gendered Theory of Female Offending." *Annual Review of Sociology* 22: 459–487.

Swart, William J. 1991. "Female Gang Delinquency: A Search for 'Acceptably Deviant Behavior.'" *Mid–American Review of Sociology* 15: 43–52.

Thompson, Linda, and Alexis J. Walker. 1989. "Gender in Families: Women and Men in Marriage, Work, and Parenthood." *Journal of Marriage and the Family* 51: 845–871.

Weis, Joseph G. 1976. "Liberation and Crime: The Invention of the New Female Criminal." *Crime and Social Justice* 6: 17–27.

West, Candace, and D. Zimmerman. 1987. "Doing Gender." *Gender & Society* 1: 125–151.

Whiting, Beatrice and Carolyn Pope Edwards. 1975. "A Cross-Cultural Analysis of Sex Differences in the Behavior of Children Aged Three Through 11." In S. Chess and A. Thomas (eds.), *Annual Progress in Child Psychiatry and Child Development 1974*. New York: Brunner/Mazel Publishers.

Williams, Joan. 2000. *Unbending Gender: Why Work and Family Conflict and What To Do About It*. New York: Oxford University Press.

Yllo, Kersti. 1988. "Political and Methodological Debates in Wife Abuse Research." Pp. 28–50 in K. Yllo and M. Bograd (eds.), *Feminist Perspectives on Wife Abuse*. Newbury Park, CA: Sage.

Zager, Mary Ann. 1994. "Gender and Crime." Pp. 71–80 in T. Hirschi and M. Gottfredson (eds.) *The Generality of Deviance*. New Brunswick, NJ: Transaction Publishers.

Zahn-Waxler, Carolyn, and Joann Robinson. 1995. "Empathy and Guilt: Early Origins of Feelings of Responsibility." Pp. 143-173 in Tangney and Fischer (eds.), *Self-Conscious Emotions: The Psychology of Shame, Guilt, Embarrassment, and Pride*. New York: Guildford Press.

6

Genocide and General Theory

Augustine Brannigan and Kelly H. Hardwick

Introduction: Criminological Theory and the Problem of Genocide

The last decade has been marked by momentous acts of human violence—brutal genocides in the former Yugoslavia and in Rwanda and Burundi, and breath-taking acts of terrorism in New York and Washington. In the aftermath, the United Nations has created international criminal tribunals in The Hague and in Arusha to bring offenders from Yugoslavia and Rwanda to justice. Steps have also been taken to create a permanent international criminal court that could become a general venue for trying international war criminals (Schabas, 2001). In the area of terrorism, the Taliban in Afghanistan has been toppled, and its sponsorship of Al-Qaida terrorist training camps has been ended, though worldwide terrorism continues to flourish. In the past decade, noncombatants increasingly have become targets of state-sponsored and independent projects of mass murder in cases of both genocide and terrorism.

The last decade has also been one of the most fruitful in terms of the development of criminological theory, especially with respect to the debates sparked by Gottfredson and Hirschi's (1990) *A General Theory of Crime* surrounding self-control and social-control as explanations of crime and analogous behaviors. If Gottfredson and Hirschi's general theory is truly general, should we not expect it to shed light on events such as terrorism and genocide? Since their general theory does not require that the activities (i.e., "crimes") that form the basis of genocide and terrorism be contrary to law, we might ask whether they are part of the subject matter that properly occupies criminologists, and what makes them so. While *A General Theory* is careful to resist the determination of its dependent variables by acts of state legislation, it finds a commonality in crime, deviation, sin, and recklessness. "The theory of sin is also a theory of crime and of immorality and of accident" (Gottfredson and Hirschi, 1990: 9). In fact, genocide and other acts of mass violence *are* contrary to international conventions and contrary to the customary rules of war.

The United Nations defines genocide in Article II of the 1948 Convention of the Prevention and Punishment of Genocide (cited in Chalk and Jonassohn, 1990: 44):

> In the Present convention, genocide means any of the following acts committed with intent to destroy, in whole or in part, a national, ethnical, racial, or religious group as such:
>
> a. Killing members of the group;
>
> b. Causing serious bodily or mental harm to members of the group;
>
> c. Deliberately inflicting on the group conditions of life calculated to bring about its physical destruction in whole or in part;
>
> d. Imposing measures intended to prevent births within the group;
>
> e. Forcibly transferring children of the group to another group.

The UN definition of genocide was developed in a highly politicized context. The definition curiously omits political groups or classes. According to Orentlicher (1999: 154) "too many governments, it seems, would be vulnerable to the charge of genocide if deliberate destruction of political groups fell within the crime's compass."[1] For example, Soviet policies of food seizure in the Ukraine in 1932 led to the starvation of several million peasant farmers in what historians characterize as a man-made famine (Mace, 1997). A parallel problem arises in the annihilation of Kurds by the regime of Saddam Hussein. In 1988, an estimated 50,000 Iraqi Kurds were killed by the use of chemical weapons. Were they killed because they were Kurds "as such," i.e., ethnic rivals, or because they were political opponents to the Iraqi regime who had conspired with the Iranians during the Iran–Iraq war? In addition, the killing fields in Cambodia that resulted in the slaughter of some 1.5 to 2 million civilians during the rule of Pol Pot and the Khmer Rouge from 1975 to 1979 would escape the UN's definition since the perpetrators and their victims were from the same ethnic/national group.

Despite the anomalies that might arise from limitations in the *actus reus* of genocide, we would include all such cases in the scope of our inquiry since they were murders of innocent civilians on a massive scale. They are also universally condemned as barbaric. The Nuremberg Court (1945) put Nazi officials on trial for "crimes against humanity," even though the orders that resulted in the destruction of the European Jews had the stamp of official authority and the Nazi rule of law (Arendt, 1994). Should they be viewed as an expression of "criminality"? The breakup of the former Yugoslavia following the dissolution of the Soviet Union was marked by a series of armed conflicts between Bosnians, Serbs, and Croats. As each group sought to consolidate a racially and religiously homogenous territory, policies of "ethnic cleansing" displaced millions of people from their homes and villages. Such conflicts frequently led to the physical elimination of noncombatants solely on the basis of religious or ethnic differences.

The Recent Genocides in Bosnia and Rwanda

What made Yugoslavia so prone to genocide and ethnic cleansing? There had been historic divisions between the Bosnian, Serb, and Croat groups based on religion, Croats (like the Austrians) were Roman Catholic, Serbs (like the Russians) were Eastern Orthodox, and the Bosnians (like the Turks) were Muslim. There was a considerable history of conflict and feud extending back centuries. The consolidation of Yugoslavia under Tito's communist leadership following World War II led to substantial integration of this population mosaic. Intermarriage across religious boundaries was common. With the demise of the Soviet block in Eastern Europe, Serbian leader Slobadon Milosovic rejected the ideals of a mixed society and pursued policies to create ethnically homogenous states (Markusen, 1999). Franjo Tudjman acted similarly in Croatia. The Serbs forcibly removed non-Serbs (Croats and Muslims) from Serbian-controlled territory. In the early 1990s, there was evidence of massacres committed on all sides against civilian populations. The Serbian leadership in particular mobilized the resources of the former Yugoslav army and created new bands of paramilitaries for "self-defense." Part of the Serbian fury was arguably kindled by atrocities suffered during the Second World War. When the Nazis occupied Yugoslavia in 1941, the Croat Ustasha Party created the Jasenovac concentration camp in which an estimated 400,000 Serbs, 30,500 Jews, and 20,000 gypsies were murdered (Hirsch, 1999).

The "Bosnian War" (1992–1995) erupted on the Bosnian–Serb border when the Yugoslav army attacked key cities and villages and put Sarajevo, the Bosnian capital, under siege, subjecting the civilian population to indiscriminant mortar bombardment, looting of humanitarian shipments, and random shooting by snipers. This resulted in a sustained campaign of terror designed to separate the communities and expunge the enemy.

> Bombardments of the civilian population, first of Sarajevo, then of besieged villages; massacres during the conquest, then the forced evacuation of civilians to modify the ethnic structure of the particular area; illegal internment of the civilian population in concentration camps; torture; systematic rape; summary executions; appropriation and pillage of civilian property; systematic destruction of the cultural and religious heritage with the sole aim of eliminating any trace of non-Serbs in the conquered territories; using detainees as human shields on frontlines and in minefields; and starvation of civilians who resisted—these were only some of the violations of

> international humanitarian law and the laws of war of which the Serbs were guilty. (Hartmann, 1999: 55–56).

By late 1994, intense pressure from NATO air strikes eased the threats to civilians in Sarajevo. The Serbs turned their attention in the spring of 1995 to the UN safe haven for Bosnian refugees at Srebrenica. In July, the enclave was overrun by the Serbs resulting in the single largest act of genocide in Europe since the Nazi period. After neutralizing the Dutch peacekeepers, the Serbs evacuated the enclave in thirty-three hours, sending some 7,000 Bosnian males to shallow graves within days (Honig and Both, 1999). Milosovic, Radovan Karadzic, the former Serb president of Bosnia Herzegovina, and General Ratko Mladic, commander of the Bosnian Serb army, were indicted by the international tribunal at The Hague for war crimes and genocide for attacks at Sarajevo and Srebrenica. Only Milosovic had been arrested as of the summer of 2003.

Another notorious instance of genocide involved the murder of an estimated 500,000 to 1 million people, primarily ethnic Tutus and moderate Hutus at the hands of the majority Hutus in Rwanda in 1994. The Rwandan conflict was the third largest genocide of the twentieth century. Where the Balkans had been marked by historic conflicts between the various communities, traditional Rwandan society was highly integrated, despite the fact that the society was peopled by what would appear to be three different races—the Twa (or "pygmies") who comprised some 1 percent of the population, the Hutus who comprised some 85 percent, and the Tutsis who comprised the balance (according to the 1933 census, Gourevitch 1998: 57). The Hutus and Tutsis were traditionally characterized by quite different physiques—the former similar to the Bantu-speakers of central Africa, the latter more resembling the taller, thinner people of Ethiopia. Over time, the various groups evolved a common language and system of governance. In the twentieth century, the majority was converted to Catholicism by the Belgian colonial authorities who displaced the German colonial powers in 1916.

The major division between Tutsis and Hutus was in terms of livelihood. The former were traditionally cattlemen, the Hutus were farmers, and there was some economic advantage associated with wealth in cattle. When Europeans expropriated the control of Rwandan society, they delegated the Hutus to demeaning work and a degraded political status, and brought them under the control of Tutsi chiefs and civil servants. The Tutsis enjoyed favoritism in education and enjoyed a monopoly of administration and political jobs. In 1933 the Belgians issued mandatory identity cards specifying tribal origins. For the European colonialists, the Tutsis were viewed as one of the lost tribes of Israel (the Hamites), and the Hutus little better than savages. A society that had enjoyed harmony and prosperity was brought into a state of discrimination and resentment under colonial control. However, there was no significant expression of this politically until the Hutu manifesto of 1957. Rather than seeking an abolition of the identity cards and their underlying racist presuppositions, Hutus organized for "democracy," meaning majority rule, social emancipation, and restrictions on the political and educational opportunities for Tutsis. The tide changed against the Tutsis as a new generation of European post-colonialists sided openly with the majority against the minority. The Belgians supported a popular rebellion against the Tutsis, and the first of many waves of Tutsis fled in exile to neighboring countries.

In the early 1960s, attacks on Rwanda by displaced Tutsis resulted in reprisal massacres against Tutsis within Rwanda followed by more refugee departures. Hutus in neighboring Burundi were massacred by Tutsi refugees followed by more reprisals in Rwanda. A generation of Tutsi refugees began organizing in Tanzania, Uganda, and Zaire for the right of return, for the end of the de facto apartheid system in Rwanda, and for an end to the one-party dictatorship of Hutu ultra-nationals. In 1986, the Kigali government dismissed out of hand the right of refugees to return home. The Rwandan Alliance for National Union, a foreign-based alliance of moderate Hutus and Tutsis, was superceded by the Rwandan Patriotic Front (RPF), a political movement created to change conditions in Rwanda by military force. Civil war broke out in 1990 with the invasion of Rwanda by the RPF. The first invasion turned out to be a disastrous military event for the RPF and was repulsed with the help of French military aid. Three hundred thousand new refugees left the country as thousands of Tutsis were massacred and tens of thousands detained as RPF sympathizers. The government of Juvenal Habyarimana began to acquire massive levels of small arms and explosives in a series of secret purchases from Egypt and France. The army was expanded from 5,000 to 28,000, and the security forces began to organize civilian militias, the "interahamwe," or "those who work together." The Hutu political elite began to talk openly about the need to remove every Tutsi from Rwandan society. In April 1994 President Habyarimana's plane was shot down as it approached Kigali en route back from peace talks with the RPF. This incident changed the low levels of killings that had become increasingly frequent into a total genocidal bloodbath that lasted three months. It came to an end with the defeat of the army by the RPF in July, 1994. At that point, 1 million Hutu refugees left Rwanda.

Can criminology shed light on these events? And what has to be established for their inclusion in the repertoire of activities properly defined as "the use of force and fraud in the pursuit of self-interest" to follow the definition given by Gottfredson and Hirschi?

In this chapter, we advance the case that crimes such as genocide can be comprehended within the broad boundaries of the control tradition as articulated by Hirschi (1969) and Gottredson and Hirschi (1990). But first, we must outline the key elements of *A General Theory*.

Criminality versus Crime in Control Theory

Gottfredson and Hirschi describe an approach to the explanation of crime that is twofold. On the one side is the motivation or the appetite of the offender. From this perspective, offenders *choose* the course of action that constitutes the social transgression. Persons with low self-control are more prone to making choices that are hedonistic and short term in scope. While this is critical to the perspective described in 1990, it is not the whole story. In their discussion of the "logical structure" of typical crimes, they emphasize that in addition to criminality (low self-control), offenders require structures of circumstances and opportunities. A burglary, for example, requires not only a motivated actor, but also an unguarded premise. Drawing on "routine activities" theory, they point out that homes are entered because doors and windows are left unlocked, valuables disappear when left unguarded, and targets of vandalism are often close at hand. Crimes typically do not take much planning or expertise. Our point is that Gottfredson and Hirschi's general theory is not premised exclusively on low self-control but a combination of this trait ("criminality"), on the one side, and the social circumstances ("crime") that constrain and/or expedite the behavioral outcomes, on the other. In the following paragraphs we reiterate the elements of each.

The Elements of Low Self-Control (Criminality)

In *A General Theory of Crime*, Gottfredson and Hirschi (1990: 15–44), to their credit, go to lengths to illuminate the nature of criminal acts. It is from their description of the nature of crime that the elements of low self-control or "criminality" are gleaned. For example, since *criminal acts provide immediate gratification of desires*, a major characteristic of low self-control is the tendency to "respond to tangible stimuli in the immediate environment" (1990: 89). In other words, those with low self-control have a "here and now" orientation which predisposes them to act with little regard for the future consequences of their actions. Since *criminal acts provide easy or simple gratification of desires*, those lacking self-control will also lack diligence, tenacity, or persistence in a course of action (1990: 89). Furthermore, *criminal acts are exciting, risky, or thrilling* and, thus, those lacking self-control will be adventuresome, risk-taking, active, and physical. At the same time that criminal acts are risky and exciting, they *provide few or meager long-term benefits*. Therefore, people with low self-control will "have unstable marriages, friendships, and job profiles" (1990: 89). *Crimes require little skill or planning*. It follows, then, that those with low self-control will not value or possess cognitive skills. And, importantly, since *crimes often result in pain or discomfort for the victim*, low self-control individuals will be indifferent and insensitive to the needs and suffering of other individuals.

Gottfredson and Hirschi (1990: 90) ask us to recall that crime involves the pursuit of immediate pleasure. Consequently, individuals with low self-control will also "pursue immediate pleasures that are *not* criminal: they will tend to smoke, drink, use drugs, gamble, have children out of wedlock, and engage in illicit sex." However, one of the major benefits of crime does not necessarily follow from the pursuit of pleasure but instead from the avoidance of "pain" or the relief from "momentary irritation." Thus, people with low self-control will have "minimal tolerance for frustration and little ability to respond to conflict through verbal rather than physical means" (1990:90). Gottfredson and Hirschi (1990: 90) summarize the characteristics of the low self-control actor in the following passage:

> In sum, people who lack self-control will tend to be impulsive, insensitive, physical (as opposed to mental), risk-taking, short-sighted, and nonverbal, and they will tend therefore to engage in criminal and analogous acts.

But crime requires more than just "criminality" or "appetite." Although the discussions of the elements of "crime" tend to be less systematically laid out in *A General Theory*—at least compared to the discussions of criminality—they are no less important to understanding criminal acts.

The Elements or Structure of Crime

For Gottfredson and Hirschi, the logical structure of crime includes opportunity. They state (1990: 23) that "there is every reason to believe that the necessary conditions strategy of opportunity theory is compatible with the idea of criminality." In fact, crimes are the product of the appetite of the actor situated within a context of opportunity. For instance, the burglar "searches for an unlocked door or an open window in an unoccupied single-story house," the robber "victimizes available targets on the street," the embezzler "steals from his own cash register," and the car thief "drives away cars with the keys left in the ignition" (Gottfredson and Hirschi, 1990: 17). Often, drugs and/or alcohol are factors contributing to the actor's perception of opportunity by lowering his inhibitions. In addition, group membership can play a role in criminal behavior. Groups facilitate certain activities that are more difficult to accomplish alone. In fact, Gottfredson and Hirschi (1990:157) state that self-control is a major factor in determining group membership. But group membership is not responsible for criminal activity. Instead, groups merely "facilitate acts that would be too difficult or dangerous to do alone" (Gottfredson and Hirschi, 1990: 159). Thus, some of the key elements of crime include:

1. group mediation of action, i.e., the power of peers or action in a group context to lower the threshold of actually perpetrating the crime,

2. the effects of drugs or alcohol in lowering inhibitions,
3. the environmental conditions of surveillance or nonsurveillance of potential targets of exploitation.

The Application of General Theory to Genocide

Both criminality and circumstance act conjointly to create the potential for crime and analogous behaviors. Gottfedson and Hirschi describe their focus as the use of force and fraud in the pursuit of self-interest. When it comes to genocide and mass murder, there is little doubt that the activities of genocide and mass murder involve the use of force—deadly force. However, the activities of genocide do not necessarily point to an individual-level trait of impulsivity or low self-control. Nonetheless, the use of deadly violence to achieve political ends is consistent with certain elements of low self-control. The Serbs in Srebrenica liquidated their foes in 1995 with massive violence, taking the lives of 6,000–7,000 Bosnian men and boys in an orgy of killing that lasted several days. The Hutu political leadership provoked citizens against neighbors in 1994. From one-half to as many as a million men, women, and children were murdered with machetes, clubs, and guns within three months of public incitement of ordinary Hutus by their political leaders. In both cases, interethnic tensions and civil war preceded the genocides. However, rather than pursuing complicated and time-consuming political negotiations, the political leadership in both cases sought remedies that paralleled the impulsive characteristics found in studies of garden-variety crimes: the immediate gratification of desires (hatred) through the self-righteous slaughter of enemies; easy or simple steps to achieve political ends (i.e., physical displacement and annihilation); risky, thrilling, and/or exciting solutions (sadistic orgies of killing); dubious long-term benefits (since the activities attract prosecutions for genocide, and result in cycles of revenge); little skill or planning in the conduct of genocide; indifference to the suffering of the victims; versatility of criminal acts (cruelty, humiliation, and degradation of victims, theft of their property, and desecration of their cultural symbols); and an inability to tolerate frustration in the achievement of ends (through UN negotiations, political compromise, and long-term investments in peace agreements).

The Question of Collective versus Individual Action

One of the key issues in comparing acts of genocide and acts of garden-variety perpetrators of the kind customarily portrayed in general theory is the role of collective action. It is an open question whether classical theory even admits of a theory of collective action, given its hedonistic foundations. The issue of collective behavior is one tackled specifically by Gottfredson and

Hirschi in a footnote. Gottfredson and Hirschi discuss the difficulty of classifying as a crime the action of a soldier killing in war. "Our conception of crime, which focuses on the self-interested nature of criminal acts, has no difficulty excluding behavior performed in pursuit of collective purposes" (1990: 175). It is certainly conceded that soldiers shooting other combatants are not acting in a criminal fashion. Indeed, contra Hagan and Greer (2002), war as such is not crime, and the laws of war treat killing as normative. However, those same laws are quite clear on the limits to collateral damage involving the destruction of civilian lives and property in actions against legitimate military targets. While recognizing the difficulty of applying general criminological theory to killing in actions against legitimate targets of war, who would say that My Lai was not a crime (Osiel 1999)? To say that the mass slaughter of unarmed civilians done "collectively" is not a "crime" is semantic gerrymandering. Therefore, even if we accept that a soldier's killing in war as part of a collective campaign falls beyond the scope of crime and criminology, the same does *not* follow for genocide against unarmed, noncombatants done by soldiers, other government agents or civilians. Such actions are frequently labeled and prosecuted as "war crimes." Are we to infer that war crimes escape any general theory because the beneficiary of the crime is not the individual, but the collectivity to which the individual belongs? But surely the individual shares in the collective benefits as part of the collectivity. This is recognized indirectly in the treatment of white collar, organizational, and enterprise crimes undertaken through criminal conspiracies. Gottfredson and Hirschi argue that such behaviors are not troublesome for general theory. These crimes—which are often done collectively—pose no problems for general theory since "in the final analysis" actions are the actions of individuals (1990: 202). The theory raises a dilemma. On the one hand, if war crimes are not covered, then the theory is not truly general, and we need different theories for different types of offenses (including war crimes). If this were so, general theory would forfeit its claims of generality. On the other hand, if collective actions are excluded from the scope of criminology, then "group conflicts" that result in murder (Sellin, 1938; Turk, 1982) are not really crimes at all. Neither alternative is satisfactory.

Seven Hard Facts about Genocide

General theory is attractive since it identifies the major "hard facts" with which the theory has to come to terms. These are empirical generalities that must be dealt with in a principled way, while recognizing the major mechanisms that constitute the basis for the explanation. The generalities and mechanisms have to do with self-control or loss of restraint, the role of opportunity/crime structure, age, gender, and ethnicity.

I. The Context and History of Pre-existing Collective Animosities

The first hard fact is that genocide is born in the crucible of war, civil war, or violent social conflict. These circumstances demarcate the opponents and put them into a preexisting state of conflict and/or animosity. Since war often entails an immediate threat to the personal security of the civilians in conflict, it is marked by deep feelings of insecurity and dread, fear for survival, and fear of untimely and undeserved death. Whatever codes of chivalry may have excluded noncombatants from risk of extermination in the past, the rise of total war has heightened the vulnerability of civilian noncombatants dramatically by legitimating the destruction of infrastructures needed to conduct war. Civil war intensifies inter-group conflict even more than international conflict because of the proximity of enemies in the same ecological space. Sometimes the pretext of conflict is racial difference but it can be as narrow a difference as religion, language, cultural heritage, or, as in the case of the Cambodian massacres, economic philosophies. The shared boundaries heighten the opportunities for conflict and victimization. Such preexisting animosities are not unprecedented in criminology. Sellin (1938) identified crimes based on conflicts arising over norms found in different cultural groups. Usually in criminology such groups have been equated with competing gangs or ethnic peer groups, a situation too limited to explain the dynamics of genocide. Genocide simply raises the unit of analysis in conflict to the inter-group or community level. This is also true of the mechanisms to genocide. Indeed, in his "group crime" theory, Vold (1958: 217) argued that many crimes "result from the clashes incidental to attempts to change, or to upset the caste system of racial segregation in various parts of the world." Racial or ethnic stratification and its implications for the control of territories and their resources were central to the genocides in Bosnia and Rwanda, consistent with Vold's group conflict perspective.

II. Ordinary People, Righteous Rage, and Group Action

The second hard fact is that the perpetrators of genocide are frequently recruited from the rank and file of society. Browning described the professional killers who filled the ranks of the German Order Police in Poland in the early 1940s as "ordinary men." As part of the civil authority in occupied Poland, they performed many ordinary policing duties, but when called on, they participated in ghetto clearing and mass executions of Jews and Polish patriots. Goldhagen, examining the same historical records, noted that the authors of the Holocaust were not Nazi fanatics, but middle-aged German policemen, men who took leave to visit families on furloughs, and who when returned to the field volunteered for shooting missions because, at some level, they believed the Jews ought to die. He called them "ordinary Germans."[2] Without the participation of 500,000–1,000,000 of these state functionaries, the Holocaust would never have happened. Mamdani, reflecting on the Rwandan genocide of Tutsis, similarly stresses how the "genocidaires" were recruited from all levels of society including the clergy, doctors, teachers, and civil rights workers and that the low-level technological methods of killing—the use of clubs, knives, and machetes—required the mass mobilization of the population to butcher erstwhile neighbors. As Mamdani (2001: 18) stresses, the genocide was not only a state project, but a "social project"—conducted in public by ordinary citizens.

Several things are remarkable in these episodes. The perpetrators of "righteous slaughter" often do not appear to experience any lasting trauma or shame over their bloody murders. Like the perpetrators described in Katz's *Seductions of Crime* (1988), they do not appear to experience remorse, guilt, or compunction. The photos of young policemen in Browning's and Goldhagen's books show their faces beaming with satisfaction over the cruelty dealt out to the old Jewish men whose beards were shorn before they were executed, or who were urinated on, or beaten with whips as they were rounded up. Children and old people were shot indiscriminately. Often the killing took on a frenzied quality, as bodies accumulated in the streets and houses, as the perpetrators improvised cruel ways of expunging lives. Victims were often burned alive, locked in their places of worship—something that occurred repeatedly in both Poland and Rwanda.

General theory, because it presupposes a stability of low self-control over the life cycle, appears ill-equipped to explain how wholesale numbers of people were recruited into roles as insensitive killers. In point of fact, killers as a group already represent an anomaly to general theory since the majority of those who kill tend to do so only once. Katz emphasizes how persons in intimate relationships sometimes experience such intense emotional conflicts that they murder one another "in defense of a higher good." Typically, this involves an event that produces profound humiliation in one party, the resolution of which is to strike out in rage. Rage redirects the loss of face associated with humiliation and leads to a righteous violence, sometimes resulting in murder. In the cases he reports, Katz notes that the perpetrators do not try to flee, do not appear to experience any deep remorse in the aftermath of their deeds, and are often found justified at trial in their behaviors as a result of provocation. The fact that they experienced a loss of self-control is undeniable. What is more problematic is that this does not appear to be associated with a life-long profile of "versatile" dysfunctional behavior, that is, criminality.[3] The loss of self-control appears more situational. If drugs, alcohol, and/or tobacco can produce a transitory loss of self-control, the same may be argued for intense emotional breaches of experience. Gottfredson and Hirschi note the following regarding drugs: "Drugs, tobacco and alcohol serve more as indicators of limited self-control than as causes of crime, but they can, on occasion, produce criminal acts by reducing the time frame of the user to the immediate situation. With limited time and space horizons, the individual is vulnerable to spur-of-the-moment impulses" (1990: 179). Presumably, intense emotional experiences can similarly reduce the time frame to the immediate situation. Katz draws exactly this conclusion: "Rage focuses consciousness completely on the here-and-now situation with an unparalleled intensity. Rage so powerfully magnifies the most minute details of what is present that one's consciousness cannot focus on the potential consequences of the action for one's subsequent life" (p. 31). And a combination of anger and alcohol can be more potent still.

Where Katz points to situational losses of self-control arising from interpersonal humiliation and anger, the phenomenon of genocide may trade more on hatred and other deep emotional insecurities to lower the threshold to violence in inter-group mass murder. This could explain why "genocidaires" could be recruited from across the social structure, why they could be mobilized in a short, intensive spree of mass-killing, and could subsequently reenter the ranks of society with little risk of repetition or migration to other sources of misconduct.

Two other considerations come into play in the understanding of the onset and contextual promotion of genocide. The first has to do with the nature of the effects of group solidarity in the commission of crime. The second has to do with the enormous emotional intensity of the activities of genocide themselves. On the first count, general theory is clear that groups do not create criminality, but rather that persons with low self-control drift into associations with persons of similar dispositions. When low self-control is more situational, the dynamics change. The normal effect of groups continues to play its role, that is, reducing inhibitions. Gottfredson and Hirschi report as follows: "groups imply impunity from sanction; they defuse and confuse responsibility for the act, and they shelter the perpetrator from immediate identification and long-term risk of retribution. In some cases, they prevent sanctions through threats of retaliation. Groups, then, act as a mask and a shield, as a cover for activities that would not otherwise be performed (1990: 209)." Obviously, the gangs of killers who cleared the Polish ghettoes of their Jews in 1941 and 1942 acted under the cloak of group action, dispersing responsibility from specific individuals as they "mopped up" children and old people. If this is true of informal groups, it is probably of greater importance in formal groups, including persons in uniforms, persons acting in official bureaucratic capacities, as was the case in the Holocaust. This explanation disavows the perspective of Milgram whose obedience paradigm portrayed the perpetrators of the Holocaust as frightened pawns in the German bureaucracy. The evidence is quite to the contrary. The perpetrators acted as though the destruction of the European Jews was a national project—anticipating the similar perspective of Serbs vis-à-vis the Bosnians, and the Hutus vis-à-vis the Tutsis.

Also relevant in understanding the dynamics of genocide is the emotional intensity of the killing events themselves. The reports from Browning and Goldhagen from the initial ghetto round-ups in Poland in 1941 suggest that the soldiers and policemen went into a frenzy of orgiastic murder, that without specific instructions on how to clear the Jewish neighborhoods, they initiated cruel methods of killing. As with Katz's "moral dominance" in robbery, they frequently took delight in dehumanizing the victims before taking their lives. The evidence from Rwanda is similar. Many victims were dismembered a limb at a time over days before succumbing to their wounds. What this suggests is that the activity of killing unleashes an appetite of brutality, of sadism, and cruelty that is normally checked in peacetime, or found only rarely—among serial killers and psychopaths. The Rwanda case is particularly disturbing since victims were dispatched often by multiple cuts, often by mobs of perpetrators wielding machetes and knives against single unarmed victims.

In summary, the second hard fact is that the perpetrators of genocide obviously exhibit a lack of self-control that is brutal, but contrary to the condition found in garden-variety criminal populations. These cases seem to be grounded in emotional states marked by hatred, exacerbated by a condition of conflict, expedited by group actions, and often abetted by alcohol. In contrast to the model of stable, impulsive dispositions in specific individuals from backgrounds of ineffective socialization, the path to genocide involving "normal" individuals is marked by transitory shifts in self-control produced by extremely provocative propaganda, that is, emotional excitations of the sort found in cases of "righteous slaughter." Though the primary illustrations that Katz amasses come from domestic conflicts, disputes in other contexts may be just as lethal and just as transitory (e.g., "road rage"). By implication, situational conditions can produce levels of violence that are only weakly associated with generalized individual impulsiveness but more akin to transitory mob action.[4]

This is not to say that individuals with low self-control play no important role in genocide. Goldhagen's depiction of Lieutenant Hartwig Gnade and his sadistic inclinations to beat the Jews he was going to murder raise questions about the psychopathology of German officers involved in mass murder (Goldhagen 1997: 228). Melvern (2000: 44) writes regarding the "self-defence" militias created in Rwanda: "The militia contained delinquents and petty criminals, experts in thuggery who disrupted political meetings and terrorized anyone who criticized the government." Zeljkp Raznatovic (a.k.a. "Arkan"), the notorious commander of a Bosnian Serb paramilitary group (and himself a wanted criminal) recruited persons with a similar profile: "Arkan, with the help of a recruitment campaign in the state-owned media, had begun rallying unemployed soccer hooligans and criminals and training them at army facilities" (Amanpour 1999: 268). Goldhagen's position is that, from the perspective of an historian, such persons may *expedite* genocide but that it occurs whether they participate or not, and that genocide should not be attributed to persons with specific dispositions. However, for criminologists, the effect of such extreme individuals is like that of delinquent peer groups—they appear to reduce the inhibitions toward violence even if they are not responsible primarily for the violence of others.[5]

III. Righteousness and Techniques of Provocation

The next hard fact is an elaboration of the last one but points to mechanisms that play a important role in "making murderers out of victims" (to paraphrase Mamdani). Sykes and Matza (1957) advanced the idea that offenders frequently rationalize their misconduct by "techniques of deviance neutralization." These include denial of responsibility, denial of injury, denial of the victim, condemnation of the condemners, and appeal to a high loyalty. These appear to be post hoc rationalizations that mitigate the individual's culpability for misconduct. But the mental element in crime may operate in a different way. Techniques of thinking or account-giving that "neutralize" the offender's mental state *after* crime seem to be the exact opposite of the mental state needed to mobilize the righteousness and anger at the core of genocidal behavior. What are required instead are techniques of provocation and incitement. For example, when Major Trapp assembled the men of Police Battalion 101 before the extermination of the Jews of Jozefow in Poland in 1941, he tried to encourage their murderous behavior by telling them "to think of our women and our children in our homeland who had to endure aerial bombardments . . . we were supposed to bear in mind that many women and children lose their lives in these attacks. Thinking of these facts would help us carry out the order" (Goldhagen, 1997: 212).

In Rwanda, there were dozens of speeches by Hutu ultra-nationalists designed to inflame fear of Tutsi invaders. In point of fact, the RPF had staged an invasion, the country was in civil war, and there had been massacres of Hutus in neighboring Burundi as recently as 1993. Earlier, in 1972 some 200,000 Burundi Hutus were murdered by a Tutsi-dominated army. This led to the departure of hundreds of thousands of Burundi Hutus into Rwanda. As a consequence, there were Hutus in Rwanda who had already suffered gravely at the hands of the Tutsis, so threats that they were returning, that Hutu land would be seized, and that the Hutu would again become subservient to Tutsi masters, and indeed that they were being enslaved and butchered by the invading army, were extremely provocative. By 1994 the civil war had created about 1 million *internally* displaced Hutus. In addition, the first Hutu president of Burundi, Mechior Ndadaye, was assassinated in 1993 by officers of the Tutsi-dominated army. Propagandists in Rwanda seized on this as proof that political accommodation with the Tutsis was impossible. This cancelled any popular confidence in the Arusha peace accords that were designed to stop the civil war and create democratic elections in Rwanda.

The other propaganda message that struck such a deep chord was that the loss of the civil war and a UN-brokered peace with the Tutsis would end the Hutu political ascendance in Rwanda. When the state-owned radio and newspapers advocated wiping out the Tutsis in their entirety, it was heard as an act of Hutu political self-preservation. Propaganda does not neutralize deviance as much as generate the hysteria required to make it self-righteous. In such a condition, neutrality or moderation is interpreted as treason, with the consequence that moderate Hutu politicians and citizens, including tens of thousands in mixed marriages became targets for elimination.

Our position here differs from the usual role attributed to the mass media in studies of TV violence and aggression. While social learning theorists argue that normal viewers may acquire aggressive conduct as a result of exposure to violent entertainment, the evidence for this is weak (Fowles, 1999). However, this does not mean that mass media can have no important role in inciting violence. The people drawn into acts of genocide typically have experienced cycles of murder, massacre, and reprisal killing. Sometimes violence is provoked simply by news. For example, the assassination of President Ndadaye resulted in some 50,000 murders in Burundi, victims more or less evenly split between Hutus and Tutsis. Sometimes violence can be provoked deliberately by political speeches and propaganda. What they have in common is making the motive for genocide respectable, and inflaming the appetite for self-defense and vengeance. This is a media "effect" but the mechanisms have nothing to do with social learning and everything to do with hate promotion and provocation.

IV. The Role of the State and the Rule of Law

The fourth hard fact to be explored concerns the role of the state in mobilizing the perpetrators against their victims. In Rwanda, the Hutu-led government compiled lists of Tutsis, broadcast their names and license numbers by radio, purchased and distributed thousands of weapons, and used the militias to turn out the Hutus and dispatch their erstwhile neighbors. The Serbian militias (e.g., "Arkan's Tigers") were makeshift armies of nonprofessional fighters and barely disguised pawns of the Yugoslav army, armed and supplied to carry out the war against civilians. They assumed the dirty work of "ethnic cleansing" at the behest of the political elite. Gottfredson and Hirschi note: "If indeed some crime is the product of formal organization, or if indeed the mob is structured like a legitimate firm, then there may be merit invoking principles of organizational behavior to explain some criminal behavior" (1990: 202). The principles would include hierarchical structures of command, systems of reinforcement to ensure compliance with role expectations, and some overall consensus regarding the political desirability of the actions. In addition, the fact that the state becomes implicated means that the usual role of authorities in creating conditions of personal security evaporates. During genocide, people who look for succor among those who have monopolized the legitimate use of force (i.e., politicians acting through police and armed forces) are turning to the very agents of death for protection.

The state as such is not a concept found in control theory. However, Gottfredson and Hirschi do explain how pain and pleasure are regulated by various "systems"—natural, moral, religious, and political. The state is the political apparatus that regulates behavior. Horowitz (2002) outlines how states have been critical to the major genocides of the past century and he points out that they tend to be associated with authoritarian regimes. Often these regimes are dominated by a small coterie of elites who use their access to power to further their individual interests.[6] This suggests that if they are premised even nominally on the rule of law, they will tend to be unstable and dictatorial because they lack any transcendent legitimacy and reflect individual megalomanias.

In Hirschi's *Causes of Delinquency* (1969), one of the key covariates of misconduct was "belief" in societal values and respect for the law and authority figures. One of the hallmarks of the rule of law is its indifference to the specific identities of citizens of the sort that are implicated in ethnic cleansing. The logic of the rule of law in democratic societies is that it tends to valorize questions of "uniformity," and hence to create a moral dissonance between particularistic justice and the ideals of universality (Thompson, 1975). Also related is the commonsense perception of equity. The modern secular state treats the rights of citizens as equal. Historical animosities between groups motivate aggression of a collective kind that suppresses the respect for the rule of law. The state historically has assumed the role of arbitrating competing claims to citizenship and the rights it entails. In homogenous states, consensus is probably achieved relatively easily due to common values (religion, language, culture, ethnicity). The divided society complicates the task of a "transcendent" or "inclusive" rule of law for the whole state and is more prone to genocide.

V. Unguarded Targets in Ethnic Conflicts

The fifth hard fact we need to deal with is that the victims are basically unarmed and defenseless. Or they are confronted with force so overwhelming that they cannot resist effectively. This fact is co-extensive with the observation that the targets of genocide are "civilians," that is, people by definition unarmed. Who would expect children and women to be armed? This means that genocide is an act devised to destroy what Hegel referred to as "civil society," the normal transactions of everyday life based on what Durkheim emphasized as "contract law." Students of sociology will recall Durkheim's comparison on the mentality of primitive versus modern societies. The former were governed by a collective consciousness of "mechanical solidarity" in which social cohesion was based on vivid and emotional condemnation of the criminal and outcast, and based on the use of lethal force to eliminate the enemies of the community. Modern societies marked by "organic solidarity" are governed by contracts, a form of law based on trust, and policed by informal methods of social control, and by social expectations of reciprocal dependence and respect. The Tutsis lived side by side with Hutu neighbors in a civil society created by European colonial powers. The walled cities and moats defending feudal properties had been abandoned by European powers as the economies of Europe became more integrated, and material and cultural exchanges became normative, and xenophobia declined. Under such trends, why would modern people revert to ethnic bunkers? Durkheim's world emphasized interdependence in what we have come to call "open societies." Genocide flourishes under such conditions. Where social groups are differentiated in terms of collective conflicts and where they take steps to secure arms against the dominant state, civil war or feud, as opposed to genocide, is the result. Genocide is a condition that reflects the vulnerability or defenselessness of the target group. Civil war and feud are hazards during historical transition from Durkheim's closed, ethnically homogeneous (mechanical) societies to pluralistic, ethnically mixed open (organic) societies. Genocide is a condition that emerges when the state fails to broker the conflicts between its competing racial or ethnic constitutents.

VI. When Casualties Constitute Genocide

The sixth hard fact about genocide is that the casualties are considerable. In the last century, a person was far more likely to die violently as a result of a state-sponsored action like genocide than to die at the hands of a common criminal. However, there is no numerical criterion as to when murder crosses the threshold to genocide. Although there is some debate as to the precise number of victims of the Holocaust, it matters little whether the number is put at "5.5" million versus "6.0" million. The numerical ambiguity does not detract from the special category of mass murder that occurred (Horowitz, 2002: 35ff.). Likewise, when observers put the number of deaths in the Rwanda genocide at between 500,000 and 1,000,000, no one disputes that the requisite number of deaths, however indecisively identified, constitutes genocide. The magnitude of the killing may be simply a function of opportunities, methods of killing, or the vulnerability of the targets.[7] Ambiguity arises from the group nature of the conflict and the motive and opportunities to inflict injury on the group "as such." International agreements do not identify a cutpoint that turns murder into genocide. This is not an irrelevant point from a practical perspective since signatories to the UN Convention have a duty to *prevent* genocide. How many deaths need occur before the UN member states spring to the defense of the victims? This is not a "hard fact." The killing of one member of the group, or a planeload or busload may amount to "mere" murder or terrorism. Genocide implies a wholesale destruction of a group, not a targeting of individuals qua individuals, or individual Jews/Muslims/Catholics as individual Jews/Muslims/Catholics. The group qua group, whatever its identity, is the object of lethal violence. Also, this fact exploits earlier ones in which noncombatants are selected as targets and are unprepared to engage an enemy in conventional forms of armed conflict. A final relevant point here is that even if killings fail to meet the *actus reus* of genocide as laid down in the UN conventions, the normal prohibitions in respect of "mere" murder ought to apply. What is remarkable in the cases we have discussed is that there was no civil authority to bring the killers to account within ordinary criminal procedures because of the conditions of war and because the "security" forces and the agents of genocide were often the same institutions.

VII. Deterrence and Opportunity Theory

The seventh hard fact is that the behavior constituting genocide, from an international perspective, is deterrable. State officials can be called to account. Genocidal field operations can be met with force. For example, Honig and Both (1996) describe the Serb advance on Srebrenica in early July 1995, and particularly on the tentative nature of the advance into the enclave under threat of NATO F-16 airpower reprisals. Serb tanks were primary targets for air strikes. The Dutch peacekeepers briefed the terrified Bosnian population to the effect that air strikes were immanent, and indeed, the Serbs hesitated at every point under the apprehension of airborne offenses from NATO forces stationed in Italy—only minutes across the Adriatic Sea from Yugoslavia. However, NATO was so preoccupied with the appearances of bias or alignment with one side vis-à-vis the other, that the decision to bomb Serbian columns on the outskirts of the UN enclave was never made, and the Serbs overran Srebrenica without opposition, after days of approach and withdrawal, testing the NATO resolve. The enclave was cleared of every Bosnian within thirty-three hours, and the males dispatched to shallow graves on the pretext of retribution for war crimes. The Serbs forced the UN to pay for the gasoline to remove the Bosnians since their removal was characterized as a humanitarian relocation. Honig and Both are quite clear in their judgment that effective NATO action against the Serbs in the form of air strikes would have prevented the ethnic cleansing of Srebrenica.

The case for deterrence in Rwanda is similar. Powers (2001) in "By-standers to Genocide" records how the Belgian and U.S. governments colluded to prevent the Hutu-Tutusi conflict from being labeled as "genocide" despite the reports of UN peacekeepers to the contrary. For months, leading members of the Hutu political elite were calling for the elimination of Tutsis from Rwandan society at mass rallies and on the national government-controlled radio station. The peacekeepers pointed out that the destruction of the broadcast facilities would have stemmed the tide of propaganda that mobilized the Hutu population against the traditionally more "aristocratic" Tutusis. Since the state played such an important role in escalating the violence, curtailment of the organs of state would have hobbled the political mobilization essential for the killing. Even after the UN reduced the size of the peacekeeping mission, from 3,000 soldiers to about half that number (on the justification that there was civil war and no peace to keep), Canadian General Romeo Delaire found that the government-sponsored militias were reluctant to kill in the face of the peacekeepers, that killings took place after their departure, and that, however thinly spread the remaining peacekeepers, they succeeded in preserving the security of civilians under their direct supervision. In a parallel way, the record in Kosovo suggests that when Serb military units were targeted by air strikes, they ultimately desisted (Charny and Jacobs, 1999).

General theory has little confidence in the mechanisms of deterrence in the case of common criminals. This is because the trait at issue, low self-control or impulsiveness, tends to be persistent over the life course, and because the state's intervention typically occurs only *after* such traits have developed. However, where the mechanism is a transitory state, the circumstances that precede the violence (i.e., political provocations) can be challenged and targets at risk can be guarded. That is one of the awful lessons of Rwanda. Preparations for genocide were an open secret yet the international community failed to act effectively either to curb the provocation or to guard the potential targets.

Conclusion: Implication for General Theory

In the preceding discussion, our use of *A General Theory* shifted to a reference of "general theory" and not *a* general theory nor *the* general theory. The shift was deliberate since we wanted to avoid, on the one hand, the idea that the theoretical perspective, general theory, is singular ("a theory") or, on the other hand, that it is already fully articulated ("the theory"). However, we are committed to a perspective that is broad or general in scope. At the same time, our perspective is one that is not quite settled since we believe that general theory construction is ongoing in the control tradition, and that application to areas like genocide likely questions the adequacy of the perspective as articulated to date, without dismissing the explanatory power of the ambitious vision laid out by Gottfredson and Hirschi. By use of the term "general theory" we convey our indebtedness to the work of Gottfredson and

Hirschi without limiting our analysis exclusively to the issues articulated by them, while asserting our commitment to a theoretical framework that is truly inclusive.

However, Gottfredson and Hirshi's *A General Theory* seemed to us to be sufficiently, if not masterfully, articulated, and an eloquent model for the application of general criminological control theory to the phenomenon of genocide. Indeed, no other approach to date could serve as well without facing endless typologies of causes for every variety of crime. We believe that genocide and terrorism should be rightfully studied within criminology, and likely better understood as a consequence, using criminological theory. Although we incorporated phenomenological theory into our explanation, we feel that the application of *A General Theory* as the primary organizing principle has proven fruitful. While we discovered that it is likely unreasonable to assume that all those directly (or indirectly) responsible for genocide suffer from individual-level low self-control as a stable predisposing trait that can account for their criminal actions, it did not follow that the low self-control profile was irrelevant. For instance, in many cases, there does appear to be a disposition to act with little regard for future consequences. More and more, this is true with respect to the potential international repercussions or responses to genocide, however severe or swift those consequences may be in coming (Ball, 1999; Bass, 2000). Furthermore, it is quite credible to characterize genocide as providing, if not an "easy" gratification, at least a simple gratification of desires. The desire to exterminate is often manifested by simply picking up the "weapon" closest to hand whether that be a gun, axe, pitchfork, or whatever. In fact, we suggest that those actively involved in the attempt to eradicate large numbers of relatively defenseless humans *can* (and perhaps should) be characterized as impulsive, risk-taking, physical, and indifferent or insensitive to the needs and suffering of those they are attempting to annihilate. Such acts require little skill and the long-term benefits of genocide remain unclear. The difficulty, then, lies not so much in matching the profile of the low self-control actor to those who commit acts like genocide but, instead, in applying (and understanding) the distal and proximal mechanisms that create the situationally contingent "readiness" or predisposition to engage in mass destructive activities and the specific circumstances which trigger or facilitate them.

Recall that according the Gottfredson and Hirschi the distal mechanism responsible for low self-control is ineffective or poor parenting. If we could rightly assume that all of those responsible for genocide were predisposed to criminality, then the application of this mechanism would be unproblematic. However, we have discovered that it is more likely that many if not most of the perpetrators are incited to low self-control, or righteous anger by a confluence of historical, situational, and/or "momentary" provocations. Thus, it becomes necessary to propose an alternative distal mechanism or mechanisms to the phenomenon of genocide. Here, we are searching for mechanisms or processes that can reasonably explain why individuals might be willing and ready to systematically attempt to destroy large numbers of other individuals. We suggested that it is the state or culture or a combination of both that provides the predisposition to genocide by employing propaganda, selective education, subornment of group hatred, misinformation, and the creation of special militias perhaps populated to some extent by key "role models" (i.e., criminals). The fact that genocides frequently occur in cycles of retaliation is another distal condition that may motivate murder out of fear and self-defense. However, we cannot separate these processes from the historical context that is vitally important to understanding genocide. All of this creates a populous, or at least a significant proportion of the population, that is predisposed or "ready" to partake in genocide. Proximately, then, all that is required is the creation of opportunity.

Notes

1. Hitchens (2001) argues in a similar vein that Henry Kissinger was directly implicated in the murder of the Chilean chief of defense in 1973 and in the mass destruction of peasants by indiscriminant bombing in Cambodia and Laos during the Vietnam War.
2. Goldhagen said in short: "No Germans, no Holocaust." For a critique of this racial/ethnic perspective, see Finkelstein and Birn (1998).
3. One of the methodological weaknesses of case selection and the de-contextualized nature of his accounts is that Katz cannot rule out that such cases are unrepresentative or that the individuals reported on do not show other expressions of low self-control. Certainly, Katz recognizes that those who rob tend also to gamble, assault, pimp, and are involved in conflict-prone domestic arrangements. Righteous slaughter does not seem to show similar evidence of versatility. Katz argues that most persons who are confronted with humiliating conflict resolve it short of homicide. The bouts of humiliation that result in slaughter appear to be episodic and result in murder when precipitated by contextual factors resulting in provocation—the proverbial straw that breaks the camel's back. This suggests that these expressions of the loss of self-control, however deadly, are exceptional.
4. Ed Vulliamy (1999: 365) reports from an account at the Serb-operated concentration camp at Omarska: "One prisoner was forced to bite off the testicles of another who, as he died, had a live pigeon stuffed into his mouth to stifle his screams. An eyewitness, testifying later at the United Nations International Tribunal for the Former Yugoslavia (ICTY) at The Hague described the behavior of the guards during this barbarism as being 'like a crowd at a sports match.'"
5. Moffit (1993) distinguishes persons who engage in offending as a function of age ("adolescent limited") from persons with a stable, impulsive tendency toward misconduct ("life course persistent"). She argues that the latter may function as models for the former, initiating activities the latter copy. A similar process may operate in genocide where individuals prone to violence and low self-control set the pace for persons acting in a transitory or "state dependent" frame of mind.
6. Melvern (2000: 43) writes that there was an oligarchy behind the presidency of Juvenal Habyarimana involving his wife, her brothers, and other family members

that ran Rwanda as their personal fiefdom: "This group was using ethnic hatred to increase its power and was determined to resist democracy. Knowing that it would be suicidal to oppose reform directly, the group relied on propaganda to instill fear among the people about an invasion by the Ugandan army supporting the RPF."

7. When the RPF defeated the Rwandan army in July 1994, a million Hutus fled to Zaire. Subsequent attacks by the RPF on the civilian refugee camps to scotch Hutu raids on the new government in Rwanda resulted in the killing of hundreds of thousands of Hutu civilians. The former "genocidaires" became the victims.

References

Amanpour, Christiane. 1999. "Paramilitaries." Pp. 266–268 in Roy Gutman and David Rieff (eds.), *Crimes of War: What the Public Should Know*. New York: Norton.

Arendt, Hannah. 1994. *Trial in Jerusalem*, Revised and Expanded (original edition, 1964). London: Penguin.

Ball, Howard. 1999. *Prosecuting War Crimes and Genocide: The Twentieth-Century Experience*. Lawrence: University Press of Kansas.

Bass, Gary J. 2000. *Stay the Hand of Vengeance: The Politics of War Crimes Tribunals*. Princeton, NJ: Princeton University Press.

Chalk, Frank, and Kurt Jonassohn. 1990. *The History and Sociology of Genocide*. New Haven, CT: Yale University Press.

Charny, Israel, (ed.). 1999. *Encyclopedia of Genocide*, Two Volumes. Santa Barbara, CA: ABC–CLIO.

Charny, Israel W., and Steven L. Jacobs. 1999. "Ethnic Cleansing and Genocide in Kosovo." Pp. 644–654 in Israel Charny (ed.), *Encyclopedia of Genocide*. Santa Barbara, CA: ABC–CLIO.

Finkelstein Norman G., and Ruth Bettina Birn. 1998. *A Nation on Trial, The Goldhagen Thesis and Historical Truth*. New York: Henry Holt.

Fowles, Jib. 1999. *The Case for Television Violence*. Thousand Oaks, CA: Sage.

Goldhagen, Daniel. 1997. *Hitler's Willing Executioners*. New York: Vintage Books.

Gottfredson, Michael, and Travis Hirschi. 1990. *A General Theory of Crime*. Stanford, CA: Stanford University Press.

Gourevitch, Philp. 1998. *We Wish to Inform You that Tomorrow We Will Be Killed with Our Families*. New York: Farrar, Straus and Giroux.

Gutman, Roy, and David Reiff. 1999. *Crimes of War: What the Public Should Know*. New York: W.W. Norton & Company.

Hagan, John, and Scott Greer. 2002. "Making War Criminal." *Criminology* 40(2): 231–264.

Hartmann, F. 1999. "Bosnia." Pp. 50–56 in Roy Gutman and David Rieff (eds.), *Crimes of War: What the Public Should Know*. New York: Norton.

Hirsch, Herbert. 1999. "Genocides in Yugoslavia: Historical Background." Pp. 633–634 in Israel W. Charny (ed.), *Encyclopedia of Genocide*. Santa Barbara CA: ABC–CLIO.

Hirschi, Travis. 1969. *Causes of Delinquency*. Berkeley: University of California Press.

Hitchens, Christopher. 2001. *The Trial of Henry Kissinger*. London and New York: Verso.

Honig, J. W., and N. Both. 1996. *Srebrenica: Record of a War Crime*. Harmondsworth: Penguin Books.

Horowitz, I. L. 2002. *Taking Lives: Genocide and State Power*, Fifth edition. New Brunswick, NJ: Transaction.

Katz, Jack. 1988. *Seductions of Crime: The Moral and Sensual Appeals of Doing Evil*. New York: Basic Books.

Mace, James E. 1997. "Soviet Man-made Famine in Ukraine." Pp. 78–112 in Samuel Totten, William S. Parsons, and Israel W. Charney (eds.), *Century of Genocide: Eyewitness Accounts and Critical Views*. New York: Garland.

Mamdani, Mahmood. 2001. *When Victims Become Killers: Colonialism, Nativism and the Genocide in Rwanda*. Princeton, NJ: Princeton University Press.

Markusen, Eric. 1999. "Ethnic Cleansing and Genocide in Bosnia and Croatia, 1991–1995." Pp. 635–644 in Israel W. Charny (ed.), *Encyclopedia of Genocide*. Santa Barbara CA: ABC–CLIO.

Melvern, Linda. 2000. *A People Betrayed: The Role of the West in Rwanda's Genocide*. London: Zed Books.

Milgram, Stanley. 1974. *Obedience to Authority*. New York: Harper & Row.

Moffit, Terrie. 1993. "Adolescent-Limited and Life-Course-Persistent Antisocial Behavior: A Developmental Taxonomy." *Psychological Review* 100(4): 674–701.

Orentlicher, D. F. 1999. "Genocide." Pp. 153–157 in Roy Gutman and David Rieff (eds.), *Crimes of War: What the Public Should Know*. New York: Norton.

Osiel, Mark J. 1999. *Obeying Orders: Atrocity, Military Discipline and the Law of War*. New Brunswick, NJ: Transaction Books.

Power, Samantha. 2001. "Bystanders to Genocide." *Atlantic Monthly* (September), pp. 84–108.

Schabas, William A. 2001. *An Introduction to the International Criminal Court*. Cambridge, UK: Cambridge University Press, 2001.

Sellin, Thorsten. 1938. "Culture Conflict and Crime." *American Journal of Sociology* 44: 97–103.

Sykes, Gresham, and David Matza 1957. "Techniques of Neutralization: A Theory of Delinquency." *American Sociological Review* 22: 664–670.

Thompson, E. P. 1975. "Epilogue: The Rule of Law." in *Whigs and Hunters*. New York: Pantheon.

Turk, Austin. 1982. *Political Criminality*. Thousand Oaks, CA: Sage.

Vold, George. 1958. *Theoretical Criminology*. New York: Oxford University Press.

Vulliamy, Ed. 1999. "Unlawful Confinement." Pp. 365–366 in Roy Gutman and David Rieff (eds.), *Crimes of War: What the Public Should Know*. New York: Norton.

7

Sexual Harassment and Low Self-Control: A Proposed Application of the General Theory of Crime

Kevin M. Thompson and Leana Allen Bouffard

Gottfredson and Hirschi's (1990) *A General Theory of Crime* has probably generated more empirical tests in the past ten years than any other criminological theory. Cohn and Farrington (1999) note that *A General Theory of Crime* was the second most cited work of all criminological books in the 1990s. So popular and controversial has this theory become that it is rare to open an issue of *Criminology* or *Justice Quarterly* and not observe an empirical demonstration of this work. Indeed, the volume of empirical tests of this theory were sufficient enough a few years ago to facilitate a meta-analysis of the empirical status of the theory (Pratt and Cullen, 2000).

Gottfredson and Hirschi's (1990) theory is highly marketable in the deviance field because the theory portends to account for any behavior that is undertaken in the pursuit of self-interest. In this respect the theory is not limited to explaining variation in the propensity of individuals to engage only in behaviors involving force and fraud, although empirical tests have focused most intensely on how well the theory assembles data on delinquency (Brownfield and Sorenson, 1993; Cochran, Wood, and Arneklev, 1994) and crime (Burton et al., 1998; Evans et al., 1997). This general propensity, which Gottfredson and Hirschi refer to as low self-control (formerly criminality), is also associated with a host of analogous or co-morbid deviant behaviors since these acts are allegedly measures of the same latent trait. Thus, researchers have examined how well low self-control accounts for behaviors such as smoking and drinking (Arneklev et al., 1993), speeding, (Forde and Kennedy, 1997), academic cheating (Gibbs and Giever, 1995), accidents (Junger and Trembley, 1999), and resistance to school (Nakhaie, Silverman and LaGrange, 2000).

Others have found that the concept of self-control accounts adequately for variation in the risk of victimization (Schreck, Wright, and Miller, 2002).[1]

Since self-control can account for the stability of differences in the proclivity to engage in deviance (Polakowski, 1994) and is useful for organizing the facts surrounding the versatility of deviance (see Akers, 1991), the theory should also be able to assemble data surrounding civil action, such as acts involving sexual harassment. Though little research has made this connection, the nature of sexual harassment appears compatible with the scope of Gottfredson and Hirschi's theory.

Sexual Harassment

In 1980, The Equal Employment Opportunity Commission (EEOC) established guidelines on sexual harassment. These guidelines state that harassment on the basis of sex violates Title VII of the Civil Rights Act of 1964. Title IX of the Education Amendments of 1972 further protects persons from sexual harassment in schools by prohibiting sex discrimination in institutions that receive federal funds.

Sexual harassment did not become elevated as a social phenomenon however, until the Clarence Thomas hearings[2] and the Navy's Tailhook investigation in 1994 (Jaschik-Herman and Fisk, 1995). The publicity following these investigations/hearings led to a flurry of studies to assess the prevalence of sexual harassment in the workplace and in American institutions (Charney and Russell, 1994; Newell, Rosenfeld, and Culbertson, 1995).

Research on victims of sexual harassment also emerged indicating that victims often manifest psychological, physical, and economic damage (Thacker, 1992; Van Roosmalen and McDaniel, 1998). Victims report feeling helpless, depressed, shamed, and angry after being harassed (MacKinnon, 1979; Schneider, 1982). Others report post-traumatic stress disorder symptoms (Morse, 1996) and some leave jobs due to harassment (Crull, 1982; Baugh and Page, 1998). Those who choose to endure often experience a decrease in work efficiency (Morlacci, 1987–1988) and work satisfaction (Stedham and Mitchell, 1998). Sexual harassment in secondary schools and universities yields equally negative consequences, including loss of academic self-confidence, excessive absenteeism, diminished concentration (Bogart and Stein, 1989; Roscoe, Strouse, and Goodwin, 1994), and nausea and sleeplessness (Van Roosmalen and McDaniel, 1998).

Types of Sexual Harassment

While definitional ambiguities and debates abound in the literature, factor analytic techniques point to three subtypes of sexual harassment. One subtype includes quid pro quo incidents in which submission to sexual conduct is made a condition of concrete employment benefits, such as being offered a raise or a promotion (Vinciguerra, 1989). A second subtype consists of unwanted sexual attention such as when a male coworker touches a female coworker in a sexually provocative manner without her consent (Rosen and Martin, 1998). Harassment on the basis of gender characteristics constitutes a third subtype.[3] This form of sexual harassment is quite prevalent in the elementary and secondary schools and may involve teasing, name calling, and bullying (O'Donohue, Downs, and Yeater, 1998). The latter two subtypes form cause of action through the creation of a hostile environment.[4] Hostile environment harassment can involve persistent requests for sexual favors (not involving quid pro quo) and/or all other conduct of a sexual nature that demeans or humiliates the person addressed and in that way creates an offensive work or school environment (Morlacci, 1987–988).

To date, theory development on the etiology of sexual harassment has been restricted to gender-based and context-based models (Done, 2000). One popular model, sex-role spillover theory, holds that sexual harassment is due to the transfer of inequitable gender-based power from the larger social structure to the workplace (Gutek and Morasch, 1982). Context-based theories posit that sexual harassment is largely a function of organizational culture and dynamics (Caparulo, 2000). Factors here that might increase the probability of sexual harassment could include an unprofessional work environment and a lack of formal sexual harassment policies and procedures (O'Hare and O'Donohue, 1998).

Regrettably, criminologists have been somewhat silent on applying criminological principles to explain sexual harassment. We were able to identify one article written on this topic in criminology. This was a dissertation written by Done (2000) which focused specifically on self-control and sexually harassing behavior. Done found that low self-control was associated with a higher probability of engaging in sexually harassing behavior, consistent with the general theory of crime. Nevertheless, the paucity of research on this topic in criminology is puzzling. Sexual harassment is construed as a violation of a societal norm, consumes ample court resources in this country (Kandel, 1988), and fosters symptoms similar to those experienced by other victims of crime (e.g., PTSD, helplessness, depression) (Crull, 1982; Whealin, 1998). Further, sexual harassment affords criminologists the use of concepts central to criminological theories—power, control, inequality, strain, and differential association (Kelly and Radford, 1998). As a "general" theory, a theory of low self-control should be capable of organizing the facts of sexual harassment.

The Logical Structure of Sexual Harassment

The logical structure of sexual harassment appears to be consistent with Gottfredson and Hirschi's assumption that most acts require little in the way of skill, planning, and intelligence (1990: 89). Most sexual harassment acts require such rudimentary skills as whistling, grabbing, insulting, gesturing, or making sexual advances (Koen, 1989). Second, sexual harassment requires meager effort. Most victims are situated in the same operating room, ride the same bus, or occupy office space in the adjoining cubicle from the offender. Third, sexual harassment appears to satisfy self-interest primarily by providing the offender with momentary relief from the boredom, frustration, and irritation arising from attending school or working. Fourth, sexual harassment need not be constrained to the employment setting, which largely reduces the synergistic role of opportunity in accounting for variance. This may be important because opportunity has been conceived as an ambiguous concept in Gottfredson and Hirschi's work (Grasmick et al., 1993; Sellers, 1999).[5] While most legal claims have emerged from the work sphere, sexual harassment has been reported in a wide variety of settings, including elementary and secondary schools (Bogart and Stein, 1989; Land, 2001), the military (Newell, Rosenfeld, and Culbertson, 1995; Rosen and Martin, 1998), hospital settings (Duncan et al., 2001), and universities (Dey, Korn, and Sax, 1996). Fifth, sexual harassment lends itself nicely to tests of the theory through the use of either cognitive indicators of low self-control such as that used by Grasmick et al. (1993) and Sellers (1999) or through behavioral indicators such as the Impulsive Behavior Scale (Rossotto, Yager, and Rorty, 1998).[6]

This chapter examines how the principles delineated in "a general theory of crime" might be compatible with sexual harassment. We then suggest a series of testable propositions and recommend a suitable research design for testing these propositions. We conclude by offering the reader a glimpse of how Gottfredson and Hirschi's work can be employed in organizational and institutional settings to combat sexual harassment. Because most readers will be well versed with the fundamental assumptions of Gottfredson and Hirschi's theory, we will avoid offering a thorough exposition of the theory of self-control (see Cohen and Vila, 1996).

Low Self-Control and Sexual Harassment Predictions

Indicators of Low Self-Control

The central concept of *A General Theory of Crime* is self-control. While self-control is conceived to feature both behavioral and cognitive traits, the concept has been principally operationalized by employing cognitive scales (Grasmick et al., 1993). The cognitive dimension of low self-control assesses an individual's propensity to take risks, prefer impulsive acts, avoid complex tasks, be self-absorbed, and prefer physical as opposed to cerebral activities.[7] Cognitive self-control scales that have included these indicators have demonstrated adequate reliability and validity (Grasmick et al., 1993).

These traits should have implications for involvement in sexual harassment. The twelve-year-old school boy taunts and teases the girls in math class because this form of interaction requires less effort, skill, and intelligence than forging relationships and deflects attention from the difficulty of calculating exponents. The twenty-nine-year-old employee strokes the shoulder of the new female employee and attempts to pressure her into a sexual liaison because these actions require less courtship effort and patience than establishing a long-term relationship. Further, these actions deflect attention from his mundane job and are simply more pleasurable than work tasks. Persons willing to undertake these efforts will be highly impulsive, be prone to risks, be self-absorbed, and exhibit disinterest in the feelings of others.[8]

Overall Prevalence

Sources of sexual harassment data are similar to crime source data in being mined from three sources: self-reported admission of activity, official counts in the form of legal claims, and self-reported victimization. Like crime data, data on the prevalence of sexual harassment victimization are not lacking. What is lacking is consensus regarding the interpretation of what constitutes a high or a low rate of sexual harassment on the basis of existing estimates.

Published research involving representative sample surveys reveals that 25 to 45 percent of women report being sexually harassed on the job (Newell, Rosenfeld, and Culbertson, 1995; Stawar, 1999). Surveys of school environments show that anywhere between 85 to 95 percent of children and adolescents report being subjected to some form of sexual harassment (Stratton and Backes, 1997; Land, 2001). Whether these figures constitute high or low rates is subject to interpretation and is dependent on the phenomenon being measured. Scrutiny of the dependent measures used in many studies shows that researchers frequently record gestures, jokes, looks, and insults as evidence of sexually harassing behavior (Stratton and Backes, 1997). This is akin to asking employees in an embezzlement survey if they have ever taken a ballpoint pen, a nail, or a diskette from their workplace without authorized consent. These acts might constitute embezzlement but they may not be egregious enough to warrant legal action.

While we are not averse to using self-report and victimization data to test Gottfredson and Hirschi's theory, we would also advocate that a sexual harassment study focus on legal claims as the dependent measure for several reasons. First, legal claims imply that (1) victims were exposed to a series of acts, (2) these acts were severe, (3) victims may have been physically threatened, or (4) exposure unreasonably interfered with work performance. Second, the victim feels these acts have accumulated in such a way as to contribute to the probability of some kind of psychopathology (e.g., depression, anxiety, somatic disorders). In that respect, victims of sexual harassment are likely to experience emotional distress similar to other crime victims.

With this in mind, Gottfredson and Hirschi's theory would predict that legal claims in the work sphere should be relatively low. This is because the characteristics of low self-control are contrary to the traits required of persons to locate and retain employment. An examination of the number of sexual harassment claims shows that the prevalence rate resembles that of embezzlement. The Federal Equal Employment Opportunity Commission (EEOC) reported 15,475 charge receipts involving sexual harassment in 2001 (U.S. Equal Employment Opportunity Commission, 2002) and for the ten years beginning in 1992, the EEOC reported an average of 14,579 legal claims per year. Regrettably, we were not able to determine the distribution of these claims based on their context of origination but we would speculate that the bulk of these claims are work related.

Organizational Prestige

Because low self-control has implications for selection into the type of occupational structure (1990: 191), we would predict an inverse relationship between organizational prestige and sexual harassment claims. Specifically, firms and companies that are high in occupational prestige should have lower rates of harassment than firms that rank lower in prestige because presumably more-prestigious companies seek out characteristics of employees that are compatible with high self-control. Further, persons in these organizations will be less prone to take risks that might jeopardize their attaining a position in a prestigious company. Among universities, one could test this assumption by utilizing a prestige-ranking system of colleges and universities and assess levels of sexual harassment across institutions. For instance, the Carnegie Classification of Institutions of Higher Education could be employed to determine whether doctoral/research extensive universities have lower rates of sexual harassment (self-reports or legal claims) than master's colleges and universities, which in turn would record lower rates than associate's colleges. Similarly, companies that hire large numbers of temporary employees (temps) should be subjected to greater levels of sexual harassment than companies with large numbers of permanent employees.

Occupational Position

Self-control theory should also be capable of accurately predicting prevalence rates based on an individual's structural position within an organization. For instance, quid pro quo harassment is predicated on the assumption that supervisors have the authority to withhold a reward from a noncompliant employee or punish them in some way should he/she resist advances. Since being in a position of authority requires toil, attending to obligations, and making sacrifices, the theory predicts a low rate of quid pro quo sexual harassment. Persons in position of authority are unwilling to risk being divorced from their investments by being terminated on a sexual harassment complaint. Quid pro quo behavior, when it occurs, should be inversely associated with hierarchical position. An adequate test of this hypothesis could compare rates of quid pro quo harassment among persons at different levels of authority with comparable opportunities to harass. Support for the theory should reveal that senior-level executives should have lower rates than junior-level executives who in turn should have lower rates than executives in training. In military settings, colonels should have lower rates than captains who in turn should have lower rates than sergeants. Professors likewise should have lower rates than assistant professors who in turn should exhibit lower rates than lecturers.

Similarly, being admitted to an institution of higher learning is incompatible with low self-control. Getting into a university requires that students take their academic work in high school somewhat seriously, that they make sacrifices, and that they attend to obligations. Consequently, we would predict that students in institutions of higher education should have lower rates of sexual harassment than their same age peers in the working world. One could take this prediction a step further and argue that student-to-student sexual harassment should be inversely associated with university prestige using the Carnegie Classification of Institutions of Higher Education.

Gender

Gottfredson and Hirschi (1990: 147) assert that gender differences in criminal and analogous behaviors imply a substantial self-control difference between the sexes. If true, self-reports and legal claims should reveal higher rates of perpetration among males than females.[9] Critics of Gottfredson and Hirschi's theory might be inclined to focus on the greater level of opportunity afforded males in the workplace to harass as accounting for the bulk of the criterion variance. A test of this hypothesis could control for years of employment, structural position, and workplace contact with members of the opposite sex. Controls for sexual harassment opportunity at the school level (among students), whether it be kindergarten or the university would not be necessary because gender differences in opportunity should be equivalent for the sexes.

Relationship between Perpetrator and Victim

The pattern of peer-to-peer sexual harassment has received less scholarly and popular coverage than superior-to-subordinate harassment. Nevertheless, several studies show that student-to-student harassment is more common than staff-to-student harassment (Stein, 1986; Bogart and Stein, 1989; Larkin, 1993). Workplace data similarly reveals that sexual harassment by coworkers and subordinates is more common than harassment by supervisors or authorities (Schneider, 1982; Studd and Gattiker, 1991). Surveys show that between 60 and 65 percent of initiators of harassment are in nonsupervisory positions (Tangri, Burt, and Johnson, 1982; Gutek, 1985). Moreover, when *men* are harassed by *women* they are likely to be harassed by a younger co-worker or subordinate (Gutek, 1985).

Testable Propositions

Gottfredson and Hirschi's theory of self-control facilitates the following propositions regarding sexual harassment:

1. Persons low on self-control will have a higher probability of engaging in sexual harassment than persons high on self-control.
2. Sexual harassment will be positively associated with other criminal and deviant acts.
3. The overall official prevalence rate of sexual harassment that results in symptoms that are akin to crime victimization symptoms will be relatively low.
4. Sexual harassment within organizations will be inversely related to the prestige of the organization.
5. Quid pro quo sexual harassment should be less common than hostile environment sexual harassment.
6. Sexual harassment should be inversely associated with hierarchical position in the organization.
7. In all social settings, males should exhibit higher rates of sexual harassment than females.
8. Peer-to-peer sexual harassment will be more common than superior-to-subordinate sexual harassment.

Research Design

There are a variety of means of measuring the distribution and risk factors of sexual harassment. Many previous harassment studies have gathered data from representative samples of citizens to assess the prevalence of victimization (Roscoe, Strouse, and Goodwin, 1994; Kelly and Radford, 1998). While this research focus is important, it restricts our ability to ascertain the distribution and risk factors among perpetrators. Therefore, we recommend that researchers employ psychometrically accepted instruments for assessing self-control and sexual harassment using self-reports and official records.

In terms of measuring involvement in sexual harassment, researchers have asked respondents retrospective questions about the occurrence of specific behaviors (Arvey and Cavanaugh, 1995). Though initially developed to measure victimization, the Sexual Experiences Questionnaire (SEQ) (Fitzgerald et al., 1988, cited in Arvey and Cavanaugh, 1995) includes behaviorally specific items representing a variety of facets of sexual harassment and has applications for measuring offending as well. Arvey and Cavanaugh (1995) note that the strengths of this questionnaire include the specificity of behavioral definitions and the avoidance of ambiguity in the items. Another instrument that has been used to measure involvement is the Likelihood to Sexually Harass Scale (Pryor, 1987). The original instrument included ten scenarios depicting various types of male-on-female harassment and asking subjects to report the likelihood that they would engage in harassing behavior. More recent uses of this instrument have revised the scenarios to include female-on-male situations to assess likelihood among both male and female subjects (see Perry, 1998).

We would also advocate that a sexual harassment study focus on legal claims as the dependent measure. First, legal claims imply that (1) victims were exposed to a series of acts, (2) these acts were severe, (3) victims may have been physically threatened, or (4) exposure unreasonably interfered with work performance. Second, the victim feels these acts have accumulated in such a way as to contribute to the probability of some kind of psychopathology (e.g., depression, anxiety, somatic disorders). In that respect, victims of sexual harassment are likely to experience emotional distress similar to other crime victims.

With respect to assessing self-control, we recommend that researchers continue to employ psychometrically accepted cognitive instruments that have been used extensively in the crime literature. However, we also recommend that researchers attend to administering behavioral scales as well. One behavioral scale which has rarely caught the attention of criminologists is the Impulsive Behavior Scale (IBS-C/A) developed by Rossotto and colleagues (1998). This scale assesses the self-reported frequency in the past year of nineteen different impulsive and self-destructive behaviors such as risk taking, accident proneness, reckless driving, promiscuous sex, and excessive chemical consumption.[10] The observed behaviors in this scale should be associated with sexual harassment because they should come together in the same people through low self-control.

Finally, researchers should consider testing the low self-control–sexual harassment nexus by employing a quasi-experimental design. We recommend gathering data from a random sample of persons charged with sexual harassment and compare them on self-control scores to a randomly selected group of non-charged persons. A study of this nature could be conducted in the secondary schools, the military, a university, or the workplace. Gottfredson and Hirschi's theory implies that the social setting could not have influenced self-control because the trait is relatively stable and established long before people seek college life, military experience, or employment.

Such a design would resolve problems associated with the role of sexual harassment opportunity. Unlike white-collar crime, the opportunity to harass should be relatively ubiquitous and it would therefore be unnecessary to separate opportunity from low self-control. Consequently, we recommend that the theory be tested by (1) randomly selecting known offenders, (2) randomly selecting known non-offenders, (3) assessing self-control via proven instruments, and (4) assessing characteristics such as organizational or institutional prestige, occupational prestige, previous criminal behavior, gender, and the relationship between harasser and victim.

Policy Implications

What implications does the concept of low self-control have for preventing or reducing sexual harassment? The trajectory of low self-control can inform us about policies that will likely be ineffective as well as those that might prove effective in combating sexual harassment. The trajectory of self-control leads us to believe that self-control will be established some time quite early in life. Gottfredson and Hirschi assert that self-control is a relatively immutable quality by a person's eighth birthday. They further contend that "because low self-control arises in the absence of the powerful inhibiting forces of early childhood, it is highly resistant to the less powerful inhibiting forces of later life" (1990: 255). On this basis, employers who require that new employees attend workshops to learn about sexual harassment guidelines are likely wasting their time and resources on persons low on self-control. Further, requiring known sexual harassers to attend sensitivity workshops will have little impact toward reforming their sexual harassing behavior. This is because the primary value of the theory lies in the ability of policymakers to identify high-risk harassers prior to the full-blown emergence of low self-control. Delivery of the appropriate intervention thus will be mistimed and cannot function to prevent the disorder nor intervene in its reduction.

Other organizational sanctions intended to cause sexual harassers to desist will likely fail as well. In the private sector, demotions, reducing salary, and exposing the harasser to miserable working conditions will only likely contribute to their quitting rather than ceasing their harassment. Likewise, reducing sexual harassment by equalizing employee pay or improving working conditions are likely to be unsuccessful. In agencies where sexual harassment has become relatively institutionalized, it is the victims who will routinely seek alternative employment.

Organizations that are serious about combating sexual harassment can however protect themselves by conducting thorough background checks and assessments on prospective employees. Many criminal justice agencies now examine the backgrounds of prospective employees for felonies and substance-abuse histories. In addition, they routinely administer a battery of personality tests intended to sort out unstable personalities from their pool. We submit that other organizations can go far toward preventing sexual harassment by (1) determining whether a person has an arrest history, (2) demonstrating a previous history of sexual harassment, and (3) assessing persons via a self-control inventory.

Ultimately, it may be the school and in particular, teachers in the early grades that may be best positioned to prevent sexual harassment. It is in the early grades that high-risk subjects can be identified and for whom an appropriate intervention can be designed and delivered. Harassment may currently be indistinguishable from bullying and American schools have decided that bullying is degrading and detracts from the learning environment. Many schools have subsequently translated this proactive bullying posture to combating harassment. Consequently, early detection and intervention of harassing behavior by the school could be an effective vehicle for offsetting sexual harassment.[11]

Conclusion

Criminologists have been unusually silent in applying criminological principles to sexual harassment. The neglect of this topic is puzzling because sexual harassment manifests behavioral characteristics in offenders and psychopathological traits in victims that are compatible with the crime literature. We submit that the assumptions of Gottfredson and Hirschi's general theory of crime appear to be highly germane to accounting for variation in sexually harassing acts. Descriptions of sexual harassment from published accounts suggest that these acts require little in the way of effort, skill, planning, and intelligence. These acts do however, require that persons take risks, exhibit insensitivity to the feelings of others, be easily distracted, and be unwilling to delay sexual gratification. Further, the motive for sexual harassment appears to be limited to the immediate benefits provided by the act itself. Stepping out of one's cubicle to hurl an insult at a passing coworker carries the benefit of providing relief from mundane job tasks.[12] Similarly, inappropriate touching of a coworker bears immediate fruit for the offender in terms of pleasure. Such an act is preferable to a protracted courtship that carries the uncertainty of receipt of physical pleasure. The ubiquitous nature of sexual harassment also deflects attention from the disputed role of opportunity as a moderating variable in the model. Hostile environment harassment opportunities are equally available regardless of grade level, military rank, or position in the corporation.

Gottfredson and Hirschi's theory predicts that the typical workplace harasser will have a history of harassment, beginning in the early school years. Low self-control traits will subsequently work against individual's opportunity to procure and maintain steady employment because sanction systems established by federal law work against the possibility that harassers will have lengthy careers. These persons may in fact wield an episodic job history because of their willingness to sexually harass other employees. Like the white-collar offender, workplace harassers are likely to convert places of work into sources of satisfaction that are consistent with previous behavior (1990: 141). When organizations strengthen their harassment policies or enforce existing policies, persons low on self-control will be inclined to leave for less restrictive work environments. Workplace non-harassers will comply with federal harassment guidelines because they do not wish to risk losing the substantial social and financial capital they have invested and accumulated in the organization.

While we are advocating that criminologists examine how well Gottfredson and Hirschi's theory organizes the facts surrounding sexual harassment, other criminological theorists need not shy away from this phenomenon. In particular, Sampson and Laub's (1993) age-graded theory has clear implications for desistance from sexual harassment. Where Gottfredson and Hirschi see conventional organizations as either repelling persons with low self-control traits or being corrupted by them, Sampson and Laub see these same organizations as possibly redirecting self-control in the previously weakly bonded individual. Agnew's general strain theory (1992) also might have implications for assembling the facts surrounding sexual harassment. In particular, Agnew's emphasis on the desire to be treated in a just or fair manner could have implications for harassment in the work sphere. Finally, theories such as social learning theories (Akers, 1985, 1997), which attempt to identify the processes and motivational forces involved in the initiation and continuation of behavior could certainly have relevance for sexual harassment.

In closing, it is the hope that this proposal can stimulate criminologists to take a closer look at sexual harassment as well as other civil acts in which the consequences mimic criminal victimization. Criminologists have much to offer in terms of explaining crime and other behaviors that share conceptual common ground with crime (see Paternoster and Brame, 1998). Like white-collar crime, sexual harassment is costly to organizations.[13] Like sexual assault, its victims are left feeling helpless and dissociated. We submit that the assumptions delineated in the work of Gottfredson and Hirschi can assemble the facts surrounding sexual harassment and therefore make strides toward reducing this phenomenon.

Notes

1. Other analogous behaviors would seem compatible with the tenets of Gottfredson and Hirschi's theory. We suggest that low self-control might have implications for the probability of smoking cessation, traffic citations, and eating disorders. To the

best of our knowledge, low self-control has not formed the basis for an explanation of these behaviors.

2. Thomas was accused at his confirmation hearings of making lewd and indecent sexual remarks to Anita Hill while she worked for him.
3. The *Harris v. Forklift Systems, Inc.* case (114 S. Ct. 367, 1993) constituted the test case whereby the United States Supreme Court defined this form of sexual harassment. This case involved a woman who was routinely referred to by her boss as a "dumb ass woman," told she won accounts at a Nashville truck leasing company by sleeping with clients, and was asked to take coins out of the front pockets of her boss's pockets.
4. The United States Supreme Court unanimously ruled in the Harris case (114 S. Ct. 367, 1993) that a victim of sexual harassment need not demonstrate severe psychological injury to win damages in sexual harassment suit. Rather, the victim merely needed to be exposed to a workplace that is permeated with discriminatory intimidation, ridicule, and insult that is sufficiently severe or pervasive to alter the conditions of the victim's employment and create an abusive working environment. The Supreme Court ruled that such a situation constitutes a violation of Title VII of the Civil Rights Act of 1964.
5. The reader is encouraged to consult Sellers (1999) for an interpretative discussion of the role of opportunity in Gottfredson and Hirschi's theory.
6. We were unable to locate any tests of Gottfredson and Hirschi's theory that employed the Impulsive Behavior Scale. This scale is commonly employed in the field of psychology and psychiatry and provides a brief but thorough assessment of impulsive and self-destructive behaviors. The validity and reliability of the scale has been well documented and the instrument has been used extensively in treatment outcome studies. An examination of the self-reported behaviors in the scale reveals items that are indicative of low self-control.
7. The physical dimension of the cognitive scale does not appear to load adequately on the other items in the scale (see Grasmick et al., 1993; Arneklev et al., 1993). While we would not dispute these factor analytic results, we think that the preference for physicality still may be an important dimension to low self-control. We suspect that this dimension of self-control may need to be reconceptualized, rather than simply dismissed. As used in most tests, the physical activities items such as "If I had a choice, I would almost always rather do something physical than something mental" is probably not an adequate measure of self-control. This item and others in the physical dimension probably captures too many respondents who enjoy running, golf, soccer, weight lifting, and racquetball, to name a few. We suggest that persons low on self-control may attempt to avoid activities that carry some threshold of pain such as running marathons or swimming and instead may prefer physical activities with a high pleasure/pain ratio (e.g., basketball). In other words, responses to the physical dimension of self-control may depend on the nature of the activity.
8. While we recognize that the concepts of power and social structure are also highly relevant in explaining behaviors like sexual harassment, these concepts have not been incorporated into Gottfredson and Hirschi's theory. Therefore, we will not address them here.
9. The gender difference in sexual harassment is particularly germane to criminal justice since the criminal justice system is predominately male, making females working within the system vulnerable to sexually harassing behavior (see Stohr et al., 1998). If true, such a practice could erode productivity and reduce effectiveness of agencies that have crime control as their mission, thereby possibly affecting recidivism rates.

10. None of these behavioral indicators are subject to measurement tautology when assessed with sexual harassment and therefore avoid one of the pitfalls levied against the theory (see Akers, 1991; Tittle, 1991).
11. Gottfredson and Hirschi (1990, p. 106) assert that the school can be an effective socializing agent for reducing low self-control in the absence of parental support.
12. We are reminded of Rob Schneider's workplace behavior on *Saturday Night Live* in which he simply toyed with fellow employees's names as they attempted to copy materials at the photocopy machine.
13. In many ways, one of the victims of sexual harassment is the organization (Baugh and Page, 1998). Sexual harassment is costly to organizations not just in terms of lawsuits but in lower productivity, loss of work time, and negative publicity subsequent to a lawsuit (e.g., consider Mitsubishi).

References

Agnew, Robert. 1992. "Foundation for a General Strain Theory of Crime and Delinquency." *Criminology* 30: 40–87.

Akers, Ronald L. 1985. *Deviant Behavior: A Social Learning Approach.* Third Edition. Belmont, CA: Wadsworth.

———. 1991. "Self-Control as a General Theory of Crime." *Journal of Quantitative Criminology* 7: 201–211.

———. 1997. *Criminological Theories.* Second Edition. Los Angeles: Roxbury.

Arneklev, Bruce J., Harold G. Grasmick, Charles R. Tittle, and Robert J. Bursik, Jr. 1993. "Low Self-Control and Imprudent Behavior." *Journal of Quantitative Criminology* 9: 225–247.

Arvey, Richard D., and Marcie A. Cavanaugh. 1995. "Using Surveys to Access the Prevalence of Sexual Harassment: Some Methodological Problems." *Journal of Social Issues* 51: 39–52.

Baugh, S. Gayle, and Diana Page. 1998. "A Field Investigation of Gender-Based Differences in Perceptions of Sexual Harassment." *Journal of Social Behavior and Personality* 13: 451–465.

Bogart, Karen, and Nan Stein. 1989. "Breaking the Silence: Sexual Harassment in Education." *Peabody Journal of Education* 64: 146–163.

Brownfield, David, and Ann Marie Sorenson. 1993. "Self-Control and Juvenile Delinquency: Theoretical Issues and an Empirical Assessment of Selected Elements of a General Theory of Crime." *Deviant Behavior* 4: 243–264.

Burton, Velmer S., Jr., Francis T. Cullen, T. David Evans, Leanne Fiftal Alarid, and R. Gregory Dunaway. 1998. "Gender, Self-Control, and Crime." *Journal of Research in Crime and Delinquency* 35: 123–147.

Caparulo, Barbara K. 2000. "Men's Violence against Women: Toward a Transtheoretical Model of Sexual Harassment." Unpublished dissertation, Massachusetts School of Professional Psychology, Boston, MA.

Charney, Dara A., and Ruth C. Russell. 1994. "An Overview of Sexual Harassment." *American Journal of Psychiatry* 151: 10–17.

Cochran, John K, Peter B. Wood, and Bruce J. Arneklev. 1994. "Is the Religiosity-Delinquency Relationship Spurious? A Test of Arousal and Social Control Theories." *Journal of Research in Crime and Delinquency* 31: 92–123.

Cohen, Lawrence, E., and Bryan J. Vila. 1996. "Self-control and Social Control: An Exposition of the Gottfredson-Hirschi/Sampson-Laub Debate." *Studies on Crime and Crime Prevention*,5: 125–150.

Cohn, Ellen, G., and Farrington, David P. 1999. "Changes in the Most-Cited Scholars in Twenty Criminology and Criminal Justice Journals between 1990 and 1995." *Journal of Criminal Justice* 27: 345–359.

Crull, Peggy. 1982. "Stress Effects of Sexual Harassment on the Job: Implications for Counseling." *American Journal of Orthopsychiatry* 52: 539–544.

Dey, Eric, L., Jessica S. Korn, and Linda J. Sax. 1996. "Betrayed by the Academy: The Sexual Harassment of Women College Faculty." *Journal of Higher Education* 67: 149–173.

Done, Robert S. 2000. "Self-Control and Deviant Behavior in Organizations: The Case of Sexually Harassing Behavior." Unpublished doctoral dissertation, University of Arizona, Tucson, AZ.

Duncan, Susan M., Kathryn Hyndman, Carole A. Estabrooks, Kathryn Hesketh, Charles K. Humphrey, Jennifer S. Wong, Sonia, Acorn, and Phyllis Giovannetti. 2001. "Nurses' Experience of Violence in Alberta and British Columbia Hospitals." *Canadian Journal of Nursing Research* 32: 57–78.

Evans, T. David, Francis T. Cullen, Velmer S. Burton, Jr., R. Gregory Dunaway, and Michael L. Benson. 1997. "The Social Consequences of Self-Control: Testing the General Theory of Crime." *Criminology* 35: 475–501.

Fitzgerald, Louise F., Sandra L. Shullman, Nancy Bailey, Margaret Richards, J. Swecker, Yael Gold, Mimi Ormerod, and Lauren M. Weitzman. 1988. "The Incidence and Dimensions of Sexual Harassment in Academia and the Workplace." *Journal of Vocational Behavior* 32: 152–175.

Forde, David R., and Leslie W. Kennedy. 1997. "Risky Lifestyles, Routine Activities, and the General Theory of Crime." *Justice Quarterly* 14: 265–294.

Gibbs, John J., and Dennis Giever. 1995. "Self-control and Its Manifestations among University Students: An Empirical Test of Gottfredson and Hirschi's General Theory." *Justice Quarterly* 12: 231–235.

Gottfredson, Michael, and Travis Hirschi. 1990. *A General Theory of Crime*. Stanford: Stanford University Press.

Grasmick, Harold G., Charles R. Tittle, Robert J. Bursik, Jr., and Bruce J.Arneklev. 1993. "Testing the Core Empirical Implications of Gottfredson and Hirschi's General Theory of Crime." *Journal of Research in Crime and Delinquency* 30: 5–29.

Gutek, Barbara A. 1985. *Sex and the Workplace*. San Francisco: Jossey–Bass.

Gutek, Barbara A., and Bruce Morasch. 1982. "Sex Ratios, Sex-Role Spillover, and Sexual Harassment of Women at Work." *Journal of Social Issues* 38: 55–74.

Jaschik-Herman, Mollie, L., and Alene Fisk. 1995. "Women's Perceptions and Labeling of Sexual Harassment in Academia before and after the Hill-Thomas Hearings." *Sex Roles* 33: 439–446.

Junger, Marianne, and Richard E. Tremblay. 1999. "Self-Control, Accidents and Crime." *Criminal Justice and Behavior* 26: 485–501.

Kandel, William L. 1988. "Current Developments in Employment Litigation." *Employee Relations Law Journal* 14: 439–451.

Kelly, Liz, and Jill Radford. 1998. "Sexual Violence against Women and Girls: An Approach to an International Overview." In Rebecca E. Dobash and Russell P. Dobash (eds.), *Rethinking Violence against Women*. Sages series on violence against women. Thousand Oaks, CA: Sage Publications.

Koen, Clifford M. Jr. 1989. "Sexual Harassment: Criteria for Defining Hostile Environment." *Employee Responsibilities and Rights Journal* 2: 289–301.

Land, Deborah J. 2001. "Teasing, Bullying, and Sexual Harassment among Adolescents." Unpublished dissertation, University of Virginia, Charlottesville, VA.

Larkin, June. 1993. "Walking Through Walls: The Sexual Harassment of High School Girls." Unpublished manuscript, The Ontario Institute for Studies in Education.

MacKinnon, Catharine. 1979. *Sexual Harassment of Working Women: A Case of Sex Discrimination*. New Haven, CT: Yale University Press.

Morlacci, Maria. 1987–1988. "Sexual Harassment Law and the Impact of Vinson." *Employee Relations Law Journal* 13: 501–519.

Morse, Heather B. 1996. "Factors Affecting Reporting Behavior and Psychological Effects of Female Graduate Students Who Are Sexually Harassed." Unpublished dissertation, University of Kentucky, Lexington, KY.

Nakhaie, Reza M., Robert A. Silverman, and Teresa C. LaGrange. 2000. "Self-Control and Resistance to School." *Canadian Review of Sociology and Anthropology* 37: 443–460.

Newell, Carol E., Paul Rosenfeld, and Amy Culbertson. 1995. "Sexual Harassment Experiences and Equal Opportunity Perceptions of Navy Women." *Sex Roles* 32: 159–168.

O'Donohue, William, Kala Downs, and Elizabeth A. Yeater. 1998. "Sexual Harassment: A Review of the Literature." *Aggression and Violent Behavior* 3: 111–128.

Paternoster, Raymond, and Robert Brame. 1998. "The Structural Similarity of Processes Generating Criminal and Analogous Behaviors." *Criminology* 36: 633–670.

Perry, Elissa L. 1998. "Propensity to Sexually Harass: An Exploration of Gender Differences." *Sex Roles* 38: 443–460.

Polakowski, Michael. 1994. "Linking Self and Social Control with Deviance: Illuminating the Structure Underlying a General Theory of Crime and Its Relation to Deviant Activity." *Journal of Quantitative Criminology* 10: 41–78.

Pratt, Travis, C., and Cullen, Francis T. 2000. "The Empirical Status of Gottfredson and Hirschi's General Theory of Crime: A Meta-Analysis." *Criminology* 38: 931–964.

Pryor, John B. 1987. "Sexual Harassment Proclivities in Men." *Sex Roles* 17: 269–290.

Roscoe, Bruce, Jeremiah Strouse, and Megan Goodwin. 1994. "Sexual Harassment: Early Adolescents' Self-Reports of Experiences and Acceptance." *Adolescence* 29: 515–23.

Rosen, Leora N., and Lee Martin. 1998. "Incidence and Perceptions of Sexual Harassment among Male and Female U.S. Army Soldiers." *Military Psychology* 10: 239–257.

Rossotto, Elizabeth, Joel Yager, and Marcia Rorty. 1998. "The Impulsive Behavior Scale." In Johan Vanderlinden and Walter Vandereycken (eds.), *Trauma, Dissociation, and Impulse Dyscontrol in Eating Disorders*. Philadelphia: Brunner/Mazel.

Sampson, Robert J., and John H. Laub. 1993. *Crime in the Making: Pathways and Turning Points through Life*. Cambridge, MA: Harvard University Press.

Schneider, Beth E. 1982. "Consciousness about Sexual Harassment among Heterosexual and Lesbian Women Workers." *Journal of Social Issues* 38: 75–98.

Schreck, Christopher J., Richard A. Wright, and J. Mitchell Miller. 2002. "A Study of Individual and Situational Antecedents of Violent Victimization." *Justice Quarterly* 19: 159–180.

Sellers, Christine. 1999. "Self-Control and Intimate Violence: An Examination of the Scope and Specification of the General Theory of Crime." *Criminology* 37: 375–404.

Stawar, Terry L. 1999. "A Model for Sexual Harassment Behavior." *Forensic Examiner* 8: 30–34.

Stedham, Yvonne, and Merwin C. Mitchell. 1998. "Sexual Harassment in Casinos: Effects on Employee Attitudes and Behaviors." *Journal of Gambling Studies* 14: 381–400.

Stein, Nan, D. 1986. *Who's Hurt and Who's Liable: Sexual Harassment in Massachusetts Schools: A Curriculum and Guide for School Personnel*. Quincy, MA: Massachusetts Department of Education.

Stohr, Mary K., G. Larry Mays, Ann C. Beck, and Tammy Kelley. 1998. "Sexual Harassment in Women's Jails." *Journal of Contemporary Criminal Justice* 14: 135–155."

Stratton, Stanley, and John S. Backes. 1997. "Sexual Harassment in North Dakota Public Schools: A Study of Eight High Schools." *High School Journal* 80: 163–172.

Studd, Michael V., and Urs E. Gattiker. 1991. "The Evolutionary Psychology of Sexual Harassment in Organizations." *Ethology and Sociobiology* 12: 249–290.

Tangri, Sandra S., Martha R. Burt, and Leanor B. Johnson. 1982. "Sexual Harassment at Work: Three Explanatory Models." *Journal of Social Issues* 38: 33–54.

Thacker, Rebecca, A. 1992. "A Descriptive Study of Behavioral Responses of Sexual Harassment Targets: Implications for Control Theory." *Employee Responsibilities and Rights Journal* 5: 155–171.

Tittle, Charles R. 1991. "*A General Theory of Crime*: A Book Review." *American Journal of Sociology* 96: 1609–1611.

U.S. Equal Employment Opportunity Commission. 2002. *Policy Guidance on Sexual Harassment*. Washington, DC: Author.

Van Roosmalen, Erica, and Susan A. McDaniel. 1998. "Sexual Harassment in Academia: A Hazard to Women's Health." *Women and Health* 28: 33–54.

Vinciguerra, Marlisa. 1989. "The Aftermath of Mentor: A Search for Standards in the Law of Sexual Harassment." *Yale Law Journal* 98: 1717–1738.

Whealin, Julia M. 1998. "Gender Differences and Long-term Impact of Unwanted Sexual Attention during Childhood." Unpublished doctoral dissertation, University of Georgia, Athens, GA.

8

Punishment of Children from the Perspective of Control Theory

Travis Hirschi and Michael R. Gottfredson

Control theory assumes that individuals are capable of committing delinquent and criminal acts without benefit of example, training, or rewards over and above those inherent in the acts themselves. This assumption, more than any other, distinguishes control theory from other psychological and sociological theories. In control theory, criminal behavior is likely whenever its advantages outweigh immediate and long-term risks, as perceived by the individual. Given the natural ability of individuals to see the immediate advantages of delinquent and criminal acts, the task for society is to persuade them that such acts are not in their long-term interests. Given the natural ability of individuals to see the immediate advantages of crime, society should not be overly concerned with protecting them from exposure to such information. Put another way: The benefits of speeding, theft, assault, and drugs are obvious. Efforts to control them by denying or distorting their benefits are unlikely to be effective.

Control theory assumes that delinquent and criminal acts provide immediate and obvious benefits, or satisfaction of ordinary human desires, at little expense of time or energy. It assumes that they are, at the same time, costly to others and to the long-term interests of the offender. Contrary to common academic and popular images of crimes, which see them as highly motivated, complicated, and organized, control theory sees the vast majority of criminal acts as opportunistic and simple, as requiring little in the way of preparation or skill. These assumptions stress the availability of crimes to everyone, and the idea that no special motivation or training is required for their commission. The question, from a control theory point of view, is how society can efficiently and effectively monitor the behavior of so many potential offenders and convince them that crime is something to be avoided.

Forms of Control

Since Jeremy Bentham, four methods of crime control or sanction systems have been described.

1. Natural sanctions, which involve the pains of injury, disease, and loss of life as a direct consequence of the act itself.
2. Moral or social sanctions, which involve the pains of isolation, loss of reputation and affection.
3. Legal sanctions, which involve deprivations of life, liberty, and property imposed by the state.
4. Supernatural sanctions, which involve losses and deprivations in an afterlife.

Let us examine each of these control mechanisms as they apply to childrearing and crime and delinquency.

Natural Sanctions

Children quickly learn the natural consequences of many forms of behavior. Steps and stoves are dangerous, as are animals, machines, and larger children. These lessons tend to come directly from the environment, are easily learned, and are powerful shapers of behavior. They provide boundaries to natural curiosity and templates for learning the consequences of behavior more generally. Because natural penalties are so prevalent and so often harsh, parents must in fact frequently intervene to prevent or ameliorate their effects. At the same time, parents may take advantage of these mechanisms to illustrate more generally the connections between acts and their consequences. Because humans are rational and perceptive, they can presumably quickly generalize such lessons to a variety of acts and consequences.

This is not to say that all violations of natural laws are automatically or immediately punished. On the contrary, in many cases the relevant consequences of a certain line of behavior are uncertain and much delayed. Cigarette smoking more often than not produces no immediate illness or disease, and rarely produces delayed illnesses or diseases for which it can be held wholly responsible. The probability of an accident fatal to a drunken driver on a single trip home from a bar is essentially zero. Numerous risky sexual encounters may produce no untoward outcomes for their participants.

Interestingly enough, probabilistic connections between behavior and its consequences, such as these, may be better teachers of reality than deterministic connections, such as those provided by hot stoves and steep stairs. In most cases in real life, penalties are far removed and unlikely. However, the more frequently repeated the behavior, the greater the likelihood of penalty, such that, given a large enough number of occurrences, sanctions become virtually certain. This fact is a major focus of effective education. And indeed, actions with long-term uncertain consequences are more likely to be avoided by educated than by uneducated segments of the public.

Social Sanctions

Social sanctions are penalties provided by others, as when a parent expresses disapproval, a friend withdraws affection, or a stranger expresses outrage. The assumptions of modern social science make these the most serious or severe penalties faced by the individual. The major assumption is that people care for the opinion of others, and are therefore punished when others disapprove of their behavior. Unlike natural sanctions, which are automatic, social sanctions presuppose the presence of others, their awareness of the behavior in question, and their concern for it. The complexities of social sanctions obviously make them less reliable than natural sanctions and subject to greater interpretive difficulties in assessing their utility or value.

Legal Sanctions

Legal sanctions are penalties provided by the state for behavior forbidden by statute. In the contemporary United States, they are largely restricted to fines, probation, and imprisonment, but other systems employ flogging, mutilation, and execution as well. Modern social science is essentially undecided about the efficacy of legal sanctions (Blumstein, Cohen, and Nagin, 1978). The general public, however, strongly approves the use of such penalties. Until very recently, more than 8 in 10 believe that the courts should deal more harshly with criminals (Pastore and Maguire, 2003: Table 2.54).

Supernatural Sanctions

Supernatural sanctions refer to the belief that conduct during one's life is punished and rewarded in the hereafter. Belief in such sanctions is presumably conveyed to children as a means of shaping their behavior. The template established by natural, social, and legal sanctions is sufficiently clear that, in principle, such beliefs could be effective. To the extent they are effective, supernatural sanctions provide one mechanism for the generation of self-control, because the system cannot by definition depend for its success on actual consequences of behavior.

Relations among the Sanction Systems

Sanction systems may be ranked in terms of the distance between behavior and its consequences. Natural sanctions are most immediate and certain. Moral sanctions, which depend on the existence and interest of friends and family, and detection of the act, are less immediate and certain. Legal sanctions, operating at some remove from the act, are notoriously uncertain and much delayed. Supernatural sanctions are of course the most removed from the act in terms of immediacy, and their certainty is a matter of belief.

Given this hierarchy, control theorists assume that natural sanctions govern much behavior most of the time; that social sanctions can be highly influential; and that legal and supernatural sanctions are best left to lawyers and priests.

In our view, all of these systems rely ultimately on the threat of some form of physical pain to those who do not conform to their requirements or expectations. The natural and most effective system in fact operates almost exclusively on physical pain. Corporal punishment thus has logical and temporal priority in the sanctions hierarchy. Summarizing Thomas Hobbes, Michael Oakeshott put it this way: "man is a creature civilized by the fear of death" (Hobbes, 1957 [1651]: xxxvi). In recognizing that the ultimate or basic sanction is execution, Hobbes was not advocating its use, but pointing out that the task of society is to influence behavior in ways consistent with this premise without having to resort to such drastic methods. The danger that follows from ignoring ultimate sanctions is that the miscreant will as a result be more likely to be exposed to them. In the control theory view, small punishments, corporal or otherwise, by teaching moral lessons, function to prevent larger penalties.

Given such assumptions, it is hard to overstate the role of natural sanctions. They are the major shapers of behavior, and provide the conceptual and factual foundation of all other sanction systems. They teach the value of immediacy, certainty, and severity, and thereby define the limits of social, legal, and supernatural systems. Indeed, these secondary systems seek to control behavior that somehow escapes natural sanctions by augmenting or otherwise modifying their consequences. Attempts to enhance the natural system tend to take predictable forms. For example, one device is to educate potential offenders about the true risks of unwanted behavior. In this way, governments and societies use natural sanctions as effective weapons to reduce the levels of risky behaviors. It is easy to show that natural sanctions used in these ways are more effective than legal sanctions. With no change in legal sanctions, tobacco use by adults in the United States declined as a consequence of increased awareness of its effects on health and longevity.[1] At the same time, Draconian increases in legal penalties for use of marijuana, a drug not seen as having dire health consequences, had little effect on the portion of the population willing to use it. By the same token, the large shifts in sexual behavior in modern times are better explained by the appreciated risks of pregnancy and disease than by shifts in moral sanctions. In fact, the extent to which "moral" beliefs in this area have *followed* changes in the actual consequences of sexual behavior is nothing short of phenomenal.

Another device is simply to supplement natural sanctions with secondary sanctions. Thus social and legal systems often add punishments to those naturally connected to risky behavior. For example, burglars run the risk of physical injury or death when they invade a home or business. If they escape such penalties, they may still be ostracized by the community and imprisoned by the state. In this regard, greater use of legal punishments by society is evidence of weakened natural and social sanction systems. Ironically, then, societies, such as the United States, said to be more punitive than others because of their high incarceration rate are, by definition, less punitive than others at the natural or social sanction level. Thus, those who advocate lessened social and natural sanctions may be unwittingly responsible for the growth of the criminal justice system. They may also be unwittingly responsible for the severity of the punishments it imposes. A possible connection between liberty in a society and a heightened level of punitiveness within its justice system has long been noted (see Toqueville's remarks in Garland, 1990: 9). Thus, in free societies a larger portion of the population may be incarcerated for a longer period of time. Criminal sanctions tend to be more certain and severe where social sanctions are neither.

The assumption that the primary effect of sanctions, whatever their form or source, is to reduce the prevalence or frequency of sanctioned behavior, is largely restricted to control theory. Alternative perspectives emphasize the dangers inherent in sanctioning, and prefer some methods of sanctioning to others. Indeed, the standard assumption in the punishment literature is that methods equal in apparent or immediate effectiveness are in all cases to be preferred to physical pain or "verbal aggression." Thus locking a child in a room is better than slapping his or her hands; explaining the reasons for one's disapproval is better than spanking; grounding is better than epithets or bad names; the expression of wounded feelings is better than shaking the child in a vigorous manner; lengthy incarceration is preferable to caning.

In control or rational choice theory, sanctions are judged by their efficacy, by their effectiveness, and cost. Excessive sanctions exact more pain than is required; they are therefore considered cruel or unjust. Alternative perspectives are likely to find something inherently wrong with certain kinds of punishments, whatever their efficacy. Thus physical pain and verbal aggression are not seen as inferior because they are more punishing (they are not more punishing; if they were, they would be more effective) but because they are thought to have *long-term* negative effects, because they "teach the wrong lessons." A variation on this theme is the famous violence begets [teaches] violence thesis, according to which violence must be observed, felt, or learned before it can become part of one's behavioral repertoire.

Indeed, a standard "finding" in the research literature is that offenders are more likely than nonoffenders to have experienced various forms of punishment. A recent review of longitudinal research on childrearing asserts without fear of contradiction that "it is clear that harsh or punitive discipline (involving physical punishment) predicts a child's delinquency. . . . [A] follow-up study of nearly 700 . . . children . . . found that physical punishment at ages 7 and 11 predicted later convictions; 40% of offenders had been smacked or beaten at age 11, compared with 14% of nonoffenders" (Farrington, 2001: 137). Much earlier, Sheldon and Eleanor Glueck had reported that the largest difference between the disciplinary practices of parents of delinquents and those of nondelinquents was in the "extent to which the former resorted to physical punishment" (1950: 133). The Gluecks acknowledged that their delinquents may have "called forth" their own punishment, but they retained the conclusion that their findings said something about the relative effectiveness of disciplinary techniques. A control theorist would guess that the mode of punishment is irrelevant to subsequent behavior, that delinquency comes before physical punishment, and that subsequent delinquency, whatever its form, is explained by the versatility of offenders and the stability of their tendencies to commit delinquent acts. Indeed, recent analysis of the Glueck's data suggests that with appropriate controls for the tendencies of the child, the predictive power of "harsh and erratic" discipline all but disappears (Hardwick, 2002: Table 1.13).

The standard thesis of the punishment literature is thus contrary to control theory. This thesis is easily recognized as a variant of the notion that crime is [must be] learned. It is also a product of the notion that no worthwhile distinction may be made between aggressive reaction to norm violating behavior and aggression aimed at advancing selfish personal interests (for a lengthy discussion of the consequences of the failure to make this distinction, see Gottfredson and Hirschi, 1993).

With this background, we turn to a discussion of the role of corporal punishment in childrearing as seen from a control perspective.

Control Theory and Childrearing

The basic model of childrearing from a control theory perspective is easily described: Proper socialization of children requires that adults monitor their behavior and correct misbehavior when it occurs. Because monitoring and correction are time consuming or expensive, the model presupposes adults who care enough about the child to devote the necessary time and effort to the task. It also of course requires that the adult be able to identify unwanted or deviant behavior.

Affection One: Interest in the Outcome

A major premise of the model outlined is that the parent, caretaker, or guardian must care enough about the child or the child's behavior to devote the immense amounts of time and energy monitoring and discipline require. The source of this care or concern does not seem to be especially important, as long as it is reliable. Thus, the natural affection of parents for their children (based, in the mother's case, on unavoidable prior connections) may be replaced by the financial or contractual interests of nannies and daycare workers.

Interest in the outcome, whatever its source, tends to assure monitoring and discipline. It also severely limits the range of usable or acceptable sanctions. Thus, interested guardians do not allow serious accidents, whatever their teaching potential, and they tend to protect the child from the more severe penalties of the legal system, however much in some sense these penalties might be deserved. Interested guardians will tend to apply the same logic to the sanctions available to them. They will not go beyond the bounds set by their relationship with the child and by their concern for the child's ultimate deportment or behavior. Put another way, cruel or excessive punishment is strictly contrary to the explicit control theory assumption of interest in the child. Corporal punishment is not excluded by this interest, but if used would be expected to be well within the limits set by modern sensibilities.

Affection Two: Attachment to the Caregiver

The theory also assumes that attachment to the caregiver is requisite to successful socialization. The caregiver must be interested in the child; the child must have affection or at least respect for the caregiver. This too puts strict limits on the severity and nature of punishments available to the caretaker. Excessive punishments would destroy the relationship and vitiate their effectiveness. Corporal punishment is apparently in this respect risky. It may sometimes exceed the tolerance level of the child and destroy attachment to its source.

A major source of attachment is assumed to be attention, the time and effort devoted to the child by the caregiver. This "attention" is another word for supervision.

Supervision

Monitoring allows groups to determine whether or not individuals "comply with their obligations," and to sanction them accordingly. It is thus a major element in the relation between group control and individual compliance (Hechter, 1987: 51). Applied to childrearing, the concept takes on a broader meaning, extending beyond misbehavior to concern for the child's happiness, safety, and well-being. When parents give great attention to such matters, they reduce if not obviate the need for explicit punishment. So, the greater the supervision the less punishment is required. In other words, for control theory, neglect is the principal cause of punishment and especially excessive punishment; it is the primary source of violence by the parent and of misbehavior by the child.

The theoretical centrality of neglect (supervision) is supported by research, where it is routinely found to be a major predictor of delinquency (Glueck and Glueck, 1950; McCord, 1979). It is also supported by the actions of the juvenile justice system, where children neglected by their parents or guardians make up a substantial portion of the case load (Widom, 1989).

Supervision takes many forms, and poses many practical difficulties. In contemporary Western societies, daycare workers and school teachers share the supervision of children with parents or guardians, and adolescents can often arrange large blocks of time relatively free of surveillance by interested adults. All of which means that parents are often forced to rely on indirect measures of conformity (e.g., grades, curfew violations), on the reports of other adults, and on the notoriously incomplete self-reports of their own children. For present purposes, a major consequence of the breakdown of direct observation of behavior as the primary mode of supervision is that it has made certain forms of punishment less appropriate or acceptable. Slapping, spanking, and shaking often presuppose instantaneous reaction by an adult fully responsible for the behavior of the child. Any delay between commission of the offensive act and the application of sanctions, and any diminution of adult responsibility for the offender, will thus reduce the likelihood of corporal punishment. This may partially explain why we have less corporal punishment today and why we don't like it as much as we once did.

Discipline

Discussion of a childrearing model that includes care, monitoring, and punishment of misbehavior quickly reveals that these distinctions are analytic, that in reality the three elements are hard to separate from one another. Thus the research literature occasionally reports that "care" of children is an important predictor of delinquency, where care implies supervision and discipline as much as it implies affection (see Kolvin et al., 1988). And the quality of "supervision" is typically gauged as much by the imposition of rules or discipline as by parental awareness of the child's whereabouts or behavior. By the same token, when care and supervision are subtracted from punishment, the techniques that remain may not be particularly important in and of themselves (Rutter, 1985: 385). Thus, in context, it may make little difference whether the parent yells, nags, scolds, shakes, slaps, or cries. The important thing is that these particular techniques virtually presuppose the failure of supervision and put at risk the affectional relation between the parent and the child. Consistent with this expectation, use of such techniques is routinely found to be positively correlated with delinquency (see above).

In an attempt to test the effects of parental monitoring and discipline on delinquency, Larzelere and Patterson carefully built multi-method measures of both constructs. A structural equation model forced them to conclude that the correlation between monitoring and discipline was so large (.60) that these two measures could not have "significant direct paths to delinquency simultaneously" (1990: 312). As important for present purposes, none of their individual measures of monitoring or discipline was significantly correlated with delinquency independent of the effects of the parental management factor produced by combining monitoring and discipline.

The bottom line would appear to be that there is little room in current research for the conclusion that specific disciplinary techniques or forms of punishment have an important effect on subsequent behavior independent of the overall relationship between parent and child (see again Rutter 1985: 357). This suggests that in the causation of delinquency corporal punishment is typically not that important, one way or the other.

The reverse conclusions to be drawn from our analysis deserve to be made explicit. Severe punishment or abuse is predictable from control theory. It is likely to reflect the breakdown or absence of intimate caretaker–child relationships. Caretakers who have no strong interest in the child are much more likely than others to neglect the child and to resort to inappropriate disciplinary techniques. Control theory thus implicates family disintegration in violence, disputing the "normative" interpretation, which sees family violence as a product of training, learning, or modeling. Similarly, control theory explains why family violence seems to run in families. Parents with low self-control have difficulty teaching self-control to their children. As a consequence, children of violent parents tend to be violent themselves.

All of this, it seems to us, should put to rest the idea that control theory advocates corporal punishment, or that it encourages oppressive parental styles and the production of rigid or authoritarian children. It has always been a mistake, in our view, to attempt to judge theories by their basically unexamined or putative policy implications. In this case, dismissal of control theory in favor of alternatives may put at risk the very children the critics wish to save from harm.

Note

1. As governments educate citizens about the health consequences of cigarette smoking, they also tend to increase the price of cigarettes through tax hikes and legal actions against cigarette manufacturers. As a result, it is often not obvious whether reduced consumption is due to increased knowledge or to increased monetary cost. One way to separate and assess these effects might be to note that their strength should vary from one segment of the population to another. Thus, education should work best among the educated, well-to-do portion of the population, those with long-term prospects. Increases in price, in contrast, should work best among those

with little money to spare. Control theory does not deny that unwanted behavior may be reduced by making it more expensive or difficult, and is at the same time leery of the idea of addiction. However, we would point out that in the matter of tobacco, the evidence seems to suggest that awareness of long-term cost, where the long term matters, has more effect than immediate inconvenience, where the long term has more dubious value. This differential effect of current policy or information by economic status would be consistent with evidence suggesting that declines in cigarette use among adults are greater than those among teenagers.

References

Blumstein, Alfred, Jacqueline Cohen, and Daniel Nagin.1978. *Deterrence and Incapacitation: Estimating the Effects of Sanctions on the Crime Rate*. Washington, DC: National Academy Press.

Farrington, David P. 2001. "Families and Crime." Pp. 129–148 in J. Q. Wilson and J. Petersilia (eds.), *Crime*. San Francisco: ICS Press

Garland, David. 1990. *Punishment and Modern Society*. Chicago: University of Chicago Press.

Glueck, Sheldon, and Eleanor Glueck. 1950. *Unraveling Juvenile Delinquency*. Cambridge, MA: Harvard University Press.

Gottfredson, Michael R., and Travis Hirschi. 1993. "A Control Theory Interpretation of Psychological Research on Aggression." Pp. 47–68 in R. B. Felson and J. T. Tedeschi (eds.), *Aggression and Violence*. Washington, DC: American Psychological Association.

Hardwick, Kelly H. "Unraveling 'Crime in the Making': Re-examining the Role of Informal Social Control in the Genesis and Stability of Delinquency and Crime." Ph.D. dissertation, University of Calgary, 2002.

Hechter, Michael. 1987. *Principles of Group Solidarity*. Berkeley: University of California Press.

Hobbes, Thomas. 1957 [1651]. *Leviathan*. Oxford: Basil Blackwell.

Kolvin, I., F. J. W. Miller, M. Fleeting, and P. A. Kolvin. 1988. "Social and Parenting Factors Affecting Criminal-offence Rates: Findings from the Newcastle Thousand Family Study (1947–1980)." *British Journal of Psychiatry* 152: 80–90. Reprinted in *Psychological Explanations of Crime*, ed. D. P. Farrington, (pp. 269–279). Aldershot, Eng.: Dartmouth, 1994.

Larzelere, Robert E., and Gerald R. Patterson. 1990. "Parental Management: Mediator of the Effect of Socioeconomic Status on Early Delinquency." *Criminology* 28: 301–323.

McCord, Joan. 1979. "Some Child-Rearing Antecedents of Criminal Behavior in Adult Men." *Journal of Personality and Social Psychology* 37:1477–1486.

Pastore, Ann L. and Kathleen Maguire, eds. *Sourcebook of Criminal Justice Statistics* [Online]. Available: http://www.albany.edu/sourcebook/ [Accessed April, 2003].

Rutter, Michael. 1985. "Family and School Influences on Behavioural Development." *Journal of Child Psychology and Psychiatry* 26: 349–368. Reprinted in *Psychological Explanations of Crime*, ed. D. P. Farrington, (377–396). Aldershot, UK: Dartmouth, 1994.

Widom, Cathy S. 1989. The Cycle of Violence. *Science*, 244, 160–166.

9

Self-Control, Group Solidarity, and Crime: An Integrated Control Theory

Chester L. Britt

One of the issues that control theories of crime have had the greatest difficulty addressing is the effect of group processes. Regardless of the version of control theory, individual characteristics are assumed to be the most important causes of crime. By emphasizing individual characteristics that make the commission of crime more or less likely, such as self-control (Gottfredson and Hirschi, 1990) and the social bond (Hirschi, 2002), control theories have neglected the possibility that groups may in fact affect the behavior of individuals affiliated with those groups. Prior criminological theorizing on the effects of groups has generally taken one of two general approaches to explaining how groups affect criminal behavior. Neither approach turns out to be fully satisfactory. Control theories, for example, have tended to downplay the possibility that groups have any unique effect on individuals. Rather, what accounts for the apparent effect of groups is really the "birds of a feather" phenomenon—people spend time with those whom they are most similar (see, e.g., McPherson et al., 2001). When evidence indicates that there may be independent effects of groups on individual behavior beyond the characteristics of those individuals, the results are taken as evidence that control theories are wrong, since control theories do not make specific predictions about groups and are unable to account for group effects. Alternatively, social learning and cultural deviance theories of crime provide the group with such an important role in the cause of crime that individual characteristics are nearly irrelevant, since crime is solely a reflection of group processes. Thus, when evidence indicates that individual characteristics do affect crime, these theories are assumed to be wrong, since there is often no clear way to incorporate individual factors logically into the explanation without compromising the internal consistency of the theory (Costello, 1997; Kornhauser, 1978).

The focus of this chapter is the development of a control theory that incorporates both individual and group characteristics, yet remains consistent with classical perspectives on the causes of crime. Construction of this theory relies on classical criminology as well as developments in rational choice sociology and game theory that have focused on issues of individual and collective action. Fundamentally, the question for researchers studying collective action is very similar to the one motivating explanations of crime: In light of individual preferences to behave selfishly, how can a group influence that person's behavior to achieve some other goal?

Preliminaries

Defining Crime

Prior to offering an explanation of crime, it is useful to define what is meant by crime so that we are clear on what it is that is being explained. To begin, and consistent with the classical tradition, criminal acts are viewed as simply another type of behavior. What distinguishes crimes from other behaviors is that crimes are acts that involve the use of force and/or fraud (Gottfredson and Hirschi, 1990). The use of such a general definition of crime opens up the possibility for the theory to explain a wide range of behaviors, including such behaviors as cheating on an assignment at school, having an extramarital affair, taking another person's property, and physically attacking another person. Although some of these acts may be defined as crimes by the state, there is no requirement by the theory that commission of the act result in the possibility of a state-imposed sanction.

One of the apparent limitations to much of the theorizing on crime in the last century has been its focus on state-defined crime. There are numerous acts that mirror state-defined crimes, but have no laws prohibiting their commission—what Gottfredson and Hirschi (1990) refer to as analogous acts. Should a theory be restricted only to those acts proscribed by the state? If so, then what happens if the state changes its definition of the act as a crime? If the state no longer defines an act as a crime, does the theory no longer explain the behavior? More importantly, however, the consequence of limiting a theory to those acts prohibited by the state may unnecessarily limit the domain of a theory of crime.

Assumptions

It is necessary for any theory of individual action to make assumptions about the individuals it purports to explain. Without assumptions about what is being explained, the theorist may conveniently alter key parts of an explanation to account for a new research finding that might be used to cast doubt on the validity of the theory.[1] Similar to many other theories of individual action, I begin by assuming that human behavior is purposive (Axelrod, 1984; Coleman, 1990). All that this assumption means is that when an individual engages in any type of behavior, there is a goal in mind—a reason for the behavior—and the individual expects to benefit from the action in some way. An alternative way of thinking about individual action as purposive is that individual actors are assumed to be self-interested.

In economic theory, this assumption is typically stated in such a way that a rational, calculating individual is expected to act in a way that maximizes her or his utility (e.g., von Neuman and Morgenstern, 1953; Tsebelis, 1990). By maximizing utility, individuals are expected to consider the costs and benefits, the pleasures and pains, or more generally, the incentives and disincentives associated with acting in a given way. After considering the consequences of different actions, individuals are expected to act in ways that provide them with the greatest benefit or pleasure. How individuals move from a consideration of the incentives and the disincentives is through some kind of mental exercise that leads the individual to the point where the consequences of different actions are clear. To be sure, not all individual actions have a clear goal in mind. The behavior may ultimately even be harmful to the individual actor. Sometimes these actions are a result of the person acting on incomplete information or personal biases that affect individuals' ability to make a fully rational or self-interested choice (see, e.g., Kahneman and Tversky, 1979). Alternatively, actions may sometimes be a consequence of psychological states of individuals that impede the ability to make rational choices.

One of the common criticisms of rational choice theories of behavior has been the argument that people do not meet the requirements of rationality in making decisions, especially in regard to making decisions about committing crimes. People may vary in a variety of different ways that cast doubt on the idea that individuals give much, if any, thought to the consequences of their actions. For example, people vary in their ability to gather and process information, in their ability to consider the long-term consequences of an action, and in their ability to place the needs of others ahead of their own. In all cases, what is called into question is the idea of a rational, thoughtful, and self-interested person making choices about individual actions.

Much of the rational choice literature focused on behaviors other than criminal has dealt with variability in the ability of people to consider the consequences of their actions in a number of ways. For example, to address concerns about the ability of individuals to gather information and make perfectly rational decisions, attention has been paid to issues of bounded rationality (Simon, 1955), decision-making under uncertainty (see, e.g., Tversky and Kahneman, 1986), and a trial-and-error adaptive approach (Axelrod, 1984, 1997). Although the specific explanation for each approach differs, they focus on the issue of how individual behavioral decisions are made in such a way that the individual expects to avoid pain and to benefit in some way from the behavior.

Similarly, concerns about the time horizon of an individual reflects on whether people fully consider the long-term consequences of their criminal and non-criminal actions. To the extent that individuals do not consider the long-term consequences of an act, can the behavior be the result of rational self-interest? Some rational choice decision-making models have incorporated a time discounting parameter, but it is not common (see, e.g., Heckathorn, 1990). Although strictly economic models of behavioral choice may have difficulty incorporating a time horizon of the individual, game theoretic models of behavior find nothing inherently problematic with short-term, self-interested behavior (Axelrod, 1984). Rather, the question of how to elicit long-term cooperation from individuals who have selfish short-term interests is the focal point for much of this work.

More recent developments in game theoretic models focusing on individual and collective action have found that an individual's ability to place the interests and needs of others ahead of their own complicate the traditional assumptions of the self-interested individual. An attempt at addressing individual variability in game theoretic models has involved trying to account for individual characteristics. One such approach distinguishes "egoists" from "altruists" (see, for example, Heckathorn, 1991). Egoists represent the more traditional notion of a rational self-interested actor, while altruists represent individuals who may put the interests and concerns of other ahead of their own self-interests. Other research suggests the possibility that individual variability in such characteristics as generosity and contrition would also affect the nature of social interaction (Axelrod, 1997).

Ultimately, the assumption of a self-interested individual does not require the individual to be able to make a fully rational calculation (Tsebelis, 1990). Extensive research has shown that individuals rarely have complete information relevant to their decisions, would have difficulty processing complete information if it was available, and may rely on personal biases or experiences in making decisions (Kahneman and Tversky, 1979). The notion of self-interest used in this chapter is analogous to Axelrod's (1986) trial-and-error adaptation, where individuals are expected to learn through repeated social exchanges which actions and behavioral strategies will be most and least effective at avoiding sanctions.

Specifying the Goals: Human Desires and Needs

If criminal behavior is indistinguishable from other forms of behavior, then we are not required to explain any special motivation to commit crimes (cf. Akers, 1985, 1998). Instead, we are faced with the question of why individuals would choose criminal action over some other type of action. Like any other behavior, crimes are meant "to satisfy universal human desires" (Gottfredson and Hirschi, 1990: 10). The difficulty for control theories of crime has been to specify these desires and explain how it is that they affect the likelihood of committing (i.e., choosing) criminal acts. Put differently, control theories of crime begin with an assumption of individual self-interest and purposive action aimed as satisfying some goal. Left implicit in most control theories is the goal or desire that is to be satisfied. Roshier's (1989) attempt to specify a control theory of crime suggested several needs—what he views as "sources of control"—that individuals want to satisfy with *any* behavior. In this view, crime is seen as only one possible course of action. Whether crime is chosen depends on whether the individual perceives the action to be in her or his self-interest.

Roshier suggests seven different needs that may be satisfied by individual action: affection, status, stimulation, autonomy, security, money, and belief. He does not claim this list to be exhaustive or for any of the needs to be more important than any other need. Rather, the needs are present to varying degrees for all individuals at any given moment. Choices about behavior are expected to be aimed at satisfying one or more of the needs. In short, the sources of control described by Roshier represent the needs or the goals expected in a rational choice theory of individual action. It is also important to note that the different needs may conflict with each other; that in order to satisfy one need, an individual may have to postpone or ignore another need. Nearly a century ago, Thomas (1923) described a similar set of needs in his description of the "four wishes": the desires for new experiences, security, response (affection), and recognition (status). Similar to Roshier's discussion, Thomas noted how these human desires could also be used as a way to achieve social control. Specifically, that regulation of the sources satisfying these desires could, theoretically, be used to modify the behavioral choices of individuals.

Affection is a basic human need and refers to the emotional bond between persons. Similar to Hirschi's (2002) notion of attachment, affection is the tie between two or more persons that provides some kind of emotional satisfaction. Thus, affection within a family unit, say, from a parent, sibling, child, or spouse, becomes an important goal for individuals to satisfy. People have a desire to please those persons they most care about. At the same time, they fear losing the affection of others if they act in some way that may be harmful to those we care about most. There is also the need for affection from one's peers, regardless of age. While youth may be most concerned about affection from their closest friends, adults will also have a group of peers—some social acquaintances, some close personal friends, others who are peers in a work or professional context—that are important and meaningful to the individual. The potential loss of affection from those the individual cares about will simultaneously operate as a source of control over behavioral choices and as a goal or need to be satisfied. Framed within the rational choice perspective, the primary expectation is that individuals will act in ways that will gain the affection from those persons who are most important to them.

The quest for status is another universal human desire that may take many different forms. By status, I refer to the positioning of people relative to others. The basis for the positioning may be economic, social, or any other dimension on which humans have managed to rank each other. It does not matter whether the ranking or positioning is real or perceived. Some individuals may seek status within a small group, such as among other family members or friends, while others may seek status in larger groups, such as a neighborhood or a professional community (Frank, 1985). Roshier (1989) notes that status is similar to affection in the sense that most people are generally sensitive to what others think of them. However, status is much less intimate than affection and many people may not be particularly concerned with whether those persons who have less status show a great deal of affection. Again, the expectation is that most people will act in ways that improve their status relative to others (Frank, 1985).

That humans have a need for physical and emotional stimulation would seem to be apparent by the many and varied ways societies have constructed ways for individuals to experience some kind of excitement, danger, or challenge. It may also be possible for individuals to experience some form of emotional or physical stimulation vicariously, such as attending a sporting event or a concert. Across individuals, the threshold for excitement and stimulation may be quite variable. Some individuals will be satisfied by simply watching, while some individuals will not experience or feel anything unless they are actively engaged in some activity. Roshier notes that the many forms of punishment—both formal and informal—involve confinement, and have as their primary purpose the removal of any possible form of excitement: being sent to one's room as a child, kept inside a school during a "recess" or break, or incarceration (1989: 81–82).

Autonomy refers to the desire to be independent, to express oneself, and to have a sense that one is in control of the world around them. Recent publications on leadership and management, for example, have emphasized the importance of generating a sense of autonomy among employees (see, e.g., Lucas, 1994). Over time, those employees who are given more autonomy appear to be the most creative and productive because of the increased opportunities to satisfy the need for self-expression. Roshier (1989) points out, however, that the need for autonomy is not absolute and will vary across a given population, as indicated by the number of persons voluntarily serving in the military and various religious orders, where they have forfeited their autonomy and opportunities for self-expression.

The threat of physical harm, injury, or physical discomfort reflects concerns about the need for security. In contrast to the need for emotional and physical stimulation, security reflects a desire not to experience unpleasant events (Roshier, 1989: 82). Although most people can tolerate brief periods of physical discomfort or the threat of harm, it is not a situation that most people will want to experience, even for a relatively brief period of time. Rather, individuals tend to act in ways that offer protection from other people and physical surroundings that are perceived as dangerous or threatening.

The desire for money is distinct from a need for status. Status refers to the relative positioning of individuals on some dimension that may be only loosely related to money or other financial resources. For example, status within trade unions is typically based on the amount of time served within the organization. There is a basic need in virtually every society for some amount of money simply to subsist. Beyond subsistence, money opens up possibilities to fulfill other needs and create opportunities for other types of behavior. Roshier (1989) is quick to note, however, that all humans do not aspire to money to the same degree. In the same way that variation can be found in the other needs, there is also individual variability in the desire for money.

Our belief in conformity is viewed by Roshier as another need as well as a source of control on our behavior. To the extent that individuals can see the long-term benefits to an action, they will be more inclined to conform—not commit crimes—than in those cases where the long-term benefits of conformity are less clear. Our belief in conformity, or the validity of the law (Hirschi, 2002), does have important effects on the commission of criminal acts. It is not clear, however, that belief is a "need" in the same sense that the preceding six are human needs that affect behavioral choices. Given the ambiguity surrounding belief as a need, the following discussion will focus primarily on the first six needs discussed above.

In general, each of these needs, or goals, provides a way of describing what is often meant by self-interest. Put differently, these needs provide a context for understanding what the individual expects to gain or to lose as a result of any given behavioral choice. Although each of the needs provides a way for understanding individual choices, there is no clear hierarchy of importance of each of the needs. As noted above, satisfaction of one need may exclude satisfaction of another need. What remains, however, is the expectation that these needs are met in some fashion with different behaviors. Importantly, then, the relationship of each need to individual action does not require a distinct explanation for criminal behavior. Rather, crimes are simply acts involving the use of force or fraud that satisfy one or more of these needs at a given moment in time.

These goals also provide, in some sense, the motivation for behavior, whether criminal or non-criminal. All humans have needs, but the level of the different needs is as variable as the individual—some people will be more concerned about affection from others, some more concerned about status, others more concerned about autonomy, security, stimulation, or money. The key is that people are motivated to act in their self-interest to satisfy one or more of these needs. If we take the attractiveness of crime as a given—that most people will be able to discern the apparent and immediate benefits of a crime—then what is it that prevents people who are assumed to have selfish short-term interests from committing crime? The discussion now turns to both individual and group factors that may affect the behavioral choices people make, resulting in behavior that may not be clearly self-interested.

Self-control, Crime, and Rational Choice

Gottfredson and Hirschi's (1990) control theory of crime begins by noting the high degree of similarity across criminal offenders and criminal acts. In their view, crimes are events that are likely aimed at some short-term gain or pleasure, involving little planning, and occur spontaneously (Gottfredson and Hirschi, 1990, chapter 2). Offenders are expected to exhibit characteristics consistent with the nature of criminal acts—what they call low self-control. A key mechanism in their theory is the idea that the greater the individual's self-control, the less likely that person is to be attracted to short-term gains relative to long-term gains. This implies that people with greater self-control will be less likely to commit crimes, since these acts are aimed at primarily short-term benefits for the offender.

How does Gottfredson and Hirschi's control theory conform to a rational choice perspective on criminal behavior? Gottfredson and Hirschi claim, consistent with classical theories of crime, that individuals act in their own self-interest. What distinguishes individual actions is then the person's level of self-control. Those with lower levels of self-control will consider the short-term gains of some action rather than the long-term consequences. Based on the perceived short-term gains, the individual is expected to act accordingly. Gottfredson and Hirschi's claim applies equally well to criminal and non-criminal behavior—a self-interested individual with low self-control will act in ways consistent with considering short-term benefits, but be less inclined to defer benefits that may be more long-term in coming as well as the long-term negative consequences associated with some behavioral choice. Their focus on self-control as a factor that conditions the perceived benefits from individual action is analogous to the individual in game theoretic models of behavioral choice. Recall that individuals are expected to behave selfishly in the short-term, and the question becomes one of how to gain the cooperation of the individual in the long-term.

Linking Self-control with Human Needs

How is self-control related to the human needs of affection, status, stimulation, autonomy, security, and money? Since criminal behavior does not require a special explanation relative to other kinds of behavior—all individual action is aimed at satisfying a goal or a need—self-control may help to distinguish why behavioral choices vary across different circumstances. To the extent that individuals with lower levels of self-control consider only the short-term benefits and consequences of actions, then behaviors will be oriented toward achieving more immediate affection, status, stimulation, autonomy, security, and/or money. Note that this does not imply any particular behavioral choice. We cannot use the needs to predict criminal or non-criminal behavior. Consistent with the idea that these needs motivate all behavior, we can only expect behaviors to satisfy these needs. At the same time, a focus on low self-control implies that there may immediate benefits to some behavioral choice, but potentially severe long-term negative consequences that are not considered.

Although Roshier (1989) claimed that the needs could not be ranked in any way, self-control does imply a rank ordering of the different needs. According to Gottfredson and Hisrchi (1990), there are six identifiable elements of self-control: impulsivity, insensitivity, physicality, risk-taking, short-sightedness, and non-verbal (1990: 90). Individuals with lower levels of self-control tend to be more impulsive, insensitive, physical, risk-oriented, short-sighted, and non-verbal. Consequently, we might expect low self-control individuals to rank stimulation relatively more important than the other needs, especially affection and security, because of the tendency to be more likely to take risks, to be more physical, and less sensitive to others. In contrast, individuals with greater levels of self-control might be expected to rank affection and security relatively higher, but autonomy and stimulation relatively lower.

Group Solidarity, Sanctions, and Crime

The history of much of the sociological theorizing on crime attributes the causes to group process or socialization effects (e.g., Akers, 1985, 1998; Matsueda, 1982). Although group process may indeed be important for a more complete understanding of crime, this tradition has largely failed to consider two important issues. First, characteristics of individuals, such as self-control, are generally assumed to be unimportant, with any individual variation being attributed to some unidentified social structural factor. Or, alternatively, individual characteristics are incorporated into the theory on an ad hoc basis, raising concerns about the internal consistency of the theory. Second, all groups are not equal in their effects on individual members, which is due in part to the characteristics of the individuals comprising the group, and also due in part to the characteristics of the group. In other words, all groups are not the same, and consequently do not have the same kinds of effects on group members, yet the typical analysis of peer or group effects assumes this is the case (see, e.g., Warr, 1993, 2002). Some groups will be closely knit, and able to influence the behavior of any individual member, but other groups will be much more porous, where the contact among members is more sporadic and limited, meaning that the group will have relatively little influence on any single person's behavior.

Recent rational choice explanations of individual behavioral choices—whether conforming and non-conforming—offer an attempt to link individual characteristics, such as self-interest and self-control, with the effects of groups that individuals are involved and identify with (see, e.g., Clarke and Cornish, 1985; Coleman, 1988, 1990; Hechter, 1987; Heckathorn, 1990, 1991; Jankowski, 1991; Tsebelis, 1990). The utility of these different approaches to understanding individual action in a group context comes in the form of the mechanisms through which groups may (or may not) influence individual behavioral choices.

Hechter's (1987) work, for example, attempts to explain individual behavior as a choice process that is conditioned on group membership and the solidarity of the group. He says that a group is "solidary"

> to the degree that its members comply with corporate rules in the absence of compensation (that is, some tangible payment for value received or service rendered, but not mere psychic gratification). (1987: 39)

The solidarity of a family, for example, would refer to the extent that each family member abided by the family's rules and desires. If each family member contributed to the overall benefit of the family unit, then the family would be described as having a higher degree of solidarity. Conversely, if each member were involved in their own pursuits, with little consideration for how their actions affected remaining family members, then the family would be described as having a lower level of solidarity.

The same logic can be applied to peer groups. Peer groups that have greater levels of solidarity should be able to achieve a higher level of overall cooperation from all the group's members. Groups with lower levels of solidarity would not be able to get members to act to benefit the group, and would likely break up after a brief existence. Jankowski's (1991) study of gangs in Boston, Los Angeles, and New York provides evidence consistent with this expectation. His ethnographic research found that gangs with low levels of solidarity—those unable to achieve a high degree of commitment and cooperation from individual members were more likely to break apart after a relatively short time. Other classic studies of gang behavior have reached similar conclusions about the characteristics of individuals who participate in gangs (e.g., Klein, 1971; Short and Strodtbeck, 1965; Suttles, 1968).

The factors that influence the degree of solidarity within a group are, according to Hechter, *dependence* and *control capacity*. Those groups that are able to foster high levels of dependence on the group among its members will likely have higher degrees of solidarity. To the extent that each group member will not be able to have certain needs met outside the group, each member must maintain group involvement to satisfy their needs. Dependence cannot occur in isolation, however, and some level of control—monitoring—is necessary in order for the group initially to develop a certain level of dependence among its members (Axelrod, 1986). In short, both conditions are necessary to produce solidarity within a group. Without dependence, regardless of the level of control exerted by the group, the level of solidarity will be low, since the group will be unable to fulfill any need that the individual may have. Similarly, without any control over individuals, dependence will not, by itself, produce solidarity, since it will be possible for individual members to have their needs met elsewhere. Those groups with the greatest likelihood of long-term survival (i.e., those with higher levels of solidarity) must continue to meet the needs of their members, but at the same time, they must control their members' activities so they are unable to satisfy these needs elsewhere.[2]

The effectiveness of group solidarity in influencing individual behavior is related to the use of individual and collective sanctions (Axelrod, 1986; Cohen et al., 2001; Heckathorn, 1990). Individual sanctions involve some negative consequence for only the individual who has acted in a way contrary to the group's expectations, while collective sanctions involve some negative consequence for the entire group as a consequence of the individual's behavior. Heckathorn (1990) argued that there is a complex set of relationships among individual behavior, group solidarity, and sanctions (individual or collective). Not surprisingly, individuals are expected to be concerned primarily with individual sanctions—punishments that they alone will experience. Individual sanctions are also likely to cause greater discomfort to the person experiencing the sanction. To the degree that there is a high level of group solidarity, each individual member of the group should be sensitive to collective sanctions, and will try to act in ways that do not result in sanctions for the other members of the group (Axelrod, 1986). In part, Heckathorn (1990) shows that some of the apparent success of individual sanctions is really a function of concern on the individual's behalf for collective sanctions; they do not want other members of close groups, such as family members or friends, to suffer as a consequence of their own behavioral choices. Further, the possibility that other group members may further sanction the individual who elicited the collective sanction on the group is also expected to have some bearing on the individual's behavioral choices (Axelrod, 1986; Coleman, 1990).

The family and the peer group provide two interesting contexts in which to look at the effects of solidarity, since both groups are composed of only corporate obligations—that family members are not, for example, financially compensated for holding the position of father or daughter. The key to family solidarity is to make each member of the family dependent on goods that only the family can provide. These goods would likely include such things as love and affection. But, at the same time, the family needs to be able to restrict each family member's ability to obtain these goods elsewhere, such as, in a peer group or other organization. Similarly, peer groups would need to provide such goods as companionship, fun, and excitement, and to monitor members so they could not obtain these goods anywhere else. To the extent that groups are unable to provide goods to meet individual needs, the individual will be free to look elsewhere to have these needs met.

It is important to note that group solidarity is not simply a function of the number of ties within a group or the density of those ties (Haynie, 2001; Krohn, 1986). There is nothing in the theory that precludes finding individuals with a large number of ties to other individuals within a group, indicating a high level of network density, but the group may in fact have low solidarity. The number or density of ties does not imply that those ties are meaningful to the individual so connected. Similarly, measuring the level of affection individuals have for other members in the group—whether family, peer, work, or other—does not provide us with a measure of the solidarity of the group. Although a measure of affection for others in the group may provide us with an indirect measure of the level of dependence, it says little about monitoring within the group.

How can Gottfredson and Hirschi's (1990) view of self-control and crime be integrated with a theory of group solidarity and behavioral choices? If we consider Hechter's (1987) theory of group solidarity and individual behavioral outcomes, it would be difficult for any group to foster a significant level of dependence on the group for the person with low self-control. The reason being, the individual's level of self-control would affect the ability of that person to consider their long-term commitment to the group. Without a long-term commitment to a group (or at least the possibility of a long-term commitment), the individual is less likely to invest any resources in the group and the impact of the group on the individual will be limited, since the person will likely see other alternatives as equally attractive and perhaps more immediately accessible.

The relationship between group solidarity and delinquency is complex, as it depends on both the group (e.g., the family or the peer group) and the individual. First, we might expect, based on the preceding discussion, that families with high levels of solidarity will have family members—both children and parents—who are less likely to be involved in illicit activities. The basis for this expectation is that a person willing to commit to the family's rules and goals has a higher degree of self-control, and therefore, an expected lower likelihood of crime. Additionally, if the person is willing to commit to the group's goals, then it gives the group the option of further socializing and sanctioning the individual (Axelrod, 1986). Although Heckathorn (1990) has argued that under certain circumstances a high degree of family solidarity may foster criminal behavior, these circumstances may be so unique that for most of the population, most of the time, increased family solidarity should lead to lower rates of crime among the family's members.

A similar argument can be made in regard to peer group solidarity. Peer groups with greater solidarity would, again, likely be composed of individuals with greater levels of self-control. To the extent that individuals had low levels of self-control, they should be less likely to want to invest the amount of time and effort needed to maintain a peer group. In turn, peer groups with low levels of solidarity would be unlikely to influence the behavior of the individuals connected to the group. In contrast, peer groups with higher levels of solidarity should be composed of individuals with higher levels of self-control. In such a case, the peer group would then have the ability to influence the behavior of each individual in the group through the joint processes of dependence and control capacity.

The relationship between group solidarity and crime has parallels to Hirschi's (2002) social control theory linking the social bond to criminal behavior. The strength of the social bond—indicated by the level of attachment to others, commitment to conventional goals, involvement in conventional activities, and belief in conformity—directly affects the likelihood of crime. The weaker the individual's social bond, the greater the chances the individual commits a crime. What this reflects is the idea that the social bond restricts individuals from acting in their own self-interest by highlighting the potential social and emotional costs associated with the commission of criminal acts.

Coleman's (1990) discussion of social capital and the apparent constraints that it places on behavioral choices provides a more recent theoretical treatment on the effect of group ties. Coleman claims that social capital refers to the sets of social relationships that connect individuals to each other and has several different forms in which it may manifest itself: obligations and expectations between individuals, information passing from one person to another, norm creation and sanction potential, authority relations, voluntary social organization, and intentional social organizations (1990: 306–313). Social capital—social relationships—become important in the understanding of individual actions, because these relationships highlight the fact that individuals do not live in isolation and act wholly on their own self-interest. Rather, the needs of individuals are often a function of social interaction, say with other family members or coworkers. Clearly, there are variations in the number, type, and strength of ties that individuals have to other persons. This reflects variation in social capital. The importance of social capital is that it constrains people from acting only in their own self-interest and forces each to recognize, at some level, the consequences of their actions for others. Sampson and Laub's (1993) age-graded control theory of crime has incorporated elements of both Coleman's (1990) description of social capital and

Hirschi's (2002) description of the social bond, and links variation in social capital to variations in crime across the life course.

Common to all control theories of crime is the idea that society can place constraints on the behavioral choices of self-interested individuals through meaningful social ties. Individuals with lower levels of self-control are expected to have weaker ties to others, which should result in a greater likelihood of short-term, self-interested behavior, and consequently a greater risk of committing crimes.

An Example: Adolescent Peer Groups

How would the theory described above begin to explain the differences in rates of crime across adolescent peer groups? If we assume that all youths have needs, then peer groups may be able to satisfy any of the six needs described above. For example, a group of friends can provide an individual with affection and emotional support through regular interaction with each other. A peer group may also provide each youth with status at school based on knowledge of how each youth or each youth's peer group is positioned relative to other students or groups on campus. Similarly, a peer group may create opportunities for participating in a variety of fun, exciting, stimulating, and potentially risky activities.

The level of peer group solidarity is a consequence of the level of dependence each individual has on the peer group as well as the group's ability to control or monitor each member's behavior and ability to fulfill needs elsewhere. The degree to which dependence and control capacity are present will reflect on the overall level of solidarity in the group. Where does peer group solidarity come from? If we start with peer group formation, then our focus would be on the process a peer group uses to establish who is in the group and who is out of the group in order to foster dependence on the group. Initial forms of control might simply involve verbal exchanges that draw boundaries between the group and others or that try to build dependence on the group. The process of establishing or increasing the level of group solidarity is dependent on each individual's level of self-control. A person with low self-control, as explained above, will be less likely to become dependent on the group, since there is less concern with satisfying needs with any particular group. Moreover, since the person low on self-control is less likely to be dependent on a group, several other immediate possibilities (i.e., other groups) may be viewed as more fun, exciting, or risky. Alternatively, a person with a greater level of self-control is expected to be attracted to more meaningful friendships or relationships and to be less attracted to the risky behaviors that some groups facilitate.

Given that some initial level of dependence has been created, the group must monitor its members to ensure that their needs are not being met elsewhere. How would this be done? Perhaps through spending time with each other after school just talking or visiting with each other, talking on the phone at those times when they cannot be physically present with each other, or through some other kind of group activity, such as, hanging out at the local shopping mall, a pick-up basketball game, or skateboarding. Again, the self-control of individuals may make this monitoring more or less difficult. The lower the individual's level of self-control, the less likely the person is to consider the long-term consequences of actions that may be at odds with the group's wishes and to be more attracted to other short-term activities with other groups that may be more stimulating than those with the current group.

This all points to the possibility that peer groups with greater dependence and greater control capacity will have higher solidarity. Then, the expectation is that individuals who actively participate in groups with higher solidarity will be less likely to commit crimes. Groups with lower levels of solidarity should increase the chances of criminal behavior among the individuals associated with the group, since the weaker group solidarity frees individuals to act in their own short-term self-interest. In other words, groups with low solidarity will be less effective at constraining the behavior of individuals, who in turn will be less likely to consider (or even care) about the sanctions the group may impose. At work through all of this is the individual's level of self-control, meaning that we are unlikely to find high solidarity peer groups made up of individuals with low self-control. Instead, peer groups with low solidarity will likely be composed of individuals with low self-control and evidence of higher rates of criminal behavior.

The effects of group solidarity and self-control are ongoing. In any group, the processes of dependence and control capacity will interact with each individual's level of self-control to influence future behavioral choices. The more integrated the individual becomes within a group over time, the more sensitive the individual will become to the group's expectations and act accordingly, or risk being sanctioned. Since groups with higher levels of solidarity are expected to be composed of individuals with higher levels of self-control, then as a person becomes more dependent on the group, the more conforming their behavior is expected to become. Groups with lower levels of solidarity would likely have little impact on an individual's behavioral choices, since the sanctions imposed by the group will likely carry little meaning for the individual.

It may also be possible to use the approach described here as a way to understand how group processes may apply to differences in levels of crime committed by males and females (see Costello and Mederer, this volume). At first glance, several possible hypotheses regarding the effects of peers may warrant further attention. For example, does the solidarity of a peer group vary for young males and young females? Does the solidarity of a peer group vary by the gender composition of the group? For example, how does group solidarity vary across exclusively male or female peer groups? Does group solidarity vary across mixed gender peer groups? Does the ability to foster dependence among young males and females vary across peer group? How is this related to the gender composition of the peer group? Similarly, does the control capacity of peer groups vary by gender? According to the theory described above, since males commit crimes at rates higher than females, we should anticipate that there will be differences in the dynamics of peer groups that correspond to variations in group solidarity, which in turn should be related to issues of dependence and control capacity.

Conclusion

In the introduction to the Transaction edition of *Causes of Delinquency*, Travis Hirschi notes that since the original publication of *Causes* in 1969, there have been many attempts to test the theory he described in that work. Some of the results of this work have been supportive of Hirschi's theory, some of the results have not. Yet, he notes

> what is surprising is not how many researchers have tested the particular theory found in *Causes of Delinquency*, but how few have advanced alternative versions within the control theory framework. (2002: xviii)

It is in the spirit of trying to advance an alternative, but complementary, version of control theory that this chapter was written. Much that is included in Hirschi's original statement of social control theory has informed the discussion in this chapter, as has the more recent version of control theory proposed in Gottfredson and Hirschi's (1990) *A General Theory of Crime*. The theory described in this chapter linking self-control with group solidarity represents an attempt to broaden the scope of control theory in such a way that it recognizes the importance of group process without abandoning classical assumptions about human behavior and individual decision making. Whether the effort is ultimately successful will depend on the results of future analysis.

Notes

1. Costello (1997), for example, has noted that the more recent statements of cultural deviance theory have so altered the theory that it now appears to be more of a modified version of control theory, rather than a subcultural explanation of crime.
2. Gould's (1995) analysis of the Paris Commune in nineteenth-century Paris applied notions of group solidarity, emphasizing dependence and control capacity, as a way to explain collective violence. Similarly, Hechter (2001) explains how group solidarity can be used to explain nationalism and ethnic violence cross-nationally.

References

Akers, Ronald L. 1985. *Deviant Behavior: A Social Learning Approach*, Third Edition. Belmont, CA: Wadsworth.

———. 1998. *Social Learning and Social Structure: A General Theory of Crime and Deviance*. Boston: Northeastern University Press.

Axelrod, Robert. 1984. *The Evolution of Cooperation*. New York: Basic Books.

———. 1986. "An Evolutionary Approach to Norms." *American Political Science Review* 80:1095–1111.

———. 1997. *The Complexity of Cooperation: Agent-Based Models of Competition and Collaboration*. Princeton, NJ: Princeton University Press.

Clarke, Ronald V., and Derek B. Cornish. 1985. "Modeling Offenders' Decisions: A Framework for Research and Policy." In M. Tonry and N. Morris (eds.), *Crime and Justice: An Annual Review of Research*, Vol. 6. Chicago: University of Chicago Press.

Cohen, Michael D. Rick L. Riolo, and Robert Axelrod. 2001. "The Role of Social Structure in the Maintenance of Cooperative Regimes." *Rationality and Society* 13: 5–32.

Coleman, James S. 1988. "Social Capital in the Creation of Human Capital." *American Journal of Sociology* 94: S95–S120.

———. 1990. *Foundations of Social Theory*. Cambridge, MA: The Belknap Press.

Costello, Barbara J. 1997. "On the Logical Adequacy of Cultural Deviance Theories." *Theoretical Criminology* 1: 403–428.

Costello, Barbara J., and Helen J. Mederer. 2003. "A Control Theory of Gender Differences in Crime and Delinquency." In C. Britt and M. Gottfredson (eds.), *Control Theories of Crime and Delinquency, Advances in Criminological Theory*, Vol. 12. New Brunswick, NJ: Transaction Publishers.

Frank, Robert H. 1985. *Choosing the Right Pond: Human Behavior and the Quest for Status*. New York: Oxford University Press.

Gottfredson, Michael R., and Travis Hirschi. 1990. *A General Theory of Crime*. Palo Alto, CA: Stanford University Press.

Gould, Roger V. 1995. *Insurgent Identities: Class, Community, and Protest in Paris from 1848 to the Commune*. Chicago: University of Chicago Press.

Haynie, Dana L. 2001. "Delinquent Peers Revisited: Does Network Structure Matter?" *American Journal of Sociology* 106: 1013–1057.

Heckathorn, Douglas D. 1990. "Collective Sanctions and Compliance Norms: A Formal Theory." *American Sociological Review* 55: 366–384.

———. 1991. "Extensions of the Prisoner's Dilemma Paradigm: The Altruist's Dilemma and Group Solidarity." *Sociological Theory* 9:34–52.

Hechter, Michael. 1987. *Principles of Group Solidarity*. Berkeley: University of California Press.

———. 2001. *Containing Nationalism*. New York: Oxford University Press.

Hirschi, Travis. 2002. *Causes of Delinquency*. New Brunswick, NJ: Transaction Publishers.

Jankowski, Martin Sanchez. 1991. *Islands in the Street*. Berkeley: University of California Press.

Kahneman, Daniel, and Amos Tversky. 1979. "Prospect Theory: An Analysis of Decision Under Risk." *Econometrica* 47: 263–291.

Klein, Malcolm W. 1971. *Street Gangs and Street Workers*. Englewood Cliffs, NJ: Prentice-Hall.

Kornhauser, Ruth. 1978. *Social Sources of Delinquency*. Chicago: University of Chicago Press.

Krohn, Marvin D. 1986. "The Web of Conformity: A Network Approach to the Explanation of Delinquent Behavior." *Social Problems* 33: S81–S93

Lucas, Ann F. 1994. *Strengthening Departmental Leadership: A Team-Building Guide for Chairs in Colleges and Universities*. San Francisco: Jossey-Bass.

Matsueda, Ross L. 1982. "Testing Control Theory and Differential Association: A Causal Modeling Approach." *American Sociological Review* 47: 489–504.

McPherson, Miller, Lynn Smith-Lovin, and James M. Cook. 2001. "Birds of a Feather: Homophily in Social Networks." *Annual Review of Sociology* 27: 415–444.

Roshier, Bob. 1989. *Controlling Crime: The Classical Perspective in Criminology*. Philadelphia: Open University Press.

Sampson, Robert J., and John H. Laub. 1993. *Crime in the Making: Pathways and Turning Points Through Life*. Cambridge, MA: Harvard University Press.

Short, James F., Jr., and Fred L. Strodtbeck. 1965. *Group Process and Gang Delinquency*. Chicago: University of Chicago Press.

Simon, Herbert A. 1955. "A Behavioral Model of Rational Choice." *Quarterly Journal of Economics* 69: 99–118.

Suttles, Gerald D. 1968. *The Social Order of the Slum: Ethnicity and Territory in the Inner City*. Chicago: University of Chicago Press.

Thomas, William I. 1923. *The Unadjusted Girl*. New York: Little, Brown, and Company.

Tsebelis, George. 1990. *Nested Games: Rational Choice in Comparative Politics*. Berkeley: University of California Press.

Tversky, Amos, and Daniel Kahneman. 1986. "Rational Choice and the Framing of Decisions." *Journal of Business* 59: 5251–5278.

von Neuman, John, and Oskar Morgenstern. 1953. *Theory of Games and Economic Behavior*, Third Edition. Princeton, NJ: Princeton University Press.

Warr, Mark. 1993. "Age, Peers, and Delinquency." *Criminology* 31: 17–40.

———. 2002. *Companions in Crime: The Social Aspects of Criminal Conduct*. New York: Cambridge University Press.

10

Comparative Criminology: Content or Simply Methodology?

Alexander T. Vazsonyi

Introduction

"[T]he legal definition of crime is hardly broad enough for our purpose, because the crimes which the law has designated have varied greatly from time to time and from place to place. We must distinguish features which have been more or less characteristic of crimes in general at all times and places" (Parmalee, 1918: 31). In an effort to define crime, Parmalee recognized important qualities of criminality nearly a century ago. He suggested that crimes are "ordinary acts which affect another person directly" (p. 31), that they are antisocial, harmful to individuals and to society, and as such, easily identifiable. He also implied that crime and its definition should not be tied to particular laws or legal systems. In effect, Parmalee argued for a conceptualization of crime and deviance that transcends historical periods, geographical boundaries, and different groups within national contexts. This conceptualization, which was applied to crime at the turn of the twentieth century, also still applies today at the turn of the twenty-first century. The current chapter provides evidence of the usefulness of such a conceptualization of crime and deviance; furthermore, it will be argued that only this conceptualization will allow social scientists to perform theory testing cross-culturally or cross-nationally, for comparative criminology is not about content, but rather about a method that allows rigorous testing of theoretical and empirical propositions which may ultimately lead to useful generalizations.

This chapter examines work done in comparative criminology and critically assesses its progress, problems, and ultimately, its position in criminology. To do so, select research, which has focused on official data, on victimization data, and on self-reported data, will be reviewed. Next, specific tenets of the general theory of crime for comparative criminology are examined, and at a more elementary level, how they relate to recent cross-cultural and cross-national comparative efforts. Finally, implications for the general theory are discussed and with suggestions for future comparative efforts in criminology.

Comparative Criminology: Official, Victimization, and Self-Report Data

Official Data

Perhaps one of the first efforts to compare official crime data dates back to 1833, when Quetelet published *Recherches sur la loi de la croissance de l'homme aux différents ages* (Quetelet, 1984). In his work, Quetelet examined criminal convictions across time, convictions by age and sex, across French *Departments* or counties, and lastly across nations or regions of nations, namely France and the Low Countries (e.g., Belgium, the Netherlands) as well as regions part of the Austrian and Prussian empires. He also compared characteristics of convicted individuals, such as their ability to read. The explicit goals of these comparisons were to establish the probability in these different contexts to be brought to trial, the degree of what he called repression (rates of conviction), and number of crimes. He did so in an effort to establish characteristics of "The Average Man" brought to trial or convicted of a crime both within a country, but also across countries. It is very noteworthy that, in effect, Quetelet already recognized a fundamental problem of comparing official data, as differences existed in crime rates and in prevailing conviction rates—"I will remark that certain relationships could not be strictly comparable because of incorrect evaluation of the population or an unequal repression in the courts of justice" (p. 33). However, he also noted that there seemed to be remarkable similarity and constancy of crime rates and of conviction rates, especially across parts of Prussia and Austria.

Numerous similar efforts have followed Quetelet's original work. Many have focused on comparing official crime data, largely based on Durkheimian ideas, which related rates of crime in any given society to degree of modernization, industrialization, urbanization, division of labor, and level of social disorganization (Durkheim, 1964). Nations or countries, according to this view, serve as units of analysis, which can be compared in order to arrive at conclusions, and perhaps generalizations, about crime factors or the etiology of crime. Some important examples of this include Archer and Gartner's (1984) efforts to study homicide rates based on the Comparative Crime Data (CCD) from 111 nations. Among many other hypotheses, the study examined the deterrent effect of the death penalty on crime rates (none was found) as well as the relationship between homicide rates and size of cities. Key findings included,

> our cross-sectional analyses are consistent with earlier work in finding high homicide rates in large cities, not only in the United States but also in many other societies. However, we found that the rates of large cities were high only relative to the rates of their societies, *not necessarily in any absolute or international sense*. (emphasis added; p. 115)

The authors further concluded that "sociologists have been mislead" (p. 116) because the urban crime rate was not so much dependent on urban growth or size of a city, but rather nested in and dependent on crime rates in any given society. Similar efforts have attempted to compare countries characterized by low crime rates with ones that have enjoyed extraordinarily high rates (e.g., Clinard's study of Switzerland, 1978; Adler's study of ten "low-crime" countries, 1983), such as the United States. Characteristic of this work and implicit in this approach is the idea that local mores may give insights into unique causes and contributors to variability in rates of crime cross-nationally. In one study, Clinard (1978) attempted to uncover unique cultural characteristics of Switzerland based largely on qualitative data that would account for the much lower observed crime rate. Similarly, Adler (1983) examined ten low-crime countries and associated "informal social controls" which included a broad sampling of global socioeconomic and macro-societal indicators, such as rates of immigration and emigration, population growth, urbanization, industrialization, and political structure, as well as criminal justice systems (e.g., the penal code, enforcement practices and rates of arrest, prosecution, conviction, and sentencing). Both efforts attempted to uncover "certain common characteristics in their formal (criminal justice) or informal social control mechanisms which might explain their low crime status" (Adler, 1983: 124). On this issue, Adler noted that "at first glance the diversity of approaches to crime prevention and control . . . appears baffling (p. 124)—they (the countries) have . . . found their accommodation between the two tolerance levels, that of crime rates and of social restraints" (p. 134). In the final chapter of the comparative ten-nation study, Adler concluded that the most useful way of conceptualizing observed cross-national differences and apparent inconsistencies is along an anomie-synomie continuum; no conclusions could be reached regarding key explanatory characteristics of a low-crime society. Reviewing most significant streams of criminological theory over the past half century, Adler also concluded, "each has something valuable to contribute to our understanding of crime causation, but alas, no single one has been able to see it steady and see it whole" (p. 158).

These latter examples are very characteristic of cross-national comparative efforts based on official data that continue to be completed with similar goals and certainly the same findings (see Howard, Newman, and Pridemore, 2000 for a review of cross-national comparisons employing official crime statistics). Most recently, the European Council has undertaken an ambitious study of official crime indicators across European countries (Killias and Rau, 2000; Killias and Aebi, 2000), again in an effort to juxtapose the European crime situation vis-à-vis the American one. This was done in an effort to understand factors related to criminal justice systems, and how they may impact actual crime rates in different European countries. As mentioned, characteristic of these efforts is a belief that thoroughly examining factors cross-nationally will somehow give us insights into a unique etiology of crime and into similarities or differences of cultures and societies that, in effect, maintain low levels of crime. Part of the problem in making such an assumption is what Hirschi and Gottfredson (1994) have described as "when the idea of science prevailed over the tradition of rationalism" (p. 253); most attempts to understand crime, including cross-national comparative ones, have turned to inductivist explorations of "naturally occurring" phenomena. And while methods to investigate crimes cross-nationally have advanced (at least some) since Quetelet's earliest accounts, conceptualizations of what investigators have been looking for have not. In fact, in our search for crime etiology across time and places, we may have regressed to examining idiosyncratic and culture-specific phenomena much like culture-bound, anthropological accounts and descriptive observations, which in turn have been used to develop potential explanations and a greater understanding of crime, crime etiology, and crime control. Howard and colleagues (2000) have noted, "comparative analysis was conducted mainly from a legal perspective for most of this century, preoccupied with particular nuances in legal definitions and procedures" (p. 190). Similarly, Friday (1973) had previously noted that

> official statistics have long since been demised as a source of reliable data. Societal reaction to criminal acts and to the treatment of offenders cannot be considered independent of cultural and political events which coincide with such acts. Therefore, there is a contamination of official data which tend to make findings based on them suspect. In fact, even the use of such data may be inappropriate and misleading since it fails to account for significant regional and sectoral variation. (p. 154)

As a result of this focus and emphasis, comparative criminology has not progressed in developing a more profound understanding of etiological similarities or differences cross-nationally, or in understanding why individuals in some national contexts enjoy comparatively low crime rates vis-à-vis others.

This is by no means a new insight. In fact, three decades ago, Christie (1970) noted comparative criminological research often turns "out to be a waste of both time and energy" (p. 40) because criminological data may be "more useful for the purpose of understanding the system of control than for understanding of what makes people criminal" (p. 40). Also, Mannheim (1965) strongly advocated an empirical science of criminology and the scientific study of crime. He argued that "different countries or regions have often been interested in different aspects of crime, have employed different methods of study and produced greatly differing answers. As a consequence, we are not seldom faced with the spectacle of several national or regional disciplines instead of one united body" (p. 21). Beirne (1983) lamented that numerous single culture studies "provide at best additively, only the preparatory spirit of cross-cultural investigation" (p. 21). Therefore, "criminology, unhampered by the limits of any national legislation, can afford to tackle its problems in a world-wide spirit" (Mannheim, 1965: 21; see also Friday, 1973). In conclusion, while important sources of information on levels of crime across countries, official data have not provided new insights or understanding into the etiology of crime and deviance, largely because of large differences in legal systems and definitions of crime. There have been some exceptions to this. For example, Zimring and Hawkins' (1997) very critical and careful analysis of cross-national crime rates has indicated *mostly similarities* in rates cross-nationally across all types of index crimes (e.g., in Western countries); the exception to this were the observed rates of homicides found in the United States in comparison to other developed countries, which in part lead the authors to title their book *Crime Is Not the Problem*. They concluded, "what sets the United States apart from other developed nations is a thin layer of life-threatening violence that probably accounts for less than 1 percent of American crime and less than 10 percent of American violence" (p. 50).

Victimization Data

In efforts to overcome some of the weaknesses and inherent problems of comparing official crime statistics cross-nationally and as a mode of establishing Quetelet's "The Average Man" or to gain insights into etiological factors that may generalize across places, a number of studies have examined rates of criminal victimization. Victimization surveys were conceptualized to more accurately describe rates of crime and fear of crime, as well as important characteristics of victims. The use of victimization surveys, especially in cross-national comparisons, is relatively recent. In an article on the importance of comparative crime victimization surveys, Clinard (1978) suggested, "satisfactory international comparisons can hardly be made when everywhere today official crime statistics are being increasingly subjected to severe critical examination; nowhere are they really considered completely reliable" (p. 221). In 1989, Van Dijk, Mayhew, and Killias (1991) completed an important and comprehensive comparative victimization study employing a self-report methodology across seventeen (fourteen "main participating") European (mostly Western European) and non-European countries (the United States, Canada, and Australia). Their main goals included (1) to allow a comparison of crime rates across countries; (2) to allow a comparison of crime rates based on official data with victimization data; and (3) to provide "some basis for explaining major differences in crime experience in terms, for instance, of sociodemographic variables" (p. 1). In many ways, this effort indicated that some of the findings regarding differences in rates and levels of crime observed cross-nationally based on official data were also supported by victimization data (e.g., handgun ownership). The data also suggested fewer or smaller differences cross-nationally in other areas, such as theft of personal property. While there was evidence that levels of fear varied substantially across European countries on theft, the observed level of victimization between the average of all European countries and the United States was almost identical. Some similar findings were also made for fear of different types of crime. The authors concluded, "results from these surveys are extremely difficult to compare because of differences in survey administration and data analysis" (p. 95). The criminal victimization survey was repeated two more times, namely in 1992 and 1996 (Mayhew and Van Dijk, 1997), although the most recent reports focused mainly on eleven industrialized nations. Similar conclusions regarding usefulness and comparability were reached—"the number of countries with appropriate surveys was limited, and the surveys used different methods, making comparisons far from straight-forward" (p. 7; for a further discussion, see Van Dijk and Kangaspunta, 2000).

Interestingly, efforts to account for cross-national similarities and differences focused on levels of urbanization, affluence, economic strain (dissatisfaction with household income), and lifestyles of urban dwellers (frequency of nights out), much like was done previously in studies employing official crime data. The most potent variables in accounting for variability in risk for crime were urbanization ("the proportion of people living in each of six categories of size of place of residence" p. 61) and levels of affluence (World Bank data). In conclusion, while victimization surveys are an important improvement over official data from courts and law enforcement agencies, they do not allow a thorough investigation into similarities and differences in the etiology of crime and deviance, and therefore, perhaps at best only descriptively add to the accumulation of knowledge in criminology. In fact, this is something Clinard (1978) recognized based on victimization studies he completed in Swiss and Swedish cities in the early 1970s. Furthermore, he even cautioned about making comparisons between crime rates based on police data versus victimization data and about trying to establish, at a very basic level, variability of crime cross-nationally. He concluded,

> It appears difficult to judge the relative accuracy of police statistics in various countries through a comparison of them with the number of crimes reported in a victim-

> ization survey. Time periods are often found not to coincide, the police often reclassify a victim's report of a crime, and police statistics include reports of nonresidents of the local area or city. For these reasons the victims' statements that they reported crime victimization to the police is probably the most adequate comparative measure. Despite present problems, crime victimization surveys offer today a rough international comparison of the extent and nature of crime. With more agreement on uniform procedures there is hope for a true comparative criminology. (pp. 229–230)

Clinard also provided a very clear and concise description of what steps were necessary in comparative criminology to substantially contribute to our knowledge base in criminology at the beginning of his essay, based on thinking by Durkheim.

> The initial step in developing comparative criminology is to ascertain the variation in the extent of selected types of crime by countries. They might then be ranked as to the relative magnitude of crime, also the relative increases. This *elementary epidemiology* (emphasis added) of crime could then be followed by more detailed studies designed to analyze these variations. Only then can theoretical propositions be more adequately tested in a variety of social settings. (p. 221)

So, based on this thinking, it seems that cross-national comparative victimization work is important in providing the elementary epidemiology which is an important improvement over only considering official data; however, it does not allow theory tests, or at an even more basic level, replications of causal or etiological models that may account for variation in crime and deviance across social settings. Howard, Newman, and Pridemore (2000) recently noted on victimization surveys that "these surveys are usually unable to capture much information about offenders, nor can they provide much insight into victimless crime" (p. 182).

In conclusion, part of the reason why criminology has not been able to progress is what Mannheim called "the spectacle of several national or regional disciplines instead of one united body." Gottfredson and Hirschi (1990) have precisely noted that "in the end, then, the major disciplines conclude that the conceptual chaos of criminology reflects the natural chaos of a multicultural world" (p. 173), referring to the fact that deterministic schools of thought have developed the idea, based on cross-national studies, that culturally unique explanations of crime apply to culturally unique definitions of crime.

Self-Report Data

It is well-accepted today that the self-report method is a valid and reliable way to assess deviant and criminal activity, although there continues to exist concerns over its use and its importance vis-à-vis official data for example (e.g., Junger-Tas and Marshall, 1999; for a discussion, see Hindelang, Hirschi, and Weis, 1981). Over two decades ago, based on very meticulous and thorough study of the self-report method in criminology, Hindelang et al. (1981) noted that

> the self-report method easily demonstrates that people will report crimes, that they will report crimes not known to officials, that they are highly likely to report crimes not known to officials, and that their reports of crimes are internally consistent. These facts are rightly taken as evidence that the procedure is potentially useful as an alternative to traditional procedures, *particularly for studying the etiology of delinquency*. (emphasis added, p. 212)

A variety of platforms have been used to issue calls for cross-national comparative work in criminology, not so much as a substantive or content area, but as a research analytic strategy. In his presidential address of the American Society of Sociology, Krohn (1987) suggested, "cross-national research provides an especially useful method for generating, testing, and further developing sociological theory" (p. 713). Similarly, in his presidential address of the American Society of Criminology, outlining a criminological research agenda for the next millennium, Farrington (1999) called for comparative research as a method to replicate risk factors and as a way to generalize findings across countries. "Cross-national comparisons of risk factors for delinquency are important for addressing the question how far the causes of delinquency are similar in different times and places, and hence how far theories of delinquency can be generalized over time and place" (Farrington and Loeber, 1999: 300). Again, these insights are by no means new ones. Half a century ago in 1955, at the Third International Congress of Criminology in London, Clinard outlined the need for comparative criminology as one of the most important frontiers in criminological work (Clinard, 1956). That same year, the First International Congress on the Prevention of Crime and the Treatment of Offenders held in Geneva concluded that comparative criminology was necessary to determine "uniformities and differences in causal influences, in predictive factors, and in results of preventive and treatment programs" (Glueck, 1967: 304). Glueck (1965) subsequently argued that in order to make criminology a truly scientific discipline, studies needed to embrace a multifaceted approach, an approach that included information from multiple disciplines and one that was cross-culturally or cross-nationally comparative in nature. The two hallmarks of science, according to Glueck, are repeatability and predictability.

From the discussion thus far, it seems clear that the impetus for replication and generalization through the cross-national comparative method has been an elaborated idea for many years, but that action has lagged far behind. In fact, it seems as if comparative efforts were attempted, repeatedly, but that they have been very limited in their importance because they do not move far past descriptive comparisons of official data on levels of crime in different contexts. In turn, this has had very little impact on criminological work, as predictors or etiological factors could not be subjected to rigorous tests. Recognizing this, Gartner (1993) has suggested comparative studies needed to include work that moved "much beyond those addressing behavioral incidence and prevalence" (p. 204). It needs to include strong measures of known etiological risk factors or theoretically relevant variables that can be subjected to rigorous tests. The importance here is what Gottfredson and Hirschi (1990) have so aptly described:

> Science typically assumes that proper explanations of phenomena are produced by inductive examination of differences and their correlates. First one determines that, for example, the United States has a higher homicide rate than Japan. Then one locates the cultural (or perhaps structural) differences between Japan and the United States that account for homicide differences. (p. 173)

In fact, Przeworski and Teune (1966) argued, "the logic of comparative research does not differ from any other type of social inquiry" (p. 552). They further noted,

> cross-national analysis is an operation by which a *relationship* (emphasis added) between two or more variables is stated for a defined population of countries. In analysis, no proper names of societies or cultures are mentioned. The goal is not to "understand" Ghana or Cuba, not to describe Hitler, Stalin, Roosevelt, or Churchill, but to see to what extent external crises and internal control, military prowess and economic frustration, nationalism and persecutions, are related, and *to know the generality of the relationship* (emphasis added). But these are the observations that are a means to an end—the end of testing relationships between variables, even at the cost of obscuring some differences between specific units (p. 554) . . . From the point of view of scientific inquiry attempting to explain the variance of social phenomena, such concepts as "social system," "culture," or "political system" can be absorbed into the analysis as nothing but residuals of variables influencing the phenomenon being explained. (p. 555)

A small number of notable exceptions exist in the criminological literature that have attempted to test theoretical predictions across countries, or at least, to verify sets of known risk factors employing a cross-national comparative method. For example, following meetings on self-report methodology in the late 1980s, the Dutch Ministry of Justice lead the International Self-Report Delinquency (ISRD) Study effort which ultimately employed a core, standard set of crime measures and correlates of crime items across thirteen mostly "Western" countries. In 1994, Junger-Tas, Terlouw, and Klein published initial findings of this cross-national effort based in self-report methodology. The primary goal of the study and the initial book was to provide "relative rank ordering of the prevalence of specific types of crime in different countries and cities of comparative urbanization levels" (p. 3), although limited data were also collected on background variables, social reactions to delinquency, circumstances of the delinquent act, and theoretical variables. In effect, the main thrust of this comparison of self-report data (and all comparative publications to date) was very similar to previous comparative efforts of crime data based on official data. Interestingly, the follow-up report, which has yet to be published, will focus on "statistical analyses of cross-national youth crime patterns" (p. 381). In the sample and method descriptions of this initial report of findings, one is faced with the same discussion of different samples, different methods, different measures which Mannheim has so frequently lamented in official data and which has impeded progress in comparative criminology. Nevertheless, this important effort comparing rates of crime cross-national has been one of the only large, coordinated efforts to collect self-report data from youth and young adults across a number of "developed" countries. It has documented both interesting differences as well as unexpected similarities in rates of crime across nations.

Farrington and Loeber (1999) recently completed a comparison of youth part of the Pittsburgh Youth Survey (PYS) and the Cambridge Study in Delinquent Development in order to develop an understanding of the replicability of risk factors in delinquency across time (the PYS was done in the late 1980s and early 1990s, while the Cambridge study was completed in the 1960s) and place. In their study, Farrington and Loeber review work that has been cross-national comparative and note that comparisons of longitudinal studies are very rare (e.g., Farrington and Wikström, 1994; Moffitt, Caspi, Silva, and Stouthamer-Loeber, 1995; Pulkkinen and Tremblay, 1992) and point-by-point efforts are basically nonexistent in the literature. Farrington and Loeber (1999) suggest that most comparative studies to date have not employed rigorous tests to examine for similarities in the size of the relationships. They identify other known issues in comparative work that impede progress in the replication of risk factors, but also in replicating theoretical propositions and generalizing theories, namely different constructs, differential definitions of constructs, different samples, and different legal definitions. Despite these problems, the authors examined constructs and measures used from the London and Pittsburgh studies, because the studies have many similarities due to investigator overlap.

It is important to note here that most studies reviewed were not carried out with the intention of completing cross-national comparisons, but rather, comparisons were done later due to similarities. Both studies included a series of risk variables, which were dichotomized into low (75 percent) and high (25 percent) risk groups for comparisons. Subsequently, logistic regression analyses were completed in both samples using the same, or at least very similar, twenty-one measures (individual, childrearing, SES, and parental) to predict juvenile court delinquency. In addition, hierarchical linear regressions were also used to assess multicollinearity among predictor constructs. Findings based on both analyses suggested some similarity, namely the importance of a convicted parent, harsh maternal discipline, authoritarian parents, high daring, and low achievement, but also some differences between the two investigations. A number of these variables were important in both investigations, however, the strength of the relationships differed. For example, a convicted parent was more predictive of delinquency for youth in London, while a broken family was more predictive of delinquency in Pittsburgh. In conclusion, the authors point out the importance of such comparative efforts to replicate and generalize empirical findings as well as rigorously test the generalizability of theories (for a recent cross-national comparative study on etiology of marijuana use employing the same risk factor approach and analytic techniques, see Brook, Brook, Arencibia-Mireles, Richter, and Whiteman, 2001).

In a similar effort, Moffitt et al. (1995) compared correlates and predictors of delinquency in two samples, namely the New Zealand Dunedin Multidisciplinary Health and Development Study and the Pittsburgh Youth Survey, and across a number of different groups (i.e., New Zealand males, New Zealand females, Pittsburgh whites at 12/13, Pittsburgh blacks at 12/13, Pittsburgh blacks low SES, and Pittsburgh blacks average SES). More specifically, they examined the relationship between constraint, negative emotionality, positive emotionality, and delinquency. Across all groups, delinquency was assessed through self-reports and two additional measures (e.g., teacher reports, mother ratings, and court convictions in New Zealand). The "robust" finding that emerged was that greater negative emotionality was associated with higher rates of delinquency, and less constraint was associated with more delinquency. In other words, individuals low in self-control, or as stated by the authors, "with great difficulties in modulating impulses" (p. 13) were the most delinquent. Perhaps one important issue in this work is that the measures just described ranged quite widely in their associations across the different groups. For example, the correlation between constraint and delinquency ranged from $r = -.08$ (ns) for low SES blacks to $r = -.58$ for average SES blacks. No strong inference difference tests were completed to compare the associations. Also, the measures, part of the two samples, were different which further contributed to challenges when trying to draw conclusions regarding similarities or differences in the described relationships across groups and national contexts. Similar comparisons were completed for the relationship between intelligence (verbal and performance IQs) and delinquency across groups; similar findings emerged. For example, verbal IQ was correlated with delinquency based on teacher ratings between $r = -.15$ in New Zealand females and $r = -.43$ in Pittsburgh whites.

A few exceptions exist in the literature that are point-by-point; however, in general, most point-by-point, cross-national comparative studies have been efforts to validate instruments (e.g., Rosenbaum, 1980; Zuckerman, Eysenck, and Eysenck, 1978). For example, Achenbach and colleagues (1987) attempted to cross-nationally validate the Child Behavior Checklist (CBCL) by comparing the results of exploratory factor analyses and clinical cutoff scores in samples of American and Dutch youth. They found similarities—they reported correlations between the two national contexts which ranged from r = .80 to .89—but they also found some syndromes only in the United States (e.g., immature syndrome). Part of the problem in this study is an over reliance on arbitrary clinical labels and syndromes that are by definition bound to culture and may not easily replicate across contexts. Also, the authors employed an analytic method that can be characterized as exploratory (exploratory factor analyses) rather than confirmatory, which by definition does not allow for strong inferences as discussed previously. In conclusion, these self-report studies have not produced very strong insights into the etiology of crime and deviance across countries beyond providing at times extensive lists of corollaries or risk factors of criminal behaviors that replicate across different samples. In part, this is so because most studies, with the exceptions of instrument validation studies, have been post hoc comparisons of similar studies that lacked apriori theoretical propositions or hypothesis tests.

Howard and colleagues (2000) again provide an eloquent description of the current state of affairs in comparative criminology. They suggest that self-report studies are a potential remedy to the shortcomings of both official crime data and victimization data. However, they also noted, "differences in samples and survey questions among different studies, as well as varying definitions of crime and deviance from country to country, make it difficult to use the results gained from these surveys to make cross-national comparisons" (p. 182). They continue, very consistent with the thinking previously discussed by Gottfredson and Hirschi on why cross-national comparative efforts have not been able to progress, that "perhaps the major detriment to the systematic gathering of knowledge about the etiology of crime across nations is the lack of careful operationalization of theoretical models and consistency in measurement models. . . . It is vital that all of the efforts we have placed in being careful about measurement of crime must be directed toward the definition, operationalization, and measurement of our independent variables" (p. 183). In the next section, a recent "deliberate" cross-national empirical effort building on these important insights is discussed.

A Cross-National Test of the General Theory of Crime

Gottfredson and Hirschi's (1990) general theory of crime takes a rather radical stance toward previous efforts in comparative criminology (see pp. 169–179). The authors argue that positivism has impeded the progress of cross-national comparative efforts and comparative criminology as a whole because it suggests contextual relativity or conditional truths; in other words, "facts differ from culture to culture . . . and generalization from one to another is . . . dangerous" (p. 172). In making a comparison between two cultures, for example, positivistic science has called for an inductive examination of facts in each context, which ultimately leads to apparent differences. This approach to the problem necessitates finding differences, because it dictates how data are collected, what type of questions are asked, and what type of analyses are used to answer these questions. In many ways, comparative criminology has been plagued by the fact that it has lost the original conceptualization and idea of crime, namely that it is a universal phenomenon of human existence, one that is by no means unique to a specific town, region, or country. A basic starting point when studying crime and deviance to develop explanations, which are generalizable, is that crime is universal, crime varies universally, and the way political and legal systems deal with crime varies tremendously across time and place. It logically follows then that comparisons of legal systems of crime, comparisons of number of individuals caught for certain behaviors and prosecuted for behaviors will necessarily vary across time and place due to fundamentally different definitions, processes, and political climates that affect both definitions and processes. Most comparative efforts have examined socioeconomic, labor, or household composition facts across cultures in an attempt to better understand the etiology of crime. These have largely added little to our understanding of crime and deviance.

Again, Howard and colleagues (2000) provide some insights on this topic. They note,

> (t)he greatest advantage—although often considered an impediment—for research in comparative criminology is the great diversity that exists cross-nationally with regard to social, economic, and political indicators. Though their structure and organization may vary, basic social and cultural categories such as family, urban and rural life, and community are *universals of human existence* (emphasis added), so they may be used as fundamental classifications when comparing one cultural group with another. (p. 144)

These observations are consistent with what some cross-cultural psychologist (Berry, Poortinga, Segall, and Dasen, 1992) have termed an "absolutist" orientation; however, they omit other constructs important in understanding crime and deviance which have been largely ignored by criminologists, namely individual level explanations—nested within the family, community, and society. According to Berry and colleagues (1992), there are three fundamental types of comparative inquiry ranging on a continuum from searches for universals to ones for diversity, namely ones characterized as absolutist, universalist, and relativist. The authors describe the specific characteristics of each general orientation on a number of dimensions, including the sources or factors underlying behavior (biological, biological and cultural, and cultural), the role of culture, as well as principle methodological issues when investigating human behavior. An absolutist orientation assumes a substantial portion of the variability in individual behavior is due to individual differences. Therefore, "the absolutist position seems little concerned with the problems of ethnocentrism or seeing people in their own terms" (Berry et al., 1992: 257). Furthermore, this orientation suggests that we expect similarities across different groups due to species-wide, similar basic processes of human development and human behavior (for a similar argument, see Rowe, 1997). Finally, the absolutist orientation assumes that context-free measurement is possible, that standard instruments and methods can be used in a straightforward fashion for comparative work, and that comparisons can be readily, easily, and frequently made.

A further differentiation of cross-cultural comparative studies can be made on two basic dimensions, namely whether their orientation is one of hypothesis testing or one of exploration and whether contextual factors are considered or not. The current chapter largely focuses on the importance of testing generalizable hypotheses cross-nationally based on the general theory of crime. More specifically, it is interested in examining the measurement of self-control and deviance, and in testing the similarity of the relationship between self-control and deviance across national contexts. Furthermore, consistent with the absolutist orientation just described, the chapter is not interested in examining the importance of specific context or contextual variables. According to Van de Vijver and Leung (1997) this type of inquiry needs to employ convenience samples, and it needs to use *structure techniques* analytically (correlations, factor analysis, and analysis of covariance structures) in comparison to level techniques (t-tests, ANOVAS). "In generalizability studies, a theory, a correlational or causal relationship, or an instrument derived from a theory is tested in another cultural context. The goal of the study is to establish the generalizability of the theory, the relationship, or the instrument" (p. 291). Very few studies exist in criminology that have examined proposed causal relationships across different national contexts. In part, this is due to the fact that a tremendous investment of resources and time are involved for such tests. Furthermore, if cross-national, comparative studies have been completed, they have generally been exploratory in nature, have not included known theoretical constructs important in the etiology of crime and deviance (e.g., mostly measures of crime), have not included the identical measures necessary for such comparisons, or have used different methods for collecting data. Perhaps most importantly, previous efforts described in this chapter were not conceptualized a priori to examine or test specific theoretical propositions or causal relationships.

For this chapter, two analytic procedures were used to examine the theoretical relationship between low self-control and deviance across samples from four different countries. As suggested by Van de Vijver and Leung (1997), both analyses were limited to structure techniques, namely the covariance between low self-control and different measures of deviance. Key to completing such a comparison across four national contexts is employing measures of behavior that are strictly behavioral and not bound by idiosyncratic cultural or regional meaning. For example, measures of deviance must assess deviance in behavioral terms and not in a legalistic sense, so that individuals located in different cultures can relate to and assess statements in the same manner. Breaking bottles after a sports event has the same meaning in all national contexts, while writing a phony check only has meaning for Americans for example, as few other cultures use checking writing as legal tender. In a sense, measures employed in a cross-national comparative study need to be "culture-free." The same reasoning applies to all variables assessed, whether an indicator of socioeconomic status or items measuring deviant behavior.

In a first step, simple regression analyses were completed, where low self-control predicted total deviance. These analyses were done separately for males and females by country. Secondly, a more rigorous and comprehensive analytic procedure was used that examined all relationships between the measure of low self-control and seven different types of deviance by sex and by country. For this purpose, a model free LISREL approach was selected which allowed for a simultaneous estimation of similarities versus differences in 8 x 8 correlation matrices that were generated for each country (see e.g., Rowe, Vazsonyi, and Flannery, 1994). Analyses were completed where four male matrices were compared and four female matrices were compared and then evaluated for fit. Standard fit indices were used to assess for similarities/differences; they included *chi square*, *CFI*, and *RMSEA* (Bentler, 1992; Browne and Cudeck, 1993). Because model fit is known to be highly sensitive to differences in sample size, random samples of 410 males (there were only 410 Dutch males) and 219 females (there were only 219 Hungarian females) were selected from each country.

Methods

The data were collected as part of the *International Study of Adolescent Development* (ISAD), a multinational, multisite investigation consisting of 8,417 subjects from four different countries (Hungary, the Netherlands, Switzerland, and the United States; Vazsonyi et al., 2001; 2002). The purpose of ISAD was to examine the etiology of adolescent problem behaviors and deviance utilizing large, locally representative samples from different countries. A standard data collection protocol was followed across all study locations. It was approved by a university IRB and consisted of a self-report data collection instrument, which included instructions on how to complete the survey, a description of the ISAD project, and assurances of anonymity and confidentiality. The questionnaires were administered in classrooms by project staff or teachers who had received extensive verbal and written instructions. This was done to maintain a standardized protocol across all study locations. Students had a 1- to 2-hour period to complete the survey. Much attention was given to the development of the ISAD survey instrument, particularly by developing new or employing existing measures that could be used cross-culturally without losing nuances or changing meanings. The survey was translated from English into the target languages (Dutch, German, and Hungarian) and back translated by bilingual translators. Surveys were examined by additional bilingual translators, and when translation was difficult or ambiguous, consensus was used to produce the final translation.

Sample

Valid data were collected from $N = 8{,}417$ adolescents from four different countries (Hungary, $n = 871$; Netherlands, $n = 1{,}315$; Switzerland, $n = 4{,}018$; United States, $n = 2{,}213$). In all locations, medium-sized cities of similar size were selected for participation. For each country, different schools were selected to obtain representative samples of the general population. For the European samples, this included schools for university-bound students (Gymnasium) as well as schools specializing in vocational/technical training for students in apprenticeships. In the United States, the samples included high school students, community college students, and university students (for additional sample details, see Vazsonyi et al., 2001). Because these various schools represented an age range of approximately 14 to 22 years old, students within a specific "age band" with no missing data were selected for cross-national comparisons. The final study sample included $n = 745$ Hungarians (526 males, 219 females; mean age = 16.7, $sd = 1.2$), $n = 880$ Dutch (410 males, 470 females; mean age = 16.5, $sd = 1.0$), $n = 3{,}312$ Swiss (2069 males, 1243 females; mean age = 17.9, $sd = 1.1$), and $n = 1{,}302$ adolescents from the United States (535 males, 767 females; mean age = 18.0, $sd = 1.5$). There were $n = 3{,}540$ males (mean age = 17.6, $sd = 1.3$) and $n = 2{,}699$ females (mean age = 17.6, $sd = 1.3$).

Measures

Individuals in each country were asked to fill out an identical questionnaire including demographic and background variables, age, low self-control, and deviance.

Age. Participants were asked to indicate the month and year in which they were born. In order to maintain anonymity of subjects, we did not ask for the day. The 15th day of the respective month was used to calculate subjects' ages.

Sex. Subjects were asked to indicate their sex on a single item: "What is your gender?" Responses were given as 1 = male and 2 = female.

Socioeconomic Status (SES). Subjects were asked to indicate the type of work performed by the primary wage earner in the family to assess socioeconomic status. Six categories collapsed from Hollingshead's (1975) original nine categories and modified to be applicable in each of the four countries were specified that would readily map on professions found in each of the four study countries. Each category contained descriptions of sample jobs which would fit into each of them. Responses were given by indicating the number of the category that contained the closest or most accurate description of the family's primary wage earner's job. The categories, listed here with condensed descriptions, were as follows: 1 = owner of a large business, executive; 2 = owner of a small business, professional; 3 = semiprofessional, skilled laborer; 4 = clerical staff; 5 = semiskilled laborer; and 6 = laborer or service worker.

Low Self-Control. Grasmick et al.'s (1993) low self-control scale was used to measure self-control (see Appendix A). This scale included twenty-four items in six subscales (impulsiveness, simple tasks, risk-seeking, physical activity, self-centeredness, and temper) consistent with Gottfredson and Hirschi's original conceptualization. Responses were given on a five-point Likert type scale (1 = strongly disagree, 2 = disagree, 3 = neither disagree nor agree, 4 = agree, 5 = strongly agree). This was revised from a four-point Likert type scale (1 = strongly disagree, 2 = disagree somewhat, 3 = agree somewhat, 4 = strongly agree) originally used by Grasmick et al. (1993), but it was consistent with other previous studies utilizing this scale (e.g., Longshore et al., 1996; Piquero and Rosay, 1998). Reliability coefficients on the low self-control subscales for the entire sample ranged from $a = .50$ to $a = .79$. In previous work and based on rigorous confirmatory factor analyses, data suggested that a twenty-two-item version of the six component self-control measure of self-control was reliable for males, females, different age groups, and for youth from four different national contexts (Vazsonyi et al., 2001).

Deviance. Lifetime deviance was measured by the fifty-five-item Normative Deviance Scale (NDS) newly developed for the ISAD project (see Appendix B). The purpose of this scale was to measure adolescent deviance in a manner that would capture norm-violating conduct in all cultures in the present investigation to improve cross-national comparative efforts (see also Junger-Tas, 1989). This meant including instrument items that tap a more normal distribution of responses, especially for low-delinquency cultures, such as Switzerland. Few such self-report scales that include multi-item subscales with psychometric properties have been developed for use in different national contexts. In fact, this may be one of the first attempts to employ a comprehensive scalar measure of deviance on large, representative samples from different countries (see Moffitt and Silva, 1988, for a brief discussion on individual self-report studies measuring delinquency in different countries). Single item, incidence-based crime measures that have well defined reporting periods (e.g., during the past month) are more common in criminological work, that is, one item measuring vandalism, for example. However, because the current study was primarily concerned with delinquency etiology and testing specific causal propositions, not an epidemiological assessment of incidents of deviance, an open-ended reporting period (lifetime prevalence) was adopted. This method of assessing crime and deviance cross-nationally has been previously employed and has been shown to be a valid and reliable index of crime (see Moffitt, Silva, Lynam, and Henry, 1994; Moffitt, 1989). One advantage of this approach is that it captures a greater number of reports of deviance as well as eliminates the potential problems common in bounding incidence-based self-reports. Furthermore, the rates of recent participation in deviant behaviors in the general adolescent population may be too low in many individually measured behaviors (see Moffitt, 1989). And finally, and in part because of the latter issue, the NDS measures deviance and deviance subscales as trait-like constructs with good psychometric properties that are assessed by multiple, overlapping items. Such an approach yields more reliable and robust assessments of deviant behavior for etiological work in particular.

For the current chapter, analyses were done on the seven subscales of the NDS (vandalism, alcohol, use drugs, school misconduct, general deviance, theft, and assault) as well as a measure of total deviance. Responses for all items in the NDS were given on a five-point Likert-type scale and identified lifetime frequency of specific behaviors (1 = never, 2 = one time, 3 = 2-3 times, 4 = 4–6 times, and 5 = more than 6 times). Reliability coefficients on the deviance subscales for the entire sample ranged from $a = .76$ to $a = .89$. Subscales and the total deviance measure were also reliable by sex and by countries (Vazsonyi et al., 2001; 2002; Vazsonyi and Killias, 2001). Table 10.1 includes descriptive statistics on background variables, low self-control, and the deviance measures by country.

Results

Figures 10.1 and 10.2 include scatter plots of low self-control and total deviance for males and females by country. The plots include a best-fit regression lines (straight line), upper and lower 95 percent confidence intervals, and a mean deviance score (horizontal line). The data indicated that the relationship between the two variables was similar across countries. For males, low self-control accounted for between 15 percent (Dutch) and 19 percent (Americans) of the total variance in deviance, while for females, it accounted for between 12 percent (Dutch) and 25 percent (Americans). The scatter plots also nicely demonstrated that American youth reported lower levels of self-control than youth in other national contexts and that females reported gen-

Table 10.1
Descriptive Statistics of Demographic Variables, Low Self-Control, and Deviance by Country

	Total Sample N = 6,239							
	American		Dutch		Hungarian		Swiss	
	n = 1,302		n = 880		n = 745		n = 3,312	
Age	17.97	1.45	16.46	0.97	19.71	1.16	17.87	1.14
SES	4.89	1.14	4.57	1.05	3.96	1.30	4.45	1.09
Low Self-Control	2.72	0.57	2.83	0.49	2.81	0.48	2.46	0. 40
Vandalism	1.52	0.71	1.52	0.69	1.64	0.75	1.65	0.73
Alcohol Use	2.72	1.28	2.34	0.82	2.27	0.96	2.16	0.92
Drug Use	1.96	1.08	1.64	0.88	1.50	0.69	2.10	1.09
School Misconduct	2.05	0.90	2.23	0.76	2.07	0.77	2.15	0.77
General Deviance	1.86	0.73	2.02	0.71	1.79	0.71	2.04	0.77
Theft	1.39	0.65	1.38	0.56	1.34	0.57	1.55	0.74
Assault	1.46	0.66	1.55	0.62	1.60	0.67	1.62	0.71
Total Deviance	1.86	0.70	1.82	0.59	1.74	0.60	1.92	0.67

Note: Responses for the SES variable were recoded for this table, so that a high score indicates high SES.

erally lower levels of self-control than males; nevertheless, perhaps with the exception of American females, in all groups, both males and females, a highly similar pattern of association between low self-control and deviance was found.

To assess whether there existed similarities or differences across national contexts in the magnitude or strength of the relationship between low self-control and different measures of deviance, two general analytic approaches exist. First, each regression coefficient could be compared in pairwise comparisons. For example, the beta for American males based on regressing low self-control on vandalism could be compared to the beta for Dutch males, to the beta from Hungarian males, and to the beta from Swiss males. Next, the beta from Dutch males would be compared to the betas from Hungarian and Swiss males and so forth. This "piecemeal" approach of pairwise difference testing is extremely tedious (not to mention impossible to comprehend), and it is also likely to increase the risk of Type I error (inferring relationships where there are really none). Rowe et al. (1994) have suggested a more elegant, parsimonious, and perhaps sound analytical approach, where entire

Figure 10.1
Scatter Plot of Low Self-Control and Total Deviance by Country (Males)

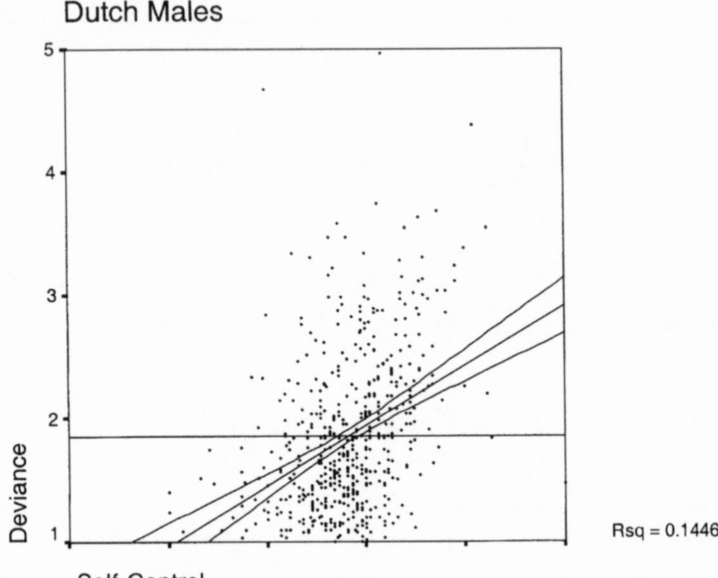

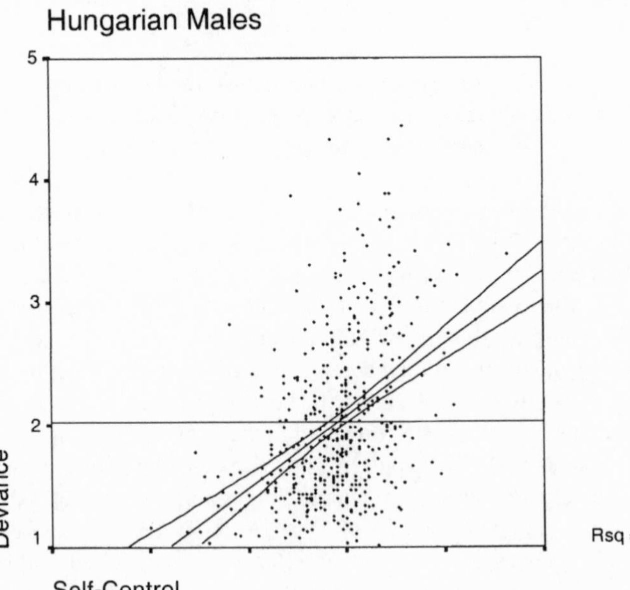

Table 10.1 (cont.)

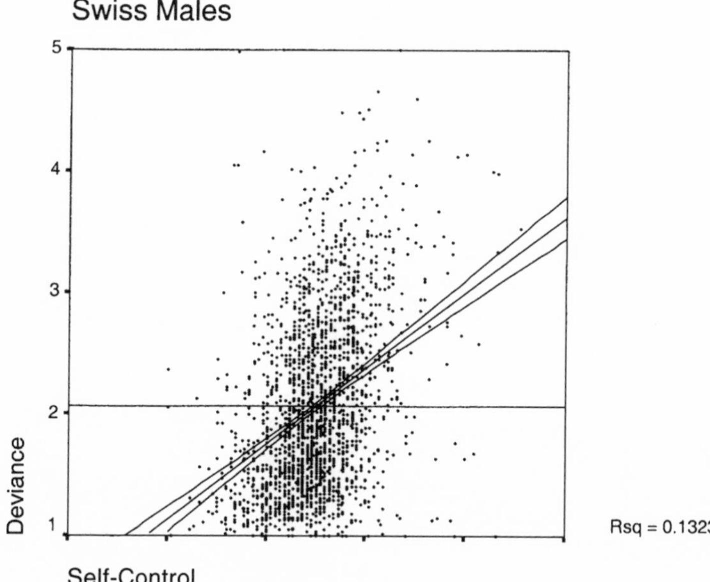

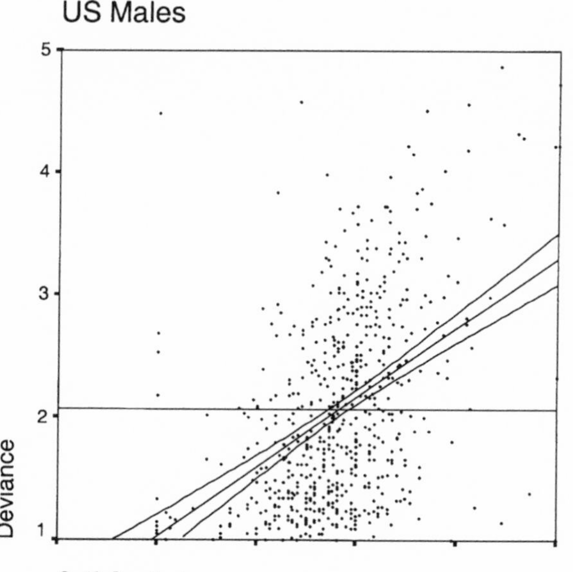

Figure 10.2
Scatter Plot of Low Self-Control and Total Deviance by Country (Females)

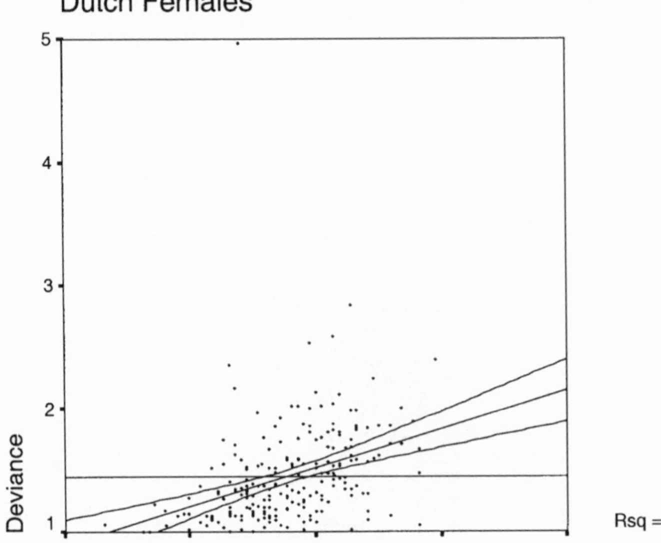

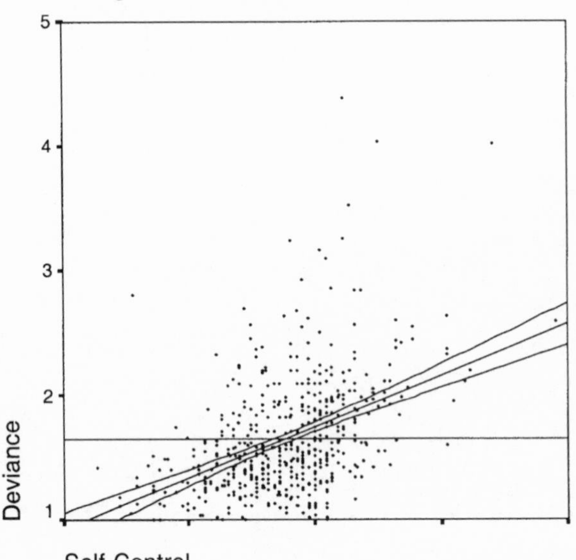

Figure 10.2 (cont.)

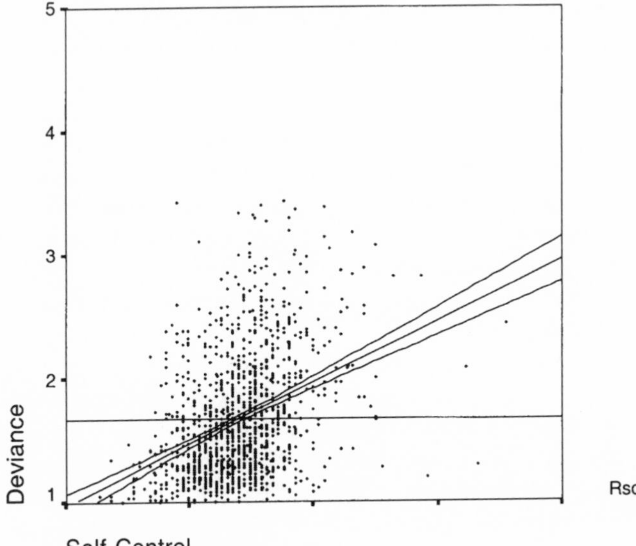

Rsq = 0.1359

US Females

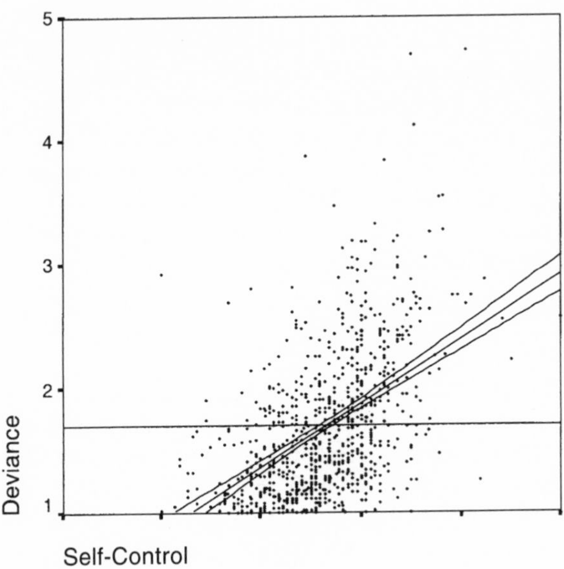

Rsq = 0.2534

correlation or covariance matrices from each group that include the antecedents, in this case low self-control, and outcomes, in this case measures of deviance, are compared. This avoids and overcomes problems associated with large numbers of pairwise tests (see also Vazsonyi et al., 2001, 2002). This approach is also more rigorous in the sense that it simultaneously compares all four 8 x 8 matrices from male self reports to each other as well as all four 8 x 8 matrices from females. In the current analyses, the latter approach was used to examine similarities or differences across countries.

To address the impact of potentially confounding variables, correlations were residualized by age and by socioeconomic status. Also, as previously described, random samples were drawn from each population to minimize the effects of different sample size in these comparisons, namely 410 males and 219 females. In this analytic approach, four matrices are input into the LISREL program, which then generated a best-fitted matrix. Subsequently, each input matrix was evaluated in terms of fit in comparison to this best-fitted matrix. Slight deviations greatly impact model fit, and final model evaluation was the cumulative assessment of each input matrix compared with the best-fitted matrix. In comparisons of the four partial correlation matrices from males, the following findings were made: *chi square* (108) = 248.25 ($p < .01$), *CFI* = .98, *RMSEA* = .05. For females, findings indicated: *chi square* (108) = 269.20 ($p < .01$), *CFI* = .96, *RMSEA* = .08. Both analyses suggested very good fit, although model fit for females was slightly poorer. To assess the fit of each group individually by sex, individual Q-plots were also inspected. LISREL only outputs the *chi square* statistic, the root mean residual (*RMR*), and the goodness of fit index (*GFI*) for each group. The *RMR* has very similar properties as the *RMSEA*; values less than .05 are considered evidence of excellent fit, values less than .08 good fit, while values less than .1 are considered acceptable fit. Also, the *GFI* can also be interpreted in a similar fashion as the *CFI*, where a fit of > .90 is considered acceptable. Model fit evaluating individual matrices by sex are presented in Table 10.2. Fit indices suggested that female matrices generally fit less well in comparison to male matrices; however, the numbers still indicated great similarity in the patterns of associations between low self-control and the seven measures of deviance across four national contexts, for both males and females.

Discussion

The findings from the cross-national comparison support one of the core predictions of *A General Theory of Crime* by Gottfredson and Hirschi (1990), namely the positive association between low self-control and deviance; this was consistently found for male and female adolescents from Hungary, the Netherlands, Switzerland, and the United States. This was so despite the fact that both levels of deviance and levels of low self-control differed across

Table 10.2
Model Fit for Individual Groups by Sex and by Country

	American	Dutch	Hungarian	Swiss
Males (*n* = 410, each group)				
Chi square	91.39	56.68	55.81	44.47
RMR	0.04	0.03	0.05	0.04
GFI	0.95	0.97	0.97	0.97
Females (n = 219, each group)				
Chi square	72.96	55.21	44.92	96.12
RMR	0.07	0.06	0.06	0.10
GFI	0.92	0.94	0.95	0.91

Note: Total *chi square* value (*df* = 108) for males = 248.25; the total *chi square* value for females = 269.20. The sum of individual country values by sex add up to the total *chi square* value.

national contexts. These findings are very consistent with the theory as it predicts that "cultural variability is not important in the causation of crime" (p. 175) and that we should find constancy rather than variability in the definitions and causes of crime. Consistent with the classical assumption, findings suggest that at least in the four national contexts sampled, human behavior may in fact be "motivated" to a large extent by the self-interested pursuit of pleasure and avoidance of pain. The theoretical conceptualization of crime "frees societies to define crime as they see fit, but in our view this freedom poses little danger to the theory" (p. 176). As examined in the current chapter, measurement of crime must be independent of legal or cultural idiosyncratic elements and rather focus on universal qualities of norm-violating conduct, much like was captured in the behavioral measures of the Normative Deviance Scale. In this sense, the evidence examined suggests that the general theory may in fact be tenable cross-nationally, and that the cross-national comparative method provides a fruitful methodology to attempt to falsify predictions made by theories or theoretical propositions. Certainly, additional cross-national comparative tests need to be completed to answer whether predictions by the general theory can stand up to further scrutiny; however, the current data have added to the already strong empirical foundation of the theory (Pratt and Cullen, 2000). The data also provide evidence that modern empirical inquiry in criminology perhaps needs to proceed by theory testing, and that this modus of trying to advance knowledge and understanding, in the end, may provide more parsimonious, more powerful answers than traditional positivistic multiple-factor approaches (Gottfredson and Hirschi, 1987). In the end, as criminologist, or perhaps more aptly, as social scientists, we are interested in strong inference, something that is only possible through hypothesis testing and by pitting competing paradigms on the etiology of crime and deviance against each other.

Content or Simply Methodology?

In the introduction, the argument was made that comparative criminology is not about content, but rather about a method that allows rigorous testing of theoretical and empirical propositions, which ultimately will lead to useful generalizations. In a fairly influential book written about comparative criminology and introduced as "the current state of the art" about two decades ago, Newman and Ferracuti (1980) suggested that "perhaps universals do not exist in a 'definitional metadiscipline' such as criminology. After all, not only natural crime has so far eluded us, but we are focusing out interests more and more on interactional aspects of crime and deviance, reaffirming the cultural relativity of our object of study" (p. 10). The authors argued that crime is a context-specific phenomenon; this implies that crime requires unique explanatory mechanisms and that crime is not universal. The majority of their edited volume also focused on "using different cultures, arranged along various relevant socioeconomic, political, or developmental continua as clinical cases, in order to test general theories against the varieties of facts and situations offered to the researcher by the existing variations in sociopolitical and economic systems" (p. 9). This misunderstanding is the very essence of what has delayed, perhaps stifled, progress in comparative criminology. It is also found in Beirne's writing and thinking (1983), where he discusses comparative criminology as being one of either "the method of agreement" (e.g., Shelly's modernization theory), or "the method of difference" (e.g., Clinard's study of an apparently low crime culture), or "methodological relativism" (Friday's replication effort of differential association in Swedish youth)—though he provides a partial resolution to the problem when he writes "to generalize is to identify a law-like regularity in social behavior . . . cross-cultural generalization . . . necessarily ignores or even forbids cultural variation" (p. 33). Of course, as previously illustrated, cultural variation can and still does exist alongside findings of generalization, findings of universality, and findings supporting a theoretical proposition as shown in the current chapter. In the end, then, comparative criminology is not about content; rather, it is a powerful methodology as suggested by the following dictum loosely adapted from Durkheim—cross-national comparative criminology is not a particular branch or subdiscipline of criminology; it is criminology itself.

References

Achenbach, T. M., F. C. Verhulst, G. D. Baron, and M. Althaus. 1987. "A Comparison of Syndromes Derived from the Child Behavior Checklist for American and Dutch boys Aged 6-11 and 12-16." *Journal of Child Psychology and Psychiatry* 28: 437–453.

Adler, F. 1983. *Nations Not Obsessed with Crime*. Littleton, CO: Rothman and Company.

Archer, D. and Gartner, R. 1984. *Violence & Crime in Cross-National Perspective* New Haven, CT: Yale University Press.

Beirne, P. 1983. "Generalization and Its Discontents: The Comparative Study of Crime." Pp. 19–38 in I. L. Barak-Glantz and E. H. Elmer (eds.), *Comparative Criminology*. Beverly Hills, CA: Sage.

Bentler, P. M. 1992. "On the Fit of Models to Covariances and Methodology to the Bulletin." *Psychological Bulletin* 112: 400–404.

Berry, J. W., Y. H. Poortinga, M. H. Segall, and P. R. Dasen. 1992. *Cross-Cultural Psychology: Research and Applications*. New York: Cambridge University Press.

Brook, J. S., D. W. Brook, O. Arencibia-Mireles, L. Richter, and M. Whiteman. 2001. "Risk Factors for Adolescent Marijuana Use across Cultures and across Time." *The Journal of Genetic Psychology* 162(3): 357–374.

Browne, M. W., and R. Cudeck. 1993. "Alternative Ways of Assessing Model Fit." Pp. 136–162 in K. A. Bollen and J. Scott Long (eds.), *Testing Structural Equation Models*. Newbury Park, CA: Sage.

Christie, N. 1970. "Comparative Criminology." *Canadian Journal of Corrections* 12: 40–46.

Clinard, M. B. 1956. "Research Frontiers in Criminology." *The British Journal of Delinquency* 7: 110–112.

———. 1978. "Comparative Crime Victimization Surveys: Some Problems and Results." *International Journal of Criminology and Penology* 6: 221–231.

Durkheim, E. 1964. *The Rules of Sociological Method*. New York: Free Press.

Farrington, D. P. 1999. "A Criminological Research Agenda for the Next Millennium." *International Journal of Offender Therapy and Comparative Criminology* 43: 154–167.

Farrington, D. P., and R. Loeber. 1999. "Transatlantic Replicability of Risk Factors in the Development of Delinquency." Pp. 299–329 in P. Cohen and C. Slomkowski (eds.), *Historical and Geographical Influences on Psychopathology*. Mahwah, NJ: Lawrence Erlbaum Associates.

Farrington, D. P., and P.-O. H.Wikström. 1994. "Criminal Careers in London and Stockholm: A Cross-National Comparative Study." Pp. 65–89 in E. G. M. Weitekamp and H.-J. Kerner (eds.), *Cross-National Longitudinal Research in Human Development and Criminal Behavior*. Dordrecht: Kluwer.

Friday, P. C. 1973. "Problems in Comparative Criminology: Comments on the Feasibility and Implications of Research." *International Journal of Criminology and Penology* 1: 151–160.

Gartner, R. 1993. "Methodological Issues in Cross-Cultural Large-Survey Research on Violence." *Violence and Victims* 8: 199–215.

Glueck, S. 1965. "Project for Fundamental Criminologic Research in Puerto Rico." *Community Mental Health Journal* 1: 5–13.

———. 1967. "Wanted: A Comparative Criminology." Pp. 304–322 in S. Glueck and E. Glueck (eds.), *Ventures in Criminology*. Cambridge, MA: Harvard University Press.

Gottfredson, M. R., and T. Hirschi. 1987. "The Positive Tradition." Pp. 9–22 in M. R. Gottfredson and T. Hirschi (eds.), *Positive Criminology*. Newbury Park, CA: Sage.

———. 1990. *A General Theory of Crime*. Stanford: Stanford University Press.

Grasmick, H. G., C. R. Tittle, R. J. Bursik, and B. J.Arneklev. 1993. "Testing the Core Empirical Implications of Gottfredson and Hirschi's General Theory of Crime." *Journal of Research in Crime and Delinquency* 30: 5–29.

Hindelang, M. J., T. Hirschi, and J. G. Weis. 1981. *Measuring Delinquency*. Beverly Hills: Sage.

Hirschi, T., and M. R. Gottfredson. 1994. "Substantive Positivism and the Idea of Crime." Pp. 253–269 in T. Hirschi and M. R. Gottfredson (eds.), *The Generality of Deviance*. New Brunswick, NJ: Transaction Publishers.

Hollingshead, A. B. 1975. *Four-Factor Index of Social Status*. New Haven, CT: Yale University Department of Sociology.

Howard, G. J., G. Newman, and W. A. Pridemore. 2000. "Theory, Method, and Data in Comparative Criminology." *Criminal Justice* 4: 139–211.

Junger-Tas, J. 1989. "Self-Report Delinquency Research in Holland with a Perspective on International Comparison." Pp. 17–42 in M. W. Klein (ed.), *Cross-National Research in Self-Reported Crime and Delinquency*. Dordrecht: Kluwer Academic Publishing.

Junger-Tas, J., and I. H. Marshall. 1999. "The Self-Report Methodology in Crime Research." *Crime and Justice* 25: 291–367.

Junger-Tas, J., G. J. Terlouw, and M. W. Klein, eds. 1994. *Deliquent Behavior Among Young People in the Western World: First Results of the International Self-Report Delinquency Study*. Amsterdam: Kugler.

Killias, M., and M. Aebi. 2000. "Crime Trends in Europe from 1990 to 1996: How Europe Illustrates the Limits of the American Experience. *European Journal on CriminalPolicy and Research* 8: 43–63.

Killias, M., and W. Rau. 2000. "The European Sourcebook of Crime and Criminal Justice Statistics: A New Tool in Assessing Crime and Policy Issues in Comparative and Empirical Perspective." *European Journal on Criminal Policy and Research* 8: 3–12.

Krohn, M. 1987. "Cross-National Research as an Analytic Strategy." *American Sociological Review* 52: 713–731.

Longshore, D., S. Turner, and J. Stein. 1996. "Self-Control in a Criminal Sample: An Examination of Construct Validity." *Criminology* 3: 209–228.

Mannheim, H. 1965. *Comparative Criminology*. Boston: Houghton Mifflin Company.

Mayhew, P., and J. J. M. van Dijk. 1997. *Criminal Victimisation in Eleven Industrialized Countries: Key Findings from the 1996 International Crime Victims Survey.* The Netherlands: WODC.

Moffitt, T. E. 1989. "Accommodating Self-Report Methods to a Low-Delinquency Culture: A Longitudinal Study from New Zealand." Pp. 43–66 in M. W. Klein (ed.), *Cross-National Research in Self-Reported Crime and Delinquency*. Dordrecht: Kluwer.

Moffitt, T. E., P. A. Silva, D. R. Lynam, B. Henry. 1994. "Self-Reported Delinquency at Age 18: New Zealand's Dunedin Multidisciplinary Health and Development Study." Pp. 354–366 in J. Junger-Tas, G.-J. Terlouw, and M. W. Klein (eds.), *Delinquent Behavior among Young People in the Western World: First Results of the International Self-Report Delinquency Study*. Amsterdam: Kugler Publications.

Moffitt, T. E., A. Caspi, P. A. Silva, and M. Stouthamer-Loeber. 1995. "Individual Differences in Personality and Intelligence Are Linked to Crime: Cross-Context Evidence from Nations, Neighborhoods, Genders, Races, and Age Cohorts." Pp. 1–34 in J. Hagan (ed.), *Delinquency and Disrepute in the Life Course*. Greenwich, CT: JAI Press.

Moffitt, T. E., and P. Silva. 1988. "Self-Reported Delinquency: Results from an Instrument for New Zealand." *Australian and New Zealand Journal of Criminology* 21: 227–240.

Newman, G. R., and F. Ferracuti. 1980. "Introduction: The Limits and Possibilities of Comparative Criminology." Pp. 7–16 in G. R. Newman (ed.), *Crime and Deviance: A Comparative Perspective*. Beverly Hills, CA: Sage.

Parmalee, M. 1918. *Criminology*. New York: The Macmillan Company.

Piquero, A. R., and A. B. Rosay. 1998. "The Reliability and Validity of Grasmick et al.'s Self- Control Scale: A Comment on Longshore et al." *Criminology* 36: 157–173.

Pratt, T. C., and F. T. Cullen. 2000. "The Empirical Status of Gottfredson and Hirschi's General Theory of Crime: A Meta-Analysis." *Criminology* 38: 931–964.

Przeworski, A., and H. Teune. 1966. "Equivalence in Cross-National Research." *Public Opinion Quarterly* 30: 551–568.

Pulkkinen, L., and R. E. Tremblay. 1992. "Patterns of Boys' Social Adjustment in Two Cultures at Different Ages: A Longitudinal Perspective." *International Journal of Behavioral Development* 15: 527–553.

Quetelet, A. 1984. *Research on the Propensity for Crime at Different Ages*. Translated by Sawyer F. Sylvester. Cincinnati: Anderson.

Rosenbaum, M. 1980. "A Schedule for Assessing Self-Control Behaviors: Preliminary Findings." *Behavior Therapy* 11: 109–121.

Rowe, D. C. 1997. "Group Differences in Developmental Processes: The Exception or the Rule?" *Psychological Inquiry* 8(3): 218–222.

Rowe, D. C., A. T. Vazsonyi, and D. J. Flannery. 1994 "No More Than Skin Deep: Ethnic and Racial Similarity in Developmental Process." *Psychological Review* 101: 396–413.

Van de Vijver, F., and K. Leung. 1997. "Methods and Data Analysis of Comparative Research." Pp. 257–300 in J. W. Berry, Y. H. Poortinga, and J. Pandey (eds.), *Handbook of Cross-Cultural Psychology* (Vol. 1: Theory and Method). Needham Heights, MA: Allyn and Bacon.

Van Dijk, J. J. M., and K. Kangaspunta. 2000. "Piecing Together the Cross-National Crime Puzzle. *National Institute of Justice Journal* (January): 35–41.

Van Dijk, J. J. M., P. Mayhew, and M. Killias. 1991. *Experiences of the World: Key Findings from the 1989 International Crime Survey*. Boston: Kluwer.

Vazsonyi, A. T. and M. Killias. 2001. "Immigration and Crime among Youth in Switzerland." *Criminal Justice and Behavior* 28(3): 329–366.

Vazsonyi, A. T., L. E. Pickering, D. Hessing, and M. Junger. 2002. "Routine Activities and Deviant Behaviors: American, Dutch, Hungarian and Swiss Youth." *Journal of Quantitative Criminology* 18(4): 397–422.

Vazsonyi, A. T., L. E. Pickering, M. Junger, and D. Hessing. 2001. "An Empirical Test of a General Theory of Crime: A Four-Nation Comparative Study of Self-Control and the Prediction of Deviance." *Journal of Research in Crime and Delinquency* 38(2): 91–131.

Zimring, F. E., and G. Hawkins. 1997. *Crime Is Not the Problem: Lethal Violence in America*. New York: Oxford University Press.

Zuckerman, M., S. Eysenck, and H. J. Eysenck. 1978. "Sensation Seeking in England and America: Cross-Cultural, Age, and Sex Comparisons." *Journal of Consulting and Clinical Psychology* 46(1): 139–149.

Appendix A: Grasmick et al.'s Low Self-Control Scale

Impulsiveness (total sample ∝ = .50; ∝ range = .45 to .62[1])

1. I often act on the spur of the moment without stopping to think.
9. I often do whatever brings me pleasure here and now, even at the cost of some distant goal.
13. I'm more concerned with what happens to me in the short run than in the long run.
20. *I don't devote much thought and effort to preparing for the future.*

Simple Tasks (∝ = .68; ∝ range = .61 to .73)

5. I frequently try to avoid projects that I know will be difficult.
7. I dislike really hard tasks that stretch my ability to the limit.
15. When things get complicated, I tend to quit or withdraw.
19. The things in life that are easiest to do bring me the most pleasure.

Risk Seeking (∝ = .79; ∝ range = .69 to .84)

3. I like to test myself every now and then by doing something a little risky.
4. Sometimes I will take a risk just for the fun of it.
6. I sometimes find it exciting to do things for which I might get into trouble.
11. Excitement and adventure are more important to me than security.

Physical Activity (∝ = .63; ∝ range = .55 to .74)

8. If I had a choice, I would almost always rather do something physical than something mental.
10. I almost always feel better when I am on the move than when I am sitting and thinking.
16. I like to get out and do things more than I like to read or contemplate ideas.
18. I seem to have more energy and a greater need for activity than most other people my age.

Self-Centeredness (∝ = .60; ∝ range = .45 to .68)

2. *If things I do upset people, it's their problem not mine.*
12. I try to look out for myself first, even if it means making things difficult for other people.
14. I will try to get things I want even when I know it's causing problems for other people.
17. I'm not very sympathetic to other people when they are having problems.

Temper (∝ = .76; ∝ range = .68 to .76)

21. I lose my temper pretty easily.

22. Often, when I am angry at people, I feel more like hurting them than talking to them about why I am angry.
23. When I'm really angry, other people should stay away from me.
24. When I have a serious disagreement with someone, it's usually hard for me to talk calmly about it without getting upset.

Notes: Items 2 and 20 are included here since they were part of the original Low Self-Control Scale; however, they are italicized to indicate that they were not included in their respective scales for current analyses. [1]Alpha ranges include reliability analyses by sex, age groups (15–19), and nationality.

Appendix B: The Normative Deviance Scale (NDS)

Have you ever . . . ?

Vandalism (total sample ∝ = .84; ∝ range = .77 to .87[3])
Smashed bottles on the street, school grounds, or other areas?
Intentionally damaged or destroyed property belonging to your parents or other family members (brothers or sisters)?
Intentionally damaged or destroyed property belonging to a school, college, or university?
Intentionally damaged or destroyed other property (signs, windows, mailboxes, parking meter, etc.) that did not belong to you?
Intentionally damaged or destroyed property belonging to your employer or at your workplace?
Slashed or in any way damaged seats on a bus, in a movie theater, or something at another public place?
Written graffiti on a bus, on school walls, on rest room walls, or on anything else in a public place?
Committed acts of vandalism when coming or going to a football game or other sports event?

Alcohol (∝ = .84; ∝ range = .76 to .90)
Consumed hard liquor (e.g., tequila, whiskey, vodka, or gin) before you were 21?[1]
Consumed alcoholic beverages (e.g., beer, wine, or wine coolers) before you were 21?[1]
Got drunk (intentionally) just for the fun of it (at any age)?
Got drunk just to fit in and be part of the crowd (at any age)?
Lied about your age to buy alcohol before you turned 21?[1]
Had an older brother/sister or friend buy alcohol for you?
Bought alcohol for a brother/sister or friend?

Drug Use (∝ = .89; ∝ range = .83 to .90)
Used tobacco products regularly (e.g., cigarettes, chew, snuff, etc.)?
Used "soft" drugs such as marijuana (grass, pot)?
Used "hard" drugs such as crack, cocaine, or heroin?
Gone to school when you were drunk or high on drugs?
Gone to work when you were drunk or high on drugs?
Gone to a concert when you were drunk or high on drugs?
Gone to a club/dance/party when you were drunk or high on drugs?
Gone to a club/dance/party to get drunk or high on drugs?
Sold any drugs such as marijuana (grass, pot), cocaine, or heroin?

School Misconduct (∝ = .76; ∝ range = .73 to .82)
Cheated on school/college/university tests (e.g., cheat sheet, copy from neighbor, etc.)?
Been sent out of a classroom because of "bad" behavior (e.g., inappropriate behaviors, cheating etc.)?
Been suspended or expelled from school/college/university?
Stayed away from school/classes when your parent(s) thought you were there?
Intentionally missed classes over a number of days for "no reason," just for fun (e.g., there was no family emergency)?
Been in trouble at school so that your parents received a phone call about it?
Skipped school/work (pretending you are ill)?

General Deviance (∝ = .81; ∝ range = .73 to .86)
Intentionally disobeyed a stop sign or a red traffic light while driving a vehicle?
Been on someone else's property when you knew you were not supposed to be there?
Failed to return extra change that you knew a cashier gave you by mistake?
Tried to deceive a cashier to your advantage (e.g., flash a larger bill and give a smaller one)?
Let the air out of the tires of a car or bike?
Lied about your age to get into a nightclub/bar?
Made nuisance/obscene telephone calls?
Avoided paying for something (e.g., movies, bus or subway rides, food, etc.)?
Used fake money or other things in a candy, coke, or stamp machine?
Shaken/hit a parked car just to turn on the car's alarm?
Stayed out all night without informing your parents about your whereabouts?

Theft (∝ = .83; ∝ range = .72 to .84)
Stolen, taken, or tried to take something from a family member or relative (e.g., personal items, money, etc.)?

Stolen, taken, or tried to take something worth $10 or less (e.g. newspaper, pack of gum, mail, money, etc.)?[2]
Stolen, taken, or tried to take something worth between $10 and $100 (e.g., shirt, watch, cologne, video game cart., shoes, money, etc.)?[2]
Stolen, taken, or tried to take something worth more than $100 (e.g. leather jacket, car stereo, bike, money, etc.)?[2]
Stolen, taken, or tried to take something that belonged to "the public" (e.g., street signs, construction signs, etc.)?
Stolen or tried to steal a motor vehicle (e.g., car or motorcycle)?
Bought, sold, or held stolen goods or tried to do any of these things?

Assault ($\propto$ = .76; $\propto$ range = .68 to .79)
Hit or threatened to hit a person?
Hit or threatened to hit your parent(s)?
Hit or threatened to hit other students/peers or people?
Used force or threatened to beat someone up if they didn't give you money or something else you wanted?
Been involved in gang fights or other gang activities?
Beaten someone up so badly they required medical attention?

Notes: [1]the age of 16 was substituted in European versions of the survey since this is the legal drinking age; [2]culture-appropriate monetary values and symbols were used in each respective country's version of the survey; [3]alpha ranges include reliability analyses by sex, age groups (15-19), and nationality.

11

Crime as Risk-Taking: Co-occurrence of Delinquent Behavior, Health-Endangering Behaviors, and Problem Behaviors

Marianne Junger and Maja Deković

There is a large amount of evidence on the risk factors for criminal behavior. This research has been adequately summarized in various publications (Farrington et al., 1990; Rutter and Giller, 1983; Rutter, Giller, and Hagell, 1998; Wilson and Herrnstein, 1985; Yoshikawa, 1994). Despite this comparatively large body of research, a number of important issues have been neglected and major questions about the origins of criminal behavior remain unanswered (Cloninger, Bayon, and Przybeck, 1997). For instance, it has been noted by several authors that there is an important gap of information regarding the co-occurrence of criminal behavior with a range of other types of risky behaviors and negative outcomes. This lack of information is surprising as the existent research suggests that criminal behavior, like many forms of psychopathology, does not occur alone: Co-occurrence is generally the rule rather than the exception (Caron and Rutter, 1991; Clark, 1999; Krueger, 1999; Krueger et al., 1996; Loeber and Keenan, 1994; Tolan and Henry, 1996; Zoccolillo, 1992). The present chapter will focus on the co-occurrence of delinquent behavior with health-endangering behaviors and problem behaviors with adverse economic consequences, such as truancy and dropping out from school. The questions which will be addressed in this chapter are: (1) Is there evidence in the empirical literature for the existence of co-occurrence between these three types of behavior, (2) what is the meaning of co-occurrence, and (3) what are the theoretical implications of co-occurrence in the explanation of criminal behavior.

Conceptual Issues

In the social sciences and related disciples such as psychiatry, different concepts have been used to refer to the same, similar, or overlapping behaviors. Criminologists study crime or juvenile delinquency, which is usually defined as breaking the criminal law. Sociologists generally use the concept of deviance, which is usually defined as breaking social norms. To the extent that these social norms have been codified in the criminal law, sociologists are thus also concerned with crime. Psychiatrists use the classification system described by the *Diagnostic and Statistical Manual of Mental Disorders* (DSM-IV, American Psychiatric Assn., 1994). For the purpose of illustration, we describe in some detail three concepts of the DSM-IV system, which are closely related to criminological concepts. Under the heading of "personality disorders" the DSM-IV describes individuals with *personality disorders* as those who "regularly disregard and violate the rights of others. These behaviors may be aggressive or destructive and may involve breaking laws or rules, deceit or theft." In childhood and adolescents, a similar concept to juvenile delinquency is conduct disorders. Conduct disorders are diagnosed when a child "seriously misbehaves with aggressive or non-aggressive behaviors against people, animals or property that may be characterized as belligerent, destructive, threatening, physically cruel, deceitful, disobedient, or dishonest. This may include stealing, intentional injury, and forced sexual activity" (diagnostic criteria for 312.8). For adults a similar concept to crime is antisocial personality disorder. *Antisocial personality disorder* is defined as (American Psychiatric Assn., 1994):

A. There is a pervasive pattern of disregard for and violation of the rights of others occurring since age 15 years, as indicated by three (or more) of the following: (1) failure to conform to social norms with respect to lawful behaviors as indicated by repeatedly performing acts that are grounds for arrest (2) deceitfulness, as indicated by repeated lying, use of aliases, or conning others for personal profit or pleasure (3) impulsivity or failure to plan ahead (4) irritability and aggressiveness, as indicated by repeated physical fights or assaults (5) reckless disregard for safety of self or others (6) consistent irresponsibility, as indicated by repeated failure to sustain consistent work behavior or honor financial obligations (7) lack of remorse, as indicated by being indifferent to or rationalizing having hurt, mistreated, or stolen from another.

B. The individual is at least age 18 years.

C. There is evidence of Conduct Disorder with onset before age 15 years.

D. The occurrence of antisocial behavior is not exclusively during the course of Schizophrenia or a Manic Episode.

The reader will note in the description above that "breaking social norms" ("deviance" for sociologists) and law breaking ("crime" for criminologists) are the outcome of interest in psychiatry.

Psychologists in the fields of clinical and/or abnormal psychology often use the psychiatric diagnostic system (see for example Loeber and Keenan, 1994; Nathan and Langenbucher, 1999; Tremblay, Pihl, Vitaro, and Dobkin, 1994). Health psychologists investigate risk-behavior, problem behavior, substance abuse, and addictive behavior (which is broader than substance abuse and also includes, for example, gambling). Obviously, the concerns of health psychologists overlap with those of criminologists when they study, for example, drug use. Health psychologists often draw up lists of health-endangering behaviors and these lists vary from study to study and author to author. These lists often include various forms of substance abuse, risk-taking in traffic, and sometimes aggression and delinquency (see for example, Basen-Enquist, Edmundson, and Parcel, 1996; Bell and Bell, 1993; Dembo et al., 1992a; DiClemente, Hansen, and Ponton, 1996b; Donovan and Jessor, 1985; Jessor and Jessor, 1977).

This brief overview illustrates that what has been defined as a crime by criminal law, and, consequently, is the dependent variable of criminology, is considered a mental health problem by psychologists, a psychiatric diagnosis by psychiatrists, and sometimes a health-endangering behavior in health psychology. It is not the purpose of this chapter to discuss in more depth these conceptual issues. However, we wish to stress that it is important to realize that under different concepts similar behaviors are studied in a relatively large number of disciplines and sub-disciplines. Consequently, the literature in these disciplines is relevant to the study of crime. This chapter is an attempt to bring together information on co-occurrence from these different fields on three categories of behavior: first, delinquent behavior (including aggression and law-breaking behavior); second, health-endangering behavior; and third, problem behavior. Globally it could be argued that delinquent behavior constitutes mainly a problem for others, while health-endangering behaviors and problem behaviors constitute risks for the individual himself. The main question in this chapter is whether those who constitute a threat to others are also a danger to themselves.

Theoretical Background / Issues in Various Disciplines: The Need for Multidisciplinary Research

The issue of co-occurrence of criminal behavior, deviance, risk-taking, or antisocial behavior has not received much attention in sociology, criminology, psychology, or psychiatry. Nevertheless, several authors in these different disciplines discussed the importance of acquiring more knowledge on co-occurring problems or behaviors and discussed the major conceptual and theoretical issues related to co-occurrence. These discussions are briefly described below. They have taken different forms in different disciplines, but at their core, the similarity in these discussions is the issue of "consistency of social behavior over situations."

The Generality of Deviance Debate in Criminology and Sociology

In criminology as well as in sociology, the debate on the cross-situational consistency of behavior has been formulated mostly as a problem of specialization versus generality of criminal behavior (Gottfredson and Hirschi, 1990). Generalists have argued that criminal behavior forms a part of a very broad and general tendency toward deviance: Individuals involved in crime commit all sorts of crimes and are involved in every type of deviant behavior; consequently, specialization is minimal (Dembo et al., 1992a; Osgood, Johnston, O'Malley, and Bachman, 1988; Osgood and Rowe, 1994; Osgood, 1990; Rowe, Osgood, and Nicewander, 1990) and, if there is some specialization, it is not relevant for theory (Gottfredson and Hirschi, 1990). In opposition with this view, others have argued that criminals do specialize in particular forms of crime. For example, many authors stated that violent offenders could be distinguished from property offenders (Brennan, Mednick, and John, 1989; Huizinga, Esbensen, and Weiher, 1991). Consequently, one of the goals of empirical research should be to discover which factors are associated with violent behavior and which factors are leading to property crime (Henry, Caspi, Moffitt, and Silva, 1996). Generalists, on the contrary, will argue that the personal risk factors are the same for every type of crime (Gottfredson and Hirschi, 1990; Jessor and Jessor, 1977).

A decade ago, Gottfredson and Hirschi (1990) presented self-control theory and argued strongly in favor of the generality thesis. They stated, first, that criminals were generalists, and, second, that delinquents were also involved in various forms of "risky" behavior, which therefore were described as "behaviors analogous to crime." In their formulation of self-control theory, they proposed that control mechanisms are needed to contain man's natural impulses toward deviance and self-interested behavior. Individuals with low self control will have a relatively high probability of succumbing to the temptations of short-term pleasures without caring for the long-term negative consequences. Therefore, they are likely to be involved in many forms of risky behaviors, and, as a result, to suffer from the negative consequences of these behaviors, such as illnesses, physical decay, and accidents.

The Cross-Situational Consistency Debate in Psychology

In psychology, a similar discussion has been conducted on the issue of the cross-situational consistency of behavior. An essential condition for the establishment of personality psychology is the empirical foundation of cross-situational consistency and the existence of personality traits (Epstein and O'Brien, 1985; Hinde, 1989; Kenrick and Funder, 1988; Krahé, 1990; Mischel and Peake, 1982; Moskowitz, 1982; Tellegen, 1991). According to personality psychologists, social behavior shows significant temporal stability and consistency across situations due to the operation of some internal disposition: a latent trait. In brief, personality dimensions are very broad behavioral tendencies. These behavioral tendencies can be described in terms of "traits," namely theoretical constructs based on "covariation of a number of behavioral acts" (Eysenck and Eysenck, 1985: 12). For example, Eysenck (1991) proposed that lower-order traits intercorrelate and make up higher-order factors or superfactors, which he has labeled "types." Eysenck (1990) proposed a hierarchical taxonomy of personality containing four levels (see Revelle, 1995 and Jang, 1998 for reviews). At the bottom level are behaviors such as talking with a friend on a single occasion. At the second level are habits such as talking with friends on multiple occasions, which are comprised of recurring behaviors. The third level is constituted by traits or factors such as sociability, which are comprised of intercorrelated sets of habits. At the top of the hierarchy are superfactors or dimensions of personality such as extraversion, which are intercorrelated sets of traits or factors. Eysenck suggests three such superfactors: extraversion (E), neuroticism (N), and psychoticism (P). These three superfactors or dimensions of personality are orthogonal to each other, which means that they do not correlate with each other (Eysenck and Eysenck, 1985; Jang, 1998). Related approaches were described by Tellegen (1991). Consequently, traits can consist of simple descriptions of the variables that they "summarize," for example, aggression, honesty, or consciousness. Other, higher-order traits have a surplus meaning and have explanatory power based on inferred structures or processes. This surplus meaning leads to new explanations and testable hypotheses. For example, positive emotionality, negative emotionality, and traditionalism are "higher-order" traits (Tellegen,1991: 13–15).

In opposition to this approach in personality research, Mischel (1968) argued that there is no cross-situational consistency. For example, he argued, there is no such thing as "honesty" or "aggression" or "conscientiousness" (Mischel and Peake, 1982; Nisbett and Ross, 1991). Although there is no cross-situational consistency of behavior, there is, however, temporal stability, namely stability of the same behavior over time. This stability will exist to the extent that situations are stable. Mischel's (1982) thesis lead to heated discussions (see, among others Bem and Allen, 1974; Bem and Funder, 1978; Burton, 1963; Chaplin and Goldberg, 1985; Conley, 1984; Emmons and Diener, 1986; Epstein and O'Brien, 1985; Funder and Colvin, 1991; Krahé, 1990; Magnusson and Ellen, 1983; Mischel and Peake, 1982; Mischel and Shoda, 1995; Murtha, Kanfer, and Ackerman, 1996; Peake and Mischel, 1984;

Pervin, 1989, 1990, 1994; Scarr and McCartney, 1983; Shoda, Mischel, and Wright, 1994; Tellegen, 1991; Van Heck, Perugini, Caprara, and Froger, 1994). The search for empirical support for the existence of traits has produced mixed results (Bem and Allen,1974; Bem and Funder, 1978; Burton, 1963; Chaplin and Goldberg, 1985; Conley, 1984; Epstein and O'Brien, 1985; Krahé, 1990; Mischel and Peake, 1982; Peake and Mischel, 1984; Pervin, 1989, 1994). All this indicates that issue of cross-situational consistency is still subject to controversy (Krahé, 1990; Rowe, 1987).

The issue of cross-situational consistency has been particularly relevant in the field of risk-taking and health psychology. There are two substantially different views on health-endangering behavior. The first view holds that the specific types of health-endangering behavior are unrelated, and each form needs specific explanatory variables. In this view, smoking, drinking, drug use, or driving behavior are each determined by specific circumstances (Ajzen, 1991; Bachman, Johnston, and O'Malley, 1998; Stroebe and Stroebe, 1995). The alternative view is that different health-endangering behaviors co-occur within the same persons, and that these behaviors are related to each other. Consequently they have something in common, and they could, to some extent, be the expressions of a single underlying dimension (Abram, 1989; Allen, Leadbeater, and Aber, 1990; Anderson et al., 1993; Baumeister, Heatherton, and Tice, 1994; Casper et al., 1980; Caspi et al., 1997; DaCosta and Halmi, 1992; DiClemente, Hansen, and Ponton, 1996a; Donovan, Jessor, and Costa, 1991; Elliott, 1993; Friedman et al., 1993; Igra and Irwin, 1996; Istvan and Matarazzo, 1984; Jeffery, 1989; Jessor and Jessor, 1977; Junger and Wiegersma, 1995; Mischel and Peake, 1982; Neumark-Sztainer, Story, Dixon, and Murray, 1998; Otero-Lopez et al., 1994; Scherwitz and Rugulies, 1992; Sikorski, 1996). In general, this view implies that the same processes lead to involvement in a variety of health-endangering behaviors.

The Co-Morbidity Issue in Psychiatry

Psychiatrists study diseases or mental disorders. Generally, mental disorders are conceptualized as dichotomies: the disorder is or is not present. Co-orbidity means that some individuals have more than one disease. The issue of co-orbidity was to some extent perceived as a "nuisance" and an embarrassment to the DSM classification system as it may imply imperfect validity of psychiatric nosology (Angold, Costello, and Erkanli, 1999; Krueger, Caspi, Moffit, Silva, and McGee, 1996). As a result, the issue of co-morbidity has received very little attention until recently. This general lack of information on the co-occurrence of problem behaviors was to some extent surprising as it appeared that most mental disorders do not occur alone: co-morbidity was the rule rather than the exception (Caron and Rutter, 1991; Krueger, 1999; Loeber and Keenan, 1994; Tolan and Henry, 1996; Zoccolillo, 1992). Several large studies were conducted to investigate co-morbidity (Krueger, 1999; Robins and Price, 1991). Recently, Angold et al. (1999) performed a meta-analysis and found substantial co-morbidity between various psychiatric diagnoses. He reported an odds ratio of, 10.7 between conduct disorders and ADHD; an odds ratio of 6.6 between conduct disorders and depression; and an odds ratio of 3.1 between conduct disorders and anxiety (Angold, Costello, and Erkanli, 1999). Most authors concluded that the issue of co-morbidity raises fundamental questions about the DSM-IV diagnosis system, the nature of psychiatric disorders, and about their causes (Angold, Costello, and Erkanli, 1999; Caron and Rutter, 1991; Krueger, Caspi, Moffit, Silva, and McGee, 1996; Nathan and Langenbucher, 1999).

In summary, interest in issues related to the co-occurrence of various types of "problems," "deviant or criminal behaviors," and "disorders"' hase been growing recently in different disciplines.

Reasons to Study Co-Occurrence

Before looking at the empirical evidence, it is important to examine the reasons why the co-occurrence of criminal behavior with risk-taking is worth studying. The co-occurrence of many types of risky behavior with criminal behavior raises fundamental questions about the nature of the outcome variables that are being studied in the field of crime and delinquency, similarly to the issue of co-morbidity in the study of psychopathology (Caron and Rutter, 1991; Costa, McCrae, and Siegler, 1999; Maughan and Farrington, 1997; Pfohl, 1999). Obviously, in some cases, co-occurrence (or co-morbidity) is artefactual or has trivial explanations, and this possibility has to be ruled out before looking for other substantive reasons. For example, in the case of traffic behavior and crime, it is possible that a particular crime and an accident are both part of the same chain of events. It sometimes happens that a robber leaves the scene of the robbery by car and has an accident, or that an individual who is suicidal has a fatal traffic accident which should actually be considered a suicide (Junger and Tremblay, 1999). Although accidents and crime can co-occur as the result of being part of the same sequence of events, this is probably very rare. For example, in a Dutch sample of 1,000 accidents, there were no occurrences of an accident and a crime taking place on the same day (Junger, West, and Timman, 2001). Other artefactual explanations of co-occurrence (or co-morbidity) can occur in clinical samples as a result of referral policies which are more likely to refer patients with multiple diagnoses (for a discussion of these issues, see Caron (199 1), Zoccolillo (1992), and Caron (1991). Nevertheless, although co-occurrence of criminal behavior with risk-taking behaviors or negative outcomes may sometimes have trivial explanations, most co-occurrence is not artefactual and needs to be explained in a substantive way. We believe three major reasons make the co-occurrence of criminal behavior and risk-taking an important issue.

1. Consequences Associated with Criminal Behavior

Knowledge concerning the extent to which criminal behavior is connected to different forms of risk-taking behaviors and negative outcomes leads to a better understanding of the dangers that are associated with involvement in criminal behavior. There are several examples of these dangers. First, the relationship of criminal behavior with truancy and dropping out from school are likely to have durable negative consequences for the individual in terms of job opportunities and income. Second, relationships between criminal behavior and accident involvement as well as other health-endangering behaviors can have considerable health implications. The association of criminal behavior with depression and suicidal thoughts has also, obviously, far-reaching implications. A better understanding of these consequences should, among other things, have implications for the policies toward criminal behavior and stresses the need for interventions for the children/individuals concerned. They might be, together with their eventual victims, the ones who will suffer most from their involvement in criminal behavior.

2. Tests for Explanations of Criminal Behavior

The fact that criminal behavior is usually associated with many other problems constitutes one of the basic facts about criminal behavior that theories should take into account. These associations can be seen as a test case for theories. The question is whether the specific theory also explain why all these additional negative outcomes accompany criminal behavior? For example, if learning theories on violence (Akers, 1994, 1996; Bandura, Ross, and Ross, 1961) argue that violent behavior has to be learned, are accidents or dropping out from school—two negative consequences associated with violence—also "learned" at the same time? Another example comes from studies on the role of toxins and nutrients on criminal behavior (Rutter, Giller, and Hagell, 1998). Several studies found that children of alcoholic parents have an increased risk of criminal behavior. But these relationships are difficult to interpret as alcohol abuse is likely to be correlated to many other form of risk-taking, including other forms of substance abuse, as well as other familial psycho-social dysfunction (Rutter, Giller, and Hagell, 1998). Taking co-occurrence into account is essential for being able to draw meaningful conclusions for the etiology of criminal behavior.

3. Prediction and Prevention

If we know more about the how traits underlying criminal personality express themselves early in life this knowledge may help in identifying children at high risks of developing this disorder. An example is childhood accidents, which have been shown to be predictive of later criminality. An interesting finding was reported by Wadsworth (1978) who showed, on the basis of a large-scale cohort study that, over twenty-one years, "the most striking and significant associations with later delinquency were found to be in the experience of injuries between the ages of 6 and 10—which, as far as we know were all accidental—and of admissions to hospital before the age of 5 years"(Wadsworth, 1978: 47). And the same relationship the other way around is also possible: Cobb et al. (1995) found that childhood aggression (assessed during the 4th or 7th grade) predicted injuries at age 14–18. Other studies also reported that accident children differ from non-accident children on the Rutter-behavior scale (Read et al., 1963; Wadsworth, Burnell, Taylor, and Butler, 1983). An explanation of this finding may be found in the fact that childhood accidents can be the result of poor parenting and/or child behavior such as impulsivity and/or ADHD (Junger, 1994). Both are also predictors of late criminal behavior (Farrington et al., 1990; Rutter and Giller, 1983; Rutter, Giller, and Hagell, 1998; Wilson and Herrnstein, 1985; Yoshikawa, 1994). Thus, accidents predict future delinquency and, accordingly, childhood accident involvement could help, within a larger framework of identifying risk factors, identify which children are at risk for future criminal behavior. If criminal behavior co-occurs with health-endangering behavior, for instance with smoking and alcohol abuse, this has implications for public health policies. If one is able to identify children who will also be at risk for developing criminal personalities early in life, these same children will also be at risk for poor health outcomes. This implies knowledge about the childhood predictors of future criminal behavior also helps to identify children at risk for poor health outcomes.

Method

The present chapter is based on a literature review that investigated whether delinquent behavior is associated with health-endangering behaviors and problem behaviors. *Health-endangering behavior*, with potentially serious negative physical outcomes was defined as: (1) risky traffic behavior such as not wearing a seatbelt, not wearing a helmet on a moped/motorcycle, disobeying stop signs, dangerous (too fast) driving; (2) substance use such as alcohol abuse, tobacco use, soft drugs (cannabis products such as marihuana and hashish), hard drugs (heroine, cocaine, methadone, crack, barbiturates, amphetamines [speed], and psychedelic products [such as LSD and XTC], and ecstasy); (3) self-medication (tranquilizers or laxatives without prescription); (4) unsafe sex (first sexual relationship without contraceptives, having sexual contact with many different partners, having sexual relations with possibly infected partner, and teenage pregnancies); (5) unhealthy diet (too fat, irregular meals); (6) lack of physical exercise; and (7) suicidal behavior (suicide, suicide attempts, suicidal thoughts). *Problem behavior* was defined as behavior with (direct) negative economic consequences namely: (1) homelessness, (2) gambling (on machines, making bets, playing cards for money), (3) dropping out from school, and (4) truancy. *Delinquent behavior* was conceptualized as (1) aggression at school (defined here as violence against other pupils and oppositional behavior at school), and (2) criminal behavior, as defined by criminal law, self-report, or registered contacts with the criminal justice system.

To find out whether these behaviors co-occur a literature search was performed in Psychinfo and Medline. We searched for the studies that examined each of the possible relationships among these sixteen behaviors (for example, the studies that examined the relationship between risky traffic behavior on the one hand and alcohol abuse, tobacco use, soft drug use, etc. on the other hand). It should be noted that our findings do not pretend to provide a complete overview in terms of the number of studies that investigated a particular relationship. For example, some relationships such as alcohol abuse and crime or crime and truancy have been well documented and it would be unfeasible—and not very useful—to find every study which reported these relationships. However, a systematic effort was made to locate studies for every specific relationship. For example, we did look systematically to find whether there were studies investigating crime and aggression in relation to an unhealthy diet and/or lack of physical exercise.

Results

The findings are presented in a matrix with the sixteen forms of risk-taking mentioned above in the rows and columns (Table 11.1). An "X" in a particular cell indicates that the literature search resulted in at least one study that found a positive relationship between two types of risk-taking. For example, we found twelve studies that report a positive relationship between alcohol abuse and risky traffic behavior. These studies can be found in a note of Table 11.1, with complete references in the appendix. An empty cell indicates that no study was found that examined a particular relationship. For example, we found no study that examined the relationship between risky traffic behavior and self-medication.

The results will not be discussed for every cell, as this would become a very long and tedious discussion. Only the global findings will be presented. Generally, the sixteen concepts that were included in our review tend to co-occur. Criminal behavior appears to be related to every other concept. Tobacco smoking also shows associations with all of the studied concepts. The other forms of substance abuse (apart from tobacco smoking) are related to most other types of risk-taking. Suicidal behavior and the three types of problem behavior, namely gambling, truancy, and dropping out from school are also related to a large variety of other behaviors. Physical exercise and self-medication were not found to have many relationships with the other concepts. In sum, the empirical literature provides a good basis for thinking that—with some exceptions—delinquent behavior, health-endangering behaviors, and problem behavior tend to co-vary together.

Discussion

The goal of this chapter was to investigate the relationships between delinquent behavior, health endangering behaviors (such as risky traffic behavior, substance use [such as alcohol abuse, smoking, soft drugs, and hard drugs], self-medication, unsafe sex, unhealthy diet, lack of physical exercise, and suicidal behavior), and problems behaviors (namely gambling, truancy, and dropping out from school). Our findings show that most of the sixteen concepts included in this review are related to each other. In the paragraphs below, the meaning of these findings will be discussed, and possible explanations of the findings will be presented.

What Is the Meaning of Co-Occurrence?

Health Implications of Delinquency

The findings presented in this chapter emphasize the health consequences of involvement in delinquent behavior. The issue of physical health is a relatively new issue in relation to criminal behavior. Several other negative consequences have already been documented in past research. The fact that criminal behavior is predictive of poor social functioning and economic prospects has been documented in the past (Kokko and Pulkkinen, 2000; Robins, 1966). Similarly, the mental health aspects of criminal behavior have also received attention in previous research (Angold, Costello, and Erkanli, 1999; Caron and Rutter, 1991; Cloninger, Bayon, and Przybeck, 1997; Fergusson, Horwood, and Lynskey, 1994; Kessler et al., 1998; Loeber and Keenan, 1994; McConaughy and Achenbach, 1994; Nottelmann and Jensen, 1995; Pedersen, 1994; Pfohl, 1999; Skodol et al., 1993; Tolan and Henry, 1996; Verhulst and van der Ende, 1993).

The present findings suggest that criminal behavior should have long-term health implications. A number of recent studies did indeed report relationships between crime and/or criminal behavior and various indicators of physical health (Bardone et al., 1998; Farrington and Junger, 1995; Junger, Stroebe, and Van der Laan, 2001) and mortality (Laub and Vaillant, 2000) and thereby confirm the health implications. For example, Bardone et al. (1998) found, in a New Zealand-sample, a "robust link between female adolescent conduct disorder and poor physical health" in a prospective study (with a six-

Table 11.1
Relationships between Risk-Taking Behaviors

	1	2	3	4	5	6	7	8	9	10	11	12	13	14	15
Health Endangering Behavior															
1. Risky traffic behavior	-														
2. Alcohol abuse	X[2]	-													
3. Tobacco use	X[3]	X[4]	-												
4. Soft drugs	X[5]	X[6]	X[7]	-											
5. Hard drugs		X[8]	X[9]	X[10]	-										
6. Self-medication						-									
7. Unsafe sex	X[11]	X[12]	X[13]	X[14]	X[15]		-								
8. Unhealthy diet	X[16]	X[17]	X[18]	X[19]	X[20]	X[21]	X[22]	-							
9. Lack of physical exercise	X[23]		X[24]					X[25]	-						
10. Suicidal behavior	X[26]	X[27]	X[28]	X[29]	X[30]	X[31]		X[32]		-					
Problem Behavior															
11. Homelessness		X[33]		X[34]	X[35]			X[36]			-				
12. Gambling		X[37]	X[38]	X[39]							X[40]	-			
13. Dropping out	X[41]	X[42]	X[43]	X[44]	X[45]		X[46]				X[47]		-		
14. Truancy		X[48]	X[49]	X[50]	X[51]		X[52]			X[53]	X[54]	X[55]		-	
Delinquent Behavior															
15. Aggression at school	X[56]	X[57]	X[58]	X[59]			X[60]	X[61]		X[62]	X[63]	X[64]	X[65]	X[66]	-
16. Criminal behavior	X[67]	X[68]	X[69]	X[70]	X[71]	X[72]	X[73]	X[74]	X[75]	X[76]	X[77]	X[78]	X[79]	X[80]	X[81]

Note: Each "X" denotes studies that found a positive relationship between each pair of risk-taking behaviors. See the appendix for specific references.

year interval). In a re-analysis of the Glueck data, Laub and Vaillant (2000) reported a relationship between antisocial behavior in childhood and mortality forty years later. By the age of 65, 29 percent of the delinquents, and 21 percent of the non-delinquents had died from natural causes.

Risk Taking as an Underlying Dimension

A second implication is that the behaviors analyzed in this chapter are indicative of a common underlying "trait," "factor," or "dimension." What could be the nature of this trait? Some authors proposed to call this dimension risk-taking (Arnett, Offer, and Fine, 1997; Dahlbäck, 1990a, 1990b), others suggested conventionality-unconventionality (Donovan, Jessor, and Costa, 1991), or stimulus seeking (Mawson et al., 1996). Basically, these authors suggest, there are differences in the tendency toward risk-taking behavior in the broadest sense. The advantage of the term "risk-taking" is that it is a rather descriptive term, without direct theoretical connotations. The behaviors described in the present chapter seem to fit very well within a risk-taking framework. These behaviors all have in common that they provide short-term pleasures or benefits but have potentially long-term negative consequences. In that sense, they are risky behaviors. These negative consequences, or "risks," are negative physical health outcomes in the case of the health-endangering behaviors; they can be negative mental health outcomes, such as depression or anxiety; or they can be negative economic consequences in the case of problem behavior. Finally, it is obvious that criminal behavior has potentially strong negative social consequences because of the likelihood of social sanctions generally, and the possibility of prosecution by the criminal justice system with all of its implications. Consequently, we suggest defining risk-taking as behavior that carries an unreasonable chance for adverse outcomes for the physical, economical, or psychological well-being. In this approach, crime is but one form of risk-taking in a series of risky behaviors. In the rest of the chapter, the term "risk-taking behavior" will be used to refer to the sixteen forms of behavior studied in the chapter.

Exposure as an Alternative Explanation

It is possible that exposure could explain at least some of the relationships described in this chapter. One could think, for example, of the relationship between traffic accidents (as an outcome of risky behavior) and criminal behavior. It is clear that exposure is a major determinant of accident involvement (Baker, O'Neill, Ginsburg, and Li, 1992; Chipman, 1982; Evans, 1984; Jonah and Engel, 1983; Li, Baker, Langlois, and Kelen, 1998; Maycock and Lockwood, 1993). Delinquents go out more often (Agnew and Petersen, 1989; Hirschi, 1969; Junger and Wiegersma, 1995; West and Farrington, 1977) and are therefore more likely to be exposed to traffic. Consequently, it is probable that in part the relationship between traffic accidents and crime is the result of a tendency of delinquents to spend a lot of time outside. However, a number of qualifications regarding this line of reasoning can be made.

First, exposure is usually not a random process but is in part the result of personality characteristics. People do create their own opportunities and level of exposure (Pervin, 1989; Tellegen, 1991). Moreover, factors related to high rates of offending are also promoting high rates of outgoing behavior. The amount of time youngsters spend outside the house and the type of leisure activities they engage in are related to the way they function in their family and at school (Junger, 1990). In addition, children who are strongly attached to their parents and closely supervised will spend less time outside their home and will therefore be less exposed to danger (Dekoviæ, 1999; Junger and Tremblay, 1999).

Second, some studies have found that passive leisure-time activities such as watching TV, which imply decreased exposure, were not related to a decrease in victimization by crime (Lauritsen, Laub, and Sampson, 1992), but instead, were related to an increase in accidents (Junger and Wiegersma, 1995).

Third, several studies were able to control for exposure and concluded that the relationship between crime and accidents did not disappear (Hilakivi, Veilahti, Asplund, Sinivuo, and et al., 1989; Junger, West, and Timman 2001; West, 1997; West et al., 1998).

Finally, the behaviors in the present chapter are so diverse, they occur is so many different contexts, and were (in most cases) found in so many different studies, that it seems very unlikely that trivial explanations (or exposure) would provide a sufficient explanation. It seems, therefore, that exposure, although a very important aspect and probably in part a common cause, is unlikely to be the only explanation of the relationship between crime and accident involvement.

More generally, it should be mentioned that in the psychological and psychiatric literature on co-morbidity, several authors (Angold, Costello, and Erkanli, 1999; Caron and Rutter, 1991; Loeber and Keenan, 1994) concluded that the co-occurrence/co-morbidity of mental disorders was not a methodological artefact, that it could not be the result of the way the data were collected (single informants), or result from problems in coding multiple symptoms, or that it was an artefact of the diagnostic system. Therefore, most authors agree that co-morbidity is a real "fact" that does not disappear after taking into account plausible trivial explanations.

All in all, it is likely that other factors besides exposure are involved in the co-occurrence of risk-taking behaviors. Although sometimes, in particular studies, or in specific cases, it is possible that the co-occurrence of these behaviors has a trivial explanation, the co-occurrence of risk-taking behaviors is real and in need of an explanation. The origin of these interrelationships cannot be determined from the findings and has to be investigated in future research. However, there a number of plausible explanations which may explain a part of the total picture. A number of options will be reviewed here.

Theoretical Implications of Co-Occurrence for the Explanation of Criminal Behavior

Causal Relationships

To some extent one type of risk-taking can be the cause of another, or create risk for another problem (Caron and Rutter, 1991). A clear-cut example is alcohol abuse. It is likely that alcohol abuse leads to dangerous driving (Ross, 1992; Soderstrom, Dischinger, Ho, and Soderstrom, 1993) and driving under the influence of alcohol directly affects the likelihood of a crash (Deery and Love, 1996; Stroebe and Stroebe, 1995). Alcohol is probably also to some extent causally related to violence (Cook and Moore, 1993; Pihl and Peterson, 1995; Pihl, Peterson, and Lau, 1993; Pihl et al., 1995). However, again it does not seem likely that the relationship between alcohol and risky driving and alcohol and violence explain the totality of the relationships.

Another relationship where causality may play a role is the relationship between crime and depression. The lifestyle of delinquents might be so turbulent that depression is a probable outcome (Caron and Rutter, 1991). However, in the probably most extensive literature review on co-morbidity to date, Angold (1999) concluded that this is probably not the case and that the available evidence indicates that it is more likely that conduct disorder and depression have shared risk factors instead of one causing the other.

For every single relationship described in this study it should be investigated whether it could be the result of one concept causing the other. It is beyond the scope of the present study to do this cell by cell. Overall, however, it seems implausible that one single risk-taking behavior is at the origin of the fifteen other risk-taking behaviors included in the present study and would provide the entire explanation of the relationships that were found.

Shared Risk-Factors/Same Causal Mechanisms

It was stated above that the interrelationships described in this study are not exclusively the result of exposure, are linked to each other by causal paths, or have artefactual explanations. Another explanation is that there are shared risk factors at the origins of risk-taking behavior. The shared factors could be either constitutional or environmental factors or, to some extent, both. Several authors have argued that, globally, risk-factors for various forms of risk-taking are similar, and/or overlap to a large extent (Dekoviæ, 1999; Donovan, Marlatt, and Salzberg, 1983; Durlak, 1997; Jessor and Jessor, 1977).

Biological Factors and Personality Characteristics

Several authors have suggested that the co-occurrence of risk-taking behaviors is the product of genetic factors (Cloninger, Svrakic, and Przybeck, 1993; McGue, Bacon, and Lykken, 1993; Plomin, McClearn, Pedersen, Nesselroade, and et al., 1988; Tellegen et al., 1988). For example, it has been suggested that differences in risk-taking are the result of a biologically determined motivation for sensation seeking (Zuckerman, 1979) or a need for arousal (Ellis, 1990). These basic traits proved an overall difference in the motivation for risk-taking activities.

One factor which may be important in explaining the co-occurrence of several forms of risk-taking is hyperactivity. Hyperactivity and a reduced ability to sustain attention have been related to crime (Farrington et al., 1990; Rutter, Giller, and Hagell, 1998), to accident involvement (Barkley et al., 1993; Bijur and Stewart-Brown, 1986; Langley, McGee, Silva, and Williams, 1983), to substance abuse, and diverse forms of mental disorders (American Academy of Pediatrics, 2000). Reviews of the literature suggest that about 80 percent of the variation in hyperactivity is genetically determined (American Academy of Pediatrics, 2000). It seems plausible that hyperactivity may be responsible for the co-occurrence described in the present findings.

In personality psychology, to the extent that broad "higher-order personality traits" are constitutional, these approaches (see above) are in line with the idea that biological factors cause the co-occurrence of risk-taking behaviors. Indeed, there is evidence that personality traits predict involvement in many types of risk-taking behavior. For example, Krueger (2000a) found that the personality factor of constraint predicted substance abuse, unsafe sex, and dangerous driving as well as conduct disorders.

Environmental Factors

In different fields, it has been proposed that individuals are globally similar with respect to these motivational forces but that they differ with respect to the internal controls on their behavior. In other words: individuals differ in their level of "self-control" or "self regulation" (Baumeister, Heatherton, and Tice, 1994; Block and Block, 1980; Caspi, Henry, McGee, Moffitt, and al., 1995; Durlak, 1997; Gottfredson and Hirschi, 1990; Logue, 1988; Logue, 1995; Mischel, 1981; Pulkkinen, 1982). These differences in internal controls are generally assumed to be (besides eventual biological factors) the result of a socialization process: one of the essential tasks of parents is to teach their children to avoid negative outcomes in the broadest sense (Gottfredson and Hirschi, 1990; Kochanska, Coy, and Murray, 2001).

The consequences of environmental or biological causation are similar: individuals who are unable to avoid negative outcomes for themselves, and accordingly will smoke or get involved in accidents, will not care about the negative outcomes experienced by others, and therefore they will be more likely to commit crimes (Gottfredson and Hirschi, 1990; Neeleman, Wessely, and Wadsworth, 1998).

A plausible causal path is that distal personal characteristics do influence negative outcomes, such as accidents, through their influence on proximal factors. For example, delinquents have been found to drive more often without wearing their seatbelts than non-delinquents (Orpinas, Basen-Engquist, Grunbaum, and Parcel, 1995; Sikorski, 1996), to have higher driving speed (Elander, West, and French, 1993; Lajunen and Summala, 1997) and to have more dangerous driving habits (Caspi et al., 1997; Elander, West, and French, 1993). This suggests that personal characteristics influence the driving style which, in turn, affects the probability of an accident (Elander, West, and French, 1993; West, Elander, and French, 1993). In sum, models are needed which integrate proximal factors as well as distal factors. Some authors have suggested that the control models, combining the concepts of "internal controls" (namely the personal characteristic of self-control) and "external controls" (namely situational and contextual factors) provide such a model (Gottfredson and Hirschi, 1990; Kornhauser, 1978).

Unique Causes

It is necessary to emphasize that, apart from a set of common causes, as was argued above, it is probable that many risk-taking behaviors also have one or more unique causes. For example, depression has a genetic factor (Zoccolillo, 1992). Interestingly this genetic factor may be particularly important for depressions without co-occurring conduct disorders and less important for those with co-occurring conduct disorders. Accordingly, co-occurrence may be important in separating out groups of individuals with different risk factors. Similarly, being unemployed may be the result of dropping out of school but can equally well be the result of changes in production systems on a worldwide scale.

Disconfirmation of Theories

A question we would like to raise is whether the co-occurrence of risk-taking behaviors, and more generally with various types of mental disorders, is compatible with specific approaches that abound in the literature. For example, explanations which focus on motivational approaches strongly emphasize a need for risk-taking or a search for sensation seeking (see above). This type of explanation seems to be in opposition with findings showing that passive forms of leisure-time activities are associated with relatively high risks of accidents as well as relatively high levels of delinquent behavior (Junger and Wiegersma, 1995). Passivity does not seem to fit with individuals whose main way to crime and accidents is risk-taking (or related concepts such as impulsivity). Future research should investigate more in depth the role of passive activities or withdrawal behavior (Gottfredson and Hirschi, 1990).

Similarly, other problems for personality models may arise. On the one hand, different traits are related to different forms of risk-taking. On the other hand, the present review shows that various forms of risk-taking are positively correlated to each other. These two statements seem in contradiction with each other. Gray's personality model can illustrate this point. Gray (, 198, 1) reformulated Eysenck's theory. At the core of his model is a division of personality traits in a behavioral activation system (BAS) and a behavioral inhibition system (BIS). People with high impulsivity are highly sensitive to reward and non-punishment, whereas people with high anxiety are highly sensitive to signals of punishment, non-reward, and novelty. The underlying system for impulsivity is the behavioral activation system (BAS), and the underlying neurological system for anxiety is the behavioral inhibition system (BIS). Both systems are located in different parts of the brain. The behavioral activation system activates approach behaviors, while the behavioral inhibition system (BIS) is the braking system. Signals of punishment, non-reward, novel stimuli, and innate fear stimuli lead to behavioral inhibition. Just as approach traits are associated with the BAS, so are avoidant and inhibitory traits associated with the BIS. Anxiety and neuroticism are believed to reflect chronically high levels of BIS function. Depression reflects high BIS and low BAS activity (see Revelle, 1995 and Jang, 1998 for reviews). In Gray's model, different types of risk-taking behaviors and mental disorders are expected to be associated with the two systems in different ways. The question is whether the co-occurrence of behaviors originating from a defective BIS, such as crime with behaviors which are the expression of too much BIS, such as anxiety (Zoccolillo, 1992), depression (Angold, Costello, and Erkanli, 1999), and a lack of activity (Gottfredson and Hirschi, 1990; Junger and Wiegersma, 1995) is in agreement or in contradiction with Gray's model.

In criminology, most theories on crime, for example, subculture- or strain-theory, do not predict the co-occurrence of criminal behavior with other forms of risk-taking behaviors. The extent to which they could accommodate these relationships is unclear. Could cultural deviance explain the co-occurrence of risk-taking behaviors? Several authors questioned whether deviance is valued by any cultural or sub-cultural group at all (Hirschi, 1996; Kornhauser, 1978) as is argued by sub-culture models. In relation to accidents and health this seems even more problematic. It seems improbable that any (sub)culture could not place a high value on health or would value accident involvement positively (Hurrelmann and Losel, 1990). Similarly, Tittle (1995: 22) has argued that it does not seem to make sense that subculture theory could explain "individualized acts totally lacking normative acceptability." Tittle (1995) mentioned suicidal behavior as an example. Accident involvement seems to be another example of such an "individualized act" lacking normative acceptability.

Second, central concepts such as learning processes involving social or non-social reinforcement have appeal in the explanation of some health-endangering behavior: smoking or drinking is agreeable in itself, this is non-social reinforcement. In addition, if one's friends smoke and use alcohol, they can reward this behavior: this is social reinforcement (Gibbons and Krohn, 1991: 153–154). In relation to accidents it seems difficult to see how the same processes could be at work. It does not make much sense to assume that accident involvement would be reinforced either by social or non-social means. An accident would rather be considered as a punishment. Therefore there is no non-social reinforcement. In addition, most accidents will happen without anyone else present to act as an immediate reinforcer. In the Netherlands, for example, accidents involving adolescents are likely to be cycling accidents or motorcycle accidents. In general, there will not be another passenger on the (motor)cycle who could act as a reinforcer (Junger, Terlouw, and van der Heijden, 1995). It is unlikely that there will be immediate social reinforcement. Consequently, it is difficult to translate the processes involved in learning deviant behavior into the "learning of accident involvement."

It might be argued however, that although accidents in themselves are not learned or reinforced, risky behavior or bravado behavior in itself is. This is argued in much of the psychological literature on health, as is explained in the next paragraph. In the field of psychology of health a number of theories are based on concepts such as attitudes, beliefs about outcomes of behavior, normative beliefs, and control beliefs (such as the theory of planned behavior; for a review see Stroebe [1995]). Some of the concepts used in these theories, such as normative beliefs and attitudes, are similar in orientation to the cultural deviance and social learning approaches in the field of deviance. These studies usually find strong correlations between their independent variables and health behavior or traffic behavior. For example, Parker et al. (1992) found that subject's normative beliefs about drinking and driving, speeding, close following, and dangerous passing are related to the intention to actually perform these four forms of dangerous driving. This type of research could be interpreted as support for a cultural deviance approach. However, it has proved very difficult to change behavior by influencing the independent variables derived from these models (Stroebe and Stroebe, 1995). For example, changing attitudes and beliefs in order to influence smoking in adolescence in a very difficult enterprise which globally has been unsuccessful (Foulds, 1996; Reid, 1996). This lack of effect does not support the idea of the causal significance of attitudes, values, and norms on health-endangering behavior.[1] On the contrary, it suggests that these values and attitudes may be the product of these health-endangering behaviors and are private self-serving explanations for it. Interestingly, the opposite line of reasoning could be true as well: the estimated risk of arrest is often found to be unrelated to driving under the influence of alcohol (Berger and Snortum, 1986). But, in opposition with this absence of a relationship, influencing the likelihood of arrest usually has a strong impact on traffic behavior (Arnett, 1992; Clarke, 1995; Ross, 1992), supporting the idea that increased chances of an arrest is causally related to traffic behavior.

In summary, it is difficult to make causal claims for the role of values in relation to risk-taking behavior. Attitudes and values are strongly related to health and traffic behavior but changes in attitudes and values do not seem to have an impact on this behavior. In opposition with this, the likelihood of getting caught is hardly correlated to crime or traffic behavior, but changing the likelihood of getting caught has a strong impact on behavior. Clearly, the causal role of values and attitudes in the field of traffic and health is still difficult to evaluate.

Finally, an essential question is whether one wishes to accept the way in which the broad way "values" and "attitudes" in the psychology of health studies are operationalized. Kornhauser (1978) explicitly defined culture and values in a confined way: culture is defined by ultimate values which act as the ultimate goals in life. When people are asked to name their main goals in life, they always mention good health as one of them (the other two goals are: a happy family life and a reasonable level of material success, SCP, 1995). Clearly, everybody values health. Therefore, the question is: is the extent to which one does or does not enjoy speeding, the reflection of a "basic value" in the way Kornhauser (1978) defined "values"? This seems unlikely, and in this sense it seems unlikely that there is a "culture of accidents" (Gottfredson and Hirschi, 1990).

It also difficult to see how strain theory could be compatible with these broad behavioral differences between delinquents and non-delinquents. Strain theory emphasizes the instrumental role of crime. However, for accident involvement it is difficult to see how they can serve any useful purpose or how they might be a means to achieve any goal. Therefore, if delinquents and non-delinquents differ in risk-taking, it is difficult to see how that would be compatible with strain theory. Brezina (1996) described the opposition between this "pathology approach" and strain theory. "Although the concept of strain is broad, strain theorists have consistently viewed delinquency as a form of adjustment or adaptation to problems stemming from frustration and undesirable social environments." This view of delinquency differs from those perspectives that conceptualize delinquent behavior as a form of maladjustment or pathological behavior (Raine, 1993). In contrast to theories that consider delinquency to be the product of individual deficiencies and aberrations, strain theory assumes that delinquency more often represents "the normal reaction, by normal persons, to abnormal conditions" (Merton in Brezina, 1996: 40).

Brezina (1996) formulates adequately how strain differs from other theories in how much "individual dysfunction or pathology" it assigns to delinquents. Overall, the co-occurrence of risk-taking behaviors seems to be incompatible with a strain perspective.

The Need for Multidisciplinary Research

As was mentioned above, the co-occurrence of risk-taking behaviors has received little attention in the scientific community. The reasons for this may lie in the fact that different types of risk-taking behaviors belong to different fields of research. As a result, many investigators are not aware of the findings outside their own field. In addition, most scientific work is organized in departments, which each study their "own" dependent variable (crime, traffic, physical health, or mental health). As a result, it usually does not come to mind to include "foreign" dependent variables into one's own research. Also, integration does not fit with the way most research is funded. For most policy departments, for example, a department of justice, it is not seen as useful to include traffic accidents or unhealthy diet in a study on crime: traffic accidents or an unhealthy diet are the responsibility of other departments. Similarly, these departments, such as the departments of transportation or health, are usually not interested in crime. Finally, it did seem to the authors that researchers outside criminology are not always eager to associate "their" outcome variables to criminal behavior. Although reasons for this lack of interest sometimes remain unclear (to a criminologist) they seem to think that including crime will lead to associations of their work to politically sensitive issues (think for instance of the association between IQ and crime). In turn these associations with sensitive issues may lead to problems in the sphere of funding or questions regarding privacy rules (see also Peterson [1994] for a similar discussion on child abuse and childhood injuries). It is interesting to note that many older studies did not stay so closely within the borders of their own disciplines as modern researchers do (see for example Glueck and Glueck, 1950; Robins, 1966; Tillman and Hobbs, 1949; West and Farrington, 1977).

Implications for Prevention and Treatment

The present study has policy implications. First, the findings indicate that social health and public health institutions deal to a certain extent with the same problematic individuals and/or their families as the criminal justice programs (Durlak, 1997; McKnight and Tippetts, 1997; Resnick and Burt, 1996). If only from a practical point of view, in order to avoid doing the same things twice, coordination and integrations seems desirable.

The findings also imply that—among others—health policies, work in traffic education, and crime prevention policies share an interest in common background factors. Thus, crime prevention programs and health policies will need, to a certain extent, to focus on the same risk factors. This is in contrast with most approaches. At the moment most programs toward risky behavior are generally focusing on one type of risky behavior (e.g., smoking, drinking, peer relationships) and they start mainly at the high school level (De Vries and Backbier, 1994; Perry and Staufacker, 1996; Stroebe and Stroebe, 1995; Windle, Shope, and Bukstein, 1996). There is not much evidence that these programs are successful. It has been argued that "literally thousands of programs addressing the problems of high-risk youth are operating without any particular evidence that they are accomplishing their goals" (Dryfoos, 1993; Townsend, 1996; Wilcox, 1993).

In a similar line of reasoning Durlak (1997) argued, on the basis of a large literature review, that many different negative outcomes are correlated to each other and do share the same risk factors. Consequently, policymakers should think about setting up programs which address problems as they usually present themselves: namely in combination with each other, concentrated within the same individuals and within the same families. Several effective health programs demonstrated beneficial effects in different domains of functioning (DiClemente, Hansen, and Ponton, 1996b; Durlak, 1997). One example of a health program which has been successful in achieving a broad range of positive outcomes on the social level as well as in preventing accidents is the Home Visitation Scheme (Olds et al., 1997). In this scheme, professional nurses visited regularly teenage, single, low-income pregnant women, starting during pregnancy and lasting until the child was two-years-old. Many positive outcomes were reported in mother's functioning and in their children. Experimental mothers smoked less, went back to school more often than controls, there was less child abuse, the children displayed better cognitive functioning, and had suffered less often from unintentional injuries (Olds et al., 1997).

Limitations of the Present Study

The data presented above should be considered as a first attempt to integrate the findings of several different fields. Some of the relationships described above, such as the relationship between delinquency and dropping out from school, drug-abuse and/or alcohol abuse, have been thoroughly investigated. However, the relationships between some other risk-taking behaviors have yet to be investigated. For example, an unhealthy diet, self-medication, or physical activity levels have not been systematically studied in relation to the other forms of risk-taking behaviors included in the present study.

Several important issues could not be studied in the present chapter but need to be mentioned. First, it is unclear at what age these interrelationships appear, and in what order they appear (Angold, Costello, and Erkanli, 1999). A literature review on the relationship between criminal behavior and accidents suggest that this relationship is present already in young children (Junger, 1994). The age at which these relationships occur may have important theoretical consequences. For example, in the case of crime and accidents, if the relationship is present in young children, this would suggest an important role for either constitutional factors or socialization as a causal factor.

Another important issue is related to gender and ethnic differences. Is the co-occurrence of risk-taking behaviors equally strong in women and in men, and in various ethnic groups? Several studies suggested that co-occurrence was stronger in females and outcomes in relation to co-morbidity were more severe (Costello, Armstrong, and Erkanli 2000; Hofstra, Ende, and Verhulst 2000; Loeber and Keenan, 1994; Miller-Johnson et al., 1998). The present authors could not find studies investigating co-occurrence in different ethnic groups.

Another issue is the extent to which risk-taking is "transmitted" from parents to children. Several studies reported that parental antisocial behavior is one of the strongest predictors of antisocial behavior in their children (Farrington, Barnes, and Lambert, 1996; Lahey, Walsman, and McBurnett, 1999). A similar intergenerational transmission has been reported for unintentional injuries in at least one study (Kolvin et al., 1990). In both cases, it is assumed that intergenerational transmission occurs through maladaptive parenting (lack of supervision and support, harsh physical discipline).

Given these important limitations there is a strong need for more research. To date, few studies have as a main goal to investigate co-occurrence of a broad range of risk-taking behaviors and even less to study theoretically relevant risk factors predicting risk-taking behaviors. Consequently, future research should try to fill this gap. It is important to investigate co-occurrence with more precision than this review could do. Attention should be paid to gender and ethnic differences, and to timing and age issues. Furthermore, the processes leading to co-occurrence of risk-taking behaviors should be studied in depth.

Notes

1. Amdur (1989) has described a similar problem of causal inference in the study of crime. According to Amdur (1989), the evidence suggests that "deviant friends" is an outcome variable, just as crime is. Deviant friends are therefore not causally related to crime.
2. *Alcohol by traffic*: Bjerver and Goldberg (1950); Perrine (1975); Perrine (1976); Asmussen and Roszbach (1987); Hansell and Mechanic (1990); Kidd and Holton (1993); Brickley and Shepherd (1995); Mayou and Bryant (1995); Miller, Plant et al. (1995); Shope, Waller et al. (1995); Deery and Love (1996); Mathijssen (1999).

3. *Tobacco by traffic behavior:* Langlie (1979); Hansell and Mechanic (1990); Elliott (1993).
4. *Tobacco by alcohol:* Donovan and Jessor (1985); Hansell and Mechanic (1990); Kuipers, Mensink et al. (1993); Stroebe and Stroebe (1995); Department of Education (1996); Junger, Stroebe et al. (2001).
5. *Soft drugs by traffic behavior*: Hansell and Mechanic (1990); Elliott (1993).
6. *Soft drugs by alcohol*: Donovan and Jessor (1985); Donovan, Jessor et al. (1988); Hansell and Mechanic (1990); Kuipers, Mensink et al. (1993).
7. *Soft drugs by tobacco*: Donovan and Jessor (1985); Hansell and Mechanic (1990); Kuipers, Mensink et al. (1993).
8. *Hard drugs by alcohol*: Donovan and Jessor (1985); Ter Bogt and Van Praag (1992).
9. *Hard drugs by tobacco*: Donovan and Jessor (1985); Ter Bogt and Van Praag (1992).
10. *Hard drugs by soft drugs:* Donovan and Jessor (1985); Ter Bogt and Van Praag (1992); Department of Education (1996).
11. *Risky sex by traffic behavior:* Basen-Enquist, Edmundson et al. (1996).
12. *Risky sex by alcohol:* Donovan and Jessor (1985); Donovan, Jessor et al. (1988); Ketterlinus, Lamb et al. (1994); Brugman, Goedhart et al. (1995); Valois, Oeltmann et al. (1999).
13. *Risky sex by tobacco:* Ketterlinus, Lamb et al. (1994); Brugman, Goedhart et al. (1995); Valois, Oeltmann et al. (1999).
14. *Risky sex by soft drugs:* Donovan and Jessor (1985); Donovan, Jessor et al. (1988); Ketterlinus, Lamb et al. (1994); Brugman, Goedhart et al. (1995); Valois, Oeltmann et al. (1999); Smith, Krohn et al. (2000).
15. *Risky sex by hard drugs:* Brugman, Goedhart et al. (1995); Smith, Krohn et al. (2000).
16. D*isordered eating by traffic*: Donovan, Jessor et al. (1993).
17. D*isordered eating by alcohol:* Bulik (1987); Goldbloom, Naranjo et al. (1992); Holderness, Brooks-Grunn et al. (1994); French, Sotry et al. (1995); Neumark-Sztainer, Story et al. (1996); Wiederman and Pryor (1996).
18. D*isordered eating by tobacco*: Holderness, Brooks-Grunn et al. (1994); French, Sotry et al. (1995); Neumark-Sztainer, Story et al. (1996); Ponton (1996); Lipscomb (1997).
19. D*isordered eating by soft drugs:* Gwirtsman (1993); Holderness, Brooks-Grunn et al. (1994); French, Sotry et al. (1995 This study did not differentiate between soft and hard drugs); Neumark-Sztainer, Story et al. (1996); Wiederman and Pryor (1996).
20. *Disordered eating by hard drugs:* Holderness, Brooks-Grunn et al. (1994); French, Sotry et al. (1995); Wiederman and Pryor (1996).
21. *Disordered eating by tranquilizers-self-medication*: Pryor, Wiederman et al. (1996).
22. *Disordered eating by risky sex:* French, Sotry et al. (1995); Neumark-Sztainer, Story et al. (1996).
23. *Less physical exercise by traffic behavior* : Langlie (1979); Donovan, Jessor et al. (1993).
24. *Less physical exercise by tobacco*: Langlie (1979); Hansell and Mechanic (1990); Stroebe and Stroebe (1995).
25. *Less physical exercise by disordered eating*: Stroebe and Stroebe (1995); Basen-Enquist, Edmundson et al. (1996).
26. *Suicide by traffic:* Romanov, Hatakka et al. (1993).
27. *Suicide by alcohol*: Merrill, Milner et al. (1992); Kienhorst, de Wilde et al. (1994); Garnefski and Diekstra (1995); Department of Education (1996); Rossow (1996).

28. *Suicide by tobacco*: Garnefski and Diekstra (1995).
29. *Suicide by soft drugs*: Kienhorst, de Wilde et al. (1994); CBS (1995); Garnefski and Diekstra (1995); Department of Education (1996).
30. *Suicide by hard drugs*: Kienhorst, de Wilde et al. (1994); CBS (1995).
31. *Suicide by tranquilizers*: CBS (1995).
32. *Suicide by eating disorders*: Noordenbos (1993); French, Sotry et al. (1995); Neumark-Sztainer, Story et al. (1996).
33. *Homelessness by alcohol:* Thomeer-Bouwens, Tavecchio et al. (1996).
34. *Homelessness by soft drugss:* Thomeer-Bouwens, Tavecchio et al. (1996).
35. *Homelessness by hard drugs:* Thomeer-Bouwens, Tavecchio et al. (1996).
36. *Homelessness by disordered eating:* Dortmans and de Bie (1991); Scholte (1994)
37. *Gambling by alcohol:* Kuipers, Mensink et al. (1993).
38. *Gambling by tobacco:* Kuipers, Mensink et al. (1993).
39. *Gambling by soft drugs*: Kuipers, Mensink et al. (1993).
40. *Gambling by homelessness:* Van der Ploeg (1991); Thomeer-Bouwens, Tavecchio et al. (1996).
41. *Dropout by traffic*: MMWR (1994).
42. *Dropout by alcohol*: MMWR (1994).
43. *Dropout by tobacco*: MMWR (1994).
44. *Dropout by soft drugs*: MMWR (1994); Smith, Krohn et al. (2000).
45. *Dropout by hard drugs:* Smith, Krohn et al. (2000).
46. *Dropout by risky sex:* Ketterlinus, Lamb et al. (1994).
47. *Dropout by homelessness:* Sikorski (1996).
48. *Truancy by alcohol:* Kuipers, Mensink et al. (1993).
49. *Truancy by tobacco:* Kuipers, Mensink et al. (1993).
50. *Truancy by soft drugs*: Sikorski (1996).
51. *Truancy by hard drugs*: Sikorski (1996).
52. *Truancy by risky sex*: Ketterlinus, Lamb et al. (1994); Sikorski (1996).
53. *Truancy by suicide:* Kienhorst, de Wilde et al. (1994).
54. *Truancy by homelessness*: Dortmans and de Bie (1991); Scholte (1994).
55. *Truancy by gambling*: Kuipers, Mensink et al. (1993).
56. *Aggression by traffic:* Orpinas, Basen-Engquist et al. (1995).
57. *Aggression by alcohol:* Pihl, Peterson et al. (1993); Orpinas, Basen-Engquist et al. (1995); Pihl, Young et al. (1995); Department of Education (1996); Hoaken and Pihl (2000).
58. *Aggression by tobacco:* Orpinas, Basen-Engquist et al. (1995).
59. *Aggression by soft drugs:* Orpinas, Basen-Engquist et al. (1995).
60. *Aggression by risky sex:* Orpinas, Basen-Engquist et al. (1995); Valois, Oeltmann et al. (1999).
61. *Aggression by disordered eating:* Orpinas, Basen-Engquist et al. (1995).
62. *Aggression by suicide:* Orpinas, Basen-Engquist et al. (1995); Department of Education (1996).
63. *Aggression by homelessness:* Van der Ploeg, Gaemers et al. (1991).
64. *Aggression by gambling:* Scholte (1994).
65. *Aggression by drop out:* Orpinas, Basen-Engquist et al. (1995).
66. *Aggression by truancy:* Junger (1990).
67. *Delinquency by traffic*: Glueck and Glueck (1950); West and Farrington (1977); Yeager and Otnow-Lewis (1990); Farrington and Junger (1995); Junger and Wiegersma (1995); Junger and Tremblay (1999); Junger, West et al. (2001).
68. *Delinquency by alcohol:* Donovan and Jessor (1985); Donovan, Jessor et al. (1988); Bö (1990); Dembo, Williams et al. (1992); Windle (1994); Pihl and Peterson

(1995); Pihl, Young et al. (1995); Huizinga and Jacob-Chien (1998); Krueger (1999); Junger, Stroebe et al. (2001).

69. *Delinquency by tobacco*: Donovan and Jessor (1985); Kuipers, Mensink et al. (1993); Junger, Stroebe et al. 2001).
70. *Delinquency by soft drugs*: Hundleby, Carpenter et al. (1982); Donovan and Jessor (1985); Donovan, Jessor et al. (1988); Osgood, Johnston et al. (1988); Gillmore, Hawkins et al. (1991); Dembo, Williams et al. (1992); Huizinga, Loeber et al. (1993); Otero-Lopez, Luengo-Martin et al. (1994); Krueger (1999); Junger, Stroebe et al. 2001).
71. *Delinquency by hard drugs*: Donovan and Jessor (1985); Abram (1989); Allen, Leadbeater et al. (1990); Jol and Dorenbos (1996); Krueger (1999).
72. *Delinquency by tranquilizers:* Pihl and Hoaken (1997); Crimmins, Cleary et al. (2000).
73. *Delinquency by risky sex*: Donovan and Jessor (1985); Donovan, Jessor et al. (1988); Allen, Leadbeater et al. (1990); Ketterlinus, Lamb et al. (1994); Smith, Krohn et al. (2000).
74. *Delinquency by disordered eating*: French, Sotry et al. (1995); Neumark-Sztainer, Story et al. (1996).
75. *Delinquency by lack of physical* exercise: Junger and Wiegersma (1995).
76. *Delinquency by suicide*: Elliott (1993); Garnefski and Diekstra (1995); Krueger (1999).
77. *Delinquency by homelessness*: Van der Ploeg (1991); Van der Ploeg, Gaemers et al. (1991); Rotheram-Borus, Parra et al. (1996).
78. *Delinquency by gambling*: Kuipers, Mensink et al. (1993); Scholte (1994).
79. *Delinquency by drop out*: Elliott (1993); Huizinga and Jacob-Chien (1998); Smith, Krohn et al. (2000).
80. *Delinquency by truancy*: Elliott (1993); Sikorski (1996); Huizinga and Jacob-Chien (1998).
81. *Delinquency by aggression:* Junger (1990); Huizinga and Jacob-Chien (1998).

References

Abram, Karen M. 1989. "The effect of co-occurring disorders on criminal careers: Interaction of antisocial personality, alcoholism, and drug disorders." *International Journal of Law and Psychiatry* 12: 133–148.

Agnew, Robert, and David M. Petersen. 1989. "Leisure and delinquency." *Social Problems* 36: 332–350.

Ajzen, Icek. 1991. "The theory of planned behavior." *Organizational Behavior and Human Decision Processes* 50: 179–211.

Akers, Ronald L. 1994. *Criminological theories: Introduction and evaluation.* Los Angeles, CA: Roxbury Publishing Co.

———. 1996. "Is differential association/social learning cultural deviance theory?" *Criminology* 34: 229–248.

Allen, Joseph P., Bonnie J. Leadbeater, and J. Lawrence Aber. 1990. "The relationship of adolescents' expectations and values to delinquency, hard drug use, and unprotected sexual intercourse." *Development and Psychopathology* 2: 85–98.

Amdur, Richard L. 1989. "Testing Casual Models of Delinquency: A Methodological Crititque." *Criminal Justice and Behavior* 16: 35–62.

American Academy of Pediatrics. 2000. "Clinical practice guideline: diagnosis and evaluation of the child with attention-deficit/hyperactivity disorder." *Pediatrics* 105: 1158–70.

American Psychiatric Assn. 1994. *Diagnostic and statistical manual of mental disorders* (4th ed.). Washington, DC: American Psychiatric Association.

Anderson, Edward R., Nancy J. Bell, Judith L. Fischer, Joyce Munsch, Charles W. Peek, and Gwendolyn T. Sorell. 1993. "Applying a risk-taking perspective." Pp. 165–185 in N. J. Bell and R. W. Bell (eds.), *Adolescent risk taking*. Newbury Park CA: Sage Publications.

Angold, Adrian, E. Jane Costello, and Alaattin Erkanli. 1999. "Comorbidity." *Journal of Child Psychology and Psychiatry and Allied Disciplines* 40: 57–87.

Arnett, Jeffrey. 1992. "Socialization and adolescent reckless behavior: A reply to Jessor." *Developmental Review* 12: 391–409.

Arnett, Jeffrey Jensen, Daniel Offer, and Mark A. Fine. 1997. "Reckless driving in adolescence: 'state' and 'trait' factors." *Accident Analysis and Prevention* 29: 57–63.

Bachman, Jerald G., Lloyd D. Johnston, and Patrick M. O'Malley. 1998. "Explaining recent increases in student's marihuana use: Impacts of perceived risks and disapproval, 1976 through 1996." *American Journal of Public Health* 88: 887–892.

Baker, Susan P., Brian O'Neill, Marvin J. Ginsburg, and Guohua Li. 1992. *The injury fact book*. Oxford: Oxford University Press.

Bandura, Albert, Dorothea Ross, and Sheila A. Ross. 1961. "Transmission of aggression through imitation of aggressive models." *Journal of Abnormal and Social Psychology* 63: 575–582.

Bardone, Anna M., Terrie E. Moffitt, Avshalom Caspi, Nigel Dickson, Warren R. Stanton, and Phil A. Silva. 1998. "Adult physical health outcomes of adolescent girls with conduct disorder, depression, and anxiety." *Journal of the American Academy of Child and Adolescent Psychiatry* 37: 594–601.

Barkley, Russel A., David C. Guevremont, Arthur D. Anastopoulos, George J. DuPaul, and Terry L. Shelton. 1993. "Driving related risks and outcomes of attention deficit hyperactivity disorder in adolescents and young adults: A 3- to 5-year follow-up survey." *Pediatrics* 92: 212–218.

Basen-Enquist, Karen, Elizabeth W. Edmundson, and Guy S. Parcel. 1996. "Structure of health risk behavior among high school students." *Journal of Consulting and Clinical Psychology* 64: 764–775.

Baumeister, Roy F., Todd F. Heatherton, and Dianne M. Tice. 1994. *Losing control: How and why people fail at self-regulation*. San Diego: Academic Press.

Bell, Nancy J., and Robert Bell, W. 1993. "Introduction." Pp. 1–6 in N. J. Bell and R. Bell (eds.), *Adolescent risk taking*. Newbury Park, CA.: Sage.

Bem, Daryl J., and Andrea Allen. 1974. "On predicting some of the people some of the time: The search for cross-situational consistencies in behavior." *Psychological Review* 81: 506–520.

Bem, Daryl J., and David C. Funder. 1978. "Predicting more of the people more of the time: Assessing the personality of situations." *Psychological Review* 85: 485–501.

Berger, D. E., and J. R. Snortum. 1986. "A structural model of drinking and driving: alcohol consumption, social norms and moral commitments." *Criminology* 24: 139–153.

Bijur, Polly E., and Sarah Stewart-Brown. 1986. "Child Behaviour and Accidental Injury in 11,966 Preschool Children." *American Journal of Diseases of Children* 140: 487–493.

Block, Jeanne H., and Jack Block. 1980. "The role of ego-control and ego-resiliency in the organization of behavior." Pp. 39–101 in W. A. Collins (ed.), *Development of cognition, affect, and social relations*, Vol. 13. Hillsdale, NJ: Lawrence Erlbaum.

Brennan, Patricia A., Sarnoff A. Mednick, and R. John. 1989. "Specialization in violence: evidence of a criminal subgroup." *Criminology* 27: 437–453.

Brezina, Timothy. 1996. "Adapting to strain: an examination of delinquent coping responses." *Criminology* 34: 39–60.

Burton, Roger V. 1963. "Generality of honesty reconsidered." *Psychological Review* 70: 481–499.

Caron, Chantal, and Michael Rutter. 1991. "Comorbidity in child psychopathology: Concepts, issues, and research strategies." *Journal of Child Psychology and Psychiatry* 32: 1063–1080.

Casper, R. C., E. D. Eckert, K. A. Halmi, S. C. Goldberg, and J. M. Davis. 1980. "Bulimia: Its incidence and clinical importance in patients with anorexia nervosa." *Archives of General Psychiatry* 37: 1030–1035.

Caspi, Avshalom, HonaLee Harrington, Terrie E. Moffit, Dot Begg, Nigel Dickson, John Langley, and Phil Silva, A. 1997. "Personality differences predict health-risk behaviors in young adulthood: Evidence from a longitudinal study." *Journal of Personality and Social Psychology* 73: 1052–1063.

Caspi, Avshalom, Bill Henry, Rob O. McGee, Terrie E. Moffitt, and et al. 1995. "Temperamental origins of child and adolescent behavior problems: From age three to fifteen." *Child Development* 66: 55–68.

Chaplin, William F., and Lewis R. Goldberg. 1985. "A failure to replicate the Bem and Allen study of individual differences in cross-situational consistency." *Journal of Personality and Social Psychology* 47: 1074–1090.

Chipman, Mary L. 1982. "The role of exposure, experience and demerit point levels in the risk of collision." *Accident Analysis and Prevention* 14: 475–483.

Clark, Lee Anna. 1999. "Dimensional approaches to personality disorder. Assessment and diagnosis." Pp. 219–244 in C. R. Cloninger (ed.), *Personality and psychopathology*. Washington, DC: American Psychiatric Association.

Clarke, R. V. 1995. "Situational crime prevention." Pp. 91–150 in M. Tonry and D. P. Farrington (eds.), *Crime and Justice*, Vol. 19. Chicago: The University of Chicago Press.

Cloninger, C. R., C. Bayon, and T. R. Przybeck. 1997. "Epidemiology and Axis I comorbidity of antisocial personality." Pp. 12–21 in D. M. Stoff, J. Breiling, and J. D. Maser (eds.), *Handbook of antisocial behavior*. New York: John Wiley & Sons.

Cloninger, C. Robert, Dragan M. Svrakic, and Thomas R. Przybeck. 1993. "A psychobiological model of temperament and character." *Archives of General Psychiatry* 50: 975–990.

Cobb, Brenda K., Beverley D. Cairns, Margaret S. Miles, and Robert B. Cairns. 1995. "A longitudinal study of the role of sociodemographic factors and childhood aggression on adolescent injury and 'close calls'." *Journal of Adolescent Health* 17: 381–388.

Conley, James J. 1984. "Relation of temporal stability and cross-situational consistency in personality: Comment on the Mischel-Epstein debate." *Psychological Review* 91: 491–496.

Cook, Philip J., and Michael J. Moore. 1993. "Violence reduction through restrictions on alcohol availability." *Alcohol Health and Research World* 17: 151–156.

Costa, Paul T. Jr., Robert R. McCrae, and Ilene C. Siegler. 1999. "Continuity and change over the adult life cycle: Personality and personality disorders." Pp. 129–154 in C. R. Cloninger (ed.), *Personality and psychopathology*. Washington, DC: American Psychiatric Association.

Costello, E. Jane, Tonya D. Armstrong, and Alaattin Erkanli. 2000. "Report on the Developmental Epidemiology of Comorbid Psychiatric and Substance Use Disorders." Duke University Medical Center, Department of Psychiatry and Behavioral Sciences, Durham NC.

DaCosta, M., and K. A. Halmi. 1992. "Classifications of anorexia nervosa: Question of subtypes." *International Journal of Eating Disorders* 11: 305–313.

Dahlbäck, Olof. 1990a. "Criminality as risk-taking." *Personality and Individual Differences* 11: 265–272.

———. 1990b. "Criminality as risk-taking." *Personality and Risk-Taking* 11: 1235–1242.

De Vries, Hein, and Esther Backbier. 1994. "Self-efficacy as an important determinant of quitting among pregnant women who smoke: The Ø-pattern." *Preventive Medicine* 23: 167–174.

Deery, Hamish A., and Anthony W. Love. 1996. "The effect of a moderate dose of alcohol on the traffic hazard perception profile of young drink-drivers." *Addiction* 91: 815–827.

Deković, Maja. 1999. "Risk and protective factors in the development of problem behavior during adolescence." *Journal of Youth and Adolescence* 28: 667–685.

Deković, Maja, E. Reitz, and Anne Marie Meijer. 2002. " Problem behavior in adolescence: Differential manifestation, developmental trends and risk factors." Pp. 317–339 in N. N. Singh, T. Ollendick, and A. N. Singh (eds.), *International perspectives on child and adolescent mental health*. London, UK: Elsevier.

Dembo, Richard, Linda Williams, Werner Wothke, James Schmeidler, Alan Getreu, Estréllita Berry, and Eric D. Wish. 1992a. "The generality of deviance: Replication of a structural model among high-risk youths." *Journal of Research in Crime and Delinquency* 29: 200–216.

DiClemente, Ralph J., William B. Hansen, and Lynn E. Ponton. 1996a. "Adolescent at Risk. A generation in jeopardy." Pp. 1–4 in R. J. DiClemente, W. B. Hansen, and L. E. Ponton (eds.), *Handbook of adolescent health risk behavior, Issues in Clinical Child Psychology*. New York: Plenum Press.

DiClemente, Ralph J., William B. Hansen, and Lynn E. Ponton, eds. 1996b. *Handbook of adolescent health risk behavior, Issues in clinical child psychology*. New York: Plenum Press.

Donovan, Dennis M., G. Alan Marlatt, and Philip M. Salzberg. 1983. "Drinking behavior, personality factors and high-risk driving: A review and theoretical formulation." *Journal of Studies on Alcohol* 44: 395–428.

Donovan, John E., and Richard Jessor. 1985. "Structure of problem behavior in adolescence and young adulthood." *Journal of Consulting and Clinical Psychology* 53: 890–904.

Donovan, John E., Richard Jessor, and Frances M. Costa. 1991. "Adolescent health behavior and conventionality-unconventionality: An extension of problem-behavior theory." *Health Psychology* 10: 52–61.

Dryfoos, Joy G. 1993. "Common components of successful interventions with high-risk youth." Pp. 131–147 in N. J. Bell and R. Bell (eds.), *Adolescent risk taking*. Newbury Park, CA: Sage.

Durlak, Joseph A. 1997. *Successful prevention programs for children and adolescents*, M. C. Roberts and L. Peterson (eds.). New York: Plenum Press.

Elander, James, Robert West, and Davina French. 1993. "Behavioral correlates of individual differences in road-traffic crash risk: An examination of methods and findings." *Psychological Bulletin* 113: 279–294.

Elliott, Delbert S. 1993. "Health-enhancing and health-compromising lifestyles." Pp. 119–145 in S. G. Millstein, A. C. Petersen, and E. O. Nightingale (eds.), *Promoting the health of adolescents. New directions for the twenty-first century*. New York: Oxford University Press.

Ellis, L. 1990. "Universal behavioral and demographic correlates of criminal behavior: Toward a common ground in the assessment of criminological theories." in L. Ellis and H. Hoffman (eds.), *Crime in biological, social, and moral context*. New York: Praeger.

Emmons, Robert A., and Ed Diener. 1986. "Situation selection as a moderator of response consistency and stability." *Journal of Personality and Social Psychology* 51: 1013–1019.

Epstein, Seymour, and Edward J. O'Brien. 1985. "The person-situation debate in historical and current perspective." *Psychological Bulletin* 98: 513–537.

Evans, Leonard. 1984. "Driver fatalities versus car mass using: A new exposure approach." *Accident Analysis and Prevention* 16: 19–36.

Eysenck, Hans J. 1990. "Biological dimensions of personality." Pp. 244–276 in L. A. Pervin (ed.). *Handbook of Personality: Theory and Research*. New York: Guilford.

———. 1991. "Dimensions of personality: Criteria for a taxonomic paradigm." *Personality and Individual Differences* 12: 773–790.

Eysenck, Hans J., and M. W. Eysenck. 1985. *Personality and individual differences: A natural science approach*. New York: Plenum.

Farrington, David P., and Marianne Junger. 1995. "Illnesses, injuries and crime, Accidents, self-control and crime." *Criminal Behavior and Mental Health* 5: 255–478.

Farrington, David P., Geoffrey C. Barnes, and Sandra Lambert. 1996. "The concentration of offending in families." *Legal and Criminological Psychology* 1: 1–17.

Farrington, David P., Rolf Loeber, Delbert S. Elliott, J. David Hawkins, Denise B. Kandel, Malcolm W. Klein, Joan McCord, David C. Rowe, and Richard E. Tremblay. 1990. "Advancing knowledge about the onset of delinquency and crime." Pp. 283–342 in B. B. Lahey and A. E. Kazdin (eds.) *Clinical child psychology*, Vol. 13, *Advances in clinical child psychology*. New York: Plenum.

Fergusson, David M., L. John Horwood, and Michael T. Lynskey. 1994. "The comorbidities of adolescent problem behaviors: A latent class model." *Journal of Abnormal Child Psychology* 22: 339–354.

Foulds, Jonathan. 1996. "Strategies for smoking cessation." *British Medical Bulletin* 52: 157–173.

Friedman, Howard S., Joan S. Tucker, Carol Tomlinson-Keasey, Joseph E. Schwartz, Deborah L. Wingard, and Michael H. Criqui. 1993. "Does childhood personality predict longevity?" *Journal of Personality and Social Psychology* 65: 176–185.

Funder, David C., and C. Randall Colvin. 1991. "Explorations in behavioral consistency: Properties of persons, situations, and behaviors." *Journal of Personality and Social Psychology* 60: 773–794.

Gibbons, Don C., and Marvin D. Krohn. 1991. *Delinquent behavior*. Englewood Cliffs, NJ: Prentice Hall.

Glueck, Sheldon, and Eleanor Glueck. 1950. *Unraveling Juvenile Delinquency*. New York: The Commonwealth Fund, Oxford University Press.

Gottfredson, Michael R., and Travis Hirschi. 1990. *A general theory of crime*. Stanford, CA: Stanford University Press.

Gray, Jeffrey A. 1981. "A critique of Eysenck's theory of personality." Pp. 246–277 in H. J. Eysenck (ed.) *A model for personality*. Berlin, Germany: Springer.

Henry, Bill, Avshalom Caspi, Terrie E. Moffitt, and Phil A. Silva. 1996. "Temperamental and familial predictors of violent and nonviolent criminal convictions: Age 3 to age 18." *Developmental Psychology* 32: 614–623.

Hilakivi, I., J. Veilahti, P. Asplund, J. Sinivuo, and et al. 1989. "A sixteen-factor personality test for predicting automobile driving accidents of young drivers." *Accident Analysis and Prevention* 21: 413–418.

Hinde, Robert A. 1989. "Temperament as an intervening variable." Pp. 27–33 in G. A. Kohnstamm and J. E. Bates (eds.), *Temperament in childhood*. Chichester, UK: John Wiley & Sons.

Hirschi, Travis. 1969. *Causes of delinquency*. Berkeley: University of California Press.

———. 1996. "Theory without ideas: Reply to Akers." *Criminology* 34: 249–257.

Hofstra, Marijke B., Jan Van Der Ende, and Frank C. Verhulst. 2000. "Child and adolescent problems predict DSM-IV disorders in adulthood: A 14-year follow-up of a Dutch epidemiological sample." *Journal of the American Academy of Child and Adolescent Psychiatry* 39: 850–858.

Huizinga, David, Finn-Aage Esbensen, and Anne Wylie Weiher. 1991. "Are there multiple paths to delinquency?" *Journal of Criminal Law and Criminology* 82: 83–118.

Hurrelmann, Klaus, and Friedrich Losel. 1990. "Basic issues and problems of health in adolescence." Pp. 1–21 in K. Hurrelmann and F. Losel (eds.), *Health hazards in adolescence*. Berlin: Walter de Gruyter.

Igra, Vivien, and Charles E. Jr. Irwin. 1996. "Theories of adolescent risk-taking behavior." Pp. 35–51 in DiClemente. R. J., W. B. Hansen, and L. E. Ponton (eds.), *Handbook of adolescent health risk behavior. Issues in clinical child psychology*. New York: Plenum.

Istvan, J., and J. D. Matarazzo. 1984. "Tobacco, alcohol, and caffeine use: A review of their relationships." *Psychological Bulletin* 95: 301–326.

Jang, KwangMin. 1998. "The PEN Model: Its Contribution to Personality Psychology." http: //www.personalityresearch.org/papers/jang.html. [Accessed April 2003.]

Jeffery, Robert W. 1989. "Risk behavior and health." *American Psychologist* 44: 1194–1202.

Jessor, R., and S. L. Jessor. 1977. *Problem behavior and psychosocial development*. New York: Academic.

Jonah, Brian A., and G. Ray Engel. 1983. "Measuring the relative risk of pedestrian accidents." *Accident Analysis & Prevention* 15: 193–206.

Junger, Marianne. 1990. *Delinquency and ethnicity. An investigation on social factors relating to delinquency among Moroccan, Turkish, Surinamese and Dutch boys*. Boston: Kluwer.

———. 1994. "Accidents." Pp. 81–112 in T. Hirschi and M. Gottfredson (eds.),*The generality of deviance*. New Brunswick, NJ: Transaction Publishers.

Junger, Marianne, Wolfgang Stroebe, and André Van der Laan. 2001. "Delinquency, health behavior, and health in adolescence." *British Journal of Health Psychology* 6: 103–120.

Junger, Marianne, G. J. Terlouw, and Peter G. M. van der Heijden. 1995. "Crime, accidents and social control." *Criminal Behaviour and Mental Health* 5: 386–410.

Junger, Marianne, and Richard E. Tremblay. 1999. "Self-control, accidents and crime." *Criminal Justice and Behavior* 26: 485–501.

Junger, Marianne, Robert West, and Reinier Timman. 2001. "The relationship between criminal behavior and risky behavior in traffic." *Journal of Research in Crime and Delinquency*.

Junger, Marianne, and Auke Wiegersma. 1995. "The relations between accidents, deviance and leisure time." *Criminal Behaviour and Mental Health* 5: 144–174.

Kenrick, Douglas T., and David C. Funder. 1988. "Profiting from controversy: Lessons from the person-situation debate." *American Psychologist* 43: 23–34.

Kessler, Ronald C., Paul E. Stang, Hans-Ulrich Wittchen, T. Bedirhan Ustun, Peter P. Roy–Burne, and Ellen E. Walters. 1998. "Lifetime panic-depression comorbidity in the national commorbidity survey." *Arch. Gen. Psychiatry* 55: 801–808.

Kochanska, Grazyna, Katherine C Coy, and Kathleen T. Murray. 2001. "The development of self-regulation in the first four years of life." *Child Development* 72: 1091–1111.

Kokko, Katja, and Lea Pulkkinen. 2000. "Aggression in childhood and long-term unemployment in adulthood: A cycle of maladaptation and some protective factors." *Developmental Psychology* 36: 463–472.

Kolvin, I., F. J. W. Miller, D. McI Scott, S. R. M. Gatzanis, and M. Fleeting. 1990. *Continuities of deprivation?—The Newcastle 1000 family study.* Aldershot, England: Avebury.

Kornhauser, Ruth R. 1978. *Social sources of delinquency: An appraisal of analytic models.* Chicago: University of Chicago Press.

Krahé, Barbara. 1990. *Situation cognition and coherence in personality: An individual-centered approach.* Cambridge, UK: Cambridge University Press.

Krueger, Robert F. 1999. "The structure of common mental disorders." *Archives of General Psychiatry* 56: 921–926.

Krueger, Robert F., Avshalom Caspi, and Terrie E. Moffit. 2000a. "Epidemiological personology: The unifying role of personality in population-based research on problem behaviors." *Journal of Personality* 68: 967–998.

Krueger, Robert F., Avshalom Caspi, Terrie E. Moffit, Phil A. Silva, and Rob McGee. 1996. "Personality traits are differentially linked to mental disorders: A multitrait-multidiagnosis study of an adolescent birth cohort." *Journal of Abnormal Psychology* 105: 299–312.

Lahey, B. B., I. D. Walsman, and K. McBurnett. 1999. "The development of antisocial behavior: An integrative causal model." *Journal of Child Psychology and Psychiatry* 40: 669–682.

Lajunen, Timo, and Heikki Summala. 1997. "Effects of driving experience, personality and driver's skill and safety orientation on speed regulation and accidents." Pp. 283–294 in T. Rothengatter and E. Carbonell Vaya (eds.), *Traffic and transport psychology: Theory and application.* Amsterdam, NL: Pergamon.

Langley, John, Rob McGee, Phil Silva, and Sheila Williams. 1983. "Child Behaviour and Accidents." *Journal of Pediatric Psychology* 8: 181–189.

Laub, John H., and George E. Vaillant. 2000. "Delinquency and Mortality: A 50-Year Follow-Up Study of 1,000 Delinquent and Nondelinquent Boys." *American Journal of Psychiatry* 157: 96–102.

Lauritsen, Janet L., John Laub, H., and Robert J. Sampson. 1992. "Conventional and delinquent activities: Implications for the prevention of violent victimization among adolescents." *Violence and Victims* 7: 91–108.

Li, Guohua, Susan P. Baker, Jean A. Langlois, and Gabor D. Kelen. 1998. "Are female drivers safer? An application of the decomposition method." *Epidemiology* July 9(4): 369–370, 379–384.

Loeber, Rolf, and Kate Keenan. 1994. "Interaction between conduct disorder and its comorbid conditions: Effects of age and gender." *Clinical Psychology Review* 14: 497–523.

Logue, Alexandra Woods. 1988. "Research on self-control: An integrating framework." *Behavioral and Brain Sciences* 11: 665–709.

———. 1995. *Self-control—Waiting until tomorrow for what you want today.* Englewood Cliffs, NJ: Prentice Hall.

Magnusson, David, and Vernon L. Ellen. 1983. "An interactional perspective for human development." Pp. 3–31 in D. Magnusson and V. L. Ellen (eds.), *Human development: An interactional perspective.* New York: Academic Press.

Maughan, Barbara, and David P. Farrington. 1997. "Editorial." *Criminal Behavior and Mental Health* 7: 261–264.

Mawson, A. R., J. J . Biundo, D. I. Clemmer, K. W. Jacobs, V. K. Ktsanes, and J. C. Rice. 1996. "Sensation seeking, criminality, and spinal cord injury: A case control study." *American Journal of Epidemiology* 144: 463–472.

Maycock, G., and C. R. Lockwood. 1993. "The accident liability of British car drivers." *Transport Reviews* 13: 231–245.

McConaughy, Stephanie H. and Thomas M. Achenbach. 1994. "Comorbidity of empirically based syndromes in matched general population and clinical samples." *Journal of Child Psychology and Psychiatry* 6: 1141–1157.

McGue, Matt, Steven Bacon, and David T. Lykken. 1993. "Personality stability and change in early adulthood: A behavioral genetic analysis." *Developmental Psychology* 29: 96–109.

McKnight, A. James, and A. Scott Tippetts. 1997. "Accident prevention versus recidivism prevention courses for repeat traffic offenders." *Accident Analysis and Prevention* 29: 25–31.

Miller-Johnson, Shari, John E. Lochman, John D. Coie, Robert Terry, and Clarine Hyman. 1998. "Comorbidity of conduct and depressive problems at sixth grade: Substance use outcomes across adolescence." *Journal of Abnormal Child Psychology* 26: 221–232.

Mischel, Walter. 1968. *Personality and assessment*. New York: John Wiley.

———. 1981. *Introduction to personality*. New York: CBS College Publishing.

Mischel, Walter, and Philip K. Peake. 1982. "Beyond déjà vu in the search for cross-situational consistency." *Psychological Review* 89: 730–755.

Mischel, Walter, and Yuichi Shoda. 1995. "A cognitive-affective system theory of personality: Reconceptualizing situations, dispositions, dynamics, and invariance in personality structure." *Psychological Review* 102: 246–268.

Moskowitz, D. S. 1982. "Coherence and cross-situational generality in personality: A new analysis of old problems." *Journal of Personality and Social Psychology* 43: 754–768.

Murtha, Todd C., Ruth Kanfer, and Phillip L. Ackerman. 1996. "Toward an interactionist taxonomy of personality and situations: An integrative situational-dispositional representation of personality traits." *Journal of Personality and Social Psychology* 71: 193–207.

Nathan, P. E., and J. W. Langenbucher. 1999. "Psychopathology: Description and classification." *Annual Review of Psychology* 50: 79–107.

Neeleman, Jan, Simon Wessely, and Michael Wadsworth. 1998. "Predictors of suicide, accidental death, and premature natural death in a general-population birth cohort." *The Lancet* 351: 93–97.

Neumark-Sztainer, Dianne, Mary Story, Lori Beth Dixon, and David M. Murray. 1998. "Adolescents engaging in unhealthy weight control behaviors: Are they at risk for other health-compromising behaviors?" *American Journal of Public Health* 88: 952–955.

Nisbett, Richard E., and Lee Ross. 1991. *The person and the situation: Essential contributions of social psychology*. Philadelphia, PA: Temple University Press.

Nottelmann, Editha D., and Peter S. Jensen. 1995. "Comorbidity of disorders in children and adolescents. Developmental perspectives." *Advances in Clinical Child Psychology* 17: 109–155.

Olds, Davis L., John Eckenrode, Charles R. Henderson, Harriet Kitzman, Jane Powers, Robert Cole, Kimberly Sidora, Pamela Morris, Lisa M. Pettitt, and Dennis Luckey. 1997. "Long-term effects of home visitation on maternal life course and child abuse and neglect; Fifteen year follow-up of a randomized trial." *JAMA* 278: 637–643.

Orpinas, P. K., K. Basen–Engquist, J. A. Grunbaum, and G. Parcel. 1995. "The comorbidity of violence-related behaviors with health-risk behaviors in a population of high school students." *Journal of Adolescent Health* 16: 216–225.

Osgood, D. Wayne. 1990. "Covariation among adolescent problem behaviours." Paper presented at the *Annual Meeting of the American Society of Criminology*. Baltimore, MD.

Osgood, D. Wayne, Lloyd D. Johnston, Patrick M. O'Malley, and Jerald G. Bachman. 1988. "The generality of deviance in late adolescence and early adulthood." *American Sociological Review* 53: 81–93.

Osgood, D. Wayne, and David C. Rowe. 1994. "Bridging criminal careers, theory, and policy through latent variable models of individual offending." *Criminology* 32: 517–554.

Otero-Lopez, Jose M., Angeles Luengo-Martin, Lourdes Miron-Redondo, Maria T. Arrillo-de la Pena, and Estrella Omero-Trinanes. 1994. "An empirical study of the relations between drug abuse and delinquency among adolescents." *British Journal of Criminology* 34: 459–478.

Parker, Dianne, Antony S. R. Manstead, Stephen G. Stradling, and James T. Reason. 1992. "Determinants of intention to commit driving violations." *Accident Analysis and Prevention* 24: 117–131.

Peake, Philip K., and Walter Mischel. 1984. "Getting lost in the search for large coefficients: Reply to Conley (1984)." *Psychological Review* 91: 497–501.

Pedersen, Willy. 1994. "Parental relations, mental health, and delinquency in adolescents." *Adolescence* 29: 975–990.

Perry, Cheryl L., and Michael J. Staufacker. 1996. "Tobacco use." Pp. 53–82 in R. J. DiClemente, W. B. Hansen, and L. E. Ponton (eds.), *Handbook of adolescent health risk behavior, Issues in Clinical Child Psychology*y. New York: Plenum Press.

Pervin, Lawrence A. 1989. "Persons, situations, interactions: The history of a controversy and a discussion of theoretical models. Special Issue: Theory development forum." *Academy of Management Review* 14: 350–360.

———. 1990. "A brief history of modern personality theory." Pp. 3–18 in L. A. Pervin (ed.), *Handbook of personality: Theory & research*. New York: Guilford Press.

———. 1994. "A critical analysis of current trait theory." *Psychological Inquiry* 5: 103–113.

Peterson, Lizette. 1994. "Child injury and abuse-neglect: Common etiologies, challenges and courses toward prevention." *Current Directions in Psychological Science* 3: 116–120.

Pfohl, Bruce. 1999. "Axis I and axis II: Comorbidity or confusion?" Pp. 83–100 in C. R. Cloninger (ed.), *Personality and psychopathology*. Washington, DC: American Psychiatric Association.

Pihl, Robert O., and Jordan B. Peterson. 1995. "Drugs and aggression: Correlations, crime and human manipulative studies and some proposed mechanisms." *Journal of Psychiatry and Neuroscience* 20: 141–149.

Pihl, Robert O., Jordan B. Peterson, and Mark A. Lau. 1993. "A biosocial model of the alcohol-aggression relationship." *Journal of Studies on Alcohol* 54: 128–139.

Pihl, Robert O., Simon N. Young, Philip Harden, Stewart Plotnick, Brian Chamberlain, and Frank R. Ervin. 1995. "Acute effect of altered tryptophan levels and alcohol on aggression in normal human males." *Psychopharmacology* 119: 353–360.

Plomin, Robert, G. E. McClearn, Nancy L. Pedersen, John R. Nesselroade, and et al. 1988. "Genetic influence on childhood family environment perceived retrospectively from the last half of the life span." *Developmental Psychology* 24: 738–745.

Pulkkinen, Lea. 1982. "Self-control and continuity from childhood to late adolescence." *Life-Span Development and Behaviour* 4: 64–105.

Read, John H., Eleonor J. Bradley, Joan D. Morison, David Lewall, and David A. Clarke. 1963. "The epidemiology and prevention of traffic accidents involving child pedestrians." *Canadian Medical Association Journal* 89: 687–701.

Reid, Donald. 1996. "Tobacco control: Overview." *British Medical Bulletin* 52: 108–121.

Resnick, Gary, and Martha R. Burt. 1996. "Youth at risk: Definitions and implications for service delivery." *American Journal of Orthopsychiatry* 66: 172–188.

Revelle, W. 1995. "Personality processes." *Annual Review of Psychology* 46: 295–328.

Robins, Lee N. 1966. *Deviant children grown up.* Baltimore: Williams and Wilkins.

Robins, Lee N., and Rumi K. Price. 1991. "Adult conduct disorders predicted by childhood conduct problems: Results from the NIMH epidemiologic catchment area project." *Psychiatry* 54: 116–132.

Ross, H. Laurence. 1992. *Confronting drunk driving. Social policy for saving lives.* London: Yale University Press.

Rowe, David C. 1987. "Resolving the person-situation debate: Invitation to an interdisciplinary dialogue." *American Psychologist* 42: 218–227.

Rowe, David C., D. Wayne Osgood, and W. Alan Nicewander. 1990. "A latent trait approach to unifying criminal careers." *Criminology* 28: 237–270.

Rutter, Michael, and Henri Giller. 1983. *Juvenile delinquency: Trends and perspectives.* Middlesex: Penguin.

Rutter, Michael, Henri Giller, and Ann Hagell. 1998. *Antisocial behavior by young people.* Cambridge, UK: Cambridge University Press.

Scarr, Sandra, and Kathleen McCartney. 1983. "How people make their own environments: A theory of genotype (leading to) environment effects." *Child Development* 54: 424–435.

Scherwitz, Larry, and Reiner Rugulies. 1992. "Life style and hostility." Pp. 77–98 in H. S. Friedman (ed.) *Hostility, coping & health.* Washington DC: American Psychological Association.

SCP. 1995. *Sociaal en Cultureel Rapport 1994.* Rijswijk, Netherlands: Sociaal en Cultureel Planbureau.

Shoda, Yuichi, Walter Mischel, and Jack–C Wright. 1994. "Intraindividual stability in the organization and patterning of behavior: Incorporating psychological situations into the idiographic analysis of personality." *Journal of Personality and Social Psychology* 67: 674–687.

Sikorski, John B. 1996. "Academic underachievement and school refusal." Pp. 393–412 in R. J. DiClemente, W. B. Hansen, and L. E. Ponton (eds.), *Handbook of adolescent health risk behavior, Issues in clinical child psychology.* New York: Plenum Press.

Skodol, Andrew E., John M. Oldham, Steven E. Hyler, H. David Kellman, Norman Doidge, and Mark Davies. 1993. "Comorbidity of DSM-III-R eating disorders and personality disorders." *International Journal of Eating Disorders* 14: 403–416.

Soderstrom, Carl A., Patricia C. Dischinger, Shiu Man Ho, and Margaret T. Soderstrom. 1993. "Alcohol use, driving records, and crash culpability among injured motorcycle drivers." *Accident Analysis and Prevention* 25: 711–716.

Stroebe, W., and M. S. Stroebe. 1995. *Social psychology and health.* Duckingham, UK: Open University Press.

Tellegen, Auke. 1991. "Personality traits: Issues of definition, evidence, and assessment." Pp. 10–35 in W. M. Grove and D. Cichetti (eds.), *Personality and psychopathology,* Vol. 2, *Thinking clearly about psychology.* Minneapolis, MN: University of Minnesota Press.

Tellegen, Auke, David T. Lykken, Thomas J. Bouchard, Kimerly J. Wilcox, Nancy L. Segal, and Stephen Rich. 1988. "Personality similarity in twins reared apart and together." *Journal of Personality and Social Psychology* 54: 1031–1039.

Tillman, W. A., and G. E. Hobbs. 1949. "The accident-prone automobile driver." *American Journal of Psychiatry* 106: 321–331.

Tittle, Charles R. 1995. *Control balance: Toward a general theory of deviance.* Boulder, CO: Westview Press.

Tolan, Patrick H., and David Henry. 1996. "Patterns of psychopathology among urban poor children: Comorbidity and aggression effects." *Journal of Consulting and Clinical Psychology* 64: 1094–1099.

Townsend, J. 1996. "Price and consumption of tobacco." *British Medical Bulletin* 52: 132–142.

Tremblay, Richard E., Robert O. Pihl, Frank Vitaro, and Patricia L. Dobkin. 1994. "Predicting early onset of male antisocial behavior from preschool behavior." *Archives of General Psychiatry* 51: 732–739.

Van Heck, Guus L., Marco Perugini, Gian Vittorio Caprara, and Joyce Froger. 1994. "The Big Five as tendencies in situations." *Personality and Individual Differences* 16: 715–731.

Verhulst, Frank C., and Jan van der Ende. 1993. "'Comorbidity' in an epidemiological sample: A longitudinal perspective." *Journal of Child Psychology and Psychiatry* 34: 767–783.

Wadsworth, Jane, Iona Burnell, Brent Taylor, and Neville Butler. 1983. "Family type and accidents in preschool children." *Journal of Epidemiology and Community Health* 37: 100–104.

Wadsworth, Michael E. J. 1978. "Delinquency prediction and its uses: The experience of a 21-year follow-up study." *International Journal of Mental Health* 7: 43–62.

West, D. J., and D. P. Farrington. 1977. *The delinquent way of life*. London: Heineman Educational.

West, Robert J. 1997. "Cross-cultural generalisability of relationship between antisocial motivation and traffic accident risk." Transport Research Laboratory, TRL, Crowthorne Berkshire, UK.

West, Robert J., James Elander, and Davina French. 1993. "Mild social deviance, Type-A behaviour pattern and decision-making style as predictors of self-reported driving style and traffic accident risk." *British Journal of Psychology* 84: 207–219.

West, Robert, Helen Train, Marianne Junger, Alan Pickering, Eric Taylor, and Anne West. 1998. "Childhood accidents and their relationship with problem behaviour." Department of the Environment, Transport and the Regions, London, UK.

Wilcox, Brian L. 1993. "Deterring risky behavior: Policy perspectives on adolescent risk taking." Pp. 7–28 in N. J. Bell and R. W. Bell (eds.), *Adolescent risk taking*. Newbury Park, CA: Sage.

Wilson, James Q., and Richard Herrnstein. 1985. *Crime and human nature*. New York: Simon and Schuster.

Windle, Michael, Jean Thatcher Shope, and Oscar Bukstein. 1996. "Alcohol use." Pp. 115–160 in R. J. DiClemente, W. B. Hansen, and L. E. Ponton (eds.), *Handbook of adolescent health risk behavior, Issues in Clinical Child Psychology*. New York: Plenum Press.

Yoshikawa, H. 1994. "Prevention as cumulative protection: Effects of early family support and education on chronic delinquency and its risks." *Psychological Bulletin* 115: 28–54.

Zoccolillo, Mark. 1992. "Co-occurrence of conduct disorder and its adult outcomes with depressive and anxiety disorders: A review." *Journal of the American Academy of Child and Adolescent Psychiatry* 31: 547–556.

Zuckerman, Marvin. 1979. *Sensation seeking: Beyond the optimal level of arousal*. New York: John Wiley & Sons.

12

The Versatility vs. Specialization Debate: Different Theories of Crime in the Light of a Swiss Birth Cohort

Henriette Haas and Martin Killias[1]

Addressing Theoretical Questions in Criminology with Empirical Evidence

The debate on the origin of crime covers a wide range of hypotheses and theories. Most of them are based on different premises and, from an empirical standpoint, it is not easy to evaluate the scientific relevance of all hypotheses in order to eliminate those which are less promising.

Traditional sociology makes the difference between so-called micro-social or individual-related variables such as psychopathology and intelligence and the macro-social variables such as unemployment, poverty, and neighborhood. Furthermore, sociology makes a clear judgment of priority, claiming that macro variables precede micro factors. As one can imagine, not all psychologists share this view, so the controversy remains unresolved. Other sociologists consider situational factors as being decisive for crime. An example is the "lifestyle" model of Hindelang, Gottfredson, and Garofalo (1978), which postulates that the risk of becoming a victim increases if the potential victim comes into contact with a motivated offender. This approach (and particularly its "routine activity" version) has ancient roots, which go back to Greek philosophers such as Aristotle (Killias, 2001: 299).

Psychological and psychiatric research progressed in another direction, integrating biological, biographical, and social causes of individuals with great relational and character problems into the theory of personality disorders. These multiaxial diagnostics are used to assess delinquents in criminal procedure. Very often (but not always), delinquents suffer from a so-called personality disorder. According to the *Diagnostic and Statistical Manual of Mental Disorders* (4th Edition), the general diagnostic criteria for these syndromes consist of:

> An enduring pattern of inner experience and behavior that deviates markedly from the expectations of the individuals' culture. This pattern is manifested in two (or more) of the following areas: (1) cognition (i.e., ways of perceiving and interpreting self, other people, and events); (2) affectivity (i.e., the range, intensity, lability, and appropriateness of emotional response); (3) interpersonal functioning; (4) impulse control. The enduring pattern is inflexible and pervasive across a broad range of personal and social situations. The enduring pattern leads to clinically significant distress or impairment in social, occupational, or other important areas of functioning. (APA, 1994: 633)

The DSM-IV mentions ten different types of personality disorders, depending on the preponderance of certain symptoms. However, since 1970, researchers in psychology and psychiatry have hardly done any studies on psychological classifications of different types of delinquents—therefore, implicitly following the assumption of the generality of deviance.

Why not assess those conflicting theories with empirical evidence, considering at the same time different competing variables? Indeed, hardly any empirical studies permit the evaluation of the weight of each different influence with respect to the others, while at the same time including sociological and psychological variables on a sufficient number of subjects. Confusion bias is therefore inevitable (Bouyer et al., 1995). Despite the undeniable rivalry between sociologists and psychologists, this is not due to bad intent on either side—it is situational. In fact, it is very difficult for researchers to make the necessary comparison because of the very structure of data. When one wants to measure crime on a large scale, covering the entire population of a given region, one opts for the official records, that is, mainly police and court statistics. These records do not contain much psychological or individual information; rather they focus on macro-social variables. Doing clinical studies, on the other hand, provides masses of psychological data, but it is not known from what section of the general population the clinical nonrepresentative specimen stems in respect of socio-demographics. Longitudinal studies and self-report studies, on the other hand, where one is free to ask any question, cover generally samples of around 1,000 to 5,000 persons only: samples which are too small to contain a sufficient number of serious offenders. Thus, we never know whether sociological variables mask psychological variables or vice versa.

While sociological criminology and psychopathology coexist, so-called control theories attempt a synthesis between sociological and psychological aspects. Instead of asking what drives people to commit crime, control theories ask why most people do not become delinquents. This is a similar starting point to psychology, which also tries to establish what makes people function normally, before addressing the issue of disturbances. The researchers most closely identified with control theories are Gottfredson and Hirschi. Their *A General Theory of Crime,* 1990, attributes the cause of crime to an individual lack of self-control. The general theory of crime also states that deviance can be observed in a variety of respects, and that offenders do not specialize. According to this approach, delinquency is a lifestyle marked by the absence of control over one's desires. Delinquents take whatever seems to be available and only consider the short-term benefit, mostly ignoring the long-term consequences that their behavior might provoke, such as incarceration, accidents, or infectious diseases. This theory, therefore, provides a sort of bridge between the competing theories of sociology and psychology. At its core is the assumption that offenders are versatile, and that specialization is the rare exception. Just like psychological theories, low self-control theory (LSC) makes individualistic causal arguments: Acts of criminal behavior are the result of unique individual factors such as traits, which are relatively persistent personality characteristics. Some sociologists also blame control theories and psychological concepts (especially the concepts of psychopathy and antisocial personality disorder) as well, of being tautological, because according to them, they explain delinquency with delinquency. This is also a controversial question that should be addressed on the basis of data and not only with purely theoretical arguments.

The controversial issues around the validity of competing crime theories are not easy to resolve with self-report studies because the samples are usually too small to include significant numbers of severe offenders, and even more so of serial offenders of serious crimes. Such data, however, would be necessary to identify, should they exist, distinctive clusters of offending. With data currently available, the "specialization hypothesis" had, indeed, no realistic chance of being confirmed or rejected. Clinical studies, on the other hand, do not take into account all offenses actually committed during a given time, because many remain unknown.

In the following paragraphs we want to examine this question in the light of our unusually large sample, which provides the necessary data on very serious (including serial) offenders, as well as on a broad array of psychological and sociological variables.

Method

Every year, Swiss Army recruits are interviewed on a topic of social or policy relevance. In 1997, the topic chosen was violence, either committed or experienced, in a biographic perspective. The present study is based on a sample of 21,314 valid interviews with twenty-year-old Swiss men. Because of the general conscription in Switzerland, this sample represents over 70 percent of the national cohort. After approximately four weeks of basic training, the soldiers were asked to complete a questionnaire containing about 900 variables on the biographic and social circumstances of their childhood and adolescence, including violent and other deviant behavior they had either committed or experienced. The questionnaire included many items concerning mental health, deviant and impulsive behavior, along with situational circumstances such as the possession of weapons. Usually about thirty-five to sixty soldiers sat in a large classroom, with ample space between them (like an exam), under the remote supervision of civilian staff. The soldiers were guaranteed complete anonymity of their responses. In order to emphasize this, the soldiers were shown a kind of "ballot box" into which they were to drop their completed questionnaires. Given that this procedure established a confidentiality comparable to an electoral ballot, very few soldiers refused to cooperate. While all recruits were obliged to attend the session, the questionnaire explicitly allowed respondents to leave any questions unanswered. As a result, on average only about 5 percent of all questions were not answered and more than 94 percent answered both the delinquency and the victimization questions. For comparison, men of the same age group who did not serve in the army in 1997 were invited to answer a short version of the questionnaire by mail. This sample of 1,160 non-recruits showed a bimodal distribution, with a disproportionate number of university students. Illegal drug use and sexual harassment were admitted somewhat more often by the men not enrolled in the army, whereas physical violence and forced sexual intercourse were admitted more by army recruits. However, the difference was not large (Haas, 2001).

The Question of Specialization and Generality of Crime Reviewed on a National Cohort

Looking at incidences in our cohort (Table 12.1), delinquency is very widespread among young men, just as shown by other studies. Only a minority of young male adults are model citizens in a strict sense of the word.

However, the picture formed from looking at the mere incidence of offenses could be somewhat misleading because it does not discriminate the severity of the cases. Many criminologists (for example Fréchette and LeBlanc, 1987) have pointed out the fact that serious offenders present quite a distinct population and that they differ considerably from the average young man who is inclined to some adolescent indulgences.

The first controversy to address concerns the issue of whether serious delinquency is a general way of life, due to lack of important social skills, or if there is such a thing as the specialized or even professional offender. If the second hypothesis were true, one would have to examine why certain people develop one type of offending and others another type. It could also mean

Table 12.1
Incidence of Different Types of Offenses among the 21,314 Recruits during the Twelve Months Preceding Recruit Training

Traffic offenses (>1x)	n=	9,191	43.1 %
Smoke cannabis (>1x)	n=	9,575	44.9 %
Take heroin or cocaine (>1x)	n=	1,048	4.9 %
Steal > 100.- SF (>1x)	n=	887	4.2 %
Commit fraud > 100.- SF (>1x)	n=	887	4.2 %
Vandalize > 100.- SF (>1x)	n=	2,329	10.9 %
Break and enter (>1x)	n=	300	1.4 %
Set fire intentionally (>1x)	n=	141	0.7 %
Sell soft drugs (>1x)	n=	2,807	13.2 %
Sell hard drugs (>1x)	n=	323	1.5 %
Any violence with or without bodily injury (>1x)	n=	5,113	24.0 %
Any sexual harassment or abuse (>1x)	n=	2,557	12.0 %
Any of the above mentioned behaviors	n=	15,992	75.0 %
None of the above mentioned behaviors	n=	5,322	25.0 %

that offending in itself, or at least certain types of offending, need special attributes such as physical force, shrewdness, and so on.

Just one short statement concerning the definition of serious and serial offenders: It is not advisable to set the level of serial offending at the same frequency for every type of crime. According to other specifications of the offense, six separate incidences can be a lot or not much at all. Therefore we chose the frequency of twenty times or more during one year for those offenses which were the most widespread, especially taking illegal drugs, traffic offenses, and dealing cannabis. On the other hand, our questions on stealing, fraud, and vandalism (not the main topic of the questionnaire) covered only those incidents which involved damage of higher than 100 Swiss francs ($70). Therefore all those recruits who often stole CDs, liquor bottles, etc., or other minor goods do not fall into this category. This means that among the property offenders we counted all those cases with at least six offenses (burglars more than six times, committed fraud or falsified documents more than six times). Intentionally setting fire to property (of others) is considered more dangerous than other property offenses and certainly much more of a tort than smoking cannabis twenty times or more during one year. The level of serial offending was therefore set at only three incidents for arson. Concerning violence and sexual violence, the seriousness of such acts is measured according to the severity of the injury caused. Because violent and sex offenses were the main topic of the survey, we counted all incidents, including less severe ones. In order to put the categories on a comparable level, we singled out the more serious violent and sex offenders with different criteria (cf. Haas, 2001). For the present purpose, it is sufficient to refer only to two categories of serious incidents: those violent offenders who caused bodily injury to a victim and those sex offenders who had committed forcible rape. Other sexual and violent offenders such as armed robbers (who did not cause bodily injury) or child molesters have not been included here.

Of course, these categories are not exclusive—one can be a drug addict and a habitual thief at the same time. Table 12.2 shows that certain types of offenses, particularly speeding and drunken driving as well as drug abuse and drug trafficking, are more likely to be repeated than others. Therefore, the relatively high overall rate of serial offenders among the recruits is mainly caused by the cannabis smokers, the cannabis dealers, and by the traffic offenders. On the other hand, given the fact that cross-sectional studies allow us to use large samples, even the least likely constellations of very serious recidivists are represented by a few dozen subjects in a sample of some 21,000 respondents. Consequently, we also find a certain number of specialists in property offenses, arson, sexual, and violent crimes. Because most self-reported surveys cover fewer subjects, the existence of serious serial offenders of certain types (according to self-reports and not police arrests) is a hitherto unknown result.

Based on these epidemiological findings, we can extract the most important factors influencing delinquent behavior and dismiss other factors that

Table 12.2
Serial and Serious Offenders among the 21,314 Recruits in a Twelve-Month Period

Traffic offenders (>20x)	n=	1,704	8.0 %
Cannabis smokers (>20x)	n=	4,794	22.5 %
Heroin / cocaine consumers (>20x)	n=	264	1.2 %
Thieves > 100.- SF (>6x)	n=	159	0.7 %
Fraudster > 100.- SF (>6x)	n=	51	0.2 %
Vandals > 100.- SF (>6x)	n=	197	0.9 %
Burglars (>6x)	n=	45	0.2 %
Arsonists (>3x)	n=	61	0.3 %
Dealers (of soft drugs) (>20x)	n=	833	3.9 %
Dealers (of hard drugs) (>6x)	n=	171	0.8 %
Violent offenders who committed bodily injury	n=	669	3.1 %
Rapists	n=	30	0.1 %
Any of the above mentioned behaviors	n=	6,413	30.1 %
None of the above mentioned behaviors	n=	14,901	69.9 %

seem to be irrelevant. Upon further analyses, those recruits belonging to one of the offender categories mentioned in Table 12.2 are candidates for meeting the criteria for a specialized type of delinquent if they exist.

Associations between Different Specializations and Other Forms of Delinquency

General theory of crime also attempts to describe what is right and wrong within the field of criminology in order to make research across the world comparable, and independent of different national penal codes. Gottfredson and Hirschi (1990: 21) refer to the classical definition of crime "as an event involving force or fraud that satisfies self-interest." Based on the majority of past surveys on the dark figure, they assert that "specific crimes, regardless of their outcome, do not tend to be repeated." However, in this very large sample, we did find a small minority of serial offenders of a given type. The question to address now is whether their apparent specialization is only the consequence of a huge number of offenses of all different types.

Looking at the incidences of different offenses committed by those recruits who had admitted a series of delinquent acts of a given type or certain serious crimes, our first impression is that, indeed, offenders are not likely to restrict themselves to only one type of crime.

In the left column of the following table (12.3), we have singled out those offenders who could be considered "specialists" by the frequency of a certain type of offense, or by the severity of their acts during the year preceding army training (cf. also Table 12.2). The top line of the following table considers incidences of offenses and makes no distinction between very serious violent acts like shooting at somebody with a gun and less serious ones such as slapping. The same is true for the incidence of sexual harassments and abuses mentioned in the top line of Table 12.3.

Table 12.3
Incidence of Different Offenses Committed by Serial and Serious Offenders over a Twelve-Month Period

Incidences	Traffic offending	Smoke cannabis	Take heroin cocain	Steal	Commit fraud	Vandalize	Break and enter	Set fires	Sell soft drugs	Sell hard drugs	Any violence	Any sex offenses
Row %												
Traffic offenders n=1,704	100%	57%	8%	9%	11%	23%	4%	1%	21%	3%	34%	19%
Cannabis smokers n=4,794	50%	100%	19%	11%	8%	21%	4%	2%	51%	6%	33%	16%
Heroin / cocaine users n=264	51%	98%	100%	36%	21%	39%	15%	8%	78%	59%	58%	22%
Thieves > 100.- SF n=159	57%	87%	52%	100%	44%	70%	48%	19%	69%	38%	67%	36%
Fraudster > 100.- SF n=51	71%	90%	65%	86%	100%	80%	65%	39%	82%	55%	86%	43%
Vandals > 100.- SF n=197	64%	89%	39%	61%	31%	100%	41%	18%	60%	25%	78%	35%
Burglars n=45	67%	84%	58%	89%	62%	91%	100%	47%	82%	56%	87%	44%
Arsonists n=61	62%	87%	52%	59%	49%	64%	51%	100%	67%	44%	69%	51%
Dealers (of soft drugs) n=833	55%	98%	41%	27%	16%	36%	12%	3%	100%	24%	50%	23%
Dealers (of hard drugs) n=171	56%	92%	89%	51%	30%	50%	26%	16%	91%	100%	69%	33%
Bodily injury n=669	53%	65%	18%	18%	11%	34%	8%	4%	35%	10%	100%	30%
Rapists n=30	43%	70%	43%	40%	27%	43%	33%	27%	60%	43%	83%	100%

N=21,314

As can be seen in the preceding table, counting incidences of different offenses among serial and severe offenders of a given type, offenders seldom specialize in one type of delinquency. Most of them commit all sort of illegal acts, a wild mix of property crimes, drug offenses, violent acts, and sexual abuse in the course of a year. This result is consistent with the "logical structure of crime" device as proposed by Gottfredson and Hirschi (1990) that defines crime as ordinary, requiring little in the way of effort, planning, preparation, or skill. Criminals just take whatever they can and whatever is available with little effort. It also means that "crime predicts crime," without going so far as to say that this would be the only reliable prediction factor.

Now, how about different specializations: Do they overlap in any typical ways or not? The top line of Table 12.4 counts only the serial or serious offenders (prevalence) according to the same definitions as in the first column at the left.

At first sight, the figures in Table 12.4 seem to contradict the hypothesis of the generality of crime. Thus, when reading the lines containing the different multi-recidivist offenders of a given type of crime, we can distinguish one type of offender who commits mainly traffic offenses (speeding, drunken driving). Traffic offenders are somewhat more delinquent in other respects than the average recruit (cf. also Table 12.2) but, mostly, they seem to be well integrated. The same holds true for the large group of cannabis smokers. We can also state that a majority of cannabis dealers seem to be more or less ordinary citizens. Those recruits (traffic offenders, cannabis smokers, and cannabis dealers) probably consider themselves as "gentleman" offenders, and they limit their activities to traffic offending and consumption of soft drugs, and sometimes selling those drugs. Therefore, certain specializations

Table 12.4
Overlapping of Different Types of Specializations among Different Types of Serial and Severe Offenders over a Twelve-Month Period

Specializations	Traffic offenders	Cannabis smokers	Heroin cocain users	Thieves	Fraudsters	Vandals	Burglars	Fire-setters	Dealers soft drugs	Dealers hard drugs	Violent offenders bodily injury	Rapist
Row %												
Traffic offenders n=1,704	•	33%	3%	2%	1%	4%	1%	1%	9%	2%	5%	0%
Cannabis smokers n=4,794	12%	•	5%	3%	1%	3%	1%	1%	17%	3%	6%	0%
Heroin / cocaine users n=264	17%	92%	•	19%	8%	14%	8%	6%	59%	45%	16%	1%
Thieves > 100.- SF n=159	25%	78%	31%	•	24%	41%	23%	14%	50%	39%	19%	3%
Fraudster > 100.- SF n=51	45%	82%	39%	75%	•	65%	47%	37%	59%	37%	31%	10%
Vandals > 100.- SF n=197	30%	75%	19%	33%	17%	•	17%	12%	37%	19%	30%	2%
Burglars n=45	40%	80%	44%	80%	53%	76%	•	40%	58%	42%	31%	7%
Arsonists n=61	25%	66%	26%	36%	31%	38%	30%	•	28%	34%	21%	10%
Dealers (of soft drugs) n=833	19%	95%	19%	10%	4%	9%	3%	2%	•	16%	13%	1%
Dealers (of hard drugs) n=171	19%	84%	70%	27%	11%	22%	11%	12%	78%	•	26%	4%
Bodily injury n=669	13%	42%	6%	4%	2%	9%	2%	2%	16%	6%	•	2%
Rapists n=30	17%	47%	10%	17%	17%	13%	10%	20%	27%	23%	43%	•

N=21,314

seem to exist, which cover domains of offending that are considered socially acceptable in some youth countercultures. These first three types of offenders seem to be more or less well integrated into society and, overall, much less deviant than the following groups of versatile multi-recidivist offenders.

We then find a set of apparently versatile property offenders: burglars, thieves, and fraudsters. These sub-groups seem to overlap quite a lot and cover a range of criminal acts caused by the same motive of getting money. It is also obvious that a property offender might use different ways to acquire money, therefore burglars may want to steal, thieves may also want to commit an insurance fraud, and vice-versa. Many of them also seem to be implicated in drug trading. This category of offenders reveals a distinct criminal profile; their rate of severe violent and sexual offenses is also quite high. The propensity for violence is easily explained, given the fact that good opportunities to steal or commit fraud are not always present and in this case, the idea of an armed robbery might come to the mind of some less successful thief or burglar. This result confirms Gottfredson's and Hirschi's hypothesis that "the reason for all of this interchangeability among crimes must be that these diverse events provide benefits with similar qualities, such qualities as immediacy, brevity of obligation, and effortlessness" (1990: 21).

Furthermore, there are the rapists and the arsonists, two types of criminals who resemble each other very much in their highly antisocial and dangerous violent activities. They are also heavily engaged in property crime and drug trading.

Concerning violent offenders in this chapter, we are confronted with another complication because the severity of the violence is often measured by the outcome for the victim. However, according to the situational theory of crime, the degree of hurt is highly dependent on coincidence: For instance, does the bullet hit the target or not. Therefore, the offense "bodily injury" can be committed with a wide range of motives, from a wrongly perceived necessity for self-defense right up to a planned vicious act of stalking and aggressing a helpless victim. This fact is clearly reflected in the figures of Table 12.4. There are those subjects who committed a single violent offense leading to bodily injury mixed with the habitually violent individuals who carry around firearms and harbor a constant aggressive tension. Incidentally, if we take another, stricter definition of severe violence (n=341 recruits) which takes into account not only the result of the violent action but also the number of violent incidents and the use of weapons, we get a similar picture to the illegal activities of arsonists and the rapists. On the other hand, if one includes minor violent offenses not leading to bodily injury into the category of the violent offenders, and less severe sexual harassments and abuses into the category of the sex offenders, those respondents will, again, belong to the group of the "well-integrated" offenders.

From a psychological point of view, the above-mentioned figures of overlapping specializations also make a lot of sense: not surprisingly, fraudsters are likely to have committed many traffic offenses, given their need for "showing off." For drug abusers, the involvement in the drug trade is certainly the easiest way of making money, and besides that, they are often involved in property crime, because of their need for instant money. Drug dealers, on the other hand, do become violent sometimes, especially when addicts do not pay their debts or when they get into territorial fights with rivals.

Furthermore, we can observe that there are some interesting combinations according to the degree of involvement in the criminal subculture. It is quite logical that dealers of mainly hard drugs often also sell soft drugs, but not the other way around. Considering different ways drug addicts hustle for money, there is a clear hierarchy. The most obvious way to make money is certainly by selling illegal drugs. However, this activity requires some degree of self-control. Addicted dealers are tempted to consume all the drugs destined for resale themselves and then they try to cheat—not only their clients but also their drug-trade bosses. The more addicted the person, the more likely they are to fall into the vicious circle of debts owed to the "main man," resulting in the need for burglaries or armed robberies to stay afloat. Because the addict has become less trustworthy, he will not be given larger quantities of drugs to sell in the future. He has, therefore, fallen socially within the hierarchy of the illegal drug market.

With this deeper insight into the question of criminal specialization provided by Tables 12.2 to 12.4, we realize that the question of the generality of crime is quite complicated, even though it is true that offenders seem to occasionally engage in any kind of illegal act. It seems to us that criminal specialization is not only determined by the absence of self-control, but also by emotional and social needs and by the presence of psychological resources and different skills.

As a whole, our figures support Gottfredson and Hirschi's (1990) hypothesis of the generality of delinquency, saying that delinquents take whatever is easily available. However, we cannot exclude the possibility of finding clusters of typical forms of delinquency in analogy to psychiatric syndromes, for example, cannabis dealers without addiction, heavily addicted heroin and cocaine dealers, rapists, arsonists, robbers, and so on. Secondly, the development of the offending career would be a topic to examine in terms of specialization. Are different types of delinquency stable, do they develop into other types, or are they abandoned in the course of time? Naturally, if such clusters exist in the present sample, their distinctiveness would have to be confirmed by another study of comparable size on young adults.

Discovering the Roots of Delinquency among the Main Known Factors of Influence

The next question to address is the comparison of the relevance of different social, biographical, and psychological variables as potential causes of crime. In this chapter, we have to limit ourselves to the logistical regression of bodily injury and rape only. The special feature of the recruits' cross-sectional study is that it permits analysis of the influence of a great number of variables. Therefore, some of the most important epidemiological questions on the origin of delinquency can be addressed in a broader perspective. As an example, we would like to present and compare the regression analyses of two forms of delinquency: on one hand it concerns intended bodily injury (669 subjects admitted that), on the other hand it concerns rape, defined as intercourse committed under threats or direct violence (30 men admitted that).

The multivariate models consider thirty-three different socio-demographic, biographical, criminological, and psychological variables (such as delinquent friends, ownership of weapons) and indicators of psychopathology.

How was personality disorder operationalized? When measuring self-reported psychiatric symptoms with an anonymous questionnaire, one is confronted with problems of measurement similar to those for self-reported delinquency. Just as it is impossible to record the precise offenses, as defined by the penal code, it is not possible to record the symptoms in the same way as a clinical diagnosis. Instead, we could record indicators of symptoms, which were then processed into composite variables serving as an operationalization of personality disorders. However, psychiatric epidemiological research has shown that this is indeed a valid method for gaining information on mental health. We categorized symptom indicators such as low frustration tolerance, social isolation, diminished reality control (in financial matters), risky sexual behavior, excessive consumption of alcohol or drugs, excessive gambling (at slot machines), attempted suicide, depression and low self-esteem, frequent boredom, paranoid projections on others, lack of moral conscience (super ego deficit), and childhood symptoms. In the following analysis we counted only the number of such symptoms.

The variables introduced into the models are listed in Table 12.5.

Causal interpretations of correlations are not problematic, when for logical reasons, one of the two possible interpretations has to be ruled out (i.e., if one variable cannot influence the other because it precedes the other in biography). Other dependent variables are synchronous in time and therefore it is not so evident which one of them is the cause. The value of those regression models lies in the fact that almost all—and not just some—of the most important known potential influences can be considered. Presently, an interdisciplinary analysis of psychological and sociological variables is much broader than what has usually been done before in criminology. Therefore, we suppose that the remaining factors in the models are not masking many meaningful underlying influences which have not been considered.

The education of the parents and the fact that the parents were dependent on social welfare (for more than one year) were two variables that we did not

Table 12.5
Listing of the Independent Variables Introduced into the Logistic Regression Algorithm

1. Lifetime frequency of accidents (0-40)
2. Having been beaten by their parents, (0=not at all, 1=less severely, 2=severely)
3. Having been sexually abused or exploited, (0=not at all, 1=less severely, 2=severely)
4. Being born to immigrant parents (0= no, 1=other countries, 2=regions in crises or war)
5. Having suffered from conduct disorder (DSM-IV) in childhood or adolescence, (0=no, 1=milder form, 2=severe conduct disorder)
6. Having had good relations with classmates in high school (being popular)
7. Having had to repeat a year in high school because of poor educational achievements
8. Having been placed in a special school for pupils with learning or behavior problems
9. Having had a good relation with teachers during adolescence (0=not at all good, 1=not very good, 2=quite good, 3=very good)
10. Having been a police suspect during childhood or adolescence (but not indicted and not convicted) (0=no, 1=yes)
11. Having been placed in an institution for delinquent, mentally disturbed, or neglected children
12. Having had to appear before a juvenile court during childhood or adolescence (0=no, 1=yes)
13. Having acquired higher education or professional training
14. Presence in many different groups and social events (sports, parties, concerts, etc.)
15. Being unemployed
16. Having moved to a bigger city after adolescence
17. Having visited prostitutes (0, 1-2, 3-5, 6-20, 20+)
18. Having been a male prostitute one-self (0, 1-2, 3-5, 6-20, 20+)
19. Having had unprotected sex with unknown partners (0, 1-2, 3-5, 6-20, 20+)
20. Number of friends (0-7)
21. Episodes of excessive drinking (0-40)
22. Episodes of heroin and cocaine abuse, (0, 1-2, 3-5, 6-20, 20+).
23. Number of criteria fulfilled for dissocial personality disorder (number of symptoms of this disorder) (0-9)
24. Frequency of gambling at slot machines (0=never, 1=1-2x/month, 2=1-2x/week, 3=more than 3x/week)
25. Frequency of watching hard core pornography and splatter videos (0-60)
26. Having a girlfriend (0=no, 1=yes)
27. Number of delinquent friends (0-7)
28. Number of handguns owned (0, 1-2, 3+)
29. Number of blunt objects owned serving as a weapon (baseball bats, nunchakus) (0, 1-2, 3+)
30. Number of knifes owned (bigger than a Swiss pocket knife) (0, 1-2, 3+)
31. Number of iron bars, chains, knuckle dusters, etc. owned (0, 1-2, 3+)
32. Number of rifles owned (0, 1-2, 3+)
33. Frequency of carrying such a weapon (0, 1-2, 3-5, 6-20, 20+)

introduce into the models of adult offending because of their lack of significance on the univariate level and in the logistic regression analysis of juvenile conduct disorder.

The selection of important influences by the logistic process, and the weight that is attributed to the remaining variables is a strong indicator for the validity of the postulates of a theory. If Sutherland's theory of differential association were to be confirmed, we would expect the number of delinquent friends to play a very significant influence on all forms of crime, outweighing biographical and personality traits. For the labeling approach and so-called critical criminology to receive empirical support in the light of other variables, the dominant influences retained in the logistic model should consist of the institutional career of a young man, such as police arrests and court records, having been placed in a institution, special school for pupils with learning disabilities, or language or behavioral problems. If Merton's functional approach of the influence of social resources on the individual's capacity to achieve culturally defined goals is to be substantiated by empirical evidence, it is immigration of the parents, educational failure, and unemployment that should appear among the most significant influences on crime.

It should be noted that the results of the logistic regression analysis were obtained using a model where missing values are replaced by *imputing* the means of the corresponding variables (for those who injured someone and those who did not). The mathematical procedure of imputing avoids a biased sample resulting from the accumulation of missing values on the many independent variables. In the case of bodily injury and using the variables listed in Table 12.5, the full sample would have been reduced to 12,620 respondents. To reduce risks resulting from any choice between two methods, we decided to conduct the logistic regression analysis both ways. The results concerning both regression analyses were similar to the results with imputing.

Factors Accounting for the Crime of Bodily Injury

This model offers a sophisticated picture of different influences on the risk of injuring somebody (see also Killias and Haas, 2002). Given the many interval-scaled independent variables that were included in the model it is not surprising that the odds ratios are small. However, with every additional level of the variable the odds ratios increase. Hence, for those who own three or more handguns the odds ratio is 3.6, and for owners of wooden weapons, the ratio is also 3.4. Furthermore, we found a heavy influence of psychopathology: those who qualify for a dissocial personality disorder who fulfill three or more criteria have an odds ratio of over 1.5, those who have had a severe conduct disorder an odds ratio of 2.1 and finally those with a tendency to have many accidents (40 or more) had an odds ratio of 2.3. Dissocial

Table 12.6
Resulting Model for Bodily Injury

N=669 recruits who had committed bodily injury
N=19,400 recruits who had not committed bodily injury

Independent variables which stayed in the model	Odds ratio	p <
Lifetime frequency of accidents	1.022	.0065
Suffered from conduct disorder (DSM-IV) in childhood or adolescence	1.433	.0001
Having had a good relation with teachers during adolescence	0.871	.0055
Having been a police suspect during childhood or adolescence (but neither indicted nor convicted)	1.488	.0002
Having had to appear before a juvenile court	1.743	.0001
Number of criteria fulfilled for dissocial personality disorder (number of symptoms of this disorder)	1.157	.0002
Frequency of gambling at slot machines	1.172	.0019
Frequency of watching hard core pornography and splatter videos	1.013	.0016
Having a girlfriend	1.372	.0013
Number of delinquent friends	1.102	.0001
Number of handguns owned	1.527	.0001
Number of baseball bats, nun-chakus owned	1.504	.0001
Number of iron bars, chains, knuckle dusters owned	1.400	.0001
Number of rifles owned	0.821	.0049
Frequency of carrying a weapon	1.024	.0007

N=20,069, Missing=1,245 recruits who did not answer the question concerning bodily injury.

personality disorder is, together with biological predispositions, closely related to incompetent, ineffective, or inconsistent parenting and dysfunctional families (cf. Haas, 2001). This disorder is also an expression of a lack of emotional bonding of the child with his mother and father, which leads later to a lack of social attachment in a general way. When other impulsive behaviors are considered, we again note that the odds ratio is 1.6 for heavy gamblers at slot machines, that watching hard core pornography and (forbidden) gory or splatter movies (for example "Texas Chainsaw Massacre") 60 times or more yielded an odds ratio of 2.2, and that having seven or more delinquent friends produced an odds ratio of 2.

Ownership of handguns and other weapons (but not rifles) as well as carrying around dangerous weapons turned out to be very important factors in explaining violence leading to bodily injury. Thus the situational approach to the explanation of violent crime can be substantiated. The possession of knives and other weapons could be a variable that is masked by carrying weapons. Knives are particularly easy to carry.

A preexisting police record (without court record) increases the odds of perpetrating bodily injury by factor 1.5, a court and police record by factor 1.7. Is this result confirming labeling theory? A priori we expect that a criminal record would significantly increase the odds of committing any crime whatsoever in the future, because those who get caught are a selected group of the most active offenders. This can be verified through our figures. With every additional ten juvenile offenses (here only counting physical violence, traffic and property offenses, arson, and drug trafficking) the probability of being officially registered increases by about 3 to 4 percent. Therefore, an increased odds ratio for registered offenders to commit bodily injury would only indicate a negative effect of the judicial system if their criminal activity at the time had been identical to unregistered adolescents or if the factor was very high—both of which is not the case. Thus, the present analysis of the Swiss juvenile court system provides no evidence for a presumed negative influence on future criminal behavior due to the prosecution of offenders.

Given the fact, that rape as a crime is an act of will and depends somewhat less on pure coincidence than (successfully) injuring somebody, we should expect that prior arrests should exercise a greater influence in rape if the labeling theory is true. However, other regression analyses on the less severe forms of violence, on sexual harassment, and on severe violence in general (including armed robbery and frequent aggressions) have shown (cf. Haas, 2001) that police and court records do not have very significant influence and mostly none at all on offending. Therefore, the appearance of official records among risk factors for future crime reflects much more the inability to learn from experience, a defect that is common in dissocial personalities. Inability to profit has also been treated as a sociological variable in Hirschi's (1969) bond of attachment since people or institutions are sources of learning.

Interestingly, the algorithm removed drug and alcohol abuse from the model. One can interpret this in light of the existing correlations of substance abuse with personality disorder.

Measuring the predictive value of the model, we can observe that it is quite capable of predicting non-violence (true negatives), but it is not very sensitive in predicting true positives (that is, those men who have injured somebody). This is what we would expect, because not injuring somebody is strongly linked to non-violent behavior and a lack of risk factors for it whereas "successfully" injuring somebody depends very much on circumstances, not solely on a violent attitude or the behavior itself.

Thus, the findings reported in Tables 12.6 and 12.7 confirm the roles of many conventional variables in criminological research, and particularly of psychopathology, of lack of control, and of guns and other weapons. We

Table 12.7
Model Fitting Information for Table 12.6 on the Logistic Regression of Bodily Injury

Model Fitting Information and Testing Global Null Hypothesis BETA=0
(Backward and stepwise procedure yielded the same model)

Criterion	Intercept Only	Intercept and Covariates	Chi-Square for Covariates
AIC	5868.182	4714.236	.
SC	5876.089	4840.747	.
-2 LOG L	5866.182	4682.236	1183.946 with 15 DF (p=0.0001)
Score	.	.	2345.752 with 15 DF (p=0.0001)

Goodness-of-fit Statistic = 48.331 with 8 DF (p=0.0001)

Classification Table

		Correct		Incorrect		Percentages				
Prob Event	Prob Level	Even	Non-Event	Event	Non-Event	Correct	Sensi-tivity	Speci-ficity	False POS	False NEG
0.032	0.500	58	19330	70	611	96.7	8.7	99.6	55.7	2.9

conclude that the main causes of bodily injury after intentionally committed violence are:

1. Lack of self-control as it is manifested by impulsive behaviors, by poor judgment and planning (accidents, gambling, not being able to resist the suggestions of delinquent friends).
2. Psychopathology (personality disorder, accidents as potential causes of neuropsychological disturbances).
3. Possessing and carrying around weapons.

Since the times of Sutherland (1934) the criminogenic factor of having delinquent friends has belonged to the credo of any criminologist. This result is also consistent with the findings that gang violence and hooliganism are prominent criminogenic scenarios, leading not rarely to bodily injury. Sutherland attributed the delinquent behavior of youthful gang members to learning processes. This hypothesis implies, though, that human beings would indiscriminately learn everything that is presented to them and absorb it without any judgment of their own. If this were the case, the inverse process, namely offender rehabilitation, would be very easy and not at all the difficult task it actually is. Therefore, we believe that the criminogenic factor of having delinquent friends should be better interpreted in terms of a lack of self-control. Those boys who become delinquent under the bad influence of others without having criminal intentions of their own are unable to distance themselves from the harmful company they keep, even though they should. In other words, youngsters who fall under the influence of gangs (as followers and not as leaders) are too weak, too chaotic, or too impulsive to determine their own actions. We can also state that the variable "delinquent friends" does apparently not have the basic importance attributed to it by Sutherland's theory when taking into account other variables.

When gambling on slot machines enters as a risk factor into the offense of bodily injury this, of course, must also be an indirect influence. For example, this influence could be due to debts or to other conflicts, which are in some way the result of pathological gambling. In other words, it is again the loss of control, which must somehow account for the elevated risk of violence among gamblers. Another interesting result is the insignificant odds ratios of offering sex for money. At first we were surprised to find that male prostitutes are not as aggressive and violent (in a non-sexual context) as they are often assumed to be. It remains to be seen whether that would hold also for a regression analysis of robbery.

Factors Accounting for the Crime of Forcible Rape

In the next model concerning the origins of sexual intercourse perpetrated under threats or under direct violence, almost the same set of variables was introduced. Based on preliminary analysis, we did not include the possession of rifles, consumption of heroin and cocaine, and gambling at slot machines into the modeling process, as they play no role as a contributing factor for rape on the bivariate level, and it were indeed not very plausible if they did. We also took behaviors of sexual *acting-out* (visiting prostitutes, being a male prostitute, and unprotected sexual encounters with strangers) as one composite variable (0-60), because the rapists showed a high rate of all those forms of sexual behaviors in general.

Again we find the similar basic set of influences that are also causing bodily injury. However, rapists distinguish themselves from "simply violent" men by the biographical risk of having been sexually abused and by their propensity to sexual *acting-out*. The four main dimensions are:

1. Lack of self-control as it is manifested by impulsive sexual behaviors of all sorts.
2. Psychopathology (personality disorders).
3. Carrying of weapons.
4. Having been sexually abused or exploited during childhood or adolescence.

Table 12.8
Resulting Logistic Regression Model for Forcible Rape

N=30 recruits who had committed forcible rape
N=17,447 recruits who had not committed rape, nor other sexual abuses or harassments

Independent variables which stayed in the model	Odds ratio	p <
Having been sexually abused or exploited	8.97	.001
Having had a good relation with teachers during adolescence	0.56	.050
Number of criteria fulfilled for dissocial personality disorder (number of symptoms of this disorder)	1.96	.001
Frequency of engaging in sexual risk behavior such as prostitution, visiting prostitutes, and unprotected intercourse with unknown partners	1.09	.001
Frequency of carrying a weapon	1.08	.010

N=17,477, Missing=3,837 recruits who did not answer the question of sexual abuse under threats and recruits who have committed lesser forms of abuse or harassment.

The general picture we get of the rapist implies that he belongs to a subcategory of violent offenders because he has suffered an additional sexual trauma: hence his propensity to take sexual risks.

Bad company does not seem to play an important part in the causes of rape. Wright and West found (1981) that only 13 percent of all rapes involved two or more assailants. Later (1989), Lloyd and Walmsley established that the rate of solitary rapes had even risen since Wright and West's data collection in the seventies. We can interpret the diminishing of group rape in civil life in the sense that sexual violence no longer enjoys a tacit general acceptance in Western society. Rape is no longer considered as an expression of masculinity or of male dominance; on the contrary, it is generally considered as a failure and has therefore become less attractive to normal undisturbed younger men or adolescents.

Many rapists do show substance abuse. Still, this factor does not contribute significantly to the crime of rape, contrary to the assertion of sex offenders themselves, who often attribute their behavior to the influence of alcohol or other substances. But again, it seems that the crucial factor is not the substance, but much more an underlying personality disorder, which precedes substance abuse.

Concerning the influence of prior police and court contacts on future rape, we are confronted with an even more unambiguous result than in the analysis above. Rapists distinguish themselves from violent offenders who had committed bodily injury and from the other recruits by their very high rate of former police and court records (73 percent vs. 52 percent vs. 26 percent).

Given their early propensity to criminal activities, it is not surprising that many of them were discovered. Nevertheless, contacts with law enforcement do not figure as significant influences—positive or negative—on the crime of rape. With respect to labeling theory and radical criminology, our figures support the conclusion of Gottfredson and Hirschi (1990: 160): "Unfortunately for labeling theory, the empirical evidence overwhelmingly contradicts its assumptions and predictions . . . the evidence shows that such labels are highly influenced by actual behavior differences." This result may be important for choosing more efficient strategies of crime control, especially DNA-registering all offenders (with the exception of those with misdemeanors only). In the light of the facts that official records seem to have a deterrent effect (Haas, 2001) and that severe offenders are generally versatile and prone to recidivism this seems a reasonable and efficient approach. Since the counter argument that police and court records would push offenders further into crime is not at all sustained by empirical proofs, it is time to change outdated criminal policies, which were based on the beliefs of the critical criminologists.

As we can see in both models, a good relationship with a teacher turned out to be an important protective factor. This is a very welcome result, indicating that preventive measures against crime in schools can work and that children in difficulties should receive good care to support their development.

Compared to the model of bodily injury, the regression model for rape (Table 12.9) is much more sensitive at predicting who had committed the crime of forcible rape (cf. Haas, 2001). This is not surprising, because the element of coincidence of adverse circumstances plays a much lesser role in the act of rape than it does in the fact of ("successfully") hurting somebody with intentional acts of violence.

Last, but not least, for our theoretical considerations, it might be interesting to look at a group of variables, which have been removed from both models by the algorithms. Those are: (1) presence in many different groups and events (such as sports, parties, concerts, etc.), (2) being unemployed, (3) having moved to a bigger city after adolescence, (4) number of friends, (5) being born to immigrant parents, (6) having acquired higher education or professional training, (7) having had good relations with classmates in high school (being popular), (8) having had to repeat a year in high school because of poor educational achievements, (9) having been placed in a special school for pupils with learning or behavior problems, (10) having been placed in an institution for delinquent or neglected children (11) having been beaten by parents.

Conclusion

First of all, it seems that purely situational variables (those which have nothing to do with acting out) do not play a very important role when it

Table 12.9
Model Fitting Information for Table 12.8 on the Logistic Regression of Rape

Model Fitting Information and Testing Global Null Hypothesis BETA=0
(Backward and stepwise procedure yielded the same model)

Criterion	Intercept Only	Intercept and Covariates	Chi-Square for Covariates
AIC	2507.358	1680.018	.
SC	2513.898	1751.953	.
-2 LOG L	2505.358	1658.018	847.340 with 10 DF (p=0.0001)
Score	.	.	1178.358 with 10 DF (p=0.0001)

Goodness-of-fit Statistic = 1.6771 with 2 DF (p=0.4323)

		Correct		Incorrect		Percentages				
Prob Event	Prob Level	Event	Non-Event	Event	Non-Event	Correct	Sensi-tivity	Speci-ficity	False POS	False NEG
0.002	0.500	13	17444	3	17	99.9	43.3	100.0	18.9	0.1

comes to the cause of incidents of severe violence or sexual violence. Other models (in Haas,2001) concerning the less severe forms of violence and sexual harassment did retain these variables. We therefore conclude that the less severe forms of delinquency are more prone to be caused by unfortunate circumstances, while severe violence is more likely to be determined by personal characteristics of the offender. These are especially psychopathological symptoms such as lack of self-control, impulsivity, poor judgment and planning, lack of moral conscience, suicidal tendencies, and so on. These symptoms are due to defects that appear early in life and tend to become chronic traits of the delinquent adult. Other situational influences are combined with personal characteristics, especially the tendency to act out. The most important of these acting-out/situational influences is the possession and the carrying of weapons. Although the majority of gun owners are indeed conformist and law-abiding citizens, we find that there is a subgroup that is not. We also found a higher prevalence of psychiatric symptoms in this population (Killias and Haas, 2002). These findings underscore the need to design better policies to control access to and ownership of guns. On balance, the best policy might be to keep guns and other dangerous devices out of the hands of people, and particularly to exclude individuals with criminal risks or psychiatric problems from gun ownership.

Overall, the so-called macro-social variables (social class, unemployment, having moved to a larger city, immigration of the parents) did not account at all for important influences on violence or sexual violence. Since much theoretical criminological thinking has focused on strain (including anxiety and stress) as being an important factor in violence, this might be surprising. We suspect that unemployment may be less threatening to army recruits during the months preceding military training. The big city effect did not occur at all. Even educational success did not influence violence or sexual violence. These may be specific results for central und northern European countries, where many possibilities exist to take up an apprenticeship and become successful in life despite a less-brilliant school record. However, based on the present data, and contrary to the beliefs of many sociologists, we conclude that the so-called macro-social variables are not variables situated on a "higher" level of explanation for crime in Western Europe. On the contrary, according to our figures, it seems that macro-social variables are confounding influences, caused by underlying individual differences. The same is true for immigration, although boys coming from immigrant families were over-represented in both the violent and the sex offender sub-samples. However, all multivariate regression analyses have shown that this variable is linked to victimization by violent and sexual abuse and not primarily cultural differences or adjustment difficulties. Therefore, according to our figures, the underlying real cause of the excess of delinquency among immigrants is the higher prevalence of traumatic life events and not a so-called "culture clash." Gottfredson and Hirschi write with respect to macro-social theories (1990: 79): "Controversy over the relation between social class and crime has occupied the sociological literature since the late 1950's. . . . An unresolved, 30-year empirical debate over one of its core propositions is not good news for a theory, . . . the issue was . . . the truth or falsity of the discipline of sociology. Somehow, academic disciplines within the positive tradition have become isomorphic with theories of behavior, and they see the defense of such theories as defense of their own interests." In this regard, it is not our intention to question sociology as a whole, especially as social circumstances in Switzerland are quite comfortable compared to other countries. Since the social welfare system in Switzerland has a high standard (Killias and Haas, 2001), we do not know whether the macro-social variables do, in fact, have a greater influence on crime in developing countries where severe poverty and even hunger are widespread with existential consequences for those blighted by it. When accounting for sociological influences, it seems that in a wealthy Western European environment only the situational approach and the control theory can be considered a valuable contribution beside psychological and biographical elements in a theory of crime.

Severe delinquency is indeed caused by a general deviant lifestyle, according to the figures on our sample, which covers nearly a full birth cohort of young men. We did find evidence for the validity of control theory, for psychopathology, and for trauma theory. From a psychological point of view, an apparent lack of self-control can itself have different origins. On a biological level, there is the possibility of a neurological disinhibition. In fact, neuropsychological research on antisocial personality disorder shows that biological factors play an important role (Raine, 1993). A second explanation of lack of self-control is that self-discipline has never been acquired, because of inadequate parental supervision or deep-rooted attachment problems in the parent-child relationship. In developmental psychopathology, seeking bad company and adopting impulsive behavior are also known as *acting-out.* There is psychological evidence that people with certain personality disorders have a tendency to "act out" when they search for risky, conflict-provoking situations and one of their most characteristic symptoms is the lack of self-control. According to developmental psychology, the lack of control that manifests itself in acting-out behaviors is not only due to poor childrearing, but its persistence is also tied to the cognitive inability to symbolize life experiences and to verbalize emotions. Instead of seeking help for their problems, these troubled and traumatized individuals will reenact their painful life experiences. They also have a tendency to convert any emotion directly into an immediate action, instead of accepting it as a communication signal in human interactions.

Having compared theoretical issues with the biographies of a near cohort of young men, we can now address the issue of whether control theories and psychological concepts of personalities who are prone to commit crimes are tautological or not. On the one hand, we found that the pillars of these concepts fit actual data much better than many other theories of crime. Crime is not solely caused by pure coincidence in someone's life (like an accident); it is not solely caused by negative labels that have stigmatized a child for the rest of his life; it is mostly not a singular biographical event; and finally, in the overwhelming majority of cases, we do not find highly specialized offenders or a master-mind who would plan his illegal activities carefully. To avoid redundancy in the statistical analysis of the Swiss cohort, personality disorder has been categorized with the concept of dissocial personality (Rauchfleisch, 1981), a definition that does not contain any delinquent behaviors at all, but only symptoms of psychological suffering, of cognitive distortions, and other deviant (but not delinquent) characteristics. Therefore, if the empirical results of regression analysis show that personal characteristics do account for crime on a large scale—which they do indeed—this demonstrates a non-tautological explanation of crime. The argument pretending that delinquency is explained with delinquency is false, because control theories and psychopathology explain delinquency with other forms of deviant personality traits. The statistical fact that offenders are often deviant should not lead to the inverse conclusion, which is logically false. Just because all Swiss citizens are Europeans, all Europeans are not necessarily Swiss citizens. In fact deviance and psychological disorders are much more frequent than delinquency. For example (Haas, 2001: 378), only 38 percent of the young men who qualified for dissocial PD (according to our definition) were at the same time severe or serial offenders, compared to 5.6 percent of the men without this disorder. While psychological problems contribute to delinquency they do not determine somebody's life-course: at the present state of research it seems more likely that the unexplained rest of the variance is caused by the free will of the individual.

Furthermore, our results indicate that it is the combination of situational and personal factors that best explain the origin of different forms of delinquency. Dogmatic and one-sided approaches, on the other hand, are often inconsistent with data when a sufficiently large sample is examined. In an overall theoretical perspective, present results indicate that criminology will benefit most from an interdisciplinary, pragmatic approach.

Note

1. The authors wish to thank Cynthia Tavares of the Home Office in England and Wales for her editing help.

References

American Psychiatric Association (APA) (Eds.) 1994. *Diagnostic and Statistical Manual of Mental Disorders DSM-IV*. Fourth. Ed., Washington DC: author.

Bouyer, J., D. Hémon, S. Cordier, F. Derriennic, I. Stücker, B. Stengel, and J. Clavel. 1995. *Epidémiologie—principes et méthodes quantitatives*. Paris: Editions Inserm.

Fréchette, M., and M. LeBlanc. 1987. *Délinquances et délinquants*. Québec, Canada: Gaëtan Morin.

Gottfredson, M. R. and Hirschi, T. (1990). *A General Theory of Crime*. Stanford Cal: Stanford University Press.

Hindelang, M. J., M. R. Gottfredson, and J. Garofalo. 1978. *Victims of Personal Crime: An Empirical Foundation for a Theory of Personal Victimization*, Cambridge, MA: Ballinger.

Haas, H. 2001. *Agressions et victimisation: une enquête sur les délinquants violents et sexuels non détectés*. Editions Sauerländer, Aarau, Switzerland.

Hirschi, T. 1969. *Causes of Delinquency*. Berkeley: Univ. of California Press.

Killias, M. 2001. *Précis de Criminologie*. Second Edition. Berne: Ed. Staempfli (first edition 1991).

Killias, M., and H. Haas. 2001. "L'assistance sociale—un moyen pour prévenir la délinquance?" in: Kahil-Wolff B, Greber P.-Y. and Çaçi M. (Eds). *Melanges en l'honneur de Jean-Louis Duc*. Faculté de Droit de l'Université de Lausanne.

———. 2002. "The Role of Weapons in Violent Acts: Some Results of a Swiss National Cohort Study." *Journal of Interpersonal Violence* 171N: 14–32.

Killias, M., J. van Kesteren, and M. Rindlisbacher. 2001. "Guns, Violent Crime, and Suicide in 21 Countries." *Can. J. Crim.* 43: 429–445.

Lloyd, C. and R. Walmsley. 1989. *Changes in Rape Offenses and Sentencing*. London: Home Office Research Study, No 105.

Raine, A. 1993. *The Psychopathology of Crime*. London: Academic Press.

Rauchfleisch, U. 1981. *Dissozial*. Goettingen (Germany): Vandenhoeck and Ruprecht. (English translation: The dissocial syndrome)

Sutherland, E. H. 1934. *Principles of Criminology*. Second Edition. Philadelphia: J.B. Lippincott.

Wright, R., and D. J. West. 1981. "Rape: A Comparison of Group Offenses and Lone Assaults. Medicine." *Science and the Law* 21: 25–30.

Contributors

Robert Agnew is professor of sociology at Emory University.

Todd A. Armstrong is assistant professor of administration of justice at Arizona State University West.

Leana Allen Bouffard is assistant professor of sociology at North Dakota State University.

Augustine Brannigan is professor of sociology at the University of Calgary.

Chester L. Britt is chair and associate professor of criminal justice and criminology at Arizona State University West.

Barbara J. Costello is associate professor of sociology at the University of Rhode Island.

Maja Deković is professor in social and behavioral sciences at Amsterdam University.

Matt DeLisi is assistant professor of sociology and coordinator of the criminal justice studies program at Iowa State University.

Michael R. Gottfredson is executive vice chancellor and professor of criminology at the University of California at Irvine.

Henriette Haas is assistant professor of criminology and forensic psychology at the University of Lausanne, Switzerland.

Kelly H. Hardwick is senior analyst at the Canadian Research Institute for Law and the Family in the Faculty of Law at the University of Calgary.

Travis Hirschi is Regents Professor Emeritus of sociology at the University of Arizona.

Marianne Junger is researcher in developmental psychology at Utrecht University.

Martin Killias is professor of forensic sciences and criminology at the University of Lausanne.

Helen J. Mederer is associate professor of sociology at the University of Rhode Island.

Kevin M. Thompson is professor of sociology at North Dakota State University.

Alexander T. Vazsonyi is associate professor of human development and family studies at Auburn University.

Index

abusive parenting, 25
abusive punishment, 159
affection, 156-157, 165
age and opportunity, 10
age relationship with crime, 28
analogous behaviors, 32
  definition, 80-81
antisocial personality disorder, 214-215
assumptions
  self-control theory, 6, 30, 39-41
  social learning theory, 39-41
attachment, 157
autonomy, 166-167

belief in conformity, 167
benefits of crime, 31
biological factors of co-occurrence, 228
border crime, 12
Bosnian genocide, 111-112

Cambridge Youth Study, 188
causes of co-occurrence, 227
causes of delinquency, 259-260, 270-271
causes of rape, 266-268
causes of violence, 262-266
childrearing, 89, 156-159
  affection, 156-157
  attachment to the caregiver, 157
  control theory, 156-159
  discipline, 158-159
  feminist perspectives, 89
  supervision, 157-158
class and crime, 81-82
classical school,
cohort of Swiss Army recruits, 252-255
collective action, 116-117
collective and individual action, 116-117
collective sanctions, 171
co-morbidity, 218-219
comparative criminology,
  data sources, 180-190
consequences of risky behavior, 220
control capacity and group solidarity, 170-171
control theory, 39
  assumptions about crime, 151
  femininity, 90
control theory and childrearing, 156-159
control theory and the cross-national analysis of crime data, 190-193
conventional moral beliefs,
  measurement, 62
co-occurrence, 219
  biological factors, 228
  causes of, 227
  culture and subculture, 230
  definition, 215-216
  environmental factors, 228-229
  implications for prevention and treatment, 233-234
  learning, 231
  personality characteristics, 228
  shared risk factors, 227-228
  strain theory, 232
  testing theories, 229-230
  theoretical implications, 227-233
  unique causes, 229
  values and attitudes, 232
co-occurrence of risky behavior, 219, 222
correlates of crime, 84-85
crime, analogous behaviors, 32
  causes of, 259-260
  definition, 80-81, 162, 214-215
  elements of, 115-116
  generality, 252-255, 257-258
  prediction, 260-261
  self-control theory, 5
crime and criminality, 114
crime and criminality distinction, 5-7
crime on the border, 12
criminal justice
  impact of self-control on, 29

impact on crime, 28
criminal propensity,
individual, 43
learning, 43, 45
socialization, 45-46
cross-national analysis,
and control theory, 190-193
general theory of crime, 190-193
self-control, 196-202
cross-national crime data, 180-190
official, 180-183
self-report, 185-190
victimization, 183-185
cross-situational consistency, 216-218
cultural and subcultural theories of co-occurrence, 230

delinquency, causes of, 270-271
health implications of, 223-225
measurement, 63
delinquent behavior
definition, 222
delinquent peer association
group solidarity, 171-172
measurement, 63
delinquent peer association and control theory, 57-58
delinquent peers, 47-49, 57
interactions with social controls, 57-59
delinquent peers and social control, 57
dependence and group solidarity, 170-171
desire for money, 167
deterrence
ecological, 13-14
interrupted time-series,13-14
perceptual, 13-14
deviance
definition, 214-215
measurement of, 195
differential social control theory, 83-84
direct control
measurement, 61-62
direct social control, 56
discipline, 158-159
discipline and parental relationship, 159

early life course, 8
elements of crime, 115-116
elements of self-control, 114-115
environmental factors and co-occurrence, 228-229
exposure to risky behavior, 225-227

family, 7-8, 22
psychopathy, 22
self-control, 22
self-control theory, 7-8
socialization processes, 22-24
female role and crime commission, 90
external constraints, 90
feminist critique of criminological theory, 79-80
feminist perspectives on criminological theory, 78-79
forms of control, 152
legal sanctions, 153
natural sanctions, 152-153
relations among sanction systems, 153-156
social sanctions, 153
supernatural sanctions, 153

game theoretic models of choice, 164
gender and caring, 90
gender and crime
assumptions, 79-80
gap in crime rates, 80
individual level of analysis, 92-95
integrated theory, 83-85
interactional level of analysis, 95-97
level of analysis, 87, 99,100
research recommendations, 99-100
structural level of analysis, 97-99
typological theory, 80-83
gender and sexual harassment, 139
gender gap in crime and delinquency
biological differences, 88
childrearing, 89
division of labor, 88-89
gender inequality, 88
gender gap in criminal offending, 80, 83
general deterrence, 13
general theory of crime
cross-national test of, 190-193
generality of crime, 252-255, 257-258
generality of deviance, 216
genocide
Bosnia,111-112
collective animosities, 118
context and history, 118
definition, 110
deterrence theory, 126-127
facts about, 117
general theory applied to, 116, 118-127

general theory of, 127-129
guilt and remorse, 119
individual action, 118-121
opportunity, 124-125
opportunity theory, 126-127
role of the state, 123-124
rule of law, 123-124
Rwanda, 112-113
techniques of provocation, 112-123
theoretical understanding, 109-110
Grasmick et al.'s Low Self-Control Scale, 195, 208-209
group processes, 161
group solidarity, 169-174
adolescent peer groups, 174
and delinquency, 172-173
and self-control, 172-173
and social capital, 173-174
and the social bond, 173
collective sanctions, 171
control capacity, 170-171
definition, 170
dependence, 170-171
effectiveness of, 171
family, 171-172
individual sanctions, 171
peer groups, 171-172
rational choice theory, 170

health implications of delinquency, 223-225
health-endangering behavior
definition, 221-222
Hobbes, Thomas, 30
hot spots, 13
human desires and needs, 164-168
self-interest, 167-168
human nature assumptions, 40-41
self-control theory, 50-51
social learning theory, 50
human nature assumptions of theory, 50

incomplete theories of gender gap, 85
individual action, 116-117
assumptions, 162-164
individual propensity to crime, 11
individual sanctions, 171
informal social control, 55-57
internal control, 56
International Study of Adolescent Development, 193-194

latent trait
risk taking, 225
learning, 42
learning processes, 43-44
learning theory and co-occurrence, 231
legal sanctions, 153
level of analysis
cross-national, 180-190
gender and crime, 87
link between self-control and psychopathy, 27
links between self-control and sexual harassment, 140
logical structure of sexual harassment, 135-136
low self-control
cross-national measurement of, 195
indicators of, 136-137
measurement of, 195

macro-social predictors of violence, 270
manifestations of self-control, 27
masculinities and crime, 78
mental disorders, 218-219
motivation, 46
motivation and propensity, 46-47
motivation to crime, 46
multidisciplinary research on co-occurrence, 233

natural sanctions, 152-153
neglectful parenting, 25
New Zealand Dunedin Multidisciplinary Health and Development Study, 189
Normative Deviance Scale (NDS), 195, 209-211

offender
self-control theory, 7
offense
self-control theory, 6
official data
cross-national analysis of, 180-182
operant conditioning, 42
opportunity, 8-9
factors affecting, 9
reductions in, 15
opportunity and risky behavior, 225-227

parenting, 22-24
abusive or neglectful, 25
socialization, 31

parenting and self-control, 24
patriarchal criticism of criminological theory, 79
peer groups, 161
  group solidarity, 171-172
  self-control and group solidarity, 172-174
peers and delinquency 47-49
personality characteristics and co-occurrence, 228
personality disorders, 214
Pittsburgh Youth Study, 188-189
policing, 15
policy implications, 13
  deterrence, 13-14
  opportunity reduction, 15
  policing, 15
  self-control theory, 13
power-control theory, 84-85
prediction, 260-261
prediction and prevention of risky behavior, 220-221
prediction of delinquency, 260-261
prediction of rape, 266-268
prediction of violence, 262-266
prevalence of sexual harassment, 137-138
problem behavior
  definition, 222

rape
  causes of, 266-268
  prediction, 266-268
rational choice and crime, 168
rational choice theory, 163-164
relations among sanction systems, 153-156
risk factors and crime, 213
risk factors of co-occurrence, 227-228
risk taking as latent trait, 225
risky behavior
  consequences of, 220
  learning, 231
  prediction and prevention, 220-221
  theories of, 220
Rwandan genocide, 112-113

self-control, 6, 114, 168
  cross-national analysis of, 196-202
  early life course, 28
  elements of, 114-115
  stability, 27
self-control and human needs, 168-169
self-control and problem behaviors, 26
self-control and sexual harassment, 136-137
  policy implications,142-143
  research recommendations, 141-142
self-control theory, 6, 24
  assumptions, 6, 30, 39-41
  family, 7-8
  learning, 45-47
  opportunity, 8
  policy implications, 13
self-interest, 162-164
self-interest as goal-directed, 167-168
self-report data
  cross-national analysis of, 185-190
sex and opportunity, 10
sexual harassment, 134
  age-graded social control, 144
  gender, 139
  general theory and policy implications, 142-143
  general theory and research design, 140-142
  logical structure of, 135-136
  occupational position, 138-139
  organizational prestige, 138
  types of, 134-135
  victim-offender relationship, 139-140
similarities of crimes, 81-82
situational factors and violence, 268-269
social capital, 173-174
social control and delinquent peers, 57-59
  interactions, 68
social learning theory
  assumptions, 39-41
  learning process, 42
social sanctions, 153
socialization, 23, 31
socialization process
  self-control theory, 45-46
socialization processes, 43-44, 45-46
specialization and versatility, 252-255
specializations in crime, 255-258
stability of self-control, 27
stake in conformity, 56
  measurement, 62
status, 166
stimulation, 166
  emotional and physical, 166
strain theory and co-occurrence, 232
supernatural sanctions, 153

supervision, 157-158
Swiss Army Study, 251-252

testing theories of co-occurrence, 229-233
testing theories of crime, 249-251
theories of risky behavior, 220
threat of physical harm, 166-167
types of sexual harassment, 134-135
types of social control, 55
    direct control, 56
    interactions among indicators, 59-60
    internal control, 56
    stake in conformity, 56

unique causes of co-occurrence, 229
University of Arizona, 11

values and attitudes of co-occurrence, 232
versatility, 26, 216
victimization data
    cross-national analysis of, 183-185
violence
    causes of, 262-266
    prediction, 262-266
violence and situational factors, 268-269
violent behavior, 258
violent crime, 11
    university, 11